Praise for Scott Ellswor

THE SECRET GA.

"A fascinating new work of cultural and sports history.... Ellsworth captures the rich human details of a whole generation of largely forgotten basketball players." —Nick Romeo, *Boston Globe*

"As a member of the Duke community, I have long been aware and proud of the secret game. Now Scott Ellsworth has brought it to light. The true story behind this extraordinary, long-buried moment goes beyond any one school or any one state. *The Secret Game* is a triumphant look at how basketball has broken down barriers and helped create a new kind of America. Every citizen needs to know this story—and to know it now."

—Mike Krzyzewski, head coach of Duke men's basketball

"There is a basketball on the cover, but this is much more than a story about basketball. Yes, there was a groundbreaking basketball game played in Durham, North Carolina, seven decades ago, and it is recounted in great detail by Scott Ellsworth. But what we really have here is indispensable social history. White people need to read this book. People of color need to read this book. Whoever you are, you need to read this book."

—Bob Ryan, writer for the *Boston Globe* and ESPN, and author of *Scribe: My Life in Sports*

"A historian with the soul of a poet, Ellsworth offers a remarkably nuanced, vibrant, and eloquent account of life in the South during World War II, and his portraits of the principal players in this secret drama are multitextured and complex."

—Wes Lukowsky, *Booklist*

"Scott Ellsworth has unearthed the facts of this little-known but hugely important moment. His research is as overwhelming as his storytelling style is accessible and engaging. If you love basketball, truly love the game and all that it means in terms of this country and its civil rights history, you'll want to read and reread *The Secret Game*."

—Roland Lazenby, author of
Michael Jordan: The Life

"It would be difficult, if not impossible, for me to overstate my admiration for Scott Ellsworth's magnificent *The Secret Game*. It's a book about race, a book about the South, a book about America, a book about the '40s, a book about change as well as how things remain the same. This is one of the smartest and most eloquent books I've come across in a long time. A masterpiece."

—Steve Yarbrough, author of
The Realm of Last Chances

"Ellsworth skillfully puts this story in the context of World War II, which forced this country to face—albeit slowly—its unjust treatment of those who also spilled blood to protect American democracy. He lets us know what happened to each of the players after the secret game—their lives and their triumph no longer lost or forgotten."

—Cliff Bellamy, *Durham Herald-Sun*

"A riveting, little-known story reminding readers of a rising generation of risk-takers who fought against Jim Crow laws and ushered in the civil rights movement."   —Genesis Jackson, *Duke Today*

"It is a mark of Ellsworth's skill as a writer that by the last page the reader cares less about the final score than about the broader questions that he raises—whether sports really do build character, whether winning is all that matters, and when it's OK to break the rules."

—Chris Lydgate, *The Oregonian*

THE SECRET GAME

A WARTIME STORY OF COURAGE, CHANGE, AND BASKETBALL'S LOST TRIUMPH

SCOTT ELLSWORTH

BACK BAY BOOKS
Little, Brown and Company
New York Boston London

ALSO BY SCOTT ELLSWORTH

Death in a Promised Land

Back Bay Books / Little, Brown and Company
Hachette Book Group
1290 Avenue of the Americas, New York, NY 10104
littlebrown.com

Originally published in hardcover by Little, Brown and Company, March 2015
First Back Bay paperback edition, March 2016

Back Bay Books is an imprint of Little, Brown and Company, a division of Hachette Book Group, Inc. The Back Bay Books name and logo are trademarks of Hachette Book Group, Inc.

The publisher is not responsible for websites (or their content) that are not owned by the publisher.

The Hachette Speakers Bureau provides a wide range of authors for speaking events. To find out more, go to hachettespeakersbureau.com or call (866) 376-6591.

ISBN 978-0-316-24461-9 (hc) / 978-0-316-24462-6 (pb)
LCCN 2014956719

10 9 8 7 6 5 4 3 2

RRD-C

Printed in the United States of America

For Betsy

Contents

A Note to the Reader

A few years back, I went looking for the history of basketball. Instead, I found the history of my country.

I had gone to see an elderly basketball coach, a long-forgotten giant whose connection to the game stretched back nearly seventy-five years. The old man had much to tell me. But there was one story—about a basketball game played in secret in North Carolina on a Sunday morning in 1944—that at first I simply could not believe. There was nothing like this story in any history book that I had ever seen.

I soon discovered that what the old coach told me was true—the game had happened. But as I tried to piece together what occurred on that lost Sunday, I found something else. There was a larger story waiting in the wings: a story not just about basketball but about the South—and about freedom, war, and the coming of a new kind of America. And that is what this book is all about.

Seven decades ago, much of this story was deliberately kept quiet. It's time that it was told.

S.A.E.
Carrboro, North Carolina

During World War II and in the decades leading up to it, African Americans called themselves colored or Negro. And while these obsolete terms may seem insulting today, they were the accepted terms during the era in which the book's story takes place. Rather than force today's terminology into a book that is set largely during the 1940s, and to better capture and stay true to the voices of the period, I have utilized the language of the day.

THE
SECRET
GAME

PROLOGUE

Spring 1944

Something was happening to basketball.

For half a century, the game had quietly edged its way toward the top level of American sport—familiar and widely played but with little true fanfare of its own. Television had not yet arrived in the nation's living rooms, and radio broadcasts of basketball games were as rare as slam dunks and turnaround jump shots. In Franklin D. Roosevelt's America, basketball coaches and players weren't household names, the NBA hadn't yet been organized, and nobody spent half a paycheck on a pair of sneakers. If you wanted to see a college basketball game, you just showed up. There were always plenty of seats.

The truth was, aside from a few hoops-mad hot spots like Indiana and Kentucky, or New York City and Lawrence, Kansas, basketball was an entertaining but short-term winter visitor, one that helped fill the sports pages of the nation's newspapers between the end of the college football season and the heart of baseball's spring training. During the lean years of the Great Depression and the turbulent days of World War II, few Americans gave the game much thought.

But along the edges of the basketball world, in musty field houses and on gravel-topped school yards, change was in the air. A handful of maverick coaches and self-possessed players had been pushing hard against the old, dull game—the human chess matches in which scoring was rare, shooting was strictly two-handed, and belts and knee pads were standard game-day apparel. Aided by rule changes and the arrival of better equipment, these coaches and players had moved beyond the boundaries of what was considered acceptable, ruffling feathers and upsetting traditions. Tinkerers and inventors, they were reaching for something different, a kind of basketball that hadn't happened yet.

Among them was a soft-spoken man with chestnut-brown eyes, a displaced Kansan whose prairie twang and enigmatic ways often caused Southern brows to furrow and heads to tilt. Not much older than most of his players, John McLendon had not played a lick of college basketball himself, and the small school where he coached was unknown to most North Carolinians, much less to the rest of the country. But he also possessed an unmatched basketball pedigree: at the University of Kansas, where he had been one of only a handful of colored undergraduates, McLendon had also been the last student of James Naismith, basketball's inventor.

Nor was that all. For in less than a half dozen years, McLendon had transformed the Eagles of the North Carolina College for Negroes into the nation's highest-scoring college basketball team, a juggernaut of speed and finesse that left opponents demolished, referees exhausted, and fans in awe. On the outermost fringe of collegiate athletics, the twenty-eight-year-old coach had crafted an approach to basketball that was, he believed, years ahead of its time.

But to know for certain, he would have to cross another kind of boundary.

He would also need some help.

And so, on one Sunday morning during the spring of 1944, John McLendon and a handful of college basketball players suddenly found themselves in a locked gym on the south side of Durham, North Carolina, going deep into uncharted territory. More than three years before Jackie Robinson first pulled on a Brooklyn Dodgers uniform, and a full decade before the *Brown* decision and the Montgomery bus boycott, they had a chance to do something that the South wouldn't see for years and an opportunity to give the country a new vision of sport. On a long-forgotten Sunday during the middle of the nation's bloodiest war, they uncovered what the future could look like—would look like—for a different kind of country.

The young men who accomplished this are largely forgotten. Most were natural athletes, accomplished competitors on the ball courts of their hometowns, while others had honed their skills through hours of practice and years of pickup games. Some were well off, others dirt poor. And, like their fellow Americans, they came from all over.

PART ONE

CHAPTER 1

━━━━━

Aubrey

Dressed in khakis and his best Sunday shirt, the young man sat on a wooden bench inside the low whitewashed building, a cheap suitcase resting at his feet. Before the day was done, he would travel more than two hundred miles, past pine forests and tobacco barns, through villages and towns he had heard of but never seen. By nightfall he would be farther from home than ever before, sleeping in a strange bed in a strange city. But for now, in the early morning stillness of the one-room station, with the September sunlight slanting in through the windows, sixteen-year-old Aubrey Stanley was sitting quietly and waiting for the next chapter of his life to begin.

A little past seven o'clock, the blue-and-white Seashore Transportation Company bus finally rolled to a halt in front of the Beaufort, North Carolina, bus terminal. Aubrey set his suitcase, marked N.C. COLLEGE FOR NEGROES, inside the baggage compartment and took a window seat in the back. On the bridge over the inlet, Aubrey looked out at the blue-green water of the channel—and, farther out, at the deeper blues of the open ocean—shimmering in the morning light. After a five-minute stop in Morehead City, the driver turned onto the state highway and headed north and west, into the bright green country that lay beyond the edge of the sea. And while Aubrey did not know it yet, just ten minutes outside of Beaufort on that bright Monday morning in the fall of 1943, he had already left his hometown forever.

It had all happened so fast.

Only two years earlier, college had been unthinkable.

The Monday before Thanksgiving, he had met his uncle at the south docks before dawn. The other men were already there, talking quietly, their faces lit by the orange tips of hand-rolled cigarettes, while the captain and first mate pored over their charts. Sticking close to his uncle, Aubrey said nothing. But inside, he was aglow with his good fortune. Like every other boy in Beaufort, Aubrey had dreamed of the day when he, too, could join the fishing fleet. And even though he was still three months shy of his fifteenth birthday, he was finally going to have his chance.

Each fall the shad would appear off the North Carolina coast by the millions, flashing and glinting in the brilliant blue waters. Traveling south, against the Gulf Stream, they came in waves. First would come the Boston and Long Island fish, then the Delawares, and finally the Chesapeakes, moving south toward Florida in schools the size of mile-long underwater armies. You couldn't eat this kind of shad—or menhaden, as the state fish and wildlife man called them—but if you caught enough of them you could make a small fortune. You could dry them and press them and grind them into fish oil and fish meal for fertilizer and chicken feed, lipstick and house paint, soap and linoleum. And when the shad were running, all of Beaufort, a usually sleepy fishing town along the coast, would suddenly spring to life. Fishermen's wives found themselves eyeing new dresses, schoolchildren suddenly had enough money to go to the movies, and the fish plants ran day and night, blanketing the town with an aroma all its own.

"Oh, that?" the locals would say to the occasional tourist who rented a room in one of the eighteenth-century captains' houses that by then doubled as guesthouses. "Why, that's the smell of money."

When the fish appeared, the fleet would be out for days at a time. Carrying a full crew with as many as thirty-five hands, Beaufort's shad boats fished all the way north to Ocracoke and south to Topsail. When a school of shad was spotted, the hands would row out in two long skiffs, engines silent so as not to spook the fish. A huge purse seine, or net, would be lowered between them, and the skiffs would draw a circle in the water around the trapped shad. Then, to the call and response of chants and work songs, the hands would haul up the net in unison and force the fish—as many as one hundred thousand at a time—into a boiling, seething mass, ready to be lifted by winches and dip nets into the hold of the trawler. It was a grueling, backbreaking business.

And it was risky as well. Sometimes the fish simply couldn't be found, while other times men caught their fingers in the nets or were washed overboard and drowned. The waters off Cape Lookout—where sudden swells could turn a glass-top ocean into a raging sea in a matter of minutes—were not called the graveyard of the Atlantic for no reason. But for young men in Beaufort, especially colored men, it was the only game in town—and the road to manhood. In 1941 it was Aubrey's turn.

And in three days it was over. Battered and bruised, aching more than he ever had in his life, Aubrey slowly limped along the gathering gloom of Marsh Street. Too short to reach far enough into the net to gain a proper handhold, and having nowhere near the muscle power that the grown men had, he could not keep up. Unused to the rising and falling of either the trawler or the skiff, he had fallen repeatedly, gashing open his right hand. Covered in blood and fish guts, he had been unable to eat for much of the trip. All he wanted was to hide.

Luckily, he still had school. Founded by a pair of Yankee schoolmarms at the close of the War Between the States, the Beaufort (Colored) School sat at the end of Queen Street on a low rise on the edge of town. And while the one-story brick building was less than ten years old, much of what it held inside was considerably older. The desks and furniture were all hand-me-downs from the white school, as was the one working microscope, an antique affair whose eyepiece would often cloud over—usually when students were viewing an amoeba or paramecium. The books were old, too, with worn and ragged bindings, and with the names of the six or eight or ten white children who had used them in years past penciled inside their front covers.

Despite all this, the school on Queen Street was nothing less than the pride of Beaufort's small colored community. Students brought their own cleaning supplies from home to help keep the halls and classrooms tidy, while honeysuckle and wax myrtle brightened the school grounds. The direct descendant of a one-room cabin—built from shipwreck timber—where newly emancipated slaves learned to read and write, the Queen Street school was a place where a handful of teachers gave dreams to the sons and daughters of fishermen, most of whom lived in houses without either electricity or indoor plumbing, and tried to prepare them for the world to come. One of the teachers, Mr. Hayes, even had all the high school students conduct a mock presidential election, complete with political parties, nominating conventions, and secret ballots, even though Negroes had not voted in Carteret County for more than fifty years.

The meager athletic budget bestowed on the school by the all-white school board did not allow for a football or a baseball team, but a full-length basketball court had been laid out on the bare ground of the school yard, the out-of-bounds and free-throw lines carefully marked off in chalk. On weekday mornings, high school boys would play before class—five on a side; first team to twenty wins; winners stay and losers sit. On weekends groups of kids would gather for pickup games whenever they could.

Although basketball wasn't the only game in town, for Aubrey it might as well have been. Not only did he get up early each morning to take part in the dusty roundball battles that erupted before class started, he also found himself hanging around the Queen Street school yard more and more in the evenings and on weekends. Part of this was to escape from the demands of his mother, but part of it, too, was that

Aubrey had gained confidence—his first, in anything—in his abilities as a basketball player. And while he did not know it, he was also a part of a quiet athletic revolution, one that would transform basketball not only in Beaufort but also across North Carolina.

Basketball had come early to the Tar Heel State. Indeed, in the very first basketball game ever played, in Springfield, Massachusetts, in 1891, not only had a future North Carolinian been among the players, he also named the new game. "Why not call it basketball?" Frank Mahan suggested. Mahan, in fact, liked the game so much that he promptly stole the world's first typewritten copy of its rules. Within months, enthusiastic YMCA volunteers, preaching the gospel of a new, muscular Christianity—a Bible in one hand, an Indian club in the other—had brought the game to North Carolina. And after that, year by year and county by county, from Elizabeth City to Blowing Rock, roundball had slowly taken root. It was played in high schools and junior highs, Bible schools and state universities. It was played by church groups and athletic clubs. Baptists and Methodists alike played the game, and there were white teams and Negro teams and teams made up of Cherokee and Lumbee Indians. And while baseball and football were still the state's most beloved sports, North Carolina was slowly becoming basketball country as well.

Aubrey was, in his own small way, part of it all.

Each winter he'd scan the sports pages of the *Beaufort News* and the *Journal and Guide,* the colored newspaper published in Norfolk, Virginia, for whatever basketball news he could find. He'd read about the nation's great teams, the Kansas Jayhawks and the Kentucky Wildcats, the Long Island University Blackbirds and the Indiana Hoosiers, and he knew about the great college stars of the era, like Hank Luisetti of Stanford, who somehow managed to accurately shoot the ball with only one hand, and Kenny Sailors, the Wyoming Cowboys scoring champ. He knew about the new postseason championship tournaments, the National Invitation Tournament and the National Collegiate Athletic Association tournament, and he had read about the fabulous "doubleheaders" at Madison Square Garden in New York City, where as many as sixteen thousand fans would line the stands.

Aubrey's own venue, of course, was at the other end of the spectrum. Unlike the white high school in town, which had its own gymnasium, the students at the Queen Street school played all their basketball outside. There on the sandy school yard, with the sky above them and pebbles in their shoes, they'd shoot crip shots and two-handed set shots — correcting, if necessary, for the wind — and battle each other beneath the creaky backboards until the sun went down or until enough of the players had been summoned home for supper. Aubrey was short, but he was also fast and good. He loved nothing better than playing ball, and on the second Sunday of December, two weeks after the fishing debacle, that's exactly what Aubrey and a handful of his friends, all of them still dressed in their church clothes, were doing.

After the boys had been playing for about half an hour, they were interrupted by a colored stranger who had been sitting in a beat-up Chevy with the radio turned up and the windows rolled down. The man suddenly jumped out of his car, waving his arms.

Over here now, he shouted. Quick.

No more music was coming in over the New Bern radio station, only the excited voice of the announcer. As Aubrey and the others sat down on the ragged grass next to the man's car and listened to the news reports, a picture started to emerge. There had been some sort of an attack, it seemed, in the Hawaiian Islands.

It did not take long for the war to come to Beaufort. By Christmas, the Army had taken over the old Confederate fort by the inlet, turning the casemates into barracks. Infantry platoons started patrolling the windswept beaches along the Shackleford and Core Banks, deserted except for the wild ponies who stared curiously at the strange new visitors dressed in olive drab. Searchlights were set up along the dunes of Bogue Banks, spotter planes from the new Marine Corps air station at Cherry Point crisscrossed the coastline, and private yachts and party boats were converted into makeshift patrol craft.

Aubrey had been aware, of course, that much of the world was already in crisis. He had watched the newsreels that were shown before the movies at the Beaufort Theater, with their flickering images of planes and tanks, bombing and blitzkrieg. And he had studied the maps—with their strange place names, such as Abyssinia, Manchuria, Dunkirk, and Danzig—that Mr. Hayes had drawn on the chalkboard. But like almost anything that was farther away than the inlet bridge or anywhere else he could ride his bicycle to, the war might as well have been happening on another planet.

Then the U-boats came.

Their first victim was an aging Great Lakes freighter renamed the *Caribsea* en route from Cuba to Norfolk. On March 11, 1942, she was steaming north inside Diamond Shoals when two torpedoes struck her amidships, buckling the deck plates and tearing two gaping holes along the starboard side. She sank in three minutes. Within a week, two more ships, both empty oil tankers, had been torpedoed off Cape Lookout, the orange glow from the explosions easily visible from Aubrey's front yard. Then, just past midnight on March 18, a torpedo ripped into the bow of the *W. E. Hutton,* a Texas-based tanker carrying a full load of fuel oil, in the sea-lanes off Atlantic Beach, shearing away both anchors. Ten minutes later, a second torpedo hit, instantly killing a third of the crew and igniting the fuel oil, which burned offshore for weeks.

By the end of the month, four more tankers had been sunk off Cape Lookout. And despite the efforts of military censors to keep the news hush-hush, people in Beaufort didn't need a newspaper or radio to know what was happening. Oil and pieces of wreckage had been washing up on the beaches for weeks, as had the half-naked, often horribly burned bodies of dead seamen. There was even a widely believed rumor that a German newspaper had been left on one of the seats in the movie theater in Morehead City, obviously by a spy or saboteur. Shad fishermen, meanwhile, started keeping a sharp eye out for periscopes.

Aubrey didn't have to go looking for the war. It had come to him.

Spring melted into summer. The chalkboards at the Queen Street school were wiped down for the last time, the textbooks were stacked neatly alongside the walls, and the ancient microscope was wrapped in cotton batting and stowed inside the principal's closet. And while summer wasn't without its obvious appeals—you could lie among the goldenrod and marsh elders down at Black Cat Beach or fish for spot or croakers off the bridge—for Aubrey, vacation had its drawbacks as well. The first was his mother. The second was work. Usually the two went together.

Strong, stern, and lean, Lottie Stanley didn't brook any foolishness or tolerate idle hands. During the day she worked on a farm just outside town, chopping cotton, slopping the hogs, and tending the tobacco, while at night, by the light of a kerosene lamp, she did laundry for white families, heating the tub of water on the cookstove and making razor-sharp creases with a hand iron. In between, she looked after her own children, her sister's children, and her aged mother as well as a garden full of collards, tomatoes, muskmelons, and Irish potatoes. Motherly love was not her specialty. She was also firmly set in her ways.

The neighbors would say, "Everybody else go right, she go left."

One morning when he was about eight years old, Aubrey was working with his mother in the garden when a white man in a car pulled to a halt in front of the sagging wood house on Marsh Street where Aubrey had been born. The man motioned for his mother to come over.

"Is he old enough to work?" the man asked.

"Yessuh," she said.

And from that day on, Aubrey worked at as many odd jobs and took on as much seasonal employment as Lottie could scare up, which, considering the fact that the Depression was still going on, was considerable. Aubrey weeded gardens, shined shoes, mowed lawns, raked leaves, hauled trash, and swept out stores. He headed shrimp at the fish market on Pine Street and dug for clams and oysters in Taylor's Creek. By the time he entered the seventh grade, he worked after school at Beaufort's sole dry cleaning establishment, mixing the solvents and running the machines. But none of these jobs held the promise of a steady future.

Sometimes, on his way home from the dry cleaner, Aubrey would ride his bike slowly past a tidy whitewashed house ringed by bayberry bushes that sat behind the Episcopal church and wonder what the family who lived there was having for supper or what kinds of toys their children had. Because although neither his mother nor his grandmother would ever talk about who Aubrey's father was, by the time he was twelve he had figured it out on his own. For Aubrey, with his high forehead, doe eyes, and nearly blue-black complexion, was the spitting image of the man who lived in that house, a fisherman named Floyd Hill. In fact, Aubrey looked more like Mr. Hill than Hill's own legitimate son, one of Aubrey's classmates, did. And even though practically every grown-up in colored town had unraveled the mystery of Aubrey's paternity, no one ever said a word to him about it.

But the pain and loss were still there. The worst came at Easter homecoming, at church, when all the other Negro boys and their dads would line up in front of the altar to be blessed, while Aubrey slumped down in the pew, hurt and embarrassed. There were times, too, when Aubrey needed guidance but didn't know where to turn. And by the time Aubrey began his final year of high school and the first summer of the war finally ended, he felt not only more alone than ever but also as if his life were fast becoming a closed book. "You don't want this kind of life," he had told himself after the disastrous trip on the shad boat. Yet the truth of the matter was that for a poor boy in Beaufort, there weren't many other options.

Aunt Lillie, however, had other ideas.

His mother's oldest sister, Lillie, was a schoolteacher way up in Scotland Neck, an ancient town near the Virginia line—where, local lore had it, Oliver Cromwell's brothers fled after the Stuart Restoration. On her visits to Beaufort at least twice a year, she was funny, talkative, and worldly—and nothing like Aubrey's mother. Childless and unmarried, she had long had a soft spot for her nephew, who, for his part, adored her. And as Aubrey began his final year at the Queen Street school, Aunt Lillie found herself edging closer and closer to the conclusion that her nephew deserved something better, even though she didn't quite know what that was or how she could make it happen.

The answer came unexpectedly that December.

It had been a good fall for fish. The first shad runs had come late but thick, darkening the waters in schools as large as half a million. And the U-boats were gone as well. Not a single ship had been torpedoed since midsummer, and back in July, a Navy bomber on routine patrol had dropped out of the clouds and surprised a surfaced German submarine off Cape Hatteras, which it quickly sank. The submarine war, it seemed, was over. But a different kind of tragedy lay just ahead.

Early on the morning of December 14, the *Parkins,* a shad boat with a largely colored crew, steamed out of Beaufort on what everyone assumed was the last run of the season. With Christmas a week and a half away and temperatures rapidly dropping, many of the men had never fished that late in the season. But with the shad running as never before, the decision was made to go out one more time—and the captain was soon glad he did. Fishing off the Shackleford Banks, the *Parkins* hit school after school of late-season Delawares. No one, not even the old-timers on board, had ever seen so many shad.

That was before the storm hit.

By the night of the seventeenth, the *Parkins* was fighting for her life. Battered by high seas and quickly taking on water, the captain ordered most of his oversize crew into the two lifeboats, still tied to the trawler, while the first mate frantically tapped out s-o-s, s-o-s, s-o-s on the wireless. Finally, a little before two o'clock in the morning, the desperate crew could make out the dim lights of a Coast Guard rescue ship rising and falling in the heavy swell off the landward side and heading their way. But before the rescuers could cut the lifeboats free of the foundering *Parkins* and tow them to shore, both lifeboats suddenly capsized, sending their occupants into the frigid, pounding sea. Thirteen bodies eventually washed up on the beaches off Cape Lookout bight. Others were never found.

The sinking of the *Parkins* was front-page news across North Carolina. And when Aunt Lillie read about it, she quickly made up her mind. Her nephew was not going to become a fisherman. He was going to college.

Aubrey could not believe the news. While his mother said little about the whole enterprise, Aunt Lillie assured him that she had enough money in savings to cover his room and board, tuition, and books. There was nothing more important, she told him, than getting an education. Nothing.

Within days Aubrey was scanning the pages of the *Journal and Guide* at the school library, carefully reading the advertisements for various colored colleges, trying to figure out where he should go. It was all rather dizzying. Overnight, it seemed, his entire future had burst wide open. In four years' time, he realized, he, too, could be teaching at the Queen Street school, in his own classroom, wearing a coat and tie.

There was — or should have been — one rather substantial problem. In truth, Aubrey had never been much of a student, certainly not the type that Negro educators had traditionally sought. But the war had changed all that: by the spring of 1943, Aubrey Stanley was exactly what every cash-strapped, draft-decimated, colored college in the South was looking for — a male student who could pay his own way.

He offered something else as well.

By his sophomore year, Aubrey had become one of the starters on the Beaufort (Colored) School basketball team. Clad in their brand-new sateen uniforms, the money for which had been raised by collecting donations from the white shop owners down on the waterfront, Aubrey and his teammates soon became the talk of the small colored community. Coached by the math teacher, they ran crisscrosses and pivot plays, man-ups and over-and-arounds, dazzling opponents with their tightly orchestrated team play. And they were good. By Aubrey's senior year, they had won both the Eastern Class B (Colored) Outdoor Basketball championship and the state Negro outdoor title, clobbering a strong team from distant Madison, North Carolina, by twelve points in the final game. Aubrey had become a state champion.

It couldn't have come at a better time. For in March, the week after his sixteenth birthday, a letter arrived at the little house on Marsh Street. Not only had his application for admission to the North Carolina College for Negroes been accepted, Aubrey was also offered a small scholarship. His new life was about to begin.

It was nearly 10:00 a.m. before the bus rolled into Kinston, where Aubrey transferred to a red-and-cream Carolina Trailways coach. The

(*Greyhound Lines, Inc.*)

countryside had changed, and the air was different, too—a hot, dry blast smelling of dust blew steadily in from the open windows. The first hills came just outside Smithfield, bringing mile after mile of pine forest, fountains of kudzu, and, once they hit Raleigh, more cars and people than Aubrey had ever seen before. The bus had even driven right past the state capitol, its huge columns bathed in colored lights. There were stores and banks and movie theaters and the Sir Walter Raleigh Hotel, with its air-conditioned coffee shop.

It was near dark when the bus finally rolled into the Durham bus station, the sunset a rose-colored smudge on the horizon. Aubrey collected his suitcase and, as he had been instructed to do in a letter from the dean, located the colored taxi stand outside the terminal and hired a cab to drive him to the college. But nothing had prepared him for what came next. For just inside the school's gates, surrounded by lofty elms and a carefully manicured lawn, stood some of the most beautiful redbrick buildings, trimmed in white, that Aubrey had ever seen.

"I never knew," he later said, "that Negroes could have anything so nice."

He paid the driver and located Mrs. Washington, the elderly dormitory matron, who showed him to his room. Happy but exhausted, Aubrey was soon asleep in one of those same buildings that, standing like a Greek chorus, would harbor his hopes and give flight to his dreams.

CHAPTER 2

Negroes with LaSalles

Perched on the highest hill in town, the tree-lined campus of the North Carolina College for Negroes was, on the surface, the very portrait of classic American collegiate life. Inside the classroom buildings, professors in jackets and ties discussed English literature, medieval history, and organic chemistry while the voices of the college chorale spilled from the school auditorium into the bright October air. Aside from the fact that the student body was 100 percent Negro, the tranquil Durham campus would not have looked out of place in a New England village or a farm town in the Midwest.

But in truth North Carolina College was nothing less than a miracle. And no one knew that better than the man sitting behind a large wooden desk on the third floor of the administration building. At sixty-seven years old, Dr. James Edward Shepard was not only the president of North Carolina College but also its founder and creator, its protector and its avatar. Tall and lean, with a Roman nose, dark brown eyes, and a deep walnut complexion, he commanded every room he walked into. He usually dressed in an immaculate three-piece suit, a gold watch chain dangling from his left vest pocket. His hair was ash gray, but his posture was still ramrod straight. And like the ordered world of his desktop—with its blotter, fountain pen, and telephone all neatly arranged—he was a man of precision, presence, and control. He was, in fact, one of the most powerful colored men in the South.

Getting there, however, had not been easy. James's father, Augustus, had been owned as a slave by no less a figure than Charles Manly, the last Whig governor of North Carolina. A lawyer turned planter and slaveholder, Manly had opposed secession, but when the war came he threw his lot with the Confederacy, losing two of his sons-in-law in the war. Still, on his deathbed in 1871, blind and racked with pain, the ex-governor made one last request.

Bring Gus, he said. Have him say a prayer for me.

And despite the fact that Manly's overseer had once whipped him brutally, Augustus Shepard, a preacher by then, rushed to Manly's side, where he ushered him from one world to another.

Four years later, James Shepard was born. The eldest of twelve children, he would come of age in a time of marvels, when Edison lamps first cast their white-hot incandescent glow, when moving pictures flickered against screens of sailcloth and white muslin, and when telephone wires and telegraph lines, hanging like confetti, could bring news from around the corner—or around the world.

And James Shepard, even as a boy, wanted to be part of it all. He read every book he could lay his hands on and followed the events of the day in the *Raleigh News & Observer*. Rising in the pitch dark to finish his chores before school, he would marvel at the Edison lamps glowing inside the state capitol or linger outside the telegraph office, listening to the rhythm of the key operator, or perhaps run alongside the new electric trolleys that rattled back and forth along Hillsborough Street. It was an age of wonder, a time for dreams and dreamers.

But for the colored people of the South, it was also an age of terror, an age when doors were closed and bodies twisted in the wind. North Carolina was no exception. The Ku Klux Klan was so powerful in the Tar Heel State that Klansmen once murdered a Negro leader in broad daylight in Graham's town square. When a white Republican state senator went to nearby Caswell County to investigate the violence, the

Klan trapped him in the courthouse. Then they slit his throat. State-wide, colored people were lynched by the score. In Salisbury, during the blisteringly hot summer of 1906, five Negro men were taken from the county jail and hanged from the branches of an ancient oak before the white crowd riddled their bodies with buckshot and bullets from smokeless cartridges. In North Carolina, colored folk learned to stand back, step down, and stay in their place.

Not James Shepard, though. He had too much to do.

By age nineteen, Shepard had graduated from Shaw University, the still-young Negro educational institution in Raleigh. At twenty he became one of the first colored druggists in the state, mixing his own salves, tonics, and medicines for rheumatism, consumption, palsy, and lockjaw and having a stake in pharmacies in Durham and Danville, Virginia. But three years later, in 1898 — the nightmare year when white mobs burned down the offices of the Negro newspaper in Wilmington, murdered more than two dozen colored men, and vowed to turn the waters of the Cape Fear River red with blood — Shepard left his native soil. Riding a Jim Crow railroad car north to Washington, D.C., he took a job as a clerk in the office of the district's recorder of deeds.

When James Shepard arrived in the nation's capital, one out of every three persons living in the District of Columbia was colored. Most lived in cramped quarters — often two families to a single room — along the back lots and alleyways of Georgetown, Foggy Bottom, Murder Bay, and Duff Green's Row. Here men rose early in the morning to work as janitors, street sweepers, ditchdiggers, and trash haulers, while women labored as cooks and maids. Here, set off from the broad avenues that connected the neighborhoods housing the capital's white majority, was a world of privation and toil, of ragged children and storefront preachers.

But there was another colored Washington as well. For in the shadow of the Capitol, there was a city within a city, the spiritual — if not actual — descendant of an older Washington, where free blacks had lived in the decades before the Civil War. Here, in James Shepard's time, was a place where the chief surgeon at the Negro hospital had pioneered heart surgery, where colored writers and scholars gathered at the American Negro Academy, and where colored children could also hunt for Easter eggs on the White House lawn. Here, in substantial brick row houses along shaded lanes in LeDroit Park and in the Strivers' Section, lived Washington's colored aristocracy, who strolled the avenues in top hats and parasols and sent their children to the Preparatory High School for Colored Youth, where youngsters studied ancient Greek and Latin, rhetoric, and plane geometry. Here, alongside the banks of the Potomac, was a city where a colored man could get ahead.

James Shepard had done just that, and in Washington his star rose steadily. Through hard work and the force of his own personality, he had rubbed shoulders with prominent Negro leaders and Republican Party power brokers and had even become, it was said, an occasional adviser to Theodore Roosevelt. But Washington wasn't home. So by the end of 1903, James Shepard, then twenty-eight, had come back to his troubled yet beloved North Carolina. Hired as the field secretary for Negro affairs for the International Sunday School Association, Shepard—who was married and the father of two daughters by that time—began to crisscross the South on a railroad pass, visiting colored churches. He also attended numerous religious meetings and conventions in the North.

Moreover, he was also about to become a man of the wider world.

By his thirty-first birthday, on a trip made on behalf of the Sunday School Association, Shepard had gazed upon the grim face of Gibraltar from the promenade deck of an ocean liner. He had walked the alleyways of the Arab quarter in Algiers, the air pungent with the aroma of cumin and coriander, and he had seen the ancient ruins of Pompeii. He had had an epiphany as well. In a packed auditorium in Rome near the Piazza della Repubblica on a sun-drenched afternoon in 1907, Shepard gave his vision a voice. "The redemption of the colored races must be largely effected by the colored race," he told the gathering of more than two thousand churchmen from around the world. "And if you lift them up they will do it."

Back home for good in North Carolina, he got to work on that vision.

On a hillside on the outskirts of Durham, Shepard had spotted a patch of rolling countryside. Choked with ragweed and Virginia creeper, and cut in half by a malodorous, waterlogged gully, it had been used most recently as a trash heap. But among its handful of huge sycamores, oaks, and elms—none of which had been cut down for firewood during the Confederacy's last grim winters, in 1864 and 1865—Shepard saw the future. And in 1910, after he persuaded local whites to donate the land, he established upon it the state's newest Negro school. Composed of, as W. E. B. DuBois said, "four neat white buildings set on the sides of a ravine," the school soon claimed more than two hundred and fifty students and faculty from seven different states as well as an impossibly long name: the National Religious Training School and Chautauqua for the Colored Race.

But this was only a beginning. Within a decade and a half, after courting wealthy Northern philanthropists and white Southern politicians, Shepard had transformed the fledgling religious institution into the first state-supported four-year liberal arts college for colored students in America. By the early 1940s, the North Carolina College for Negroes had its own library and a spacious dining hall, modern dormitories and up-to-date classroom buildings, an eight-hundred-seat auditorium, and newly constructed athletic facilities, including a twenty-five-yard indoor swimming pool. Degrees were offered in economics, education, English, the Romance languages, mathematics, and the sciences, while graduate programs had been created in public health, home economics, commerce, and law.

"I want to build the finest Negro college in the South," Shepard told the legislature at the state capitol in Raleigh one day during the school's earliest years. And if anyone knew how to do it, he did.

(North Carolina Central University Archives, Records and History Center—James E. Shepard Memorial Library, Durham, NC)

When powerful whites visited the college—especially politicians and potential benefactors—he made certain they were treated like royalty, with luncheons, concerts, and class visits, followed up with thank-you notes dripping with sophisticated graciousness and personalized praise. When he spoke to the white press or to white audiences, Dr. Shepard—who in 1912 had been awarded an honorary doctorate by Muskingum College, a *white* school in Ohio—was the voice of reason and reconciliation, boasting that race relations were better in the Tar Heel State than anywhere else in the nation. "When we read the papers and see such racial outbursts as have occurred recently in other Southern states," he intoned in one 1934 radio address, "we feel moved to exclaim in the language of the great Confederate chieftain Robert E. Lee, 'God bless North Carolina.'"

A tireless promoter of North Carolina College, he dictated reams of correspondence, addressing birthday greetings and Christmas cards to penthouses on Park Avenue and mansions in Newport, Boston, and

Oyster Bay. "I know I can get something from Mrs. Biddle," he informed a visitor from Chicago in his office one afternoon. "You know, the new chapel was named after her father." And when Shepard appeared in the marble hallways of the state capitol and faced its all-white legislators, he was the type of man they felt they could deal with, the kind of leader that Negroes needed.

In the early years he had faced funding crises, and the college had hovered dangerously close to bankruptcy on more than one occasion. If James Shepard needed to protect the future of his school, he did so without hesitation, and when he asked for funds, he usually got them.

But in 1933 a new kind of challenge arose. One morning that spring, a request for a transcript landed on a secretary's desk in the registrar's office at North Carolina College. At first she simply could not believe her eyes. There must be some kind of mistake, she thought. But once she determined that there was not, she quickly marched down the hall and handed the astonishing request directly to Dr. Shepard.

A North Carolina College graduate named Thomas Hocutt, then working as an assistant headwaiter at the Washington Duke Hotel, intended to apply for admission into the pharmacy school at the all-white University of North Carolina at Chapel Hill. Backed by attorneys from the National Association for the Advancement of Colored People, the plan — which Shepard soon smoked out — was that after Hocutt was denied admission on racial grounds, the NAACP would file a lawsuit challenging the legitimacy of the state's segregation laws. The state would then be faced with an unsavory choice: either admit Hocutt or build a pharmacy school for Negroes. Hocutt and his attorneys had even approached the editor of the *Durham Morning Herald,* the city's most influential white newspaper, and offered him the inside scoop on what they were doing. But he quickly turned them out.

"I wish all of you were back in Africa," the editor told them.

In the end, the effort went nowhere. Shepard, who feared a backlash by the legislature, simply refused to forward Hocutt's transcript.

Without it, Hocutt's application was incomplete—and he was quickly denied admission.

Six years later, a more serious challenge arose when a brilliant and determined young Negro activist named Pauli Murray, who had graduated from high school in Durham, applied for admission into the law school at the University of North Carolina. This time, however, Murray's efforts hit the press—something that soon spurred lynch talk on the campus at Chapel Hill. "Students hearing of the movement vowed that they would tar and feather any 'nigger' that tried to come to class with them," the *Daily Tar Heel* reported. "I think the state would close the University before they'd let a Negro in," one undergraduate added. "I've never committed murder yet." Once again, however, it was Shepard who cut the ground out from under the effort.

"Negroes," he told the press, "could do their best work in their own schools."

This time, however, Shepard's actions resulted in more than a little grumbling among the Negro community. Privately, some colored leaders in the South started chastising Shepard as a handkerchief-headed Uncle Tom, a Judas, even a traitor to the race. But up North, the gloves came off. A Negro newspaper in New York scathingly called Shepard the "Minister of Apology in the Department of Propaganda for the Southern States and Their Sympathizers Who Believe in Racial Discrimination."

More careful observers, however, noticed something else.

"Every time Pauli Murray writes a letter to the University of North Carolina," one colored editor noted, "they get a new building at the Negro college in Durham."

On campus, Shepard's rule was law.

"We shall avoid all excesses," he informed the student body at vespers one Sunday afternoon. His rules, which were enforced by his handpicked men's and women's deans, were legion. Female students could only venture into downtown Durham if they wore hats and gloves and traveled in threes. Students were not allowed to walk into the dining hall side by side but had to enter single file. Female students were to be locked inside their dormitories by half past six o'clock each evening. All students were required to attend vespers. Students visiting his office had to stand throughout their meeting. He was even known to read the students' mail.

"Old Shep," one correspondent saucily scrawled across an envelope addressed to an undergraduate at the college one year. "I know you reading this so hello."

Nor was the faculty exempt from Shepard's prohibitions. When a newly hired English and drama instructor named Zora Neale Hurston decided not to live in campus housing and rented a cabin in the woods, eyebrows were raised among the faculty. When it was rumored that she had started entertaining a certain male undergraduate at her cabin, the whispers began. But when Hurston had the audacity to appear at a home football game wearing pants and was seen on campus smoking a cigarette, she caught the attention — and displeasure — of Dr. Shepard, and she was soon informed that her contract would not be renewed for the following year. "He was feared," recalled a former historian at North Carolina College.

Despite his ironclad rules, Shepard couldn't be everywhere, and there were small groups of students who began to question some of his policies, especially around issues of race. Some of the students were quite audacious. The campus chapter of the Young Men's Christian Association had made contact with a white chapter across town, and there was even talk of the two groups getting together, quietly, for a joint prayer service. This was dangerous, on-the-edge thinking, which they kept to themselves.

But Shepard also had plenty of support. As important as his contacts were among white industrialists and Yankee do-gooders, as well as in the committee rooms in the state capitol over in Raleigh, he also enjoyed the solid backing of a group of people who not only sent their sons and daughters to "Dr. Shepard's College" but also wielded considerable power of their own. Moreover, they were also much closer at hand. Because in the early decades of the twentieth century, Durham, North Carolina, was like no other Southern town. And in the Negro community, there was a group of businessmen who had created a miracle all their own.

Durham's colored commercial district was one of the wonders of North Carolina.

Nicknamed Hayti — for the colored republic in the Caribbean, but pronounced "hay tie" — it stretched along Fayetteville and Pettigrew Streets from the college practically all the way to downtown. Here colored entrepreneurs owned and operated more than one hundred businesses, including a bank, two movie theaters, pharmacies, grocery stores, restaurants, dime stores, coffee shops, shine parlors, furniture stores, a hospital, and fourteen barber shops. In Hayti, there were Negro electricians who worked exclusively for colored clients, Negro carpenters who never set foot in white neighborhoods, and Negro shop owners who never, ever waited on a white customer.

Colored patrons could dine on fried chicken and barbecue at Papa Jack's Congo Grill or order a sandwich from the Grill Room inside the Biltmore Hotel, then browse the magazine racks next door at Garrett's drugstore. Housewives could get a manicure at the Bull City Beauty Parlor or, if they wanted to save a little money, have their nails done by one of the cosmeticians in training at DeShazor's beauty college. On market day, Negro customers could shop for snap beans and turnip greens, field corn and wild strawberries, scuppernongs and bright green pods of okra from the Green Inn Fruit Stand, Tucker Brothers, Cee Cee's, or the Pine Street Grocery. Well-heeled patrons could send for their clothes at the Royal Cleaners, hire a taxi at the Dixie cab stand, or buy a corsage or a spray of roses from Amey's Florist — "Flowers are the

Language of Heaven," read their advertisements. "Telephone, Day or Night, J-2971." There were colored dentists and doctors, lawyers and accountants.

The local chapter of the Negro Business League alone had more than five hundred members.

"Durham is not a place where men write and dream," groused a Negro sociologist from up North, "but a place where men calculate and work." Here, in the land of lynching and pellagra, was a place where, on payday, colored customers lined up two deep in front of the counters at colored stores. Here was a place, some said, that was living proof that Negroes could thrive and prosper under segregation.

The economic engine for all this commercial activity was nothing less than the largest Negro-owned business in the world, the North Carolina Mutual Life Insurance Company. Founded by a group of colored entrepreneurs—including, briefly, Shepard, who sat on the board of directors—in 1898, the company began as a modest effort to sell burial insurance. But despite the firm's slow start the first year, when the annual profits amounted to a whopping $1.12 after one of the first policyholders unexpectedly died, the founding partners soon discovered they had a gold mine on their hands. Offering policies for as little as five cents a month, they soon had more business than they could handle.

In truth they were selling something far more valuable than insurance. For all across the South, in sharecropper cabins and shotgun houses, maids' quarters and one-room country shacks, having a well-worn envelope from "the Mutual" thumbtacked to the wall or slipped inside the family Bible didn't just mean that one's funeral expenses would be paid. It meant that you were *somebody*. A printed insurance policy from Durham was an affirmation that policyholder 159,876 was a person of distinction—even if he was an illiterate sharecropper living in a run-down dogtrot cabin in Red Lick, Mississippi. Within twelve years of its founding, the Mutual had more than three hundred agents selling policies and collecting payments in ten states and the District of Columbia. And the money poured in.

By the spring of 1921, the sounds of steam shovels and jackhammers echoed across the edge of downtown Durham as construction crews began erecting the scaffolding for the Mutual's brand-new six-story headquarters on Parrish Street, which was to be the second-tallest office building in town. It was said that C. C. Spaulding, president of the Mutual, even had someone measure the height of the white-owned Trust Building so as to avoid building a taller structure, which would offend white sensibilities. It was from here that the company employed more than one thousand clerks, stenographers, agents, managers, actuaries, accountants, and medical examiners. In the middle of the Great Depression, when banks and insurance companies were going belly-up at an alarming rate, the Mutual had more than forty-four million dollars' worth of policies in effect and assets of nearly five million dollars.

The Mutual spawned other locally owned Negro businesses, including the Mechanics and Farmers Bank, the Southern Fidelity and Surety Company, two savings and loan associations, and a fire insurance company, all of which not only did business with each other but also had overlapping boards of directors. "Negro Capitalists" was what one awe-struck colored journalist called them, while Spaulding himself expressed it even more directly.

"Business," he wrote in a 1943 issue of the *Negro Digest,* "is my business."

Spaulding and the Mutual's other founders and chief financial and operations officers, meanwhile, had become rich. One of them built a two-story Queen Anne–style home on Fayetteville Street, complete with a turret and a porte cochere. The mansion owned by another Mutual executive featured a central staircase befitting a society matron. By the beginning of the 1940s, there were dozens of colored homes in Durham—all tied, in one way or another, to North Carolina Mutual—with refrigerators and radios, chintz drapes and broadloom carpets, and up-to-date automobiles parked in the garages.

"Man," as one old-timer put it. "They was Negroes with LaSalles."

Nor did it stop there. Not only had colored Durham's upper-crust families intermarried with each other, they had also created their own private social universe. They played tennis together at their own tennis club, the Algonquin, and swam together at the Hillside Pool. There were bridge clubs and garden parties, book clubs and missionary circles. On Sunday mornings the same families sat in the same pews at White Rock Baptist Church, which had its own nursery school, Boy Scout troop, and recreation center, or at St. Joseph's African Methodist Episcopal Church, a commanding redbrick temple of which Booker T. Washington once said, "In all my traveling, I have never seen a finer Negro church."

On the edges of Hayti's smart set there were, of course, those who longed to get in — or, at the very least, look like they already had done so. Less fortunate mothers and grandmothers kept a keen eye out for eligible marriage partners for their offspring among the children of the city's colored elite — playing matchmaker and plotting as they'd sit at church. One woman in town even had a thriving business selling dress labels stolen from the Ellis, Stone and Company department store — "the Bergdorf's of Durham" — to colored schoolteachers, who would then sew them into their own handmade frocks. Outsiders seeking entrance into the inner circles of this rarefied world had to meet almost impossible social standards. When a rising young preacher from Harlem, Adam Clayton Powell Jr., gave a trial sermon for an assistant pastorship at White Rock Baptist Church, he was quickly turned away.

"Too flashy," came the word from on high.

For membership in Hayti's upper crust required not just a substantial bank account but also adherence to an unwritten code of social behavior. Led by Spaulding, who always kept an open Bible displayed prominently on his desk, decorum was at the top of the list. While some of his executive officers might occasionally pay a call on Mitt Dixon, the bootlegger who served Durham's colored elite, and although some executives' wives might gossip about who was sleeping with whom, such was only to happen behind tightly closed doors.

Equally important was getting along with whites, especially powerful ones. And at this, Spaulding and Shepard were masters. In Hayti, colored business leaders assiduously avoided criticizing segregation and Southern-style race relations. A 1943 profile of Spaulding that appeared in the *Saturday Evening Post* even gave him a nickname. It was Mr. Cooperation.

The message from the colored Brahmins of Durham was simple.

Don't make waves, and don't rock the boat.

"I didn't make this segregation law," Spaulding had once said. "But as long as it exists I say we ought to make it work both ways."

Louis Austin felt differently. Sitting in a cramped print shop off Fayetteville Street, his desk a sea of papers and yellowed news clippings, cigarette butts and pencil stubs, he thought it was all nonsense. Didn't he live in a state where colored men were given the electric chair while white murderers went free? Didn't he live in a state where Negro teachers were paid less, Negro soldiers weren't allowed to carry sidearms, and Negro American citizens didn't have the right to live and work where they wanted or get the education they deserved, all because of the color of their skin? Segregation, he believed, was an unholy plague upon the land, an evil incarnate that needed to end. And since there was *not a single elected Negro official in the entire state of North Carolina in 1943*, Louis Austin, the editor of Durham's colored newspaper, decided to elect himself.

Forty-five years old, Austin had spent his entire life in North Carolina. The son of a barber, he had grown up in Enfield, an old colonial village set among peanut fields. Once, when he was a child, Austin had tried to earn money by shining shoes, snapping his rag and calling out "Shine, Cap'n?" to potential white customers. But his horrified father would have none of it. "Son," he told him, "never let me hear you say those words again. No man is your captain. You are the captain of your own soul." Austin's father never let him work for white folks again.

Before he turned nineteen, Austin had been forced to leave Enfield.

"I was always getting into trouble," he later recalled. "My mother told Dad one day that they would have to send me away before the white people got me. I was too out-spoken." He landed in Durham, where he attended an early incarnation of North Carolina College, then sold insurance for the Mutual before going into the newspaper business, signing on as a reporter and editor for a Negro newspaper. Four years later he had established his own newspaper, the *Carolina Times,* from which he chronicled the lives of Durham's colored citizens, published stories on Negro political news from around the country, and soon made a name for himself with his fire-breathing editorial style.

In banner headlines in the *Carolina Times*—whose logo, complete with the head of a rearing steed, declared THE TRUTH UNBRIDLED— and in the stories that ran beneath them, Austin excoriated white judges and state representatives, the sheriff, the mayor, the school superintendent, and the chief of police. The courts were a favored target. "Negroes in Durham seeking an avenue of refuge from injustices," he wrote in one 1943 editorial, "... should not enter such a court where it appears that a Negro cannot get a favorable verdict though he have Jesus Christ for an attorney and the twelve disciples for a jury." Week after week, month after month, with the presses clattering away in the background, he called for the hiring of Negro policemen, firemen, and bus drivers, equal pay for colored teachers, and streetlamps and paved roads in black neighborhoods. "He calls white people big apes and fools," noted one contemporary. "That's the kind of nerve he's got."

He was not lacking in courage. He also backed it up.

When a Negro man was charged with assaulting a white woman in one small North Carolina town, and when every colored person in the county rightfully feared the appearance of a lynch mob at any moment, Austin showed up, alone, at the courthouse to cover the trial. When a white Durham shop owner slapped a blind colored man, Austin led a picket line in front of the store. When Thomas Hocutt tried to gain admission into the pharmacy school at the University of North Carolina, it was Austin who drove him over to Chapel Hill. He told the dumbfounded white registrar, "This is Mr. Hocutt, a new student, who needs his class schedule and dormitory assignment."

Once, when one of his many enemies in town sent word that Austin had to leave Durham or be killed, Austin showed up at the man's door. "I had a pretty good idea who was back of it," Austin later recalled, "so I went around and called on the gentleman, just to let him know that I would still be here any time they wanted me." Later that same night, after Austin's thoroughly frightened wife heard low voices and rustling sounds outside their bedroom window, she shook him awake.

"I think they're all around the house," she whispered.

"Well," Austin replied, "I guess they are really going to get me this time."

Pulling on his robe, he then walked out onto the porch, where instead of assassins he discovered a half dozen of his friends standing guard.

Even though he was a native North Carolinian, some local whites, who simply couldn't fathom that a *Southern* Negro—one of their own—could actually believe the things he wrote, started referring to him as "that nigger communist from Massachusetts." The local Klan sent him regular death threats, burned a cross on his front lawn, and broke out the windows of the *Carolina Times*. "I'll tell you what's causing a lot of this trouble," one local white complained to an out-of-state visitor. "It's that bastard over there running this nigger newspaper." By the beginning of the war, Austin had even caught the attention of the Federal Bureau of Investigation in Washington. The special agent in charge of the Charlotte office wrote a memo to Bureau director J. Edgar Hoover about Austin. Because of "the inflammatory nature of editorials and articles appearing in the CAROLINA TIMES," he wrote, Austin should be considered to be "potentially dangerous to the internal security of the Country."

But in Durham itself, many people, both black and white, simply thought that Austin was too crazy for his own good. One evening, when the lyric tenor Roland Hayes was giving a concert downtown at

the Carolina Theatre, Austin refused to sit up in the Negroes-only balcony and marched past the ushers to take a seat on the main floor.
Another time, he drove his car to the white-owned and white-operated
Buick dealership downtown to get it serviced in the garage. Sitting in
the backseat was a large, vicious dog, snapping and snarling at the
windows.

"His name is *Mister*," Austin informed the nervous white mechanics. "And if you won't call me 'Mister,'" Austin added, "you damn well
will call *him* that."

In truth Austin walked a fine line between conscience and survival.
Because while almost no white people — save for the police and some
busybodies over at the state capitol — actually read the *Carolina Times,*
his stories and editorials often divided the Negro community, alienat-
ing advertisers, on whose money the paper relied, and scorching the
egos of the Hayti elite. "Negro leaders are still a bunch of spineless,
gutless, bedridden, near humans who don't give a tinker's damn about
the masses of the race so long as they are well kept and well thought of
by the oppressor," Austin wrote in his 1938 New Year's editorial. "One
million Negroes in this state cannot be led to do better things by persons more concerned about their own welfare than they are about the
entire group."

For the movers and shakers in Hayti, the unavoidable truth was
that Louis Austin was a joker in the deck, a dangerous man who had
the power to scuttle, or at least compromise, the relationships they had
so carefully developed with local white politicians and businessmen.

Equally ominous, others had caught Austin's spirit of defiance, as more
than a few Southern whites had noticed.

"Negroes are getting worse and worse here all the time," one white
policeman complained. In April of 1943, a sixteen-year-old high school
sophomore named Dorris Lyons was riding to school on a city bus one
morning when an off-duty white detective ordered her to move farther

away from the white section, up front. "You niggers get up and get in the back," he said. When Lyons refused, he grabbed her, knocked her schoolbooks across the floor, and kicked her off the bus. Then he arrested her. Especially loathsome, many whites felt, were the colored soldiers from Camp Butner who would come to Durham on three-day leave. "I'd rather lose the war," one white Southern politician had complained, "than see these niggers strut around here in officer's uniforms." Like other small cities across Dixie where Negro servicemen had a regular presence, Durham was a powder keg ready to explode.

And it all came to a head in April of 1943, when a group of colored GIs on furlough tried to make some purchases at the white-run but Negro-patronized liquor store on Fayetteville Street in Hayti. When a clerk noticed that one of the colored soldiers had more than his share of ration books, a heated argument erupted, and the clerk struck the GI. Within moments all hell broke loose. Fists and bottles went flying, and the store's plate-glass windows cascaded out onto the sidewalk. The all-white Durham police, meanwhile, attempted to control the pandemonium, but they were fast outnumbered by a group of angry soldiers who surrounded a patrol car, slashed its tires, and tore out its radio antenna and microphone. By the time jeeploads of military police, hastily dispatched from Camp Butner, rolled into Hayti, crowds of onlookers filled the streets and tear gas had to be used to restore order.

Life appeared to return to normal the next morning, but the Durham police still had a score to settle.

A week later, a little before midnight, a Negro named Thomas "Skeet" Allen, who worked at the Liggett & Myers cigarette plant, heard pounding on the front door of his home. When his mother-in-law nervously answered the door in her robe and pajamas, a half dozen white policemen brushed past her and found Allen in bed. A detective shone a flashlight in his face and asked him his name. When he gave it, the officer said, "You are the one we want." As soon as the detective spoke, Allen realized it was the same officer who had confronted him when the riot broke out the week before, the one who had told him to move on while he watched the commotion with the GIs. "I'm a citizen," Allen had told him. "I pay taxes, I have a right to look."

When his mother-in-law asked to see the warrant, the lawmen wouldn't show it to her. Within minutes Allen was riding toward downtown in a police cruiser, surrounded by six officers. When they arrived at the county courthouse, they all got into an elevator. But between the second and third floors, one of the men pulled up on the switch and stopped the elevator. "They asked me what did I know about that mess that took place in Hayti last Saturday, and I told them I didn't know anything about it," Allen later recalled. Then the officers got to work. The first blows knocked Allen to his knees. But when he tried to get up, one of the men smashed a heavy metal flashlight over Allen's right ear. After that, Allen couldn't remember too much. Except for one thing.

"They asked me about the Draft Board, and I told them I was on Board Number 2," he remembered.

The white newspapers in town, the *Durham Morning Herald* and the *Durham Sun,* dismissed the incidents as anomalies, the work of a few hotheads and troublemakers. But Louis Austin knew better. Something else was happening. It wasn't just that a high school girl wouldn't move to a different seat on a bus or that a group of colored soldiers had smashed up a liquor store. On the sidewalks of Hayti, where Shepard and Spaulding and others preached caution and moderation, respectability and prosperity, the temple walls were shaking. On the streets of Durham, there were colored folk who weren't afraid of whites anymore.

CHAPTER 3

———

Big Dog

All that fall, while the warm weather held, groups of North Carolina College students clustered each morning along the edges of the grassy hollow in front of the dining hall before class, trading gossip and lecture notes. By tradition, the stone bench on the south side was reserved for senior men, an exclusive set dominated by a towering Pennsylvanian whose legal name was Henry Thomas but whom everyone simply called Big Dog. Already nearly twenty-four years old, he was built like a modern-day Apollo, with massive hands, legs like tree trunks, and a devil-may-care smile. He was by far the most talented and dominant athlete on campus, the kind of player who could shape and mold a basketball game practically all by himself.

Like Dr. Shepard, Thomas was a force all his own. Born Henry Wilson Thomas, he had been raised in Farrell, Pennsylvania, a gritty steel town near the Ohio line, where the blast furnaces ran all night, the winter winds howled up and down the Shenango River valley, and the local high school football and basketball teams faced some of the toughest competition in the country.

Farrell was also a city of immigrants. Indeed, even though the population never rose much above fifteen thousand during the years that Henry Thomas was growing up there, Farrell could boast its own miniature galaxy of ethnic fraternal lodges, homeland clubs, and non-English-speaking church services. Union organizers who came to town soon discovered that they had to hold their meetings in a minimum of six different languages, while native-born landlords tried to adjust to tenants who raised rabbits in backyards and turned basements into henhouses.

Scattered about were a handful of colored families as well, former sharecroppers and ex–tenant farmers from Virginia and Alabama and South Carolina who had ridden the rails north on the "chickenbone specials"—so named because Negro travelers weren't welcome to eat in the dining cars—carrying with them their suppers as well as their hopes. The men found work in the steel mills, where a kind of bootlace democracy began to emerge. Inside the mills, where the temperature of molten steel could rise to nearly three thousand degrees Fahrenheit, timing and communication meant everything. Amid the smoke and clatter, ex–cotton pickers from Georgia suddenly found themselves having to communicate with former potato farmers from Silesia, goatherds from Sardinia, and ragpickers from the last tattered remnants of the Austro-Hungarian Empire. Andrew Adams, a colored worker at American Steel and Wire, ended up learning how to speak fluent Croatian and German as well as a smattering of nearly a dozen other languages. Inside the mills, you worked with everyone.

You lived with them, too. For aside from Little Italy, a grim stretch of rooming houses near the river, everyone in Farrell lived next to everyone else—Negroes included. Because his father, Abe, worked at the Carnegie mill, Henry Thomas and his brothers and sister grew up on Hamilton Avenue, a street lined with soot-covered company houses having identical high-pitched roofs, brick chimneys, and postage stamp–size front yards. "The porches were so close together," recalled Johnie Bloodsaw, one of Thomas's childhood playmates, "that you could spit from one to another."

The Thomases, like the other Negro families in Farrell, were by and large left alone. But there was more to life in the North than that.

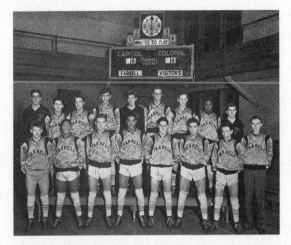

HENRY THOMAS, "*Slim*"
December 13, Farrell, Pa.
General Course. Junior Police 1-2-3;
Junior Patrolman 1-2-3; Basketball
Varsity Team 3-4; Football Varsity 3-4.

Henry Thomas (front row, center), Farrell High School, 1939. *(Farrell Area School District)*

Colored shoppers could try on clothes at the white-owned department stores in nearby Sharon and eat at nearly every restaurant in town. "You could go anywhere," Rudy Hammond, whose parents had come up from North Carolina, recalled. "You see, most of the white folk around here were from Europe. They were more strangers than we were." For the children, the social barriers were even lower. And in Farrell, the white and colored kids all went to school together—including, of course, Henry Thomas.

"He was well liked," Hammond recalled. "A hard worker."

Thomas joined the Junior Police Club when he entered Farrell High School and served as a reporter for the student newspaper. He was a B student, and his best marks were in social studies—civics, American history, modern European history, and a class called the Problem of Democracy. But his true notoriety developed out on the basketball court and the football field, where he grew into the kind of athlete that coaches dream about, one who could haul down overthrown passes, dodge entire defensive backfields, or sink a tear drop from seventeen feet. "Oh, he was a *player*," Bloodsaw remembered.

During Thomas's junior year, the Farrell High basketball team had its best season ever, defeating tough teams from New Castle, Youngstown, and Newark and winning the Mercer County and district 10 championships. They would have won the western Pennsylvania regional championship as well had the officials not waved off Joe Kratowski's left-handed shot at the buzzer. But Thomas's play that year was simply spectacular. Playing center, he not only accounted for nearly half of the team's offense but also became the first Farrell athlete—and one of the first Negroes ever—to be named to the Pennsylvania all-state basketball team. The next season, 1939, promised to be even better. Not only would the Farrell varsity team be returning most of their starters, they would also have a stunning new home.

Built by the Works Progress Administration and still smelling of fresh paint and floor wax, the new Farrell High School gymnasium was a cavernous, 2,400-seat affair, complete with a marble-and-travertine entryway, fully appointed home and visiting team dressing rooms, an all-acoustic ceiling, and glistening yellow tile walls. But for gritty Farrell, where railroad crews used to throw chunks of coal to groups of children shivering alongside the tracks and where the gutters along lower Broadway still ran black with soot after a spring rain, their shining New Deal gymnasium meant something far more important. Here, in a land where illiterate steelworkers could send their children to school for free, was nothing less than a temple of democracy. Here was living proof that the decision to leave the old country had been the right one.

That fall, when he played left end for the varsity football team, Thomas's athletic résumé grew even sturdier. Farrell High opened the season by crushing Erie Tech, 27–0. By December, not only had they beaten their bitterest rival, the powerful Sharon Tigers, for the first time in eleven years, Thomas and his teammates also compiled the best football record in the history of the school. Even better, they clinched both the county and district championships—no small accomplishment in the Keystone State, home to some of the best high school football in America.

Later that school year, however, it came out that two of the Farrell players were ineligible because of their age. And Henry Thomas, who had turned nineteen on December 13, 1938, was one of them. All that fall's football games were declared forfeits, and Farrell's magnificent season as well as the county and district titles were erased. Even worse, the same punishment was meted out to the basketball program. Although the 1939 season hadn't been quite as successful as the previous year, it, too, was purged from the record books.

On the surface, Henry Thomas had ended his high school career as a loser.

But out on the floor of the new gym, or on the grass and hard-packed dirt of the Farrell High football field, he had been something rare and special: he was the kind of player whose athletic accomplishments would not only be remembered by his classmates for decades to come but also the type of player who, many in Farrell felt, would simply get better and better.

And those people weren't alone in their thinking. More than a few college coaches had reached the same conclusion about this double-threat athlete, and by the end of his senior year the offers started to arrive in the mailbox in front of 1105 Hamilton Avenue. Despite the forfeited seasons, Henry Thomas's future glistened before him like a fistful of brand-new silver dollars, each offering a different pathway to success. He was going somewhere, and he was going to be somebody. Together with his parents, he finally reached a decision on which college to attend.

And so, on a sweltering morning during the late summer of 1939, just in time for preseason football practice, Henry Thomas boarded a westbound train at the Pennsylvania Railroad terminal in Pittsburgh and left home for good.

Set near the heart of Jefferson City, less than two miles from the marble-topped dome of the Missouri state capitol, Lincoln University had blossomed into one of the sturdiest Negro colleges in America. But its pedigree was unlike any other. Established at the end of the

Civil War by members of the United States Colored Troops, the college was founded by runaways, ex-slaves, and free blacks who had taken up arms against slavery—men who had been taught to read in the light of the campfire by their white officers. When the war ended, the Negro soldiers dug deeply into their pockets and raised nearly six thousand dollars, an enormous sum in those days, for the establishment of a school "for the special benefit of free blacks." They also asked one of their former officers, First Lieutenant Richard Baxter Foster, to lead the effort. He agreed, but it took some doing. Finally, up on a desolate promontory named Hobo Hill, Foster spied "a shell, a wreck, a ruin," which was an abandoned former schoolhouse. "The rain pours through the roof scarcely less than outside," he wrote. "I could throw a dog through the side in twenty places. There is no sign of a window, bench, desk chair, or table." But it was a beginning. First called the Lincoln Institute in honor of the slain president, it became the only college in America founded exclusively by veterans.

Seventy-three years later, in 1939, when Henry Thomas arrived on campus, Lincoln University had grown into a sturdy fixture of Negro life in the Show Me State. The campus featured an array of up-to-date buildings, and the student body was drawn largely from the highly regarded colored high schools of Kansas City and St. Louis. Even though the college enrolled fewer than seven hundred students, there was a debating society and an artist's guild, an a cappella choir and a classical string ensemble, a Negro history club and campus YMCA and YWCA chapters. The fraternities and sororities, which dominated the student social scene at Lincoln, held black-tie dances, a rush week, and initiation ceremonies and built elaborate floats for the annual homecoming parade. Less easy to see, but nonetheless present, was an unspoken belief that here, in the heart of Missouri, was a place where Negroes were destined to move ahead. And despite the Depression, with its ever-present wants and sorrows, there was a palpable sense of pride on campus, a sense of forward motion, a feeling of belonging.

But Henry Thomas didn't find it. He joined no club, acted in no play, took part in no debate. Maybe he was homesick. Perhaps, as the son of a mill worker, he didn't fit in with the campus big shots. Maybe he didn't dress quite as sharp or know the things that the students from St. Louis and Kansas City did. But whatever the reason, the well-liked, hardworking student—the Henry Thomas that everyone knew back in Farrell—began to disappear. Indeed, during his time at Lincoln, he didn't even have his class picture taken.

Where he did show up was in a Tigers uniform. Out on the football field, pushing around the blocking sled with the prairie wind in his face, or waiting on the sidelines for his chance to get into the game, he was, as the tallest player on the squad, instantly recognizable. During his freshman year, Thomas, wearing number 18, had a respectable if not spectacular football season.

Out on the basketball court, however, it was another matter. As the 1939–40 basketball season opened, Thomas emerged as an immediate star. Starting in his first game, and teamed with a veteran forward and an all-conference guard, the newcomer from Farrell dazzled fans with his passing and shooting. Midway through the season, the Tigers—who played a zone defense paired with an innovative wheel offense—had notched a 12–2 record, knocking off strong teams from Philander Smith, Le Moyne, Louisville Municipal College, Langston, Kentucky State, and Wilberforce, and were on track to win the Midwest Conference championship. In locker rooms both at home and away, the sweat-soaked Tigers got used to changing into their street clothes with huge grins on their faces.

Then, like a prairie rainstorm, the smiles suddenly disappeared. Embarking on a twelve-hundred-mile road trip in February, the Tigers lost two close matches to West Virginia State. A week later they were crushed by a newly energized Kentucky State team, 45–33, losing the conference championship as well. Five days later they were on the road again, this time to Langston, Oklahoma, where they lost two games in a row. That was not all that the Tigers lost, however. Because whatever Henry Thomas was looking for, he couldn't find it in Jefferson City. Sitting in his dormitory room, or walking alone at night by the football field while the nameless stars wheeled above him in the blue-black Missouri sky, Henry Thomas was no longer the young man that everyone knew back in Farrell. By the time of Lincoln's commencement that year, when the seniors bid farewell to their alma mater, he was gone as well.

But he didn't just leave. He disappeared.

Where Henry Thomas went next, and for how long, remains a mystery to this day.

Some said he went back East.

"His birth certificate might've said Farrell, Pennsylvania, on it," one old acquaintance recalled, "but he was all Harlem."

"He must've spent some time in New York or something," remembered another. "I mean, he *knew* things that the rest of us simply did not know."

But the truth of the matter is that for most of two and a half years, Henry Thomas walked off the map. We don't know what he did or where he was when he turned twenty-one or even how he kept himself fed. Even his folks, it seems, didn't know.

He reappeared, briefly, in the fall of 1941. He was playing football again, this time in Durham. This was thanks to William Franklin Burghardt, the North Carolina College football coach. Originally a Midwesterner—he had played center at tiny Eureka College in Illinois alongside a guard named Ronald Reagan—Burghardt had made it his business to keep tabs on every talented colored football player between the Alleghenies and the Missouri River. He had known about Henry Thomas, and he liked what he knew.

Coming in as a transfer student brought complications. Not only would Thomas have to attend summer school and complete a successful year academically, he would also have to sit out of athletics for a year. But Burghardt wasn't the type of man who cottoned to waiting, especially after starting the previous season undefeated only to lose his last two games. So at the beginning of the nation's final peacetime fall, Henry Thomas, age twenty-one, was quietly enrolled as a brand-new freshman at Dr. Shepard's college.

Burghardt didn't like losing, either. Once, when his Eagles had beaten Saint Paul's, the small Virginia school that was the perennial football doormat of the Colored Intercollegiate Athletic Association, by only one touchdown, he halted the team bus out in the middle of the country on the ride back home. Sending his players into a nearby field, a still-fuming Burghardt had his players run play after play — until a sour-faced farmer arrived with a 12-gauge shotgun. "You better get your boys out of here," he said, "or I'm gonna pepper y'all."

But as the 1941 football season got under way, Burghardt had no such problems.

After a close win against Bluefield, the Eagles turned into a CIAA juggernaut. They crushed Saint Paul's, 66–0, and Pennsylvania's Lincoln, 36–6. Within a month, North Carolina College became the talk of the conference, while the halftime shows in Durham — with the one-hundred-member drill team, dressed in matching skirts and blouses, spelling out NCC in thirty-foot letters — became the talk of Hayti. And even though their opponents soon double- and even triple-teamed their star players, the Eagles kept winning. On a cloudless Halloween afternoon, with the smell of burning leaves in the air, they beat their only likely competition, undefeated Shaw, 16–0. Not only did Burghardt's team looked unstoppable, there was already talk that the Eagles would likely play in the newly created Peach Blossom Bowl to be held in Columbus, Georgia — for the Negro national championship.

And Henry Thomas, who played offensive end, was now a part of it all.

Only Eddie Jackson, the coach at Johnson C. Smith, the Presbyterian university in Charlotte, which was next on the Eagles' schedule, had a card up his sleeve. And right before the game started, he played it. Knowing that Thomas was ineligible because he had not sat out a season after transferring, Jackson confronted the North Carolina College coach.

"If you play him," Jackson said, "I'm going to report you."

"You don't know what the hell you're talking about," Burghardt shot back.

The North Carolina College players, meanwhile, had caught wind of what Jackson had threatened to do and asked that Thomas not suit up. But Burghardt waved them off, and late in the game, near the Smith goal line with the Eagles trailing by three, he sent Thomas in on a set play. Thomas scored, the Eagles won, and North Carolina College won the conference championship.

Three weeks later, things exploded. Letters were written. Telegrams were sent. Inquiries were made. And it was all over.

Every game that Thomas played in was declared a forfeit, and North Carolina College's undefeated football season was wiped away. It was too late to cancel the trip to the Peach Blossom Bowl, but the Eagles lost that game anyway.

For the second time in his twenty-one years, Henry Thomas had caused a victorious football season to be erased. Once again, the raucous cheers of November had been swept away. And as before, he dropped from sight. Though not, as it turned out, for long.

In the fall of 1942, Henry Thomas was back on campus.

This time, however, it was not at a Negro college but at the University of Toledo, a small but up-and-coming school in the northwest corner of Ohio. A former trade school with roots in the city's glass industry, the University of Toledo had blossomed into a full-fledged four-year state college, complete with a handsome new collegiate-Gothic campus, fraternities and sororities, glee clubs and chemistry labs, a course called Principles of Modern Mathematics, and bespectacled professors in rumpled tweed jackets with elbow patches. While the overwhelming

majority of its undergraduates were white, handfuls of Negro students—
mainly athletes—had been attending the school for years.

Toledo was hardly alone. By the beginning of the 1940s, colored
football players and track-and-field athletes were no longer a true rarity
at white colleges in the North and West, and a few white schools even
had a Negro basketball player or two on their rosters as well. While
some of these colleges and universities were more racially enlightened
than others, the truth of the matter was that they wanted to win, and
once they realized that Negro athletes could help them in that endeavor,
they cracked open their doors—not much, but just enough for a few
highly talented colored athletes to slip through. And even though the
newcomers routinely had to endure second-class treatment—including
being barred from the hotels that their white teammates stayed in and
being left behind when their team played a Southern school—once-
common threats of overt violence against them had largely evaporated
north and west of the Mason-Dixon line. Moreover, some white players
had begun to rally around their Negro teammates. When Georgia
Tech threatened to not take the field in a 1934 football matchup against
the University of Michigan because the Wolverines had one colored
player, Willis Ward, on their roster, star Michigan player—and future
president—Gerald Ford threatened to boycott the game.

Eight years later, at the University of Toledo, Henry Thomas wasn't
particularly worried. After all, he had played on teams with whites all
his life. He could handle it. More important, he'd been sought after.
And as soon as he arrived on campus, it wasn't hard to see why. Something was happening to basketball at the University of Toledo. For its
first twenty years, the Rockets had posted season after season of roundball mediocrity, pegging an occasional win against the likes of Heidelberg, Findlay, Bluffton, and Bowling Green but usually winding up
with a losing campaign. But no longer. In 1934, after six straight losing
seasons, the university administration hired a thirty-one-year-old local
high school coach named Andy Anderson to lead the Rockets.

Anderson hadn't coached at the collegiate level, and during his senior year at Otterbein College in Westerville, Ohio, the basketball team lost all eleven of its games. But the Rockets' gamble paid off. At the University of Toledo, Anderson's impact was immediate. The Rockets never had a losing season under his watch, and by the end of 1938 they boasted their first All-American — Chuck Chuckovits, a sure-handed shooter who averaged more than seventeen points a game. Bill Reinhart, the basketball coach at George Washington University, called Chuckovits the greatest player he ever saw. "There's nothing like him in the East," Reinhart said. Even more remarkably, the Toledo star often shot the ball a bit... unusually. "Some of the high school coaches around here wouldn't let their kids come out to watch us play because I was throwing one-handers," Chuckovits later recalled. By the time he graduated in 1939, the Toledo field house was drawing in five thousand fans for its home games. "Seven thousand for Michigan," Chuckovits added.

A year later, Anderson snagged Bob Gerber, a pale, skinny, glasses-wearing scoring machine who became a two-time All-American, smashed the existing school records, and tore up team after team on the hardwood floors of the Midwest. By his junior year, Gerber had not only set a national scoring record but also led the Rockets to the semifinal round of the National Invitation Tournament, held at Madison Square Garden in midtown Manhattan. In the span of only eight years, Coach Anderson had completely turned the program around. And although he would soon depart for greener pastures, he had firmly placed the University of Toledo on the national collegiate basketball map.

When Henry Thomas arrived on campus the following fall, the future of Rockets basketball still shone brightly. Even though Chuckovits had graduated, Bob Gerber — by then the nation's leading scorer — was still on the roster, while the team was on a thirty-five-game scoring streak. And the new Toledo basketball coach was Burl Friddle, a legendary former Indiana high school and college player who was also a two-time high school state championship coach. Henry Thomas had noticed something else about the new coach. Not only was he determined to win: two of the former Indiana high school players he brought with him to play for the Rockets—Davage Minor, from Fort Wayne, and Chuck Harmon, from Washington—were colored. Friddle, it appeared, didn't have a quota for Negro players.

At last Henry Thomas had found his team.

After multiple colleges, false starts, and unhappy endings, he had found a coach and a team whose abilities, he believed, were on par with his own. He had finally found a home.

Or he should have.

Because one afternoon that fall, just as basketball tryouts began at Toledo, Henry Thomas received a letter. It wasn't postmarked from Farrell or Jefferson City or Durham. It wasn't from his mom or dad or any of his old teammates. Instead it was from his uncle.

CHAPTER 4

"Nobody Wanted to Mess with Him"

Pearl Harbor had hit America like a blow from a sledgehammer. A way of life that had existed for more than one hundred and twenty-five years, since the last British ship sailed out of Mobile Bay at the end of the War of 1812, suddenly disappeared. Overnight the idea that the country's shores were invulnerable had evaporated, and within weeks the entire nation was put on war footing. Civil defense activities were organized, entire assembly lines went from manufacturing Fords and Frigidaires to producing M1s and Sherman tanks, while twenty-five Japanese American families, under the first Civilian Exclusion Order, were forced from their homes on Bainbridge Island, outside Seattle. The country was in it now, and—as every mother of teenage sons knew all too well—in it for good.

For the president, his cabinet, and the military planners in the War Department, this would be a new kind of war. Not only would it be fought across two oceans and on three continents, it would also require new weaponry and tactics, novel solutions to unfamiliar problems, and a new inventiveness fostered out of necessity. Long-range, high-altitude bombers would have to be mass-produced by the thousands. The longest oil pipeline in the world, stretching beneath ten states for eleven hundred miles, would be dug from Texas to New York. Lightweight boats constructed of plywood, an aerial sighting mechanism utilizing an analog computer, the world's first synthetic rubber, the atomic bomb—these and more would arise out of the nation's accelerated war effort. With them would come new names and new groups—Flying Fortresses, the Big Inch, the Norden bombsight, landing craft, the Manhattan Project—all of which would play major roles in the struggle ahead.

So, too, would another entity—one not as well known, perhaps, but of equal importance. The Seabees, as they were called, were one of America's secret weapons during World War II.

Established to build port facilities, roads, ammunition and fuel dumps, warehouses, and advance base hospitals, the Naval Construction Battalions—or CBs, hence Seabees—turned out to be nothing short of magicians. They hauled 155 mm artillery over roads made from coconut logs, carved airstrips out of the jungle, built pontoon causeways and floating dry docks, and cooked thousands of hot meals for weary Marines and naval aviators from the Marshall Islands to Salerno. Inventive, and older than most naval recruits, they were lumberjacks and roughnecks, surveyors and steamroller operators, ditchdiggers and electricians, sandhogs and ironworkers—men from the building trades in civilian life who became part of what one journalist called "History's Greatest Construction War."

Operating under tremendous time constraints—and oftentimes under enemy fire—the Seabees blasted the pathway through the steel-reinforced concrete bunkers at Omaha Beach on D-day, patched the bomb craters and kept the Henderson Field airstrip open on Guadalcanal, and ferried GIs across the Rhine at Remagen. They carried with them Marston mats, generators, floodlights, and water distillers, and when they lacked the necessary tools to do their jobs, they made their own—from barbed wire and artillery shell casings, beached landing craft and burned-out tanks. On the beach at Treasury Island in the Solomons one day in 1943, a Seabee named Aurelio Tassone, machinist's mate second class, wanted to know why the invasion was being held up. When he was informed that heavy fire from a Japanese pillbox was keeping the Marines and GIs pinned down, Tassone charged the machine gun nest with his bulldozer and, using its heavy blade as a shield, crushed all twelve Japanese soldiers to death. From the Aleutians to Tunisia, the Seabees were in on the ground floor of America's first counterattacks against Axis forces.

And by early 1943, Henry Wilson Thomas, serial number 7232538, was among them.

Assigned to the Eightieth Naval Construction Battalion—all colored, except for its white officers—he was sent to Virginia, first to Camp Allen, a pocket-size Marine Corps camp located within the city limits of Norfolk, Virginia, for three weeks of boot camp, then on to Camp Bradford, a brand-new training base that only six months earlier had been the waterlogged bean fields of a family farm outside Virginia Beach. There he learned how to shoot and break down an M1, hiked miles in the piney woods, splashed through the surf and sand of a dozen mock invasions along the coast, and drilled endlessly out on the parade ground—column left, platoon forward, left-right-left. But as Thomas got to know his fellow Negro recruits, who were from all over the Eastern Seaboard, he also got some further lessons in American democracy.

For starters, many of them had been shanghaied.

For example, at a crowded midtown Manhattan draft office one day in 1943, where men of different colors and backgrounds were filling out forms and undergoing their initial physical exams, the soon-to-be-former civilians were soon divided by race. As reported by a witness, all the white draftees were registered in their preferred military branch. But for the forty-one Negro draftees in the office that day, all of whom had requested induction into the regular Navy, they were instead marched, en masse, over to the Seabee recruitment headquarters at 383 Madison Avenue and summarily sworn in to the Naval Construction Battalions.

They were not alone. Negro college graduates, thinking they were joining a naval engineers unit, instead found themselves cleaning out latrines, hauling cargo, slinging hash, digging ditches, or shining the shoes of the all-white Seabee officer corps. Colored men, seeking to fight the nation's enemies by enlisting in the Army or the Navy, discovered that they were on the very bottom of the American military machine.

In addition, as Thomas and the other newly minted members of the Eightieth Construction Battalion soon learned, Uncle Sam spoke with a Southern accent below the Mason-Dixon line.

"I have niggers working for me now." That is how one of their white officers greeted them at Camp Allen, where whites and Negroes ate on separate sides of the mess hall and where WHITES ONLY and COLORED ONLY signs suddenly appeared one morning outside the entrances to the PX. At Camp Bradford, there was more of the same. Colored Seabees had separate living quarters and chow halls, while armed Negro guards were posted outside the all-white latrines. "The reason they put Southern officers over you," one white chief petty officer explained, "is because they know how to handle niggers."

This, however, was merely a dress rehearsal for what lay ahead. On March 13, 1943, the Eightieth was transferred to a new deepwater port that the Navy had built along the Gulf Coast. The advance base depot, as it was first called, had transformed sleepy Gulfport into a neon-lit Babylon of bars, whorehouses, gambling dens, cheap cafés, and rented rooms that had become, practically overnight, the second-largest city in the state of Mississippi. But despite the influx of Navy men, civilian contractors, and wives and camp followers, and despite the constant hum of bulldozers, dredges, and power launches, Gulfport remained firmly antebellum in its race relations. So did the Navy.

Here colored recruits had a new name: Sambo, a derogatory term dating back to slavery. They also had a new way of life. The barracks and the latrines, of course, were segregated, as was the camp movie theater and beer parlor. Even though they were outnumbered three to one, whites ate first in the mess halls, which usually meant that the colored Seabees were rushed. There were no dances for Negroes on base, and when they were off duty, the colored Seabees found themselves hemmed in. The Navy brass had promised the civic authorities of Gulfport that Negro personnel would be kept out of the city, so local bus drivers often refused to seat colored Seabees and sailors, even if they had tickets. And even though the colored Seabees hauled construction materials, built roads, and took part in the mock amphibious invasion of Cat Island, a barrier island located some ten nautical miles offshore, they were forever reminded of their second-class status. Even for full-dress drills on the camp's parade ground, the Negro units appeared without colors.

"There was no flag waving before us," Thirkfield Montgomery, officer's cook second class, later reported. "Not even the sound of a drum or the blare of a bugle. We were as men without a flag or a country."

Yet when the colored Seabees protested, nothing happened—or at least nothing good. The white clerks at the base personnel office refused to put any white officers on report, while Negro complainants were cussed out, put on KP or guard duty, or threatened with lynching. "You people think you are smart," wrote one white officer with the Eightieth in early June of 1943. "But the time will come when we will either have to have about half of the outfit up for court martial or start a racial war and I don't care what time it starts."

A week and a half later, the men of the Eightieth set sail for Trinidad, where for nearly a year they would begin to pave runways and construct a gigantic blimp hangar—all as part of the so-called South Atlantic Road, the twelve-thousand-mile seaway that would bring the war across the ocean to Morocco, Tunisia, Sicily, and Italy. But only hours into the eighteen-day voyage, the white officers of the battalion booted the sole Negro officer out of their on-board quarters. Then they strung ropes across sections of the deck, upon which they hung signs reading WHITES ONLY.

But Henry Thomas wasn't there to see them, because one day he had simply had enough.

"He started a race riot because they would not let him and another black Seabee go into the canteen," one of his companions later recalled. Court-martialed, Thomas was charged with shirking his duty and was discharged on July 15, 1943, as being "*unfit* for Naval training."

Thomas reset his compass after that, and a month later he turned up—again—at North Carolina College. The school's 1943 football season had been canceled, a casualty of the war. But there was another sport, and with it came one more chance.

Henry Thomas was different by then. Gone was the Junior Policeman at Farrell High. Gone was the young man who made good grades in the Problem of Democracy.

"He was Big Dog now," recalled Harry Boatner, who had known him both in Farrell and at North Carolina College. "He was big. And he treated everyone like a dog."

"Basically," another classmate added, "he was a thug."

Perhaps. At times, though, like one of the brief autumnal rains that would sometimes blow up from the south, flashes of a softer side would suddenly appear. "He was just in touch with his feminine side," remembered Edith Sanford, a classmate. "Man, he would give you the shirt off his back," another former associate recalled. He could be flamboyant, too. Sometimes he'd wear a cowboy hat to class. Other times it was knee-high English riding boots and jodhpurs. What he really wanted, though, was a zoot suit. "But he could never find one that fit," a classmate remembered.

What was certain was that he was not, to say the least, Dr. Shepard's model student. On a campus where drinking, gambling, and unchaperoned visits with members of the opposite sex were cardinal sins, Big Dog was a devoted practitioner of all three. He loved to play cards, especially Georgia skins, bid whist, tonk, and coon can—"Some coons can," he'd bellow, "and some coons *can't!*"—while laying out an unending stream of bull. Life was a party. And he intended to live it as fully as he possibly could.

Drinking was the chosen ritual. When they could, Big Dog and his buddies would toss back shots of Old Crow—"Those in the Know," declared the magazine ads, "Ask for Old Crow"—Four Roses whiskey, homemade dandelion wine, or whatever liquor they could scare up. But if available, the lubricant of choice was a corpse-reviving, crystal-clear concoction known as CCC. An abbreviation for Craven County corn, it was a blindingly powerful bootleg whiskey favored by Durham's colored mill workers and tobacco hands. Sold in Mason jars, with an aroma as strong as kerosene, it even demanded its own particular drinking etiquette, one that Dog steadfastly followed. With a box of salt in one hand and a jar of the whiskey nearby, he would lick the skin between his thumb and forefinger, salt it, lick it again, and then take a gulp from the jar. Indeed, Big Dog purposely selected a room in Old Chidley—a sagging, out-of-the-way wooden dorm—not only because it offered private access for his pals in the bootlegging business but also because it was far from the prying eyes of Mother Washington, the dormitory matron.

"She was very protective," one of Dog's classmates later remembered. "And very nosy."

She also had a habit of walking into the men's dormitory rooms unannounced. So one afternoon, Big Dog and a buddy laid a trap for her. "We were laying on the beds in Dog's room, buck naked, when Mrs. Washington came barging in," the classmate recalled. "She didn't do that no more."

Big Dog's fame—and infamy—on campus sprang from other sources as well. "If Dog wanted something, he simply took it," one former North Carolina College student remembered. "Nobody wanted to mess with him." Dashingly handsome, even with a chaw of twist tobacco tucked inside his cheek, he had lots of girlfriends and was always on the lookout for more. "He'd grab them by the hair and try and kiss them," one former student recalled. Moreover, there was always a climate of excitement and uncertainty whenever Big Dog was around. "You never knew when he was going to go off," recalled a friend. Like a meteorite looking for a planet to hit, he was hard to ignore. Yet despite it all, he was also beloved.

"Everybody loved Dog," recalled one classmate. "Everybody."

Almost everybody, that is.

"That Mr. Thomas your son is running around with—I wouldn't take him to church," Dr. Shepard informed the concerned parents of a North Carolina College student one day. Shepard was not alone. When Richard L. McDougald, who was an executive officer at both the Mutual and the Mechanics and Farmers Bank, learned that Big Dog had taken an interest in his daughter, Arona, then a sophomore at North Carolina College, he took immediate action. Paying an evening visit to Old Chidley, the well-mannered businessman, dressed in an impeccable three-piece suit, had a little message for the Pennsylvanian.

"Mess with my daughter," he informed Dog, "and I'll blow your brains out."

Big Dog had a running buddy a little more than half his size. Edward Boyd—known as Pee Wee—was, by the fall of 1943, both a junior at North Carolina College and the student manager of the varsity basketball team. And while he did an admirable job at the latter, few could determine how he maintained his status as the former. Pee Wee had never been spotted on campus with any kind of book. He skipped class when it interfered with either his sleeping or social schedule, and he was better known to local gamblers and con men than he was to the college librarian. His sole academic interest, in fact, appeared to be learning dirty words in German from his language professor. Dressed like a movie star—in aviator sunglasses, imported loafers, silk shirts, and triple-pleated gabardine trousers—Pee Wee looked more like an out-of-place refugee from Hollywood or the Côte d'Azur than a barely passing junior at an all-Negro college.

In truth he was the son of a post-office janitor in Oxford, North Carolina, one who earned a substantial second income by maintaining and repairing the machinery at a local spinning mill. But Pee Wee yearned for bigger things. Sixteen months earlier, he had persuaded his parents to allow him to spend the summer in New York City, where, he argued, he could not only earn some "real" money for school but also be exposed to the city's rich cultural life — the Old Masters at the Metropolitan Museum of Art, weekend visits to the zoological gardens in the Bronx, classical music concerts in Central Park. Reluctantly, his parents had agreed to the plan, and Pee Wee and a classmate had ridden the Colonial Express north to New York, where they rented half a room in a roach-infested Harlem walk-up. As soon as Pee Wee hit the streets of the city, he couldn't believe his eyes.

"They popped right open," he later remembered.

That was only the beginning. Through the help of a friend, he landed a job as a deliveryman for a well-known furrier and high-society dry cleaner in Astoria, Queens. Already a clotheshorse with a preference for finery, Pee Wee had been ordering drape-cut suits with slash pockets and balloon-pleated sleeves for $19.50, COD, from the National Clothing Company in Chicago, whose advertisements he'd seen in the pages of the *Pittsburgh Courier*.

But the back room in Astoria was of an entirely different magnitude, and for Pee Wee it was nothing less than King Solomon's mines.

"Tailor-made English suits, cashmere blazers, you name it," he later recalled. "Once, I delivered a pure white full-length Russian sable worth twenty-five thousand dollars." And when Pee Wee wanted something, he simply took it. "I'd just try it on in the back. If it fit, it was gone. Nobody ever said anything." His favorites were a beige jacket — "collarless, lambswool, just as soft as a baby's behind" — and a single-breasted two-button gray sharkskin suit. "With double vents, you know — English style. Lay down on it and it wouldn't even wrinkle."

Pee Wee's cultural education that summer, meanwhile, consisted of playing snooker at the poolrooms on 116th Street, drinking rum and Cokes at the Orange Blossom Bar and Grill and Lucky's Rendezvous, and jitterbugging to the new sounds that were being cooked up by Dizzy Gillespie and Charlie Christian after hours at the Cotton Club and Small's Paradise. By Monday morning he'd be so broke that he'd have to jump the turnstile at the 135th Street subway station in order to get to work.

It was the greatest summer of Pee Wee's life.

"I came home from New York with two steamer trunks full of clothes," he later recalled. "And not one dime."

Back on campus, Pee Wee and Big Dog rekindled their normal social schedule. They went out when they had four quarters to rub together and pitched pennies when they didn't. They never missed Silas Green's tent show — SILAS GREEN FROM NEW ORLEANS, BEST DAMN SHOW YOU EVER SEEN! — when it rolled into town, especially its notorious "Midnight Rambler," the most infamous burlesque show in all of Dixie. Its honey-hued strippers, dressed, temporarily, in high heels and nylons and scanty satin-and-lace outfits, did the bump and grind in front of audiences across the South. Dog and Pee Wee also tried to sneak into the Negroes-only nights downtown at the armory, whose attractions went beyond what was advertised on the printed handbills. In the colored men's room in the basement, a bootlegger named Bob Hayes sold corn liquor — dispensed from a rubber douche bag, which he wore underneath his jacket — by the shot. They loved movies, too, especially cowboy shoot-'em-ups starring Tim McCoy, Hoot Gibson, and Buck Jones. One night at the Regal Theater, the colored movie house on Pettigrew, the on-screen hero, surrounded by bad guys, was running low on ammo when one of the other patrons, juiced on moonshine, rose unsteadily from his seat.

"I'll help you, Hoot!" he called out.

Then he opened up with his own revolver, plugging half a dozen holes in the screen.

Beyond these social activities, Pee Wee had two other interests.

One was a raven-haired beauty named Ruth Spaulding, one of *the* Spauldings—of North Carolina Mutual fame. Pee Wee had first met her at the College Inn, a six-booth hangout on Fayetteville Street where students could sip Cokes, eat hot dogs and hamburgers or a bowl of pinto beans or homemade banana pudding, and trade gossip out of earshot of the school authorities. Ruth was doing just that one afternoon when she suddenly felt a light tap on her shoulder.

"You gotta hairpin?" Pee Wee asked.

She did, and after he had twisted it into a roach clip so he could smoke the last of a cigarette, romance was in the air. Pee Wee soon started calling on Ruth, a day student who lived with her parents in a towering frame home on Fowler Avenue. He'd take her on walks and, when he had money in his pocket, to movies downtown at the Carolina Theatre, where they'd make out up in the "buzzard's roost" with the other colored couples—that is, they'd make out until the management sent "that black guy with a flashlight to put the spot on you," Pee Wee complained.

Once, Pee Wee even accompanied Ruth and her family to church. Dressed in his favorite zoot suit—"brown, with wide white stripes"— he hummed along to "In the Garden" and "Take My Hand, Precious Lord," then flamboyantly dropped a silver dollar, taken from his card money, into the collection basket. Over time Ruth's mom soon came to like, or at least tolerate, the young man for whom her daughter would iron her skirts, rouge her cheeks, and dab a drop of Evening in Paris perfume behind each ear. But her father, Israel Royal Spaulding, an executive with the Mutual, couldn't even stand to stay in the same room when Pee Wee came calling.

"Doesn't that boy have any *regular* clothes?" he complained one evening.

"The more you talk about him, the more I'm gonna love him," Ruth replied.

Pee Wee's other interest was doing what a certain kind of

upperclassman did best, namely, hazing. And one morning that October, while sitting on the stone bench outside the dining hall as the last warm winds of autumn sighed through the trees, Pee Wee surveyed the small, draft-depleted crop of freshman males. "Nothing but 4-Fs," he later recalled. "Rejects, underage guys." It was a sorry assortment, he thought to himself, with very, very little potential. Then he found what he was looking for. Standing alone by the bushes was a new student who looked uncomfortable in his too-small, out-of-style outfit—a short, doe-eyed, coal-black freshman, clearly from the country.

"Hey, boy!" Pee Wee called out. "Does your mama know you're wearing them high-water pants?"

College was not at all what Aubrey Stanley had expected. Back home in Beaufort, all the colored kids pretty much lived in the same world. They lived in houses that had neither electricity nor indoor plumbing, they wore the same kinds of clothes, most of which were either home-made, hand-me-downs, or castoffs from whites, and they had the same teachers and used the same tired old books. When any of them had any spending money, which wasn't very often, the entertainment choices were limited. You could buy a Pepsi-Cola or a pickled pig's foot at the Gatlin, the colored café and bar on Queen Street, or you could sit in the balcony at the Beaufort Theater downtown. Every year there'd be a Negro Day at the tent show that would pass through town in the fall. And once in a blue moon you could watch a motion picture with an all-colored cast at Fred King's part-time movie house on Broad Street.

In Beaufort, everybody knew everybody. While at North Carolina College, Aubrey didn't know anyone.

And once he got to know people, he quickly realized just how different he was.

There were students from Raleigh and Wilmington, Charlotte and Richmond, Washington, New York, and even California. Some of the guys in his dorm, smelling of Aqua Velva and Murray's hair pomade, wore houndstooth sport coats, double-pleated trousers, and English-style neckties to class, while the fashion rage among the women students that fall was two-piece suit dresses, saddle shoes, and Peter Pan collars. Sitting—usually by himself—at meals or in the hallways before class, Aubrey overheard fragments of conversations about radio shows and piano lessons, the new Duke Ellington record, and "Daddy's old Dodge." These were the families he'd read about in the society pages of the *Journal and Guide,* the ones who had things that he hadn't even dreamed about.

It was even worse in the classroom. For despite the best efforts of Mr. Hayes and the other teachers at the Queen Street school, Aubrey was decidedly unprepared for college-level work. Compared to his classmates, some of whom could already speak French or provide, with ease, examples of iambic pentameter, Aubrey soon found himself lost in classroom discussions, unsure of the boiling point of water or the value of pi or what the Supreme Court actually did or even what a gerund was supposed to be in the first place. By the end of his first month in school, Aubrey was barely scraping by, lost in a maze of words and ideas he didn't understand.

Two hundred miles from the sea, he was drowning.

"Get up!" The voice cracked open the dead of night. "Get moving. Let's go!"

Rousted from sleep, Aubrey and the other freshmen were jarred awake by bright lights, angry voices, and a gang of upperclassmen. Shoved out into the hallway, where blindfolds were tied over their heads, they were led, barefoot and in pajamas, on a half-hour forced march across wet grass and gravel. Brought to a halt, at last, at a spot where he could make out firelight flickering through his blindfold, Aubrey was grabbed by two sets of strong arms while a third ripped the front of his pajama top open. Told that he was about to be branded, he instead felt the shock of a block of ice pressed against his bare flesh.

Twenty minutes later, alone and shivering, Aubrey and the other freshman removed their blindfolds and discovered that they were all sitting on top of gravestones at Beechwood Cemetery.

The hazing, however, did not end there.

Like all freshmen, Aubrey had to wear mismatched socks every day, wait outside the dining hall until all upperclassmen had been served, and memorize the full names, nicknames, positions, and hometowns of eleven former North Carolina College athletes now serving in the United States Army and be able to recite that information, upon demand, to any current letterman. "All freshmen who do not conform to the rules," read one mimeographed sheet that made the rounds in the men's dormitory, "will be greatly surprised after the Athletic Night Program."

And Aubrey received some special attention as well. As one of the smallest and youngest male students on campus, Aubrey soon found himself the target of an almost daily dose of pranks and practical jokes, usually orchestrated by Big Dog and Pee Wee. His clothes were tossed onto the roof of the dorm. Buckets of water rained down on him as he left for class. One time in gym class, he discovered—to his horror—that someone had switched his athletic supporter with that of a senior thought to have a case of the clap. Then there was the near-constant verbal abuse.

You sure are a *country* mother.

Your mama's so black she pee ink.

Boy, you sure do smell.

Stinky. That's what we gonna call you. Stinky.

Stinky Stanley.

But there was one place that hard, lonesome fall where Aubrey could more than hold his own. In the pickup basketball games that took place every night in the gym after supper, Aubrey's abilities soon stood out. Although he barely stood five feet seven, he was a skillful ball

North Carolina College Eagles, 1943–44, from left to right: George Parks, Aubrey Stanley, James "Boogie" Hardy, Floyd Brown, Henry "Big Dog" Thomas. *(©Alex Rivera)*

handler, an accurate passer, and a deadeye shooter. "He had the purest shot I'd ever seen," Pee Wee later recalled. "He'd stay in that gym and shoot all day." And because Aubrey had spent his entire high school basketball career playing outdoors on makeshift sandy courts, his legs were unusually powerful. On the hardwood floor of the North Carolina College gymnasium — the first indoor basketball court that Aubrey had ever played on — the other players soon discovered that the freshman from the coast was very fast indeed.

Then, one week in November, Aubrey got his chance to put his abilities to use. Invited to try out for the varsity basketball team, he made a good showing and became the youngest — and smallest — member of the 1943–44 North Carolina College Eagles. Big Dog, of course, was the team's incumbent star. But there were other talented players as well, including a pair of former high school classmates from Indiana and a lean forward from Kentucky. Pee Wee was the team manager.

And then there was the well-built man carrying a whistle and a black notebook. As the first practice opened, all eyes were fixed upon the young coach of the Eagles, who was still in his twenties and barely older than some of his players. But experience can't always be measured on a calendar. And in more ways than one, John McLendon was, even then, already wise beyond his years.

He was also no stranger to tragedy.

CHAPTER 5

Fathers and Sons

Hiawatha, Kansas. Late fall, 1918.

At a yellow house with white trim, death had come calling. Inside 111 North 11th Street, on the colored side of town, thirty-two-year-old Effie Hunn McLendon had become another grim statistic, leaving behind four children, all under the age of seven, who waited in the parlor beyond the beaded glass curtain in front of the bedroom, all wanting to see a mother who had already passed into another world.

In that terrible year, when men fell by the thousands in the trenches of Flanders and France, a new, silent killer had come, creeping across doorways, lingering along city sidewalks and country lanes, slipping into cribs, and stealing into tenements and train stations. By the end of September, the Spanish flu, as it was called, had raced across six continents, killing millions of men and women and leaving broken hearts, panicked family members, and dumbfounded scientists and public health officials in its wake. By the end of the year, more than five hundred thousand people had died in the United States alone, most within days, if not hours, of falling ill with the pandemic's dreadful symptoms—high fever, fatigue, bleeding from the mouth and ears, skin turning blue, lungs filling with fluid.

Effie's widower had been left with a broken heart—but also with a pressing problem. A mail clerk for the Rock Island railroad, he was usually gone from home for days at a time, sorting, guarding, picking up, and delivering sacks of mail to scores of Kansas towns from Hiawatha all the way to the Oklahoma state line. Unable to keep his job and look after his children, he summoned his extended family for help. Uncle Clarence would take daughter Elsie, while other family members would take Anita. But Johnny and Arthur, the two boys, would go and live out West with their grandparents and a set of aunts and uncles on their mother's side. And so one bright prairie morning, the mound of dirt on his wife's grave still bare of grass, the grieving father placed his two young sons on a westbound train, headed for a ranch outside of Model, Colorado.

Tucked into the far southeastern corner of the state, not far from the New Mexico border, Model was a different country, with sudden snows and pounding winds, the Spanish Peaks shimmering in the distance, and skies that went on forever. Here was a place where the neighbors weren't just white or Indian but also Hispanic. Here was where families traced their roots not to Mexico but to Spain, whose settlers had first come to this land more than three centuries earlier. And it was here, for two years, where young Johnny McLendon and his brother, Arthur, would sleep in an adobe dugout, learn to ride their own slant-eared mules—named Jack and Jenny—and tag along beside their uncles, who would round up wild horses and break them in the corral. For supplies—fifty-pound sacks of beans, tins of sweet-smelling saddle soap, and, for the younger set, a nickel sack of peppermint sticks as bright as barbers' poles—the family would drive over to Trinidad, a mining town along the Old Santa Fe Trail. For drinking water they'd have to tie barrels on the buckboard and drive past the sagebrush and prairie-dog towns to a spring near the mountains. Once, a pack of wolves was waiting for them, hidden among the rocks and wood violets.

There were other dangers as well. For not every dry-land farmer or rancher in Las Animas County liked having Negro neighbors. One time, when the family was away, someone tied a rope around the posts in the hay barn and tried to pull it down. Another time the family came home to discover that someone had dynamited the well. And while Johnny's grandmother, a devout woman, would make sure that everyone started each day with Bible study, his grandfather never left the house without his 12-gauge shotgun, which he set alongside the jockey box in the front of the wagon, its twin barrels telegraphing a message all their own. Here, beneath the broad blue Colorado sky, dressed in boots, jeans, and a cowboy hat and with the endless wind in his face, young John McLendon began his boyhood in the twilight hours of the Old West.

Then, just before he turned six, John found himself with his brother, Arthur, rattling back across the plains, bound for Kansas City. Their father, by then a railroad clerk, owned a house on the edge of a colored neighborhood known as Rattlebone Hollow. When his dad bought it, McLendon later recalled, he and another colored man, the first Negroes to move into the neighborhood, "had to hide in the bushes at night, armed with my dad's railroad .45, to keep people from destroying their property."

And along with a new house, John and his brother had something else—a new mother.

An energetic, ball-of-fire schoolteacher, Minnie Jackson McLendon had big plans for her stepchildren.

"You are going to be a lawyer," she informed Arthur one morning. "And you, John, are going to become a doctor."

John would just chuckle and think to himself, No, I'm going to be a fireman. But one spring afternoon not long after his tenth birthday, when he was a student at the nearby Dunbar School, John McLendon's future suddenly and irrevocably came into view. It happened on the day of the sixth-grade field trip to Northeast Junior High, the new colored school that he would attend the following year. By that time McLendon had already seen his first basketball goal, the one that sat out on the playground at Dunbar. Since the school didn't have a basketball, the kids would toss "rocks and socks and everything else" at it. But at the new junior high school, it was a different story. Here was a brand-new full-size *indoor* basketball court, complete with a polished wood floor, brightly painted boundary lines, electric lights, and rows and rows of pristine bleachers. John McLendon had never seen anything so beautiful in his life.

What was even more transfixing, however, was the lone individual out on the court, a young man named P. L. Jacobs. Hired as Northeast Junior High's new trainer and coach, he shot the ball while he spoke to the wide-eyed students from Dunbar that morning. And as he talked, he kept moving farther and farther away from the goal — and kept making shot after shot after shot, all the way to the half-court line. "I just couldn't get over it," McLendon later said. "I had never seen anything like it in my entire life."

Then he added, "And that's when I decided to have a life in basketball."

There were two problems. The first was that he couldn't make the team. Not at Northeast Junior High School. And, after that, not at Sumner High School, either. For while John McLendon had found his life's calling, he had neither the skills nor the height — as a sixteen-year-old, he barely edged five feet eight — to play competitively. But he loved the game so much that, at both Northeast and Sumner, he took on the decidedly unglamorous job of team manager, refilling the water pail, toting laundry bags filled with sweat-soaked uniforms, and keeping handy a supply of gauze bandages, friction tape, bright orange Mercurochrome, and foul-smelling Unguentine. Going to practice every day, watching each drill, listening to the coach's instructions, and sitting on the bench at every game, he got his first inside look at what made some teams great while others faltered. At Sumner High School, named for the fiery abolitionist senator from Massachusetts — the only all-Negro high school in the state of Kansas — John McLendon marked the beginning of his basketball education.

His second problem was at home. Basket-Ball, as it was then often spelled, was not the career that Minnie McLendon had in mind for her elder stepson. But as a former schoolteacher, Minnie also knew a few things about adolescent psychology. Hoping to change John's mind, she made him take a solemn oath. If he wanted to pursue this crazy idea—this *bas-ket-ball,* she'd say, as if she had just swallowed a mouthful of castor oil—he had to make certain, solemn, as-God-is-my-witness promises.

He could never taste a drop of liquor, she told him. He could never drink a cup of coffee or a bottle of soda pop. He could never dip snuff or smoke a cigarette. And he had to attend church twice a week, study the Bible daily, and go to bed at an early hour every night.

Minnie's plan was a good one, but she had misjudged the level of John's interest.

John followed every rule. He had made up his mind.

In the meantime, despite not being able to make it onto a basketball team, he nonetheless developed into an athlete. At the Sumner High School gymnasium, he trained as a gymnast. For hours, he would practice L-sits and iron crosses on the rings and drop kips and handstands on the parallel bars. In the backyard at home he'd lift bricks and other makeshift weights or do scores of jumping jacks, push-ups, and deep knee bends. While he would always be on the slim side, beneath the freshly ironed shirts and trousers that Minnie would send him off to school in each morning, John McLendon was slowly developing a body to match his determination. And his biggest physical challenges, it turned out, lay just around the corner.

Kansas City, in those days, was the nation's second-largest slaughterhouse. Most of the big meat packers—Armour, Swift, Wilson, and Cudahy—had plants in the city, while the Kansas City stockyards, straddling both sides of the state line, from 12th to 23rd Streets, could hold more than seventy thousand cattle, fifty thousand hogs, and more than fifty-five thousand sheep, horses, and mules, all ready to be processed into meat, leather, and other products.

It was smelly, dirty, ghastly work. Men stood all day in pools of blood and piss. Piles of offal swarmed with thousands of green bottle flies, while the livestock, the whites of their eyes showing, had to be pushed and shoved into the chutes and holding pens. Most of the work was performed, at first, by bone-tough Irish immigrants fresh off the boat from Galway and Cork, looking for a way up. They had seen worse. Over time, Germans, eastern Europeans, and Mexicans found their way onto the killing floors as well. But even from the beginning, a few colored workers were hired by the slaughterhouses and packing plants, usually to perform the worst jobs. And during the summers of his late teenage years, McLendon was one of them.

"I worked in a hide cellar," McLendon later remembered, adding that he and his partner reeked so horribly after a full shift that nobody wanted to be near them. "We couldn't even ride the bus," he said, so they'd run home all the way from the industrial district on the other side of the Missouri River. On most afternoons they'd make a stop along the way at Edgerton Park.

Located eight blocks from his family home, it was the sole public outdoor Negro recreational facility in Kansas City, Kansas. It was a two-acre plot of sunburnt Bermuda grass, graced with half a dozen wooden picnic tables and a handful of scrawny oaks and elms. But on summer afternoons and evenings, the park was also the scene of impromptu amateur boxing matches, held beneath the twilight skies until darkness—and mosquitoes—sent everyone packing. "We'd just come up and pick an opponent," McLendon recalled. "You *tried* to pick someone in your own weight class." The fights were fought bare-chested and with gloves, but not with a whole lot of anything else. "The rule was that if you had a chance to knock a man out, you had to stop, something like bullfighting in Mexico. You just get ready to kill him, and that's it."

He added, "Sometimes, though, it didn't work, and guys got knocked out."

Already toned by his job at the hide plant, McLendon fought night after night, dodging jabs and uppercuts, absorbing body blows, and further toughening both his mind and his already well-muscled body. While he proved to be a smart, capable boxer, his days in the hide cellar and the summer nights at the park taught him something far more important. "I found out that when you go up to the park after you do that all week—working in all that salt and ham hocks and rot— *conditioning* was key."

But as much as John McLendon loved basketball and wanted to study the game at Springfield College in Massachusetts, where the game had been invented, there was a problem that simply could not be avoided: lack of money. So after he graduated from Sumner High, he worked out a plan: he would live at home and attend a local junior college while working at the hide plant until enough money could be cobbled together to get him to New England. And despite the fact that the Depression was already in full swing, with no end in sight, it was a solid plan. It would have worked, too, had his father not begun to do a little research of his own. Because the old man discovered that there was no need for John to go all the way to Springfield, Massachusetts, when the inventor of basketball worked only forty miles from their front door, at the University of Kansas.

By the fall of 1933, James Naismith was like a great-uncle who was still invited to all the family weddings but who was always seated off to the side with distant cousins, his counsel no longer needed and his opinions no longer actively sought. His defining moment, the one he would always be remembered for, had occurred more than forty years earlier, before all the students—and much of the faculty and staff—at the University of Kansas had even been born. Pushing seventy-two years of age, with old-fashioned eyeglasses, faintly Victorian three-piece suits, and wispy gray hair parted down the middle, Naismith seemed like a relic from another age. Even the formal, distant way that he was addressed, as *Dr.* James A. Naismith—a practice that continues to this day—promoted the image of a dowdy, slightly rotund old fogy smelling of tweed and pipe tobacco.

But the real Jim Naismith, the child of strict, hardworking, penny-wise Scottish immigrants, was nothing like that at all. Born and raised in the rocky, river-strewn forests and farmland of eastern Ontario, he was a life-toughened former country boy who spoke with God on a daily basis, had endured his own full measure of ups and downs, and knew how to fight when he had to. Naismith's early years were marked by unrelenting tragedy. When he was eight years old, his beloved grandfather died. Then the family sawmill was destroyed by fire, and his father contracted typhoid fever and passed away soon after. Three weeks later, on Jim's ninth birthday, his mother died as well. He missed her most of all. And for years afterward, whenever he was sad or upset, he would crawl alone into a grain bin and "talk" with her, seeking guidance.

Although he was passed off to be raised by a bachelor uncle who lived not far from the village of Almonte, the truth of the matter was that Jim Naismith largely raised himself. A hard worker, he bundled wheat and sheared sheep, went duck hunting in the fall, and on summer nights speared pike and muskie by the light of a pine-knot torch. Unable to afford a pair of ice skates as a child, he made his own—from a couple of discarded iron files, some hickory slats, and a pair of old boots.

Though he had a good sense of humor and enjoyed a rough-and-tumble time as much as the next fellow, by nature he wasn't a trouble-maker. So when some of the other boys began experimenting with tobacco and alcohol, Naismith held tight to the lessons he'd learned at the local Presbyterian church and steadfastly refused to join in. But the issue did not go away, and up and down the back roads of Almonte and Bennies Corners, word got around that Pete Naismith's nephew was too damned high-and-mighty to take even a sip of whiskey. One winter afternoon, while out driving a sleigh, Jim's path was blocked by a gang of local men who were determined to end his teetotaling once and for all. "I reached forward and loosened a sleigh stake and told them that I would brain them if they did not go about their business," he later recalled.

Naismith wasn't much of a student, and he dropped out of school at age seventeen. But after two years of working full-time, both on his uncle's farm and elsewhere, as a hired farmhand, he yearned for something more. He decided at first that he wanted to become a physician — but he later recoiled at some of the moral predicaments that sometimes arise in medicine. "Some things that a doctor should do I did not feel that I could do, such as letting a badly deformed baby die," he later wrote. He then decided upon a career in the ministry. But to become an ordained Presbyterian minister, he needed to attend college. So at age nineteen, Naismith returned to the local high school — where the administration, in a fit of spite, made him start over as a freshman.

But he persevered. Taking his schoolwork seriously for the first time in his life, James Naismith became a model student, mastering algebra and geometry and, after a considerable struggle, proper English grammar. Eventually allowed to skip two grades, and hoping to gain admission to McGill University in Montreal, the most prestigious college in all of Canada, he began to study ancient Greek, which, along with Latin, was one of the two required languages on the entrance examination. It was dreadfully slow going. It took Naismith two full weeks, studying at night by the light of a hurricane lamp, to understand just the first two sentences of *Anabasis* by Xenophon — an account of a Greek military force that outwitted a Persian army many times its size. But by the following fall, he had mastered enough of the two-thousand-year-old text to pass the exam. Two months shy of his twenty-second birthday, Jim Naismith headed off to college.

Though it was only a hundred and twenty-five miles away, McGill was so foreign to him it might as well have been Paris or Peru. Here, beside the polished oak tables in the reading room at the Redpath Library, or in the Elizabethan splendor of the physics building's lecture theater, was a world that had little in common with rough-hewn Almonte. But Montreal itself was an even greater wonder. Bright red electric trolley cars rattled up and down Saint Catherine Street, while docked at the city wharves were oceangoing steamships from Liverpool, Bristol, and Southampton, their dank holds filled with Saskatchewan wheat and English manufactured goods. Chorus girls danced the cancan in the tenpenny music halls down by the river, pickpockets and prostitutes prowled the narrow streets and alleyways of the old city, and during the annual winter carnival, when horse-drawn sleighs whispered along the icy streets, Montreal's nighttime sky shimmered with the glow of ice palaces and torchlight parades.

But Naismith was not distracted. Wavering between medicine and the ministry, and determined to find a career through which he could help make the world a better place, he plowed into his studies and stuck to the straight and narrow. And along the way, something unexpected happened: Jim Naismith discovered athletics. Or, rather, athletics discovered him.

James Naismith. *(Public domain)*

One fall afternoon he was watching the McGill rugby team practice when one of the players—a center—left the field with a broken nose. When one of the team captains asked the spectators if anyone would fill in, Naismith volunteered. Even though he had never played rugby before, it did not take a genius to figure out the basics of the game, and Naismith made a respectable showing. A week later he was a full-fledged member of the team.

He turned out to be a magnificent athlete. In the rough-and-tumble world of rugby—football in Canada—Jim Naismith had all the right stuff. A farm boy, he had no trouble handling the predawn practices held in the iron cold of Ontario's fleeting fall or the late-season matches played in mud and freezing rain. With fifteen players to a side and few rules, and played with no helmets, pads, or other protective equipment, the games were like miniature wars, leaving a trail of busted bones and bloody noses. And Naismith, with his square jaw, piercing gaze, and full mustache, could take it as well as he could give it. Once, after a brutal Saturday afternoon game in Ottawa, he gave the following morning's Scripture reading in church sporting two black eyes. On another occasion he coldcocked a rugby teammate—with a single right-handed punch—after he had called Naismith a sissy for not going out drinking with the team.

After graduating—with honors—in both Hebrew and philosophy from McGill in 1887, Naismith enrolled in the Presbyterian College, the theological seminary next door. He did not, however, abandon his athletic activities, something that didn't sit well with his professors. Future men of the cloth were supposed to behave at all times with an understated, black-robed decorum, and more than a few churchmen believed that sports, like divorce, alcohol, and Sunday streetcars, were the handiwork of the devil. But Naismith began to see something else. Could sports, he wondered, be used to spread the Gospel? Could his behavior on the playing field help win souls for Christ?

The answer arrived during his final year at Presbyterian, and it did not come in class. Instead it came during a rugby match.

The game, played on a brilliant autumn afternoon, had been a brutal, knuckle-busting affair. Neither team could break out, and tempers flared. Finally a teammate on Naismith's immediate left, a guard, let loose with a string of profanity—then he cut himself short, even though Naismith hadn't uttered a word. "I beg your pardon, Jim," the guard said. "I forgot you were there."

For Naismith, the incident was the tipping point.

"It set me to thinking about personal influence," he later explained. And after discussing the incident with a trusted friend and adviser, D. A. Budge, the secretary of the local branch of the Young Men's Christian Association, Naismith reached a momentous decision.

Nine months later, Jim Naismith came to America.

During the bright New England fall, when the sugar maples and oaks and poplars put on their annual color parade, students at the International YMCA Training School in Springfield, Massachusetts, could play American football on the athletic field, toss lacrosse balls out on the quadrangle, or go for long walks in the brisk autumn air, which smelled of wood smoke and burning leaves. Come spring, when the nickel-gray blanket of ice covering the Connecticut River heaved and broke and the first bluebirds and song sparrows appeared on windowsills and backyard clotheslines, there were baseball gloves to oil, soccer balls to reinflate, and spirits on the rise. But during the grim winter months, when the sun was a pale imitation of its summer self and nighttime temperatures in western Massachusetts could drop well below zero for days on end, physical education instructors at the school had a new foe to fight. It was boredom.

Arriving completely unannounced in Springfield some fourteen months earlier, Naismith had talked to Luther Halsey Gulick Jr., the training school's superintendent of physical instruction, who hired him on the spot. In truth it hadn't been a hard sell, as Naismith was an almost perfect match for the college. Not only was he a devout

Christian who had both university and seminary degrees, he was also an accomplished athlete. Moreover, he added a slightly international flavor to the faculty at a time when both the college and the YMCA itself were looking to have a global impact. Naismith, for his part, was ecstatic. He felt he had found his life's calling.

What he hadn't counted on was a classroom full of troublemakers.

The eighteen students in Naismith's physical education class during the fall semester of 1891 were a mouthy, high-spirited lot, easily bored and quick to criticize anything that smacked of being unnecessary busywork. And as the autumn days blew away and the winter gloom settled in, their boredom and fidgeting increased. Efforts to teach new gymnastics routines or introduce other games had all failed miserably. Finally it got so bad that Gulick stepped in. What was needed, Gulick decided, was a brand-new game for the students to play indoors during the winter months. So one week before Christmas, he told Naismith to invent one. By Monday morning.

At first Naismith toyed with the idea of creating an indoor variation of the game he knew best — rugby, or English football — one in which two opposing teams would try to move a leather ball toward a goal at opposite ends of the gymnasium. But he faced an immediate problem, namely, how not to make the game too rough, as tackling on a hardwood floor would inevitably result in broken bones. He solved this by requiring players to pass the ball to one another rather than run with it. Tackling could then be outlawed. And this, in turn, also helped determine the shape of the ball that would be used. Rather than an English rugby ball or an American football, whose elongated shapes allowed them to be carried, one-armed, by players, a round ball would be ideal. And since one didn't want the players to get injured by a flying ball, a larger ball — like those used in soccer — would work best.

It was a beginning.

But there were other equally vexing issues. The most difficult was the size and shape of the goal. In terms of area, a gymnasium, of course, is much smaller than a soccer or football field. Furthermore, with the

number of players out on the floor—there were eighteen students in
Naismith's class, so he figured on nine to a team—it would be difficult
to get any kind of a straight shot at the goal. There would simply be too
many bodies in the way. "I was sure that this play would lead to rough-
ness," Naismith later wrote. "And I did not want that."

This was the stumper. And as Friday gave way to Saturday and then
Sunday with no solution in sight, Naismith began to lose heart. Then
by chance he remembered a game that he had played as a child back in
Bennies Corners. Known as Duck on the Rock, it combined rock
throwing with a form of tag. In order for one player to tag another, he
or she had to first knock a small rock—called a duck—off a large
boulder. But before the thrower could tag someone, he or she had to
first locate and set his own rock back on the boulder. As a result, throwers soon learned that if they threw their own rocks too hard, the rocks
would usually ricochet too far away to be easily found, which left the
throwers with little time to tag someone. The better players soon discovered, however, that a high, arcing shot was best.

It was the first big breakthrough. By thinking about an *upward* shot
toward the goal, one that arced over the heads of the other players, Naismith was entering new territory—in fact, a new dimension—and
leaving rugby behind. The goals for the new game could be, he decided,
two boxes, set at either ends of the court, that the players would try to
throw the ball into. The second breakthrough came when he wrestled
with the idea of where to place the boxes. Realizing that the goals
would be too easy to defend if he kept them on the floor, he kept looking upward. By having the boxes elevated, *above* the heads of all the
players, scoring would depend on skill. It was his eureka moment.

The next morning Naismith asked the school janitor, James Stebbins, if he had a couple of spare wooden boxes—about eighteen inches
by eighteen inches—wide enough to comfortably hold a soccer ball.
Stebbins did not, but he did have a couple of peach baskets that the
instructor could have. Naismith then borrowed a ladder and nailed the
baskets to a wooden railing that happened to hang exactly ten feet

above the gymnasium floor. Then he closed the door to his office and wrote out thirteen rules for the new game, which he handed to the school stenographer to type. When class began that day, Naismith tacked the rules onto the bulletin board. His students winced.

"Another new game," one groaned.

But this one was an immediate, unqualified, and unparalleled success.

Not only did the young men who first tried out Naismith's invention at the small Massachusetts school want to play again, so did practically everyone else who was introduced to the new game. And in spreading the word, basketball had a powerful, built-in ally—the Young Men's Christian Association. Indeed, less than two months after the world's first basketball contest was played, the rules of the game were published in the *Triangle,* the Springfield College journal, copies of which were posted to YMCA chapters all over the country. And Springfield College students, all of whom were "Y-men," soon spread the game themselves—and with astonishing speed. A NEW GAME OF BALL, read the headline in the *New York Times* on April 26, 1892, A SUBSTITUTE FOR FOOTBALL WITHOUT ITS ROUGH FEATURES. Basketball had been introduced to the city three days earlier, and by midsummer it was being played in Brooklyn and out in Iowa and in many places in between. A year later, the game had debuted in California. By the end of the decade, basketball was being played in all forty-five states. Without intending to, James Naismith had lit an athletic fire the likes of which the nation had never seen.

From the outset, basketball had a lot going for it. It required very little in the form of equipment. It was also unabashedly democratic. The new game appealed to bluebloods and immigrants, farmers and city folk, girls as well as boys. Yale University fielded a team in 1894, and Harvard and Princeton soon followed suit. All-Jewish teams blossomed across Manhattan; there was a Hull House team in Chicago; and basketball became so popular in Philadelphia that some gymnasium managers, tired of their limited floor space being overrun by the new roundball craze, tried unsuccessfully to ban the game. There were all-Catholic teams, women's college teams, small-town teams, military teams, industrial teams, teams composed of theological seminarians, and colored teams and white teams. In South Dakota during the summer of 1892—less than eighteen months after the massacre at Wounded Knee and the coming of the Ghost Dance—young Lakota men and boys were introduced to basketball by a former instructor at the International YMCA Training School in Springfield. "We cut small saplings for uprights, and in place of baskets we used a rim made of willows and fastened to the uprights," he later wrote.

Even more remarkably, the new game soon spread across the globe as well. The very first contest, in fact, had been witnessed by Genza-buro Ishikawa, a visiting student at Springfield College, who subsequently helped introduce basketball to Japan. Other YMCA enthusiasts, joined by Christian missionaries, quickly carried Naismith's invention overseas. In England, basketball was first played at Shaftesbury House, in Margate, in 1894. By 1896 it was being played in Brazil, and it had spread to China by 1898. US Marines on gunboat diplomacy duty outside the Forbidden City served as referees for local Chinese teams, while six thousand miles away, along the eastern coast of Madagascar, it was French soldiers who brought the game to Africa.

And as the new American game spread farther and farther across the globe—to remote barrios in the Philippines, beneath the Acropolis in Athens, or in Jerusalem, a short walk from the Temple Mount—it sometimes had unintended effects. "In Cairo we were told that eleven teams participated in the anniversary games at the 'Y,' which were attended by three thousand people," Laurence Locke Doggett, a YMCA official, would write decades later. "There were three girls' teams, and when it is remembered that five years before no woman would appear in public without the traditional long cloak and veil, it will be realized what a tumbling of traditions was represented by the appearance of three teams of girls in gymnasium shorts."

Naismith, meanwhile, was flabbergasted by it all. Once, on a family vacation out West, he drove across what was then the world's highest suspension bridge, hovering almost one thousand feet over the Arkansas River. But what thrilled him the most was not the stomach-churning ride across the Royal Gorge but the deserted work camp at the bridge's south end, where he spied two basketball goals nailed to a pair of pines. Along the Boulevard Saint-Michel in Paris one raw spring day in 1918, while working with American doughboys on behalf of the YMCA, Naismith ducked into a bookstore only to discover a slender red volume published more than twenty years earlier that contained a French translation of the rules of "Le Basket-Ball." His friends and former classmates, meanwhile, would regularly report to him on the growth of the game worldwide. "In all parts of different cities we saw basketball goals everywhere," wrote one correspondent from Asia. "Lots of spectators from all kinds of social levels, coolies besides the soldiers, and the family carrying a baby in hands, the referee in a long Chinese skirt or coat...You can just feel what the game means to them."

As the game sped away from Naismith and around the country, it also changed.

Peach baskets were replaced by iron rings, a nest made of metal chain dangling below. At first there were no holes in the bottom of the goals, so the ball had to be retrieved either by someone climbing up on a ladder and fetching it or by pushing the ball out with a pole. Teams were limited to five players on the court rather than nine. Fouls were standardized, and free throws were introduced. Dribbling was allowed, while the chicken-wire walls surrounding some courts—which bequeathed the term "cagers" to generations of future basketball players—began to disappear. Backboards were introduced, preventing spectators seated up near the goals from "helping" the ball into the basket. By the start of the new century, the zone defense had appeared.

Uniforms evolved as well. Heavy, long-sleeved woolens, paired with lace-up, high-top leather boots, gave way to lighter, short-sleeved jerseys, cotton shorts, and rubber-soled shoes. The actual basketballs themselves changed, too. At first, the laces covering the slit where the India rubber bladder was inserted were so prominent and rode so high above the surface of the ball that players could only dribble low lest an errant bounce send the ball careening off to the side.

But during the 1930s a new kind of basketball made its debut. It was molded and laceless, thirty inches in circumference rather than thirty-two. Not only did it bounce true but players could also move across the court much faster while dribbling it. Footwear was improving as well, and in 1932 the Converse Rubber Shoe Company added the signature of its ace salesman and promoter — a fast-living, hokum-spewing, former barnstorming basketball player and marketing wizard named Chuck Taylor — to the ankle patch on its bestselling basketball shoe. The rules kept changing as well. The new emphasis was on faster play and, most of all, continuous motion. Slowly but steadily, the ground had shifted. And while it was unclear where all the changes would lead, one thing was certain. Basketball was on the move.

So was Naismith. In 1898, after marrying his landlord's daughter in Springfield, earning a medical degree out in Denver, and becoming a father, Naismith and his family moved one final time, to a new home and a new life on the edge of the Great Plains. And while Lawrence, Kansas, undoubtedly struck most newcomers in the fading years of the nineteenth century as little more than a quaint college town, there were plenty of local residents who knew otherwise. Hired as the new college chaplain at the University of Kansas, Naismith also became the school's one-man physical education department. Working out of a cramped office in the basement of Snow Hall, he taught classes on personal hygiene and gymnastics, led regular church services in the university auditorium, and ministered to the spiritual needs of the student body. He soon added another responsibility as well.

When Naismith arrived at KU, basketball there was practically nonexistent. Considered by most male undergraduates to be a "sissy game"— in large part because it had first been played on that campus by women — there was no men's basketball team at the school and no plan to create one. Naismith decided to change that. Recruiting players from his classes and teaching them the rules of the game, he served as both the coach and promoter of the brand-new Kansas Jayhawks basketball team. Its first game was played against the Kansas City, Missouri, YMCA, in February of 1899. They lost 16–5, but it was a beginning.

The early games were haphazard affairs, to say the least. Because there was no suitable place to play basketball on campus, games were played at a local skating rink, in a livery stable, and on makeshift, odd-size courts, many with support poles out on the floor. Moreover, Naismith, who also refereed many of the first games, often bent over backwards to make sure that his calls did not favor his team, to the everlasting annoyance of his own players. But in truth Naismith often didn't care about the final score anyway. For him basketball was always about recreation, not winning. And it showed. For the nine years that he coached the Kansas basketball team, the Jayhawks posted only two winning seasons.

But even in that first, brief season, fate had been busy. In the closing week of March 1899, Naismith's Jayhawks headed east, to Independence, Missouri, to play two games against the local YMCA chapter. And sitting high up in the hayloft for both games — low-scoring affairs ending in defeat for the visiting Kansans — was a stocky thirteen-year-old boy, his narrowly set blue eyes catching every bit of action on the floor below. Already known as a hell-raiser and a bad hat, one who liked to smoke penny cigars and drink glasses of beer, his brow would soon be permanently scarred by a billiard cue in a pool-hall fight. As Forrest Allen watched the two teams move deliberately back and forth across the wooden floor of the stable, his eyes aglow in the shimmering lantern light, no one present that evening, and most certainly not James Naismith, would have imagined that one day, because of this young man, basketball would never be the same.

CHAPTER 6

Lawrence

Growing up outside of Kansas City, the six Allen boys were a boisterous and lively lot who swam and ice-skated at a nearby pond, got into their share of fistfights, and organized endless corner-lot baseball games. Often joining them was the neighborhood tomboy, a striking brunette named Bess Wallace, who rode horses, played tennis, and could swing a mean bat. She was also "the only girl in Independence who could whistle through her teeth," recalled one childhood friend. A less frequent playmate was another neighborhood lad—and Bess's future husband—a glasses-wearing, piano-playing mama's boy named Harry Truman.

Like his older brother Pete, Forrest blossomed into an outstanding athlete, particularly after he left his beer-drinking and tobacco-smoking days behind. By the time he reached his late teens, in addition to the neighborhood baseball games, he played tackle football without the benefit of a helmet or pads and launched a brief, teeth-jarring career as a boxer down at the Kansas City stockyards. But no sport caught his attention more than basketball. The new game first came to Independence in 1894, when some members of the local athletic club knocked the bottoms out of a couple of old wooden chairs, nailed them upside down on walls at opposite ends of a barn, and shot at them with a bounceless, twelve-pound medicine ball. Five years later, when he watched Naismith's team in the stable, Forrest was hooked. By the time he entered high school, Kansas City had become a basketball hotbed, and he was well known as one of the game's best players, a six-footer with a flawless push shot. Not only had he and his brothers formed their own barnstorming team — the Amazing Allen Brothers, who lost only one game in five years — he also dropped out of high school to play for two other Kansas City basketball teams. And in 1905, when he was only nineteen years old, Forrest Allen, by then nicknamed Fog, pulled off one of the greatest feats in basketball's first decade and a half of existence.

That year, the best basketball team in America, if not the world, was in all likelihood the Buffalo Germans out of Buffalo, New York, a YMCA outfit that had won the Amateur Athletic Union basketball tournament the year before. They had also swept the competition at the 1904 Olympics in St. Louis, where basketball was played as an exhibition sport, and declared themselves to be world champions. For Fog Allen, who was then playing for the highly successful Kansas City Athletic Club team and was naturally competitive to begin with, this was simply too much to bear. So he promptly sent a telegram to the Buffalo club challenging them to a playoff. He also told them that he would cover their expenses.

His impetuousness had all the makings of a disaster. The Germans accepted, but Allen had failed to consult the management of the Kansas City Athletic Club. When the club officers told him to call off the games for fear of losing money, he dug in his heels. "Forrest was in too deep and had to come up with a plan to suit all parties," his biographer, Blair Kerkhoff, later wrote. Remarkably, that was exactly what he did.

Recruiting a group of well-heeled local businessmen whom he had met through the club as financial backers, Allen told the Germans that the three-game series was on. Then, incredibly, this son of a produce salesman rented not just any building but Convention Hall itself — the massive auditorium in downtown Kansas City that had hosted the

Democratic Party's national convention only five years earlier. The skeptics thought Allen was nuts. A five-thousand-seat auditorium for *basketball?*

But Allen was just getting warmed up. He started planting stories in the local newspapers, declaring that never had such a momentous sporting event been scheduled to take place in Kansas City before. With his brother Pete's help, he stirred up interest in the series at the University of Kansas and arranged to have Naismith take part. Moreover, Allen cleverly scheduled two nights of *women's* high school basketball games to open the so-called world's championship series, stoking local rivalries while at the same time broadening his potential audience.

And it worked. Not only did Kansas Citians flock to the series, it also turned into a drama all its own. The Germans won the first game, 40–36, on what the *Kansas City Star* declared was nothing short of a series of monstrously bad calls by one of the referees. The second game—a roundhouse brawl during which Pete Allen got a busted jaw, the tripping of players was allowed, and one of the visitors staggered off the court with a black eye and a bloody nose—went to the home team. Finally, during the title match, which Naismith was called upon to officiate, the Kansas City club, led by Fog himself, decimated the Germans, 45–14. "We beat the tar out of them," Allen later remembered. Not only had he promoted a successful tournament, the spectators inside Convention Hall also formed what was probably, up until that time, the largest audience for basketball anywhere.

There was one other detail.

"We gave them [the Germans] six hundred dollars," Allen later recalled. "And," he added, "we made five thousand."

It was a lesson not lost on the nineteen-year-old. And it was only a beginning. Six months later, Forrest Allen, by then one of the best-known basketball players in America, arrived at a university along the banks of the slow-moving Kansas River, thirty-five miles west of the Missouri state line. He had come to Lawrence to play basketball and get an education. But what he ended up doing, almost single-handedly, was creating basketball's first great college town.

It took him most of four decades to do it.

After a stellar career as an athlete and student at the University of Kansas, and then a busy dozen years crossing back and forth across the Kansas-Missouri border as a coach and medical student, Forrest Allen returned to Lawrence for good in the summer of 1919. University of Kansas school officials hired him thinking they were getting a new basketball coach and a physical education director. What they got instead was a human dynamo. Within three seasons Allen utterly transformed the fortunes of Jayhawks basketball. Using a combination of man-to-man, set, and a newly refined zone defense, as well as scissors plays and one-handed shooting and passing, his 1922 and 1923 teams were considered by many to be the best in the country.

Much of Allen's genius was in his single-minded, comprehensive approach to the game, which he outlined one year later in his first book, a 445-page omnibus that dwarfed every other book on basketball that had been published before then. Bound in delft-blue leatherette, its pages edged in gold, *My Basket-ball Bible* served up its share of practice drills, play diagrams, and grainy photographs of the proper way to shoot an underhand set shot or guard a pivoter. But for Allen, whose nickname sportswriters by then were writing as "Phog," this was only the beginning. There were entire sections on the proper heating and ventilation of indoor basketball courts, how to entertain fans between halves, and the proper remuneration of officials. Nearly one-third of the book focused on athletic injuries, including detailed instructions on how to wrap a figure-eight knee bandage, the use of massage to relieve back pain, and how to deal with charley horses, hemorrhoids, and jock itch. The new Kansas coach also aired his thoughts on how to create an ideal schedule, how to form a bond with your players, how to inspire your team, and, most important, how to build a tradition. *My Basket-ball Bible* wasn't just another coaching guide. It was basketball's New Testament—and Allen's personal road map to conjuring up new levels of passion for basketball and, in the process, creating a new kind of college game.

And that was exactly what he did. Not only did his Jayhawks teams quickly become winners, regularly toppling Oklahoma, Nebraska, Kansas State, and, especially, Missouri, the games themselves also grew into miniature spectacles, all orchestrated by Allen himself. He made certain that the interior of Robinson Gymnasium, the somber, castle-like stone edifice on the western edge of what was known as the Hill, where Kansas played its home games, was festooned with brightly colored bunting, flags, and pennants for each team in the Missouri Valley Conference. On game days, Allen persuaded the university chancellor to shorten morning classes in order to allow the KU student body—"the thundering thousand"—to attend a pep rally. During halftimes, there were acrobatic stunts, musical performances, and three-minute boxing matches. One year, on Washington's Birthday, a home game was preceded by a parade. Led by an eight-year-old boy who was dressed to the nines in a pint-size naval uniform, the Jayhawks, wearing three different sets of red, white, and blue uniforms, filed onto the court holding aloft a huge American flag while the college band played "The Star-Spangled Banner." For those who couldn't get into Robinson gym, Allen arranged with Western Union to have the halftime and final scores announced at a local theater. Basketball had found its first P. T. Barnum.

In time there would come the Phog Allen basketball shoe, "Designed for fast, sure footwork," according to the advertising copy. "Be sure—be safe—be fast—wear 'Phog' Allen Basketball Shoes." There was also the number 202 Phog Allen basketball, with its red and black laces, as well as more books and pamphlets, including *Better Basketball, Basket-Ball Injuries and Their Care,* and *Coach "Phog" Allen's Sports Stories for*

Forrest C. "Phog" Allen. *(University Archives, Kenneth Spencer Research Library, University of Kansas Libraries)*

You and Youth. The books were ghostwritten by his wife, Bessie—his high school sweetheart from Independence—whom he cut in on half the royalties.

Allen's most memorable creation might have been Goal-Hi, a playground version of basketball in which the players shot at a single goal—a backboardless metal contraption from which the ball exited at an unpredictable angle. Despite sinking his own money into the goals' manufacture and planting stories in friendly newspapers—NEW GAME SWEEPS CITY, declared the headline in a Sioux Falls newspaper—Goal-Hi was largely a bust. Allen's unusual creation did, however, have one long-term consequence. By giving a higher score to successful shots made from beyond fifteen feet than to those made nearer to the goal, Allen helped lay the groundwork for the three-point shot.

He also barnstormed for basketball. Not only did Allen give as many as one hundred talks about KU basketball a year—at high schools, public libraries, churches, service clubs, and whatever organization could pay his rather modest speaking fee—he also hosted a program on radio station KFKU, appeared in various training films, and became a regular on the summertime coaching clinic circuit. Allen also stirred up newspaper stories whenever he could, such as those offering his opinion on the perfect food for athletes—which he claimed was the orange—and explaining why basketball goals should be raised to twelve feet. "He liked to get into controversies," Paul Endacott, one of his first star players, later recalled. "He liked the publicity. He'd try anything."

But it wasn't all snake oil and self-promotion.

A larger-than-life character, one who once demonstrated to his players the proper way to gargle while standing on his desk in his underwear, Phog Allen truly believed in basketball, in himself, and, as it turned out, in a pioneering approach to sports medicine and physical therapy. He had trained as an osteopath, and his ability to manipulate bones and muscle tissue was legendary. "He had a system where he'd pull your legs," one of his former students recalled. "If one leg was longer than the other, that meant your spine was out of order, and he'd go up and down your spine with his thumbs." Not only did he help relieve countless dislocated shoulders and sore backs, but as word of his success grew, professional athletes, some from as far away as New York City, also began to show up in Lawrence seeking relief. And in one particularly incredible moment, he even revived a young man who had been pronounced dead at an army training camp during World War I.

But the greatest magic that Phog Allen worked was upon his players. In the early years, they were by and large Kansas and Missouri boys, a number of whom—like a seldom-used second-string guard named Adolph Rupp, the son of German-born farmers from Halstead, Kansas—would go on to make an impact on basketball. Allen drilled them, incessantly, in fundamentals. Sometimes he'd have each of them shoot fifty free throws—then start over and shoot fifty more. Most important, he taught them his beloved half-court game. Not only did his players have to memorize a playbook, he also diagrammed the actual plays by painting long lines for each player—in washable yellow, blue, orange, and green paint—on the gymnasium floor. But Allen could also capture their imaginations, reach down into their hearts and souls, and encourage them to go beyond themselves. "He'd make these talks in the dressing room just before we'd go out," Endacott recalled. "We didn't remember just what he did say. It could have been anything. But it got us to play hard."

By 1926, the overflow crowds at the Robinson Gymnasium had grown so large that the university president agreed to include, over the faculty's howls of protest, a basketball court inside the soon-to-be-constructed college auditorium. The resulting architectural arrangement for Hoch Auditorium—which also had to host plays and concerts, lectures and convocations—was far from ideal. But it did provide Allen's team with an unexpected secret weapon. Because of design limitations, the wooden basketball court sat directly on the auditorium's concrete foundation. This meant that the floor had no give whatsoever, and anyone playing on it too long would end up with rubber legs, shin splints, or both. "If you practiced there a day or two," Allen's son Bob remembered, "there's no way you could play a game."

So, he added, they never did. Instead the Jayhawks would practice back at the old gym and not show up at Hoch Auditorium until the day of the game. Not only were their legs fresh, they also, unlike their opponents, knew what to expect. Moreover, the teams that played against KU in Lawrence usually did so as part of a multigame road trip. And on many occasions, playing at Hoch so drained their reserve that they often lost their next games. For the Jayhawks, it was almost like getting two wins for the price of one.

But KU's basketball prowess didn't need to depend on tricks. Allen was a master coach who understood basketball inside and out and could effectively communicate his insights to his players. And his teams won: by 1927, after a decade of Allen's coaching basketball in Lawrence, the Jayhawks had won 161 games against 35 losses. They'd also won eight Missouri Valley Conference championships, and two of Allen's teams had been widely considered to be unofficial national champions. Allen himself, meanwhile, had become the winningest coach in college basketball, a title that he, and then his former Kansas players Adolph Rupp of Kentucky and Dean Smith of North Carolina, would hold on to for the next eight decades. Basketball may have been born on a college campus in Massachusetts, but it was in Lawrence, Kansas, where the college game learned how to walk.

Phog's success, of course, bred enemies. When the Jayhawks played in Lincoln, Nebraska, fans hurled apple cores at his head. At Iowa State, not only did angry spectators once toss a dead chicken at his feet, on another occasion they literally chased him into the locker room. Over in Manhattan, Kansas, the home of Kansas State, the animosity ran even deeper. "He was a great contributor to the game," Jack Gardner, the coach of the Wildcats once remarked. "Too bad he was such a jerk." Even in Lawrence, Phog had rubbed more than a few folks the wrong way. After some alumni complained that basketball had been unfairly elevated over football, Allen lost his title as athletic director. And there were plenty of faculty members, especially during the grim, cash-starved years of the Great Depression, who felt that too much of the university's resources were being sidelined for a game.

It did not matter. Because all across Kansas, from the dry, windblown wheat country near the Colorado border, where the dust clouds rolled and traveling rainmakers hawked their harebrained schemes, to the oak- and elm-lined streets of suburban Kansas City, where dentists and insurance men gathered on jacquard davenports alongside console radios to listen with their families to the latest news bulletins from overseas, everyone knew about Jayhawks basketball. And they knew in Norman and Columbia, Boulder and Omaha—as well as in New York, Chicago, and Los Angeles. By the early 1930s, Phog Allen hadn't just built a sporting dynasty at Kansas. He had also created the world's first true basketball town.

Only something—or, rather, someone—was missing.

Jim Naismith.

*   *   *

His once-black hair, still parted in the middle, was now dusted with gray. Crow's-feet creased his temples, and a fondness for his wife's cooking had added a noticeable girth to his waistline. Their children—there were five—were all grown, while Naismith's responsibilities at the university had slowly dwindled. Back in 1924, the president of the university forced Naismith out as the chair of the department of physical education. As the Great Depression deepened and a newly elected US president encouraged the nation to have faith in itself, James Naismith, the inventor of basketball, was the old fogy over in the PE department, a kindly, gray-haired relic from another age.

The game had in fact passed him by. While basketball steadily grew in stature, not just in Lawrence but also around the world, Naismith held fast to his own beliefs about how the game should be played. He never cared about winning—as his losing record coaching the Jayhawks basketball team from 1898 to 1907 attested—and he felt that the game should be played for its own sake. Naismith detested the increasing physical contact and commercialism of the sport and still held to his belief that nine or more players on a team was just fine. While he dutifully attended KU home basketball games, he sat quietly in the stands, never cheering. And even though Naismith and Allen were on cordial terms with each other, on a philosophical level they were polar opposites.

Naismith had other concerns as well. Money, for one, had never been overly plentiful. Not only had he refused to cash in on his invention, he also regularly loaned—or gave—funds to students in need throughout his years at KU. During his early years in Lawrence, he had supplemented his income by serving as a guest minister at a number of small rural congregations and by spending one summer working as a laborer on a road crew. And when the Depression hit, finances in the Naismith household became even tighter. After the university cut faculty salaries, he started missing mortgage payments and eventually lost the house that he and his wife, Maude, had built on Mississippi Street.

But despite these troubles, Naismith kept as busy as ever. He gave in to the automobile age and bought first a used Studebaker and then a Ford, but he proved to be a horrible driver. Once, when he had been pulled over by a traffic cop in Kansas City for running a stop sign, he had to ask the officer what the sign meant. Out of his small office at Robinson Gymnasium, he kept up with his research into the functioning of the human body, often involving his handful of students in the process. Once he had tried to find out whether regular stretching could make short people grow taller.

But by the dry, hot summer of 1933, when corn prices bottomed out, ranchers fretted about how to feed their cattle, and the first dust storms had already begun to blow across Kansas, James Naismith knew that his days at KU were numbered. What he didn't know was that, with a knock at the door that fall, the final chapters in his basketball journey would begin.

CHAPTER 7

"That's How You Do It!"

John McLendon wasn't the first colored student at the University of Kansas.

Not by a long shot.

A Negro woman had been admitted in 1870, only four years after the school opened. The first colored graduate came fifteen years later, and the Jayhawks baseball and football teams featured Negro players on their rosters throughout the 1880s and 1890s. By World War I, there had been scores of colored KU graduates, while in the late 1920s, the number of colored students on campus in any given year was more than one hundred. When McLendon showed up in Lawrence in the late summer of 1933, Negroes had been attending KU for more than half a century.

But they also lived a most precarious existence. For in Lawrence, despite Kansas's storied past as a so-called free state, the abolitionist flame had flickered and all but gone out. In 1882, three Negro men accused of murder were taken away from authorities by an angry white mob and led to a nearby bridge, where they were lynched. "Pete Vinegar, George Robertson and Isaac King were each swung over the bridge and their bodies left dangling over the muddy Kaw," the *Lawrence Daily Journal* reported, adding, "Prayers were short." Colored citizens, who made up nearly a quarter of the town's population by the turn of the century, were now barred from downtown restaurants, shops, and theaters. Many also felt that after three o'clock in the afternoon, it was unwise to be out on the streets of town. "Lawrence was a nasty old hole," recalled Arthur Lloyd Johnson, who grew up in the town's small colored community.

Dark clouds had appeared over KU as well.

In 1902, a group of white students stole a Negro cadaver from the medical school and hung it, in plain sight, on campus. Within a decade, colored athletes disappeared from Jayhawks teams, while some professors began insisting that all Negro students enrolled in their courses sit at the back of the classroom. Segregation was part and parcel of campus life. Negro students were banned from living in the dormitories and had to rent rooms from colored families or live in makeshift fraternity houses in North Lawrence or East Lawrence. When the Memorial Union opened a new cafeteria in the 1920s, colored students had to sit in a designated section, even though whites could eat anywhere. A similar mind-set limited the classes Negro students were allowed to take. "The administration would keep blacks out of engineering and blacks out of medicine," one former KU student recalled. "[They] frowned on law. Music department was wide open. But that was it. See, it was a double, crooked deal."

Conditions only worsened in the 1930s, as the Great Depression took its toll and fewer and fewer colored families could entertain dreams of a college education for their children. Not only did the number of Negro undergraduates at KU begin to decline, the students themselves had also become less visible. Colored students were barred from attending on-campus dances and could no longer take part in intramural athletics. Unease and uncertainty regularly hovered over their day-to-day lives. The old Lawrence and the old KU were gone, and what would replace them, in the year 1933, was far from clear.

John McLendon was about to find out.

His father, however, wasn't taking any chances. For even though it was boiling hot on that late-summer day when he took his son to school, the railroad man didn't slip off his jacket, loosen his tie, and roll up his sleeves, though other men did. Instead he kept his wool jacket on all day long, both outside, in the blazing late-August sun, and inside the classroom buildings, where the air felt like it was coming from a blast furnace. Anyone watching him closely that day would have noticed that his jacket hung a little lower on the left side. For in the inside pocket—grip up, loaded, but with the safety on—rested a small revolver. You just never knew, the father reasoned; you just never knew for sure.

His son, however, soon had a pretty good idea.

On the very first day of school, John McLendon walked up the steps of the hulking, neoclassical administration building, located his classroom, found an empty desk near the back, and sat down. The class was an introduction to economics. Once the professor arrived, he kicked off the semester in his usual fashion. First he introduced himself and talked a little about the class, which was, as a result of the ongoing economic crisis, more relevant than ever. He called roll after that and greeted the students, many by name. Then he told a nigger joke.

"I just walked right on out," McLendon later recalled. "The way the classroom was set up, I had to walk behind the instructor," he said. "He just looked at me, and he looked puzzled. But I didn't say anything. I just kept on going."

Welcome to KU, McLendon thought to himself.

It was basketball, of course, that had brought John McLendon to Lawrence, and he wasted no time trying to get involved. In those days, players on the KU basketball teams were usually from Kansas. Some were farm boys who had spent long hours shooting at an iron hoop nailed to the side of a barn, and some were from country towns like St. Marys or Osage City. Others, from Topeka and Wichita, had played their high school ball in brick gymnasiums and had traveled to away games on team buses. And being a native Missourian, Phog Allen had no problems with crossing the state line in search of talent. "To hell with Kansas," grumbled the University of Missouri fans, but it didn't matter. Phog snagged his fair share of Kansas City boys as well.

The Jayhawks were also white. There had never been a Negro basketball player at KU. None had played for Naismith early on, nor had any been on the roster during the years when the Jayhawks played in the Missouri Valley Conference. When the Big Six Conference was formed in 1928, there weren't any regulations barring colored athletes. Instead there was an unwritten agreement by which all the member universities, including Kansas, agreed not to allow Negro athletes on their teams. Basketball, like all the other varsity sports at KU during the 1930s, was for whites only.

But at the open tryouts for the Jayhawks varsity team, held in Robinson Gymnasium each fall, McLendon arrived, dressed and ready to play, and took a seat in the bleachers with all the other hopefuls. "I was sitting there with the other guys," McLendon recalled, "and Phog Allen is calling some of the guys out to do some of the drills that he's doing. But he never did call me. And so I said to myself, 'Well, this is a hopeless situation.' And then I went around to the other students, and they said, 'They don't allow you to play on anything.' "

McLendon was beginning to get the picture. Or at least some of it. For even though Allen honored the gentleman's agreement and kept the Jayhawks lily-white, his personal life revealed a different side. For years, Phog's next-door neighbors on Louisiana Street in Lawrence were a colored family named Holland, whose patriarch, born a slave in Tennessee, had served in the Civil War as a private in the Fortieth Regiment of the United States Colored Troops. Not only did the Allens and Hollands get along, Phog also spent time in the homes of other Negro families in Lawrence as well. "I'd say six to ten times Phog Allen was in my living room," recalled Arthur Lloyd Johnson, whose family ran a market garden. "I don't know anything about him negative. When they started integrating, he was ready to coach blacks. I wouldn't scratch him up as a racist."

"He was a just a prisoner of the system," McLendon reflected decades later. "If he tried to change it, he'd've lost his job, as great a coach as he was." In order to build his basketball dynasty in Lawrence and create the first modern version of college basketball, Allen also went along with what the university administration — and, by extension, the all-white state legislature — wanted, especially when it came to matters of race. "I always say that he was a victim, because the first chance he got he showed where his heart was," McLendon said. For his part, McLendon — who was the first colored physical education major at KU — didn't hold a grudge. "He was my teacher," he said, "and we got along well." Not only did Allen teach him physical therapy, first aid, athletic administration, and the principles of physical education, he also taught him something about coaching.

Like a number of his classmates, McLendon used to go down and watch the Jayhawks practice at Robinson Gymnasium. Sometimes he would sit high up, where the indoor track was, and get a view of the floor. But other times he would sit on the bench, where from time to time one of the students would be called out onto the floor to help run a play. "The first time I went," McLendon recalled, "I went ready to practice, just to see if he would let me come out on the court. He never even looked my way. But then it wasn't embarrassing. I was just trying him out."

Sitting quietly in the stands while the sounds of balls bouncing and sneakers squeaking echoed off the walls of the Robinson gym, John McLendon studied everything that Allen was doing. It was there that he followed the plays painted on the court and unlocked the secrets of the zone defense, and it was there that he learned the little tricks and unusual drills that the KU coach had been perfecting for more than a quarter of a century. "He had his players shoot free throws with blindfolds," McLendon remembered. It was an exercise in muscle memory — and it worked. "In a free throw, the body has to remember without your mind being a concern. If you aim that ball, you miss. If you get worried about missing it, you will." In the Robinson gym, what

McLendon did get was an unofficial advanced degree in coaching basketball.

By the early 1930s, the number of colored students at KU had been cut in half.

Negro wage earners—"last hired, first fired," the saying went—had been hit hard by the Depression, and many could no longer entertain dreams of college educations for their children. In Lawrence, most of the sixty or so colored undergraduates made ends meet with part-time jobs, such as washing dishes at the white fraternity houses and working on the serving line or in the cafeteria kitchen in the Union. Forced to live off campus, they were held together partly by KU's four Negro sororities and fraternities. Not only were these groups an oasis away from the daily sting of segregation, they were also *the* source of scuttlebutt on what classes to take, which teachers to avoid, and what, in fact, a Negro student could and could not do at the University of Kansas.

But not for John McLendon. Though he lived at the Kappa house, he refused to join. Part of it had to do with the hazing and initiation rituals. "My roommate," McLendon recalled, "had his kidney ruptured because of the beating they gave him. He was a little guy, about one hundred and five pounds. They ran all the way across the room and hit him with a paddle with holes in it." When the Kappas approached McLendon about joining, he had an alternative proposal. "I said, 'I'll join if you let me hit you every time you hit me.' But I never had anyone take me up on that." There was another reason as well. "If you were a Kappa, you weren't supposed to date Deltas. And if you were an Alpha, you weren't supposed to date AKAs. And I told them it was stupid," he said. "I mean, there's just a few of us here, and you've got all these stupid things. Why should we divide ourselves any further?"

McLendon's troubles with status quo did not begin and end in KU's tiny colored community. Elected as the first-ever Negro member of the student council, he soon found himself wrestling with phantoms. "They had some little rules that weren't written, you know. These were the hardest to get rid of." For example, whites and Negroes weren't supposed to play snooker together in the student union, so one evening McLendon and one of his roommates ended that prohibition. Negroes couldn't get served at some of the soda fountains downtown, either, but fixing that took longer. "I'd order something, and then they'd wait on everybody else." Finally one day McLendon noticed that a white classmate he knew was working behind the counter. "I said, 'Man, give me a milk shake. What's wrong with you?'"

And then there was the spring dance. The biggest social event of the year, it was a dreamscape of floor-length ball gowns and corsages where farm boys in rented tuxedos danced the box step and small-town bankers' daughters, with their hair up and Mama's good earrings on, wondered whether the young man they were dancing with was "the one." Because Kansas City, one of the true capitals of the jazz world, was located only forty miles away, the dance bands were always top-notch. For three and a half hours each year, KU students could forget what it had taken to get them there, forget the Depression, and forget the jobs that weren't waiting for them when they graduated. But not the colored students. In order to avoid the possibility of "physical contact" between the races, especially between colored men and white women, Negroes had been barred from the dance—even though they, too, had paid their student activity fees. "Most of our colored students understand," the university chancellor had declared.

McLendon had other ideas. After he learned one year that Andy Kirk and His Clouds of Joy—a nationally known Negro band that operated out of the Pla-Mor Ballroom in Kansas City—would play at the spring dance, he decided to go, too. But none of the other colored students would hear of it.

"You can't go," they said.

"We're paying a fee, aren't we?" McLendon said.

"Yes."

"Well," McLendon said, "I'm going."

McLendon then called on his girlfriend, Alice Hultz, a local high school student, and asked her if she wanted to go.

"Can we get in?" she asked.

"We'll have to see. Put on your stuff and let's go."

McLendon was playing a dangerous game. Even in Kansas—crazy Kansas, where a colored person never knew for sure what he or she could or could not do—he had already been skating along the edge. In truth, in spite of all his bravado, as he and Alice walked up the Hill that early spring evening with the sounds of "Bearcat Shuffle" and "Moten Swing" drifting out into the night air, he hadn't a clue as to what lay ahead.

It turned out to be a white student standing at the door.

"You going to the dance?" he asked.

"That's what we came for," McLendon replied.

"Okay."

And that was that. "We walked on in and started dancing," McLendon remembered. "And they [the white students] were always worried whether I was going to dance with one of them. But we didn't want to dance with anyone except each other."

He added, "We had a good time."

Not everything would run so smoothly, but one place where it did was in Naismith's orbit. McLendon had met the old man on his very first day in Lawrence when he rapped on the door to Naismith's office—a windowless, cramped cubbyhole packed with papers and books, located below one of the stairways in the Robinson gym. Naismith had asked the new freshman why he had come to KU, and McLendon had explained that his folks didn't have enough money to send him to Springfield College and that when his dad discovered Naismith was in Lawrence, the decision took care of itself.

"So your dad told you to come here and find me?" Naismith asked.

"Yeah."

A slight smile appeared beneath the old man's salt-and-pepper mustache.

"Fathers are always right," he said.

But the real beginning of their relationship came on the first day of school, when McLendon reported what had happened in his economics class. "You did right to leave the class," Naismith said. After that, John McLendon simply couldn't get enough of James Naismith. And the elderly professor, for his part, found his new advisee to be a delight. It wasn't long before McLendon started haunting the office below the stairs.

On the surface they were an odd pair. Divided by age, race, nationality, and even size, there was much that could have kept John McLendon and James Naismith apart. But there were other things that, revealed over time, helped draw them together. Both had lost their mothers at a young age. Both had spent some of their earliest years on a farm. And both, for different reasons and in different ways, were outsiders.

McLendon soon learned that as an instructor Naismith had his own distinctive style. "He taught gymnastics with folded arms," McLendon recalled. "He'd tell you exactly what you were supposed to do, and he'd stand there with his arms folded. And then you'd get up there and kill yourself." When the old man learned that McLendon could box, he had him lace up his gloves with a white student who had a reputation as a bully. "I caught the fellow flush in the face with my second punch, and he was counted out in a sitting position," McLendon recalled. Another time Naismith asked McLendon if he wanted to learn how to fence, then whacked him on the head with a fencing foil. "Talk about 'Old Naismith was so quiet,'" McLendon later recalled. "I know better than that." So that they could master human anatomy, he had each of his students purchase his or her own cadaver.

Soon there was another issue that would draw the student and the teacher even closer together. But unlike the situation in the economics class, it was not an issue from which, in the end, either of them could simply walk away.

In 1924 a new requirement had suddenly appeared in the university catalog. All graduating students, it declared, had to know how to swim. While many students welcomed the opportunity to learn, others, out of fear or anxiety or simply stubbornness, tried to worm their way out of the requirement. "Some students, I fear, received their degrees in this period under false pretenses. Many and varied were the schemes to 'get by' the swimming examiner," a retired KU chemistry professor later recalled.

Colored students, however, didn't need schemes to get out of the swimming test.

"Although the university was integrated, the pool at Robinson Gymnasium was not," Milton Katz, the biographer of John McLendon, has written. Negro students, including those who were about to graduate, simply had the swimming requirement waived and were given an automatic A in swimming—even if they couldn't do the dog paddle or hadn't ever seen the pool. Among white students, however, the clamor over the hated requirement grew so loud that, in 1933, the university administration dropped it—except, that is, for physical education majors, all of whom were white. McLendon's arrival changed that.

At first the plan had been to waive his swimming requirement altogether. But McLendon had other ideas. One afternoon he simply showed up at the pool, located in the basement of Robinson Gymnasium, and jumped in. Afterward, the manager drained the pool. When McLendon showed up the next day, the manager drained it again—and then called in help from the administration. While the other PE students could swim whenever they pleased, McLendon was informed that he could only swim on Friday afternoons. And so, once a week, he swam alone. Afterward the manager drained the pool. The compromise, it appeared, would work.

Only the incident wasn't over. McLendon and some supportive white students arranged a meeting with the university chancellor and proposed a test run. For two weeks, they proposed, let the pool be open to all students, regardless of race. But if there were any racial incidents, the pool would remain all white. The chancellor agreed, and the test was on. But Naismith was worried.

"What are you going to do?" he asked McLendon.

"I'll think of something."

That night McLendon sent the word out that all the Negro students at KU were to meet him at the Ninth Street Baptist Church. "I told them not to go to the pool," he remembered. "If they weren't there, there couldn't be an incident." It worked. The colored students stayed away, and nothing happened, while in the meantime a sympathetic white KU football player delivered a petition to chancellor Ernest Lindley, signed by a thousand students, requesting that the color line be erased at the pool. Lindley capitulated, and two weeks later, according to the agreed-upon conditions, swimming at KU should have been open to all students.

Only the pool manager wasn't finished, either. Instead he put up signs announcing that colored students would have their own "privileged swim" on Thursday afternoons at three o'clock. "So," McLendon said, "I took them all down." But the manager still wouldn't give in. That time he went directly to Phog Allen, who immediately called McLendon in for a meeting.

"If you plan to graduate," Allen told McLendon sternly, "you can't do this."

"You can go cross the street right now and ask Dr. Lindley about this."

"Oh, never mind," Allen said. "That's not the way I meant it."

And with that, it was all over. McLendon had won. The pool was open to all.

*   *   *

The bond between John McLendon and James Naismith, meanwhile, grew stronger.

The old man had helped McLendon find ways to fulfill his practice-teaching requirements, first at Lincoln School, a Negro elementary school across the river, and then at Lawrence High School, where McLendon coached the colored varsity basketball team (the school had an all-white team, too) all the way to a state championship. But Naismith also had his protégé help him teach gymnastics to a mixed group of white and colored students at one of the junior high schools. The white students, McLendon recalled, didn't care who was teaching. "They just wanted to learn something."

John McLendon. *(North Carolina Central University Archives, Records and History Center—James E. Shepard Memorial Library, Durham, NC)*

But the heart of their relationship was always basketball. While the rest of the world no longer really cared what James Naismith had to say about the game he invented, McLendon did—and their discussions were long and numerous. Naismith, for example, hated the zone defense, which Phog Allen's KU teams were then using. "Dr. Naismith abhorred the zone," McLendon recalled. "He abhorred any idea in the game that would have you retreat and wait for the offense to come to you." For Naismith, the game had always been, first and foremost, about recreation. And whether they were talking in class or in Naismith's office, McLendon—regardless of his own opinion—drank it all in.

But their most important conversation, as it turned out, came by chance. One bright and sunny afternoon, with a hint of autumn in the air, the two men were quietly sitting outside a local elementary school watching a group of first and second graders "play" basketball out on the playground. None of the children could dribble very well, and there was practically no scoring. Instead, whenever one of the boys or girls got hold of the ball, the other children would suddenly converge on the ball handler. To an outside observer it was just a mass of arms and legs with a ball in the middle moving quickly yet aimlessly up and down the playground. Only Naismith saw something else.

"That's it!" he suddenly cried out. "That's how you do it!"

Although John McLendon did not know it yet, this fleeting episode would turn out to be one of the key moments in his life, a turning point that would forever alter all that lay ahead. He would think of it many times. Naismith's seven words were more than a simple declaration. They were also the beginning of a brand-new approach to basketball, one that focused on speed and a relentless attack. There, on a dusty Kansas schoolyard during the depths of the Great Depression, the future of basketball suddenly shifted. There, for McLendon, another door had swung open.

*　　*　　*

For James Naismith, there would be one final act, one last public moment with the game he had given to the world. After decades of effort, basketball was finally to become an official Olympic sport at the 1936 summer games in Berlin. And Phog Allen cooked up a plan to make sure that Naismith was there when it happened. He called it Pennies for Naismith.

Allen's idea was simple and direct. During one week in February of 1936, every high school and college in America would declare one of its basketball games to be a special "Naismith game." And out of each and every paid admission ticket sold, one cent would be donated to a special fund that would allow James Naismith and his wife, Maude, to travel to Germany and be on hand to observe basketball's official Olympic coronation. "If there is enough money left after financing the trip to Berlin," one newspaper story announced, "an annuity will be founded on behalf of the Naismiths." Others talked of building a permanent memorial or buying the Naismiths a new home.

The campaign got a head start in late January. Not only did Lawrence High School officials shave off a portion of the gate receipts of a home game against a team from Ottawa, but at halftime cheerleaders paraded in front of the stands with outstretched blankets, upon which cascaded handfuls of pennies, nickels, and dimes. KU followed suit three weeks later, as did other colleges and universities across the country. Before the campaign had run its course, Boy Scouts and Girl Scouts had been enlisted to help pick up donations, YMCA and church teams had joined in, and all across Kansas, schoolchildren collected money on their own.

McLendon, meanwhile, wanted to contribute, too, but, as always, money was an issue. "So I asked Dr. Naismith if I could do some work for him over at his house," he remembered. "And he said, 'Yes, I need my grass cut.'" It turned out to be an all-day job. When McLendon was finally finished, Naismith gave him fifty cents — no small payment for someone who had been living on thirty-five cents a day. "I gave it right back to him," McLendon said, "and told him that this is all I could handle in regard to a contribution for his going to the Olympics. He thought a lot of it. And I did, too."

But it takes a lot of pennies and nickels and dimes and quarters to establish an annuity, create a memorial, or build a new house, and in Depression-era America, money was scarce. When the Pennies for Naismith campaign ended, less than five thousand dollars had been raised—more than enough to get the Naismiths to Berlin and back but nowhere close on the grander schemes.

In the end, even the basic plan had to be modified, for in March of 1936, Maude Naismith was hit by a heart attack and judged too weak to travel. But four months later, James Naismith boarded the gangway of the SS *Samaria,* a workhorse Cunard Line steamship bound for Glasgow, by himself. And after looking back at the New York skyline getting smaller in the distance, he turned his face, one last time, to the larger world.

CHAPTER 8

————

Berlin, 1936

Verrückt. Crazy. Berlin had gone crazy.

From the tony shops and swank coffeehouses along the Kurfürstendamm to the new concrete barracks on the outskirts of town, *das Olympische Fieber*—Olympic fever—had swept through the German capital. You could see it in the jam-packed subway stations near the massive new stadium and hear it in the voices of high school students marching along the Königstrasse, waving flags and singing songs. Ordinary citizens who had never given much thought to pole-vaulters or fencers or long distance runners now spoke knowingly of Khadr El Touni, the record-breaking Egyptian weight lifter, or blond-haired Gisela Mauermayer, the Munich-born discus thrower, or the games' unlikely superstar, Jesse Owens, the colored American track-and-field athlete who won four gold medals. Even Adolf Hitler, an opera buff who had only planned on attending the opening and closing ceremonies, was so entranced by the competition that he kept coming back, day after day. And he wasn't alone.

For the games themselves, the leadership of the Third Reich had spared no expense. In addition to a gigantic new stadium—with seating for one hundred and ten thousand—the Reichssportfeld featured state-of-the-art athletic facilities, massive sculptures and public art, and the world's most complete Olympic Village, all built literally from the ground up. There were cutting-edge technological breakthroughs as well. Collaborative work by Zeiss and Agfa, two German photographic firms, had resulted in a special new camera capable of filming more than one hundred frames a second, while starting pistols would be directly linked to precision chronometers. German engineers designed soundproof studios for the more than one hundred radio reporters from around the world, while in two dozen special viewing rooms across Berlin, spectators could watch fuzzy images of the games on a brand-new medium called television. For two breezy, breathtaking weeks in August of 1936, Berlin had the attention of the world.

And basketball was to be an official part of it all. Twenty-one nations had sent basketball teams to the games—there had been twenty-two, but since civil war had broken out in Spain two weeks earlier, the Spaniards stayed home. The basketball competition was to be played outdoors, on the Basketballplatz, which in reality was four sunken tennis courts whose playing surface was a special mixture of pounded clay, salt, and sawdust. The German officials, however, hadn't seen the need to build many bleachers; they did not think there would be many fans of this American game, which was still unknown to most Germans.

But on the first day alone, more than ten thousand fans showed up. At the biggest sporting event in human history, basketball would hold its own.

James Naismith, meanwhile, wasn't faring quite as well.

On his first morning in Berlin, he made his way to the Olympic ticket office and presented himself and his American passport, with its crimson cover stamped in gold foil, to the officials. To his shock and dismay, however, Naismith learned that no tickets or special passes awaited him and that his name appeared on no special pass lists. Schoolchildren in Wichita and Topeka may have collected pennies to send the inventor of basketball to the Olympics, but nobody in Berlin seemed to know anything about it. Inquiries to the US delegation yielded the same result, until finally an American basketball referee, a no-nonsense New Yorker named Jim Tobin, caught wind of the fact that the elderly gentleman in the rumpled linen suit was, indeed, James Naismith himself. "We managed to get him a pass for all Games, but it was not through the American Olympic Committee's efforts," Tobin told a reporter for the Associated Press. "What's more, no ceremony was planned for Dr. Naismith, who is naturally the most important figure in basketball."

In short order, calls were made, German officials were contacted, and a small celebration was quickly cobbled together—for the only individual in all of Berlin who had actually invented one of the Olympic events. Held in the massive House of German Sport, it featured brief speeches by a handful of Olympic officials and a miniature parade of nations, in which the flag of each nation competing in the basketball competition was dipped as it passed Naismith. Naismith spoke as well, though it is uncertain just how many of the athletes or the small crowd of two hundred spectators who had gathered for the quickly patched-together event understood a word of what he said.

The basketball competition got off to a rocky start. The head of the Uruguayan delegation tried, unsuccessfully, to enact a rule barring any players over five feet eight, which would have excluded practically every member of the US team. The American players, meanwhile, were eager to get going but had to sit out their first game—against the Spanish team, which did not show up. Once they started playing, they realized that the official ball that was being used was hardly up to North American standards. Manufactured by Berg, a German firm, it was lopsided, featured prominent laces, and the leather itself wasn't grained, making it difficult to control.

Still, the games themselves, played over the course of five days, were a minor hit. Thousands of Berliners ringed the courts, anxious to see this unusual game, which, in Germany, was mainly played by the military. Moreover, the complicated competition schedule, combined with the fact that more nations had sent squads to Berlin for basketball than for any other team sport, resulted in a virtual mother lode of games — forty-six in all. And because the matchups were often so unusual — Mexico versus Belgium, Peru against China, the Philippine Islands playing Estonia — the games featured not only a wealth of languages but radically different styles of play as well.

And then there was the weather. For the first two days of the competition, the weather was practically perfect — dry and in the mid-sixties. But by Sunday, August 9, the Olympic meteorological service had taken note of a scarcely perceptible wind fluttering the banners hanging on top of the stadium and rustling the leaves of the birch trees lining the nearby walkways. By Tuesday, when the third-round games were held, the wind was strong enough to be, in the words of the

Basketball in the rain, Berlin Olympics, 1936. *(Der Deutsche Olympische Sportbund)*

official reports, "equally disadvantageous to both opponents." The wind died down the next day, but by Friday's medal rounds, a front had moved in off the North Sea, bringing cooler temperatures into Berlin. And rain. Lots of rain.

It poured steadily throughout the championship game between Canada and the United States, turning Basketballplatz number 4 into a muddy mess. Not only was dribbling impossible, the smooth-textured Berg balls, wet and slippery, were even more difficult to catch and hold on to. The American team, whose uniforms had been stolen out of their lockers in the Olympic Village, eventually tossed out their original game plan and concentrated on "simple passes and close shots." It worked, and the United States won, 19–8. Indeed, basketball's first regular Olympic competition turned out to be a North American sweep. The United States won gold, Canada took home silver, and Mexico captured the bronze.

And James Naismith, who had sat through it all, was no longer the forgotten man. As the basketball competition unfolded, he found himself invited to lunch with Olympic officials, and he even attended a dinner where the Führer himself was present. And at the awards ceremony, when oak-leaf crowns were placed upon the heads of the victorious players, the aged inventor of basketball was approached by two members of the League of German Girls, the female arm of Hitler Youth, who presented him with two bouquets of roses. Afterward, Naismith bumped into Bill Mifflin, a KU grad from Coffeyville, who was attending the games as well.

"Doctor," Mifflin said, "this should be the crowning event of your life. What an honor."

"Billie," the old man replied, "it is. The land of my birth played the land of my choice, and the land of my choice won."

Naismith had not been the only one to enjoy himself. "I'm afraid the Nazis have succeeded," William L. Shirer, the brilliant Chicago-born correspondent for the Universal News Service, wrote in his diary on August 16, the night the competition ended. American movie stars, businessmen, radio and newspaper correspondents, and everyday citizens were impressed as well. Even Shirer, who after two years in Berlin was no longer a babe in the woods when it came to National Socialism, had largely enjoyed the Olympics. "I got a kick out of the track and field, the swimming, the rowing, and the basket-ball," he wrote, "but they were a headache to us as a job."

The feel-good flavor of the Berlin Olympics had not happened by chance. Once Joseph Goebbels, the new minister of public enlightenment and propaganda, convinced Adolf Hitler of their potential propaganda value, the games became an enormous public relations campaign. Not only were the competition sites a wonder to behold, every effort was made to ensure that foreign visitors to the games, regardless of their standing on the Nazis' scale of racial superiority, had a pleasant, trouble-free visit. Even more important was the message, to be sent at all times, that the new Germany was a modern, progressive nation where, contrary to the scandalous news reports that often appeared overseas, people were happy and the trains ran on time.

Altogether, it worked.

"The Nazis have put up a very good front for the general visitors, especially the big businessmen," Shirer scribbled in his diary. "Ralph Barnes [of the *New York Herald Tribune*] and I were asked to meet some of the American ones a few years ago. They said frankly they were impressed by the Nazi 'set-up.' They had talked with Göring, they said, and he had told him that we American correspondents were unfair to the Nazis."

But the Jews knew better.

For three and a half long years, ever since Hitler had been appointed chancellor, Berlin's one hundred and fifty thousand Jews had watched their world grow ever smaller, ever grimmer, and ever more dangerous. At first there had only been words. They had heard them before. But a new chapter had begun at ten o'clock on the morning of April 1, 1933, a busy shopping day, when storm troopers wearing swastika armbands and freshly shined boots appeared at the entrances of Jewish-owned department stores and boutiques in the heart of Berlin. DON'T BUY FROM JEWS! their placards read. Six days later, the Nazi-controlled Reichstag passed its first anti-Semitic laws. It was only the beginning.

By the early fall of 1935, Jews in Germany could no longer serve in the military, Jewish newspapers couldn't be sold on the street, Jews and non-Jews could no longer marry, and Jews could no longer employ any non-Jews younger than age forty-five. Then, on November 14, an even bigger hammer fell. "A Jew cannot be a citizen of Germany," article 4 of the First Regulation to the Reich Citizenship Law declared. Jews could no longer vote or hold political office.

Even in cosmopolitan Berlin, where Hitler had fared poorly in the election of 1933, conditions were declining. Across the city, Nazi activists targeted Jewish-owned businesses, smearing storefronts with paint, covering over display windows with placards, and scaring away potential customers. When *The Rise of Catherine the Great*—an English movie starring Elisabeth Bergner, an Austrian Jewish actress who had fled to London—opened at a Berlin theater, gangs of brownshirts showed up, harassing ticket buyers and interrupting the movie. More and more, the city's Jews simply stopped going out in the evenings, avoiding potential trouble at restaurants, nightclubs, and beer halls where they had gone for years. During the rain-streaked summer of 1935, when Berliners carried umbrellas under their arms on evening strolls in the Tiergarten or at the zoo, local members of the Hitler Youth even launched a campaign against the city's Jewish-owned ice cream parlors. Gathering on warm summer evenings, the uniformed youth—some as young as ten and eleven years old—threatened the owners and employees and knocked the ice cream cones and other purchases made by the increasingly rare customers to the sidewalk.

At number 8 Derfflingerstrasse, in the fashionable blocks just south of the Tiergarten, the future looked somewhat different. A large, substantial house furnished with hand-carved oak furniture, broadloom rugs, Viennese crystal, and delicate Dresden china figurines at that address was the home of Otto Bernhard and his wife, Lili. Shaded by the lindens that lined the quiet residential street, the house was just a half block from the Kurfürstendamm, home to some of the city's finest hotels, shops, and fashion houses. Two blocks to the north stood the American embassy, with its heavily draped windows and its high, wrought-iron fence, while closer in were the homes of bankers, industrialists, and company presidents. By any reasonable standard, the Bernhards had arrived.

Otto Bernhard was an executive with the German-owned affiliate of the Ford Motor Company, one who made not infrequent journeys back and forth to Detroit. Both creative and practical, he was also a part-time inventor. He had, in fact, already drawn up plans for a hybrid farm truck–half-track. His wife, née Lili von Portheim, who had been born in the glory days of the Austro-Hungarian Empire, was of aristocratic stock—*Hofjuden* who had been on speaking terms with the emperor. The couple also had two unmarried daughters, both in their twenties, living at home, Gabriela and Marianne.

Marianne was a budding artist. Petite, with chocolate-brown hair and deep brown eyes, even as a child she had been dazzled by the treasures in Berlin's art museums—the works by Botticelli, Raphael, and Rembrandt at the Kaiser-Friedrich-Museum; the impressionist paintings at the Nationalgalerie; the ancient Greek and Roman sculpture at the Pergamon and the Neues Museum; and the Islamic art at the Vorderasiatisches. But she had also drunk in the revolutionary new art that had burst across Germany like an artillery shell—the groundbreaking design coming out of the Bauhaus, the shocking and mysterious works of the city's Dadaists, and the dark, bold prints and paintings of Käthe Kollwitz, Oskar Kokoschka, Emil Nolde, and George Grosz.

At a time when most of her friends were seeking suitors, Marianne would stroll along the Unter den Linden, sketchbook in hand, taking mental photographs of a woman's hat or an old man's hands and watching the swans in the River Spree craning their necks. She could spot

Marianne Bernhard. *(Ancestry.com)*

Titian red in a restaurant awning and Van Dyck's black in a rain-drenched street. The nearby art supply houses knew her well, and when she joined the family for dinner in the evenings, more often than not her hands were still streaked with traces of cobalt blue, burnt orange, and titanium white. In truth, at age twenty-five, Marianne was on the verge of launching her own career as a painter.

But that was before.

Now, like other Jewish families across Berlin, the Bernhards had to face the one question few wanted to ask and fewer still had answers for. Like many nonobservant Jews, they considered themselves Germans first and Jews second. They spoke German at home and rarely, if ever, entered a synagogue. Moreover, Berlin was *home*. It was where Lili and Otto had raised Gabriela and Marianne, it was where their friends were, and it was where, in 1914, Otto had willingly donned a German army uniform in order to fight for the Fatherland. And as horrible—truly horrible—as

Hitler and his gang were, no one knew, really, what they were planning or how much longer they would be in power. But no longer could the dreaded question be avoided. Should they leave the country?

The consequences were enormous. Not only would they lose their home and most of their belongings, the Nazis had also passed new laws preventing the transfer of large amounts of money overseas. Unlike many others, the Bernhards had options: there were other countries where they could go, and they had the resources to make it happen. But if they did leave Germany, Otto and Lili both knew that in effect they would be starting over from scratch. Their old life, the only one that they knew, would be gone for good. But deep in their hearts, they also knew something else. The old life was already gone. On the Kurfürstendamm, gangs of Nazi toughs had beaten up anyone they thought might be a Jew, while Jewish parents, fearing for the safety of their children, had pulled their sons and daughters out of public schools. Even in the Tiergarten, signs had appeared in the parks telling Jews which benches they could sit on and which were off-limits.

Marianne left first.

Five months before the start of the Olympic games, on a warm and muggy afternoon in late March of 1936, she picked up her *Heimatschein für den Aufenthalt im Ausland,* a certificate for travel abroad, from the police headquarters downtown, paid the necessary fees, and carefully placed the official document, stamped with eagles and swastikas, inside her purse. Then she walked into the cavernous Anhalter Bahnhof railroad station, purchased a one-way passage at the ticket office, and caught an overnight train, one that would carry her south past Nuremberg and Munich and across the broad, flat waters of the Elbe and the Danube, swollen with early spring rains. When night fell and the ancient stars appeared in the blackened sky outside the window to her sleeping compartment, the train would be well into the Alps, still snow-draped and iron cold.

By morning, Marianne hoped, she would be on her way to a new life, in a new land.

What she hadn't planned on was North Carolina.

CHAPTER 9

Racehorse Basketball

Well, what are you going to do now?" Naismith asked.

As their black robes rustled in the late afternoon breeze, James Naismith and John McLendon walked alone together across the broad lawn in front of Robinson Gymnasium, the wind whispering in the already brown grass. Nearby, newly minted members of the University of Kansas class of 1936 and their families, shielding their eyes from the late July sun, lingered in front of the classroom buildings, still chattering about Governor Landon's commencement address.

In truth McLendon wasn't exactly certain. He had wanted to go to graduate school to study kinesiology, but money, as always, was the barrier. So he figured he'd go back to Kansas City. Jobs of any kind were hard to come by in those days, college graduate or not, especially if you were colored. But McLendon was fairly sure he could get hired again back at the packinghouse and do a little lifeguarding on the side. In time he should be able to save up enough tuition money for a master's degree. But Naismith wouldn't hear of it.

"You shouldn't drop out of school to work and then plan to go back, because most of the time you never get back," he said.

"Well," McLendon replied, "you know my problem. I've already told you."

James Naismith and grandsons, Lawrence, 1930s. *(University Archives, Kenneth Spencer Research Library, University of Kansas Libraries)*

The old man stood stock-still for a minute in the blazing Kansas sun. Finally he spoke.

"Come with me," he said.

Inside his office, Naismith picked up the telephone and dialed the operator, telling her that he wanted to place a station-to-station long-distance call to E. G. Schroeder in Iowa City. Schroeder was a pioneering wrestling and tennis coach who, McLendon would later learn, was next in line to become the athletic director at the University of Iowa.

"I've got a young fellow down here who needs help bad," Naismith spoke into the receiver. "Can you give him a job? He can't get there unless you do."

"Yes. Send him on."

And that was that.

One month later, McLendon traded the wheat and cattle lands of Kansas for the cornfields of Iowa.

*   *   *

McLendon had wanted to study under a pioneering research scientist named Charles McCloy. Working out of his lab and on the playing fields at the University of Iowa, where he carefully measured and recorded athletic performance, McCloy had been quietly overturning a good-size chunk of what passed for accepted wisdom in physical-education circles. In particular, he directly challenged the notion, held dearly by most coaches at the time, that "the lifting of weights would cause an athlete to become slow, ill-coordinated, and inflexible, in short, musclebound." A true believer in the value of lifelong daily exercise in an era when few Americans felt the same way, McCloy also practiced what he preached. At precisely half past three each day, he would stop working, drink a glass of tea, and rest for half an hour, then engage in a strenuous, heart-pounding workout. It worked. On his fiftieth birthday, he did forty-three pull-ups in a row.

McLendon did study with McCloy, creating a method to directly challenge the claims, aired by some, that Jesse Owens's headline-grabbing accomplishments at the Berlin Olympics had been the result of his skin color—that is, the difference in physical characteristics between Negroes and whites. But, as always, finances were an issue. So McLendon finished his master's degree in nine months. "That's all the money I had," he later told Milton Katz. But there was something else as well, for during his time in Iowa City, McLendon married his sweetheart from back in Kansas, Alice Hultz. And with plans to have a family, it was time to leave school and get a job.

Despite his accomplishments, there was simply no way that McLendon would be employed at a predominantly white school. He could have been hired at a Negro high school, but he wanted, more than anything else, to coach *college* basketball. And the vast majority of colored colleges were down south. Luckily, a colored classmate had put in a good word for him, and before the semester was over John McLendon was offered a job at the North Carolina College for Negroes, coaching basketball and teaching physical education.

Back home in Kansas City, the news raised eyebrows.

His stepmother, who had grown up in Mississippi, was dead set against any kind of move below the Mason-Dixon line. She knew what *those people* were like. But his father pointed out that there were some mighty successful colored businesses in Durham, and that if they could do okay, so could John. Privately, however, he said a bit more. "My daddy told me when I left for North Carolina what to look out for. He said it's a little different down there," McLendon recalled. "The biggest difference is that here, you might have the law to back you up. But there, the law is the same as the people who attack you."

Three weeks later, John McLendon, age twenty-two, was on his way to Dixie.

"If I had known you were this young, I never would have hired you."

Dr. Shepard, as usual, was seated behind his desk in his office in the administration building. It wasn't the greeting that the new basketball coach at North Carolina College had been expecting. But for John McLendon, it had already been a long week. He had left Kansas City by rail, then in Cincinnati he and all the other Negro passengers had been moved to a segregated car just behind the locomotive. In Lynchburg, Virginia, where he saw his first COLORED and WHITE signs on a pair of drinking fountains, he had begun to wonder whether he had made the right decision, a nagging doubt that surfaced again when the taxi dropped him off at the main entrance to North Carolina College. For right there, McLendon came face-to-face with his first chain gang, carrying shovels and pickaxes. It was a group of colored prisoners who were shackled together, widening Fayetteville Street under the hair-trigger gaze of a pair of armed white guards. "I waited for them to sing, like they did in the movies," he recalled. "But they didn't sing anything. Not one note."

There was more. As he walked toward the administration building, he saw a group of male students gathered around the circle drive, where, for tips, they would help carry the luggage of new students and faculty members to their lodgings on campus. But before McLendon could get his bearings and figure out where he should go first, he was approached by a middle-aged colored woman who had just stepped out of another taxi. "Sonny," she asked, "would you mind helping me with my bags?" She was, he later recalled, "looking right at me. So I said, 'Yes, ma'am' and took her bags over to the dorms. She gave me ten cents."

Then, two days later, on his first day in the classroom, dressed in a band-new sport jacket, while he was writing the title of his course—The Care and Prevention of Injuries—on the chalkboard, he was thrown off guard by an eruption of giggling behind him.

"Can someone tell me what's so funny?" he asked.

But all he got was nervous glances. Finally, a student—a slip of a gal named Yancey, from outside Oxford—spoke up.

"Mr. Professor, you haven't even taken off the tags on your new coat," she said.

McLendon's salary that first year was not recorded on the books. "Dr. Shepard paid me from a collection of fellows who brought the money to him, and he paid me in cash," he said. If the new basketball coach was going to survive in his new job, he would have to prove himself.

Fortune smiled upon him, because the very same year that McLendon began his coaching career in North Carolina, a game-changing revolution occurred in college basketball. After years of effort, a group of reformers finally persuaded the national basketball rules committee to eliminate the center jump after each basket. From the beginning of the 1937–38 season onward, no longer would both teams gather at center court after each and every successful field goal to replay the opening tip-off. Instead, the team that had just been scored on would inbound the ball from underneath the basket, and play would resume. If there was ever a moment ripe with opportunity for a brand-new basketball coach, this was it.

The rule change was, in fact, a sea change. In the old game, whichever team had the tallest player—or the one who could jump the highest—usually controlled the center jump, giving his team a distinct scoring advantage. That situation no longer applied. But there was an even bigger change as well. For as each team raced to get the ball back into play after a made basket, the game itself suddenly got a whole lot faster. No longer did players have to reorganize themselves at midcourt after a center jump. Instead, an offensive set could begin immediately after the other team scored. And as the pace of play picked up, scoring increased as well. Basketball had suddenly found its legs.

The fans loved it. All over the country, basketball games were no longer human chess matches—"Slow, slower, and slowest" was how one old-timer described the previous style of play—in which the team with the tallest players essentially played keep-away. Now speed, especially with ball movement, became just as important. Players who could dribble downcourt at a fast pace or quickly hustle to their defensive positions became weapons who were just as valuable as accurate shooters and lofty centers. Practically overnight, basketball had become a wide-open kind of game, one where the keys to success had changed. And John McLendon was ready to take advantage of it.

He had his work cut out for him. McLendon's first team was composed largely of holdovers from the winless, bottom-dwelling Eagles of the previous season—players who, in the words of Alex Rivera, later the Durham field representative for the *Pittsburgh Courier,* "flew too low and entirely too slow." They went 9–9. The next season his North Carolina College team climbed further up the ladder, winning sixteen and losing eight, and a year later, McLendon's players broke out of the pack. The 1939–40 Eagles won twenty-one games, lost only four, and were runners-up to that year's Colored Intercollegiate Athletic Association conference champions. In Negro coaching circles, McLendon had arrived.

Dr. Shepard, on the other hand, hadn't felt any need to publicly recognize the accomplishments of his young basketball coach. Even though he'd quit paying McLendon under the table and put his salary on the books, Shepard had also kept the young Kansan on a form of probation. Even though it was McLendon who had done all the work with the basketball teams, Shepard had him listed simply as the assistant coach—William Burghardt, the football coach, was officially the head basketball coach as well. But after the 1940 triumph, McLendon was named the head basketball coach. And while Dr. Shepard always maintained a distance from his faculty, he found McLendon to be useful in other endeavors besides basketball.

"One day he came into my office with the dean of women and asked if it was true that I had a method of teaching swimming where I did not have to touch the students. When I told him yes, I did, he walked out with a smile on his face," McLendon recalled. A few days later, McLendon learned that he had been tapped to teach swimming to the female students as well as to the male students. And when Shepard discovered that McLendon liked to read popular Western novels—like Zane Grey's *Code of the West,* Ernest Haycox's *The Silver Desert,* and Max Brand's *Trouble Trail*—among other things, he would borrow them after McLendon had discreetly wrapped them, like copies of a girlie magazine, in newspaper or a manila envelope.

But McLendon's struggles with Shepard were not over. After the incident with his new jacket on the first day of school, McLendon's work clothes grew more and more casual. In the basketball team portrait for the 1938–39 season, he wore a leather jacket and slacks, while in other photographs from the period he can be seen wearing a baseball cap or a pair of work pants. When he wanted to, McLendon could dress up with the best of them, with spit-shined shoes, a perfectly starched shirt, and a silk handkerchief peeking out of his jacket pocket. But he had an aversion to ties. "He couldn't tie one," Pee Wee remembered. "He'd have to ask someone else to do it for him." Once, when he showed up tieless, with an open collar, for services on Sunday morning at St. Joseph's AME Church—something that was unheard of in the church home of half of Hayti's elites—the Reverend James Valentine phoned Dr. Shepard, who called on McLendon the next day.

"Is this true?" Dr. Shepard asked.

"Yeah," McLendon replied. "I don't wear ties."

"Well," Shepard said, "I think it would be a good idea to wear one if you're going to church."

Nor was his boss the only source of snobbery that McLendon ran into. As on most college campuses across the country, many of the other faculty members at North Carolina College—especially those who had gotten advanced degrees—looked down on McLendon's players and the other athletes.

But McLendon's wife, Alice, had it worse. She had not, in fact, come to Durham immediately. As the child of a most protective mother, one who worried about her daughter venturing into the South, Alice had not arrived in North Carolina until Christmas of her husband's second year at North Carolina College. And even though they lived, at first, right on campus, most of the faculty wives turned up their noses at the newcomer and would have little to do with her because she hadn't attended college at all. That got even worse when she took a job at the Regal Theater on Pettigrew, selling tickets for low-budget cowboy shoot-'em-ups, murder mysteries, and romance movies to tobacco stemmers, maids, and cotton-mill workers. But membership in Hayti's smart set wasn't a priority for Alice, and in 1939 she gave birth to a baby boy. Named after his father, young Johnny became the apple of his parents' eyes, as did their second child, a daughter named Querida, born two years later.

By the beginning of the 1940–41 school year, John McLendon was deep into parenthood and deeper into basketball than he could ever have imagined. Back in Kansas City, when he first saw the court at Northeast Junior High on that fateful afternoon, he had fallen in love with the game. But now he was practically obsessed with it. Morning, noon, and night he would run plays in his mind, moving the dishes on the kitchen table as though they were players in a game. The desk in his cramped office in the gymnasium overflowed with diagrams and play-books, newspaper clippings and stat sheets, while in bed late at night, with Alice sleeping softly beside him, he would trace imaginary lines and arrows on the ceiling, directing his players to fake a dribble drive to the left, hit an open man in the corner, or launch a four-footer from the lane. And the deeper he went, the more challenging—and fulfilling—it all became.

In truth he had already worked some minor miracles. Guided by the principles he had learned firsthand from Phog Allen, and from his own hands-on experiences in Kansas City and Lawrence, McLendon had begun by replicating the Kansas game at North Carolina College. Out came the jars of washable paint to mark off plays on the gymnasium floor. In came plays and drills that could be found in his well-thumbed copy of *My Basket-ball Bible* and *Better Basketball*. And in came actual Kansans as McLendon created a small but effective recruiting pipeline for colored players from high schools back home. From Emporia he brought in the Mack brothers—Dick and George. A year later, in came Leo Fine, Buford Allen, and Monroe Collins from Kansas City as well as Rocky Roberson from Atchison, skilled athletes who had played basketball all their lives.

But McLendon also knew, in his gut, that he could do more. And it didn't take long to figure out how.

The first breakthrough came in conditioning. In the old game, basketball players needed to be tall, coordinated, and relatively strong. They also needed to be good ball handlers and able communicators. "Teach your men to be smart, heady basketball players," advised Sam Barry in 1926, three years before he became the head coach at the University of Southern California. "It is well to have them aid one another by yelling when to 'take a shot,' 'dribble,' and 'take your time.'" Mark Peterman, in *Secrets of Winning Basketball,* advised his fellow coaches to look for players with long arms, even tempers, and deep inner desires. *How to Play Basket Ball* by George Hepbron, published in 1904 as part of Spalding's Athletic Library, recommended that "agility and alertness are two of the fundamental and principal characteristics of a forward"; it added that guards must possess "the ability to receive hard knocks without a murmur" and that a center "must be a man of a cool head with the ability to size up conditions." The 1937–38 edition of *Basketball Hints*—"Written by Famous Coaches"—advised, "Do not allow an opponent to get your 'Goat' by talking with you in an ungentlemanly way." Other experts stressed footwork, ballhandling, and endurance. But *speed* was mentioned far less frequently. Here was an area where McLendon could make his mark.

Others had gotten there first. Even before the center jump had been retired, basketball players and coaches across the country had been tinkering with ways of moving the ball more quickly down the court, something that was soon dubbed the fast break. William Jennings Bryan Reinhart introduced one version of the fast break at the University of Oregon as early as the 1920s, then carried it out to George Washington University when he became its head coach in the 1930s. Reinhart was a cigar-smoking tactician who liked to fire up a dime-store stogie in the locker room and whose best-known former player was the outspoken Red Auerbach, later of Boston Celtics fame. Auerbach, an equally committed cigar aficionado, was also Reinhart's staunchest supporter. "I don't know who claims or is given credit for introducing the first organized fast break, but I know who did it—Bill Reinhart," Auerbach said, adding, "There are coaches in the Hall of Fame who couldn't carry his jock."

Perhaps. But in terms of over-the-top personality, Red's mentor couldn't hold a candle to another author of the fast break, Ernest Artel Blood. Short in stature, he caught the fitness bug in his youth and served as a physical-education instructor at a number of YMCA chapters scattered around New England, where he started playing—and coaching—basketball soon after its invention. Blood's Y teams were so successful that he parlayed their success into a career as a high school basketball coach, calling himself Professor Blood despite the fact that he never attended a lick of college. He even coached for one season, 1925–26, at the United States Military Academy at West Point, where his star forward, John Roosma, became one of the first players to score more than one thousand points in a collegiate career.

But it was in Passaic, New Jersey, a blue-collar manufacturing town located a forty-minute train ride west of New York City where Blood notched a place for himself both in basketball history and in local lore. An early advocate of strength conditioning—"He was built like a top, with the neck, shoulders and chest of a heavyweight boxer and a waist as slender as a chorus girl's," wrote one newspaper reporter—he used to work out with sixty-pound barbells and had a trick in which he would toss an iron shot put into the air and catch it on the back of his neck. (He also would go for days at a time eating nothing but ice cream and kept a pet alligator living beneath the kitchen sink in the family home on Carlton Place.)

Blood's ability to motivate his players was magical. Stressing offense above all else, he had his players rifle a quick outlet pass after a successful center tip and launch a shot before their opponents had a chance to set up their defense. Yet he also allowed his players to shoot the ball in any fashion they saw fit—including hook shots and one-handers—during an age when the underhand two-handed set shot was still the norm. As a result his Passaic High School teams were a marvel. In nine seasons, from 1915 to 1924, they won two hundred games and lost only once, racking up a 159-game winning streak. Nor was that all. Blood also brought Zep, his four-hundred-pound pet black bear, to all the games, where it sat on the bench and, during halftime, shot free throws.

They talked about Blood for years.

A more likely architect of the fast break, however, was another New Englander, a big-boned Bostonian named Frank Keaney. He had grown up on the rough-and-tumble streets of East Cambridge, where fistfights and tenements were as common as Methodist hymnals and white-collar jobs were rare. But despite his size and talent as an all-around athlete, Keaney also developed a love for books. After graduating from Cambridge Rindge and Latin School, he was a Phi Beta Kappa scholar — and a four-sport varsity letterman — at Bates College, up in Maine. He had planned on becoming a high school teacher or perhaps a principal, but once he got a taste of basketball coaching (first at the high school level), there was no looking back. And in 1921 he was hired as the new head basketball coach at Rhode Island State College.

In truth there hadn't been anyone like him. While most other coaches discussed blocking out, screens, and attacking the zone during their pregame pep talks, Keaney quoted Virgil, Homer, Socrates, Sophocles, and Shakespeare. From *The Iliad:* "I, too, shall lie in the dust when I am dead, but now let me win noble renown." From *Henry V:* "This day is called the feast of Crispian: / He that outlives this day, and comes safe home, / Will stand a-tiptoe when this day is named, / And rouse him at the name of Crispian." In the makeshift locker room on the top floor of Lippitt Hall, where basketball games were played on the combined dance floor and drill hall, Keaney invoked ancient Greek warriors and wine-dark seas; he spoke of Marathon, Thermopylae, and Agincourt. "We few, we happy few, we band of brothers; / For he today that sheds his blood with me / Shall be my brother." Shakespeare again. Keaney's players were mesmerized.

There was more to Keaney than that. Also serving as a professor of chemistry, he sorely disliked the commonplace royal-blue uniforms worn by the Rams. So in the school laboratory, he concocted a new, lighter shade, dubbed Keaney blue, that Rhode Island athletes wore for decades. To help toughen up collegiate military recruits, he invented a free-for-all game — nicknamed murder ball by the students — that "combined the more violent features of football and basketball" and was played until "no one was able to continue," wrote one Rhode Island historian. Keaney even had his own special lingo. A fried banana was a nearsighted player, a dewdrop was an idiotic one, and a player who was afraid to "give 'em the old gazazza" clearly belonged in the Strawberry League.

Built like an icebox, with bright red cheeks and a usually unkempt shock of snow-white hair, Keaney had a repertoire of game-time antics that was equally memorable. Once, in a postseason matchup, he sent a five-feet-four guard to jump the opening tip against a six-eleven center. In another contest, a barn burner in which all but four of his Rhode Island players had fouled out before the end of regulation, he scowled at the referee, then kicked an empty chair onto the court. "Here's my fifth player," he said. "Let's get on with the game."

But it was Keaney's focus on speed that rattled his opponents the most. Impatient with the slow-as-molasses tempo of most basketball contests, he created a new, quick-paced offense—nicknamed racehorse or fire engine basketball—that relied on rocket passes, little extraneous ball movement, and, above all, lots of shots. "If we shoot more," he declared, "we'll make more." And he was correct. In his first contest as head coach, a home game in early December of 1920, his Rhode Island team demolished Providence, 87–25. And while other coaches eventually found ways to slow down the Rams, by the end of the decade his Rhode Island squad had become the nation's first "point a minute" team—averaging more than forty points a game, a far cry from the basketball of three decades earlier. On the western edge of Narragansett Bay, the fast-break era was springing to life.

McLendon would take it a step further. His was a lightning break, a roundball blitzkrieg. Under his system, the Eagles wouldn't just dash to the other end of the court at the beginning of each possession. They would do so in less than four seconds—an unheard-of pace during the late 1930s and early 1940s—and by the time they got there they would have already taken a shot as well. Using an outlet or a long overhand pass when possible, the North Carolina College players would attack the basket on the run, usually by feeding the ball with a short pass to a cutter, who would then attempt a driving layup. It was a breathtaking, high-speed departure from the era of the center jump, one that dazzled fans and befuddled opponents as the Eagles racked up one quick basket after another.

But for McLendon, the fast break became more than a technique for putting points on the board. Difficult to guard against, it had a psychological dimension as well. Not only did it sow confusion among the members of the other team, but, like a right-handed boxer suddenly having to fight a southpaw, it also forced them to change their entire game plan. "The high pressure tactics of the fast break are calculated to disorganize and, subsequently, demoralize the defense," McLendon later wrote. "The fast break exploits one of the basic stratagems of the game of basketball, which is to force the opponent from the game they have planned to play."

It also wore the other team out. For as the North Carolina College players raced up and down the court, they sapped the strength of the defenders. "I am thinking now of the fast break not only as a scoring device but as a weapon for undermining the physical conditioning of the opponents," McLendon said. Only there was more. Because for McLendon, his fast break possessed a *defensive* quality as well. "Offense becomes defense, a defense against loss," he wrote. "You can defeat some teams if you possess only a semblance of defense by overwhelming them with field goals." McLendon's fast break wasn't just a coaching gimmick. It was a new kind of basketball.

To make it work, however, he needed a new kind of player—fast ones who had to stay fast all game long. And that was a problem. In those days, most basketball training programs had a different set of priorities. There were ballhandling drills, footwork drills, and shooting drills. Some coaches had their players dribble the ball, slalom-style, in and out between a row of chairs lined up on the court. Others diagrammed intricate exercises in which the entire team, scrubs and all, would endlessly pass the ball back and forth to each other. Phog Allen had his players do push-ups and heel-and-toe stretches and practice mass-formation boxing. "Nothing is better" to help train a basketball player, he declared, "than open-handed boxing." Allen also focused on the diet of his team, emphasizing grains and vegetables and allowing sweets but frowning on meat. "An orange eggnog," he wrote, "is a splendid tonic for a languid and appetiteless player."

While Allen believed in the necessity of working his players hard and drilling them in the game's basic skills, he also worried about boredom and fatigue. He was not alone. "One of the greatest dangers, especially on the part of the new or inexperienced coach," advised the authors of *Modern Basketball,* "is the tendency to overwork his men." Other coaches recommended breaking up practices with games like twenty-one or H-O-R-S-E. "For the best results," one 1938 coaching manual intoned, "these drills should not be drudgery." Rather, they should be "interesting and enjoyable."

Such advice, however, was of little help to McLendon. So he created a training program all his own. While other college basketball coaches across the country had their players doing deep knee bends and side-straddle hops, the members of the North Carolina College basketball team found themselves living in a far different world. While McLendon sat in the bleachers, stopwatch and notebook in hand, they ran half-court suicides — dashing out from the end line, touching the midcourt line, and then running back — and full-court suicides, sides aching, minds numb, sweat pouring from their heads and chests. There were speed drills for dribbling and speed drills for shooting, followed by rope skipping, Joe Louis–style, while McLendon's voice echoed off the walls of the brick gymnasium.

Let's go. Pick it up. Faster, faster.

Then came the passing drills — forty-foot bounce passes and fifty-foot baseball passes and short passes on the fly, all designed to move the ball downcourt in a blaze of speed, practiced again and again and again. There were jumping exercises and fast-paced footwork — feint, pivot, cut — followed by a barrage of shooting drills, including those designed to help players master the seven kinds of layups. "A coach never wastes time if he spends time on fundamentals," he would later write. But for McLendon, this meant fundamentals on fire — fast-break drills to match his new offensive strategy. Let's go. Faster. Pick it up.

And it worked. By his third season as head coach, not only had the revved-up Eagles become regular contenders for the Colored Intercollegiate Athletic Association conference championship, they were also recognized in Negro newspapers as one of the best colored basketball teams in America. They even made national news when Rocky Roberson scored a then-jaw-dropping fifty-eight points against Shaw, busting the record held by Stanford's Hank Luisetti, the first college player ever to score fifty points in a game.

McLendon was obsessed, on a mission to create a new kind of game. But there were still other steps to be taken.

The first involved his players — not what they had to do but who they were. McLendon knew well that he had to have a certain kind of player, one who had not only been drilled in the game's fundamentals but also had the athletic and mental ability to play the new high-speed, rapid-fire game. For as much as John McLendon loved his Kansans and Missourians, he also knew that to compete at the highest level he was going to have to cast a wider net. And he knew just where to look.

CHAPTER 10

Hoosiers

Nowhere on earth did people love basketball as they did in Indiana. A land of farmers and small-town merchants where you knew your neighbors, went to church on Sunday, voted Republican, and did your drinking at home, the Hoosier State was also a place where businesses ground to a halt during tourney time. Whole communities went into the red to build a bigger gym, and the ownership of season tickets to local high school fives became adjudicated in divorce decrees. Every Friday night from December to March, in heated gyms smelling of popcorn, hair tonic, and BO, the people of Indiana gathered to take part in their civic religion, their own roundball *Oresteia*. "They know it, love it, live it," wrote John Tunis, who penned a weekly sports column for the *New Yorker,* adding, "A Hoosier talks basketball for an hour after he's dead."

Imported into the state during the 1890s by members of the Young Men's Christian Association, basketball seemed to be tailor-made for Indiana. Here was a sport where the basic equipment—a ball, two goals, and a relatively level floor—was within reach of even the most meager educational budget. It was a game in which even the one-horse towns, with a handful of talent, could take on the city schools. Here was a sport that farm boys and farm girls, dressed in bib overalls, could practice for hours on end, tossing a leather ball at an iron ring fashioned from a barrel hoop or the iron rim of an old wagon wheel nailed to the side of a barn. Some Hoosier kids played with balls made out of balled-up socks or rags tied together with binder twine. Branch McCracken, later a coaching legend at Indiana University, started his basketball career on the family farm outside Monrovia by shooting an inflated hog bladder at a fruit basket. But however they first saw it, Indianans took to the new game like flies to buttermilk. Within a decade basketball was being played in every county and practically every town in the state. But the most explosive growth was still to come.

The engine of change was the Indiana State High School Basketball Tournament. First held in 1911, the inaugural tournament was a low-key affair played over the course of two days with only a dozen teams participating—one for each of the state's congressional districts. The team from Walton brought along only twelve fans, while the players from Clinton had to be informed that caroming shots off the walls or ceiling at Indiana University's Assembly Hall was not allowed. Ten years later, in 1921, by which time regional and sectional tournaments had been added, 394 teams participated. By 1927, when the number had grown to 731, the Indiana State High School Basketball Tournament had become the largest athletic competition in America.

The game, meanwhile, had become far more than something with which to pass the time while at the local café, feed store, or church picnic. "Winning was everything," Hoosier roundball historian Phillip Hoose observed, as were efforts to secure victory. Talented players were lured from competing school districts with the promise of better jobs for their dads; the starting salaries of high school basketball coaches jolted ever upward; and the atmosphere at home games edged out of control at times, with fans tossing objects at opposing players, fistfights erupting in the stands, and referees' whistles getting drowned out by raucous, earsplitting cheers.

Give 'em the old elbow,
Sock 'em in the jaw,
Take 'em to the graveyard,
Rah! Rah! Rah!

A New York writer, witnessing a small-town Indiana high school basketball game on a frigid, ice-bound night, became entranced by a demure elderly woman sitting quietly in the stands nearby, seemingly oblivious to the unrestrained cacophony all about her. "She wore a faded gray dress," he later wrote, "an especially ancient gray hat, and held in her right hand an umbrella." But when a member of the opposing team stole the ball and started driving toward the basket, the little old lady could bear it no more.

"Get the son of a bitch!" she yelled. "Get the son of a bitch!"

In the Hoosier madness, however, something else was happening as well. For out of the great Indiana basketball laboratory, where countless kids shot sock balls at countless hoops nailed to innumerable barns, where red-hot teams captured the attention of entire towns, and where the world's greatest high school tournament flourished, a distinct style of play emerged. Disciplined and carefully executed, Indiana basketball featured tough, constant defense and a highly planned offense. Hoosier ballplayers were anything but gunners, and in that pre–shot clock era, they would patiently pass the ball, set screen after screen, and run half a dozen backdoor cuts until the right shot, the *perfect* shot, eventually appeared. Rigorous, diligent, and prescribed, this was, above all, a team game. When it worked, which was often, it was a thing of both beauty and power.

Here in Indiana flowered a new, democratic game for a new century. A sport in which two-bit schools could take on the city slickers. A game in which Davids could take on Goliaths. A game in which it shouldn't have mattered who your daddy was or what church you went to or what part of town you lived in. Only in some cases, it did.

*   *   *

When it came to race, Indiana had long displayed a split personality.

More than two hundred thousand Hoosier men and boys—nearly one-sixth of the population of the entire state—clad in Union blue, had fought in some of the deadliest battles of the Civil War. Not every Hoosier, though, had stood by the Union cause. Despite the fact that Abraham Lincoln had grown up in the southern part of the state, more than twenty Indiana counties voted against him in the presidential election of 1860. And during the war itself, smuggling goods across the Ohio River into pro-Confederate Kentucky was common. Indiana, despite the bravery of its regiments, was also famed as the land of the Copperheads, the antiwar Northern Democrats who wanted to let the South go.

By the 1920s, the Hoosier State had become known for having one of the largest and most powerful Ku Klux Klan organizations in America. Targeting Catholics, Jews, immigrants, Negroes, liquor interests, and elected officials deemed to be soft on crime, Indiana Klansmen formed scores of local chapters, held massive parades, and became a force in politics. They also burned crosses on front lawns, forced Catholic teachers out of their jobs in public schools, and warned Negro house hunters to keep away from white neighborhoods. In 1924, more than a dozen Klan chapters from across the state even hosted a Junior Klansmen basketball tournament at the armory in Elwood. And while the Klan tournament soon disappeared, Klan thinking about basketball in the Hoosier State, and who should be involved in it, did not.

There had, of course, been colored ballplayers in Indiana from the very beginning, and Negro athletes had been members of high school teams that played in the state tournament. But like the number of colored people in Indiana in general—less than 4 percent of the population before World War II—their numbers had been small. The truth was, in almost every part of the state there were never enough Negroes to justify the creation of separate schools, so colored kids in Indiana attended white schools, where, like everyone else, they played basket-ball. On the road, colored high school players often had to contend with more than their fair share of flying elbows, crowd abuse, and homer refs. But in high schools across much of Indiana, having an occasional Negro teammate wasn't all that unusual.

In 1927, however, the situation changed. With the opening of the state's first all-colored high school, Crispus Attucks High School in Indianapolis, and plans for a second in Gary the following year, Arthur Trester, the powerful head of the Indiana High School Athletic Association, issued an extraordinary edict, declaring that because they were not open to *all* students, the state's Negro and Catholic schools were henceforth banned from taking part in the championship tournament. Barred from participating in the most important athletic event in Indiana, these young men were also denied the spotlight that the Hoosier rite of spring provided. While the Catholic high schools would develop their own state championship tournament, there weren't enough Negro high schools in Indiana to do the same. Both part of and cut off from the state pastime, these colored players would in many ways have to develop their game on their own. And anyone who was interested in finding out what they were doing would have to go looking.

John McLendon was looking, and it didn't take long for him to hit pay dirt.

His first stop was North Vernon, a brick-front railroad town set in the Limestone Belt of the southeast corner of the state. McLendon was after a pair of colored ballplayers who literally had to be seen to be believed. Six-feet-five-inch Harold Colbert—whose mother, Josephine, took in laundry to keep food on the table after her husband died—was as graceful a big man as McLendon had ever seen, a master of perfectly timed rebounding and relentless put-backs. At North Carolina College, Colbert, who was nicknamed Slam, would play center and become the school's first all-conference player.

Norbert "Slim" Downing and two of his North Carolina College teammates, Richard Mack and Walter Warmick, 1941. *(North Carolina Central University Archives, Records and History Center—James E. Shepard Memorial Library, Durham, NC)*

But it was Colbert's teammate who caught everybody's eye.

The eldest son of a blacksmith, Norbert Downing stood six feet eleven at a time when the average height for American men was five feet nine. Light-skinned and willowy, he could reach the bottom of the net standing flat-footed, had to duck through every doorway he entered, and had his clothes specially made. But what was equally amazing about Downing—who, of course, was nicknamed Slim—was his ballhandling ability. Not only was he a graceful dribbler, a wizard at fingertip passing, and an able scorer, he was also almost impossible to guard. He was the kind of player whom every basketball coach in the Big Ten dreamed about having on his roster.

Or at least he should have been. Because while a few Big Ten football and track coaches had erased the color line on their teams, there wasn't a single Negro basketball player in the Midwest's top conference, and there wouldn't be for years. So Slim went south, where McLendon's stroke of genius was to have Downing play guard. Together, Slim and Slam helped win the Eagles their first CIAA conference championship in 1941.

That same season, McLendon brought in three more Indianans. They came, however, from a much different kind of Hoosierdom. Built along the southernmost tip of Lake Michigan, the city of Gary could not be mistaken for the small-town, family-farm, corn-bin-and-church-steeple Indiana that songwriters, novelists, and advertising copywriters liked to invoke. Here was one of the most industrialized areas in the entire world, a smokestack landscape that was home to more than 175 steel mills, oil refineries, cement plants, soap factories, roller mills, slaughterhouses, and packing plants. Built on reclaimed marshland and sand dunes, where the glow of the blast furnaces and refinery flares could be seen all night, it was a place where housewives knew never to leave the family wash out on the line in the backyard too long lest the bedsheets become speckled with soot.

While colored citizens in Gary could vote as well as ride on the city's streetcars and buses, they couldn't use the parks on the north side of town. They had to sit in the balcony in movie theaters and were placed in segregated wards in local hospitals. They also knew to avoid the city's notoriously tough police department, known for breaking strikes, roughing up labor organizers, and knocking out the teeth of any Negro unlucky enough to fall into their custody.

The school system was largely, though not entirely, segregated. At the high school level, some colored students had gone to school with whites for years, even though the Negroes were barred from attending the prom or joining most of the extracurricular activities. They even had their pictures kept out of the yearbooks. But in 1927, when twenty-four Negro students were transferred—temporarily, because of overcrowding—to the Ralph Waldo Emerson School, a previously all-white school on the city's north side, more than six hundred white students walked out and led a protest march downtown, carrying signs that read WE WON'T GO BACK UNTIL EMERSON'S WHITE. In the ensuing turmoil, plans quickly moved forward for the construction of an all-colored high school, Theodore Roosevelt, which opened in 1930.

And it was there that McLendon found his most durable talent. In the fall of 1940 alone, he brought in three players from Roosevelt: a dazzling, sinewy guard named James Hardy—nicknamed Boogie—and two named Brown, a sharpshooting intellectual named Floyd and a six-feet-four, 208-pound guard by the name of John, whom everyone called Big. The addition of the trio from Gary meant that the 1940–41 North Carolina College basketball team, the first to win a conference championship, was composed of five Indianans, seven Kansans or Kansas Citians, and only three players from somewhere else.

McLendon's recruiting pipeline to the Midwest depended, of course, on an honest assessment of talent, and he did a masterful job of creating relationships with high school coaches in Kansas and Indiana and of scouring box scores and statistics. "You had to be careful, though, with some of the recommendations," he later recalled. "Because the closer some of these guys got to Durham, the shorter they got." But McLendon also had to convince the families of these players that it was safe to send their sons to school down South—especially in Gary, where the parents were almost always Southern-born and -bred.

"They all knew what the situation was," McLendon said. "But they also knew that if you have someone to look after you—that's the term they used—then that person will keep you out of problems, out of trouble." To potential recruits who admitted that they were afraid to go, McLendon was direct. "Well, I was too," he told them. "But I found out that you can get by without a lot of things. I told them that you don't have to go to the movies on a certain day. You don't have to ride the bus, because you could walk. Some of these things are not going to bother you, because we'll all be together."

But it was the parents who were key.

"I never took a player that I didn't know his parents," McLendon said. "And most of the parents that I recruited had one thing in their favor. And that was they wanted their kid to get an education. And they were willing for them to take that risk."

Once America entered World War II, McLendon had to contend with another issue, namely, finding top-quality new recruits who hadn't already enlisted or been drafted into the armed services. It was a battle that, in the long run, he knew he could never win. The photos of his wartime teams at North Carolina College tell the tale just as effectively as anything else. From a high of seventeen players in 1941, the number dropped to fifteen the following season and eleven a year later. As the 1943–44 basketball season opened, McLendon was down to seven players.

But it didn't matter. For in his obsession with perfecting his game, he knew that the fast break, which had spread like wildfire across America, was not, in itself, enough. He needed another weapon as well, and, working deep into the night in his small office in the gymnasium, or letting his mind drift back and forth to the problem over dinner, during practice, or late at night at home, he had finally figured out what it was.

Naismith, he thought to himself. I should have known. From a hilltop in North Carolina, John McLendon was about to push basketball even farther into a brand-new age.

PART TWO

CHAPTER 11

City of Stone

Three miles away, on the other side of Durham, sat not just another school but another world.

Rising out of the pine forest that bordered the western edge of town, Duke University was a picture postcard come to life. Its West Campus, modeled after the five-hundred-year-old architectural masterpieces of Tudor England, was a wonderland of spires and parapets, cloistered walkways and vaulted ceilings, stained-glass windows and oak-paneled reading rooms. On late autumn afternoons, the light-colored Hillsborough stone used to construct the campus, with its mix of tan, gray, rust, and green, could shine like bars of copper against the sunset. Duke was an architectural gem, an idyll in glass and stone.

When Aldous Huxley, the English novelist, visited in the early summer of 1937, he was flabbergasted. Driving south from New York City on what would be a three-thousand-mile road trip to a new life in Los Angeles, he had at first found the North Carolina countryside to be likable but bland—"Pine forest, tobacco fields, more pine forests succeed one another interminably.... It is a pleasant land, but unexciting; a land where one would never expect anything in particular to happen," he wrote in *Time and Tide,* a London magazine, "And then, all of a sudden, something *does* happen. One emerges from yet another

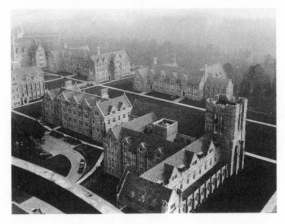

Aerial view, West Campus, Duke University, 1932. *(Duke University Archives)*

of the warm, sweet-smelling pine woods and there, astonishingly, is by far the largest Gothic building one has ever seen—larger than the Houses of Parliament, larger than St. Pancreas Station, far larger, certainly, than any church or abbey or castle set up by the original inventors of the style. The eye wanders in amazement over a whole city of grey stone."

Huxley wasn't the only one impressed. Newlyweds and grandmothers, dentists and schoolteachers, and farm families clad in bib overalls and two-dollar dresses would all gape in awe as they made the long, slow climb up Chapel Drive and laid their eyes, for the first time, on the ancient-seeming wonderment before them. Even some of the stone steps, the keen-eyed noticed, had already been worn down, as though from centuries of use.

Of course, they weren't that old. Wrote William Blackburn, a missionaries' son turned Rhodes scholar turned English professor: "Old in idea as the Middle Ages, the West Campus is, nevertheless, a new creation." From the blue-gray exhaust and the grinding gears of the buses pulling to a stop in front of the main quadrangle to the quantum mechanics and theories of superconductivity being researched in the physics and chemistry departments to the Technicolor movies shown in the campus auditorium, Duke was a fully modern university at the dawn of the 1940s. Armed with a substantial bankroll, the school's founders had not only happily raided the faculties of the nation's most prestigious colleges and universities, they had also created first-class facilities for them, including laboratories, lecture halls, and the largest library south of the Potomac. It was, some said, the Oxford of the South. "Duke became a great university because it *looked* like one from the start," one campus administrator would later write.

Moreover, it had happened practically overnight. Regardless of the fact that the school had ties to Trinity College, a small North Carolina college whose roots went back to the 1830s, the truth of the matter was that despite its ancient feel, the entity known as Duke University—created by a headline-making bequest from the Duke family, a clan of local farmers who had made their first fortune by selling brightleaf tobacco to Union soldiers—was all of fifteen years old in the fall of 1940. The school's most recognizable building, the magnificent chapel, with its bell tower reaching more than two hundred feet into the ever-blue North Carolina sky, had been completed only eight years earlier, in 1932.

Despite all the millions that had been poured into the university's creation, it was an open question at first as to just how *good* a school Duke would become. But what was not open to debate was that, Oxford of the South or not, Duke would be a *Southern* school with Southern ways. Negroes, of course, would not be allowed to enroll, although—unlike a number of Northern schools—Duke put no quota on the number of Jewish students. A statue of Robert E. Lee stood alongside the front entrance to the chapel, while the initiation regalia for one campus fraternity bore more than a slight resemblance to the hoods and robes of the Ku Klux Klan. And even though Duke attracted students from all over the country, the majority of the undergraduates, like many members of the faculty and administration, were Dixie-born and -bred. So, too, was the campus mind-set.

In the spring of 1941, nine days before Easter, a special choral concert was scheduled to take place in the chapel. The Duke Chapel Choir would perform, as would the Farmville College Choir, from Virginia. The highlight of the program, however, would be the appearance of the Harvard Glee Club, singing selections from Bach and Josquin des Prez as well as English composer Gustav Holst's "A Dirge for Two Veterans." With much of the rest of the world already at war, it was a thoughtful, masterfully designed program, a choral prayer in a time of global crisis.

But when it was discovered that there was a colored member—Drue King, a doctor's son, from Tuskegee, Alabama—among the forty-strong Harvard singers, the authorities at Duke moved swiftly to bar his appearance. "Duke University let it be known that no colored man would be allowed to sing in its chapel," journalist Ted Gup later wrote. And King didn't. Faced with a choice between canceling their Southern tour or leaving King at home, the president of the club chose the latter, though not without stirring up some commotion in Cambridge. "Your cause is to spread good music, not to solve race-relations problems," one glee club alumnus wrote. "That's somebody else's problem."

At Duke, there was exactly one murmur of protest.

"This column is strictly for Northerners," wrote a student named C. F. Sanborn in the *Chronicle,* the student newspaper. "Southerners read it at peril of their blood pressure." After laying out the facts of the case, the columnist went on the attack. "Should not the intellectual aristocracy in a vauntedly Christian institution be setting a different example?" Sanborn asked. "Granted we must fight fire with fire and Hitler with his own barbarism but how can we justify the rubbish in our own backyard."

Apparently without difficulty.

Not everyone, of course, viewed Duke the same way. Negroes in Durham generally avoided the campus, while eight miles down the road, at the vastly older University of North Carolina, smiles would fade and expressions would sour at the mention of the new upstart over in Durham. Others across the state chafed at how well-off the Duke student body seemed or at the number of Yankees and other outsiders who had taken up residence on the Gothic campus. When the chapel was struck—twice—by lightning soon after a faculty ball, an editorial in one North Carolina newspaper declared that it was a sign that God did not approve of dancing at Duke.

Nor did everyone who pulled up in front of the chapel and gazed out at the stone archways, battlements, balustrades, and cloistered walkways do so with a smile. One such visitor, a hardscrabble farmer in overalls and a straw hat, climbed slowly out of his truck, then glanced from one end of campus to the other.

"Well," he was overheard to say, "now at least I know where the money went."

And in the eastern part of the state, in the Depression-ravaged tobacco and cotton country, one late 1930s ditty began this way:

> *I'm a prostitute, from Dear Old Duke,*
> *Ain't nothin' could be finer.*
> *Get off of me, you S.O.B.,*
> *If you're from Carolina.*

Duke and basketball hadn't exactly been love at first sight, either.

The game was first introduced on campus during the old Trinity College days, but the school didn't hold its first intercollegiate game until 1906, didn't pay its coach until seven years later, and didn't play an exclusive schedule against other college teams until World War I. It also took some time to settle on a team name. The original name, the Methodists—some folks referred to the campus as Methodist Flats—didn't win much favor among the student body, so a number of potential replacements were bandied about in student-initiated polls and newspaper articles, including the Polar Bears, the Dreadnoughts, and the Royal Blazes. But nothing stuck. Finally, in the early 1920s, the editors of the *Chronicle* simply started calling the team the Blue Devils, after the Chasseurs Alpins, elite units of French mountain infantry who were known for their daring, their resourcefulness, and their distinctive blue uniforms. The French Blue Devils, as they were nicknamed, were even the subject of a song by Irving Berlin: "With their glistening sabers, / Among the shot and shell," went the lyrics to "The Blue Devils of France," "They visit their Austrian neighbors / And give them H-E–double L."

But it wasn't until the end of the decade that the North Carolina version of the Blue Devils started to give anyone hell in basketball. When they did, it came largely at the hands of one talented and determined individual. His name was Edmund McCullough Cameron.

Born and raised in Pennsylvania, Cameron had been a star football and basketball player at Washington and Lee University, in Virginia. Charismatic, outgoing, friendly, and handsome—"perhaps the most admired and best known man on Campus" is how the *Calyx,* the W&L yearbook, described him—he was also a student government leader, a model student, and a first-rate sportsman. After graduation, he gave the banking business a shot, but the pull of athletics was too strong. In 1926, when his former W&L football coach was hired at Duke, Cameron tagged along to coach the freshman football team.

It proved to be a smart move. Football had taken the South by storm, and the higher-ups at Duke were bound and determined to raise the gridiron prowess of the Blue Devils. When they lured the already legendary Alabama coach Wallace Wade to Durham, it might have spelled the end of Cameron's aspirations at Duke. But Wade liked the transplanted Pennsylvanian from the start and retained him as an assistant football coach. Moreover, Cameron had already found an additional athletic niche of his own, one where he was already making a name for himself.

While basketball still very much existed in the shadow of football in those days, especially in the South, Eddie Cameron knew an opportunity when he saw one. His roundball career took off when he was assigned to be the new head basketball coach at Duke at the beginning of the 1928–29 season. As the newest addition to the twenty-three-member Southern Conference, Duke didn't have particularly high expectations. But after losing their first three games in a row, the Blue Devils went on a tear, toppling North Carolina and N.C. State, Wake Forest, and South Carolina. And their greatest glory was still to come.

Founded in 1921, the Southern Conference Basketball Tournament was the oldest collegiate championship tournament in the country. Held every spring until the early 1930s in Atlanta's Auditorium and Armory, it had already crowned seven different champions, including Auburn, Kentucky, Virginia, and Tulane. And despite the Blue Devils' string of victories in the spring of 1929, nobody in Atlanta expected them to make much noise, at least not anytime soon.

But Duke came in and flat-out wowed everyone. Playing a high-tempo, ball-hawking, upset-minded game, they not only won over the crowd but also sent Dixie's normally florid set of sportswriters digging for superlatives. "The Blue Devils from Durham look like the cleverest team in the tournament," reported a columnist for the *Atlanta Georgian,* while the *Charlotte Observer* declared that Duke guard Bill Werber was "the greatest guard ever to play on the tournament floor." And although the Blue Devils lost in the semifinals to N.C. State, the leading sportswriter for the *Atlanta Journal* had been duly impressed. "That Duke is going to be a big factor in conference sports is certain," journalist Morgan Blake wrote. "And we don't mean maybe."

One year later, they came back and did it again. Coming into the tournament with an 18–2 record, Duke knocked off Louisiana State and Georgia Tech before facing Kentucky in what one columnist declared was the greatest basketball game ever played in Atlanta. A high-speed battle whose movements one reporter breathlessly described as being "too quick for the casual eye," the game featured perfect foul shooting by the Wildcats, howling fans, and Duke players diving to the floor to intercept Kentucky's famous submarine passes. "They were as nimble and as sure-fingered as newsboys scrambling for pennies," sportswriter Ed Danforth claimed. The Blue Devils won the game, 37–32, but lost the tournament championship to Alabama. In the long run, however, it didn't matter. It wasn't just Duke that had arrived. So, too, had Eddie Cameron.

His personality was one key to his success. Not only did he try to make certain that his players enjoyed themselves—"Basketball," he later recalled, "was fun when I coached it"—he was also a master recruiter. Largely ignoring the rather slim pickings in North Carolina, Cameron instead built Duke basketball by looking north, especially toward his native state. For most of his career as basketball coach, nearly one-third of the Blue Devils basketball lettermen were Pennsylvanians, while other players were imported from Washington, D.C., New York, and New Jersey. Duke might have been a Southern school, but under Eddie Cameron's watch, its basketball teams largely spoke with a Northern accent. They played well, too. Not only did Cameron's teams log in only one losing season, they were also a perennial threat in the Southern Conference tournament.

In early 1933, however, in a game against North Carolina, the fortunes of Duke basketball changed once again.

Though their campuses were less than ten miles apart, Duke and the University of North Carolina had been playing each other in basketball for less than fifteen years. The first decade had belonged to the Tar Heels, who won seventeen out of their first nineteen contests against Duke. When Eddie Cameron took over the Blue Devils, however, the tide turned. By the end of the 1931–32 season, Duke had won seven out of the previous nine games. But when Carolina came to Durham on January 31, 1933, it looked like the run was ending. Not only were the Tar Heels on fire, they were also undefeated. The game itself was a barn burner. Duke built a solid lead at the break, but Carolina fought back, and the lead seesawed back and forth throughout the second half. Finally the Blue Devils staged a rugged comeback and won the game by four points. What mattered the most about the game, however, was neither the victory nor the final score. Instead it had to do with where it was played.

Less than three years old, the Duke gymnasium was a first-class athletic facility. Built from the same Hillsborough stone that graced the rest of West Campus, it housed athletic offices and training facilities and served as the modern, up-to-date home court of the Blue Devils—and it was positively elegant compared with the "Tin Can," the Tar Heels' dusty, poorly lit, and barely heated home floor. With seating for more than three thousand fans, at a time when undergraduate enrollment hovered around eighteen hundred, the Duke gym undoubtedly would be big enough, the university administration reasoned, for decades to come.

When the gymnasium was built, basketball was such a low priority on campus that it didn't even rate a mention on one of the four stone shields—for football, tennis, baseball, and boxing—that hung above the building's entrance. But that was before the Carolina game. That night the fans weren't just packed in like sardines. They were everywhere. They had come from Chapel Hill and Roxboro, Creedmore and Bahama, Bynum and Cedar Grove. They had come in cars, buses, farm trucks, and Model A's; they had walked across town in the oncoming twilight. They filled every seat and every walkway, crammed every corridor, and were massed by the hundreds, shoulder to shoulder, beneath each goal. Along the slender balcony that ringed the court, spectators were standing on the windowsills or sitting with their hands on the rail, their feet dangling below them. In an era where sellouts to college basketball games were rare, even in the game's true hot spots, an estimated *five thousand* spectators had crammed themselves into the Duke gym.

Something was happening to basketball in North Carolina. Eddie Cameron knew it. So did Wallace Wade. For the roar that the crowd made that evening wasn't just shouts and clamor, whistles and catcalls, foot-stomping and rebel yells. It was also the sound of the future. On a chilly North Carolina night in 1933, a whole new kind of Southern basketball was stirring to life, one that would ignite lifelong passions, witness the crowning of numerous national champions, and give rise to a fabled conference. First, however, it would have a brand-new home.

One day in 1935, two years after the Carolina game, Wallace Wade and Eddie Cameron were discussing the future of the athletic programs on campus. When the subject of basketball came up, the two coaches agreed that what the Blue Devils needed was a new field house. Excited about their ideas but not having any paper handy, Wade and Cameron proceeded to design the new facility on a matchbook cover. "It's definitely a true story," Cameron's daughter told a reporter nearly half a century later. When planning began in earnest for the new field house, skirmishes soon broke out over the proposed number of seats. The original proposal called for seating for five thousand, a number that struck more than a few observers as extravagant. But Wade and Cameron were bullish on Duke basketball, and the number kept growing. When the call for a new field house that could seat *eight thousand* people hit the offices of Horace Trumbauer, the university's Philadelphia-based architect, jaws dropped and tempers flared. "For your information, Yale has in its new gymnasium a basket ball court with settings for 1600," the self-made, self-assured Trumbauer wrote to the president of Duke. "I think the settings for 8,000 people is rather liberal." But the two Duke coaches won the day. The next set of plans called for seating for 8,800. There would be nothing like it in Dixie.

Of special interest was the fact that the man who was primarily responsible for designing the new field house would never have been allowed to sit in one of those seats.

Born and raised in Philadelphia, Julian Abele had roots that ran deep into the city's colored aristocracy. A skilled artist, even as a child, he attended the Institute for Colored Youth, a Quaker school located just off South Street, where his aunt Julia taught drawing. But it was his hometown's renowned architecture—from the elegant Federal-style town houses and Greek revival banks and churches to the soaring new office buildings, banks, and train stations—that won his heart. As a lad, he decided to become an architect.

Brilliant and prodigiously talented, Abele—pronounced "able"—was equally determined. He entered the Pennsylvania Museum and School of Industrial Art at age sixteen and the University of Pennsylvania one year later. At Penn, he was not only the first Negro to graduate in architecture but was also elected president of the student architectural society. Abele then enrolled in the prestigious Pennsylvania Academy of the Fine Arts, where he studied architectural design. By the time he left the academy in 1903, Abele was the most talented and highly trained colored architecture graduate in America. But actually getting a job as an architect was another matter. Luckily, fortune glanced his way.

Horace Trumbauer was not an architect's architect. He blazed no new design paths and studiously stayed away from radical new approaches and novel ideas. But what Trumbauer, a salesman's son, did know was how to appeal to the status-hungry new millionaires of Gilded Age America, people for whom a stately mansion, giving off an aura of timelessness and old money, was a ticket to social success. In Philadelphia, where Trumbauer opened his own firm, he hit the jackpot. Catering to the nouveau riche, he designed fourteen-bedroom French chateaux, Georgian mansions dripping with mahogany, and magnificent Tudor palaces. As Trumbauer's practice flourished, he also needed employees, especially designers. "I hire my brains," he once said, and in 1906 Trumbauer showed both courage and business savvy by hiring Abele. Not only did he risk losing clients by taking on a colored architect, he also sent Abele on a tour of the Continent, where the young graduate could study firsthand the great houses, cathedrals, and public buildings of Europe.

It proved to be a smart move. Back home in Philadelphia, surrounded by blueprints and diazotypes, Julian Abele's quiet genius emerged. "He drew," remembered one associate, "with unmatched facility." Dressed, impeccably, in a jacket and tie—he even wore a suit and a straw bowler when he went to the beach—Abele designed churches and private homes, hotels and hospitals, for clients all up and down the East Coast.

But Duke was his masterpiece.

Closely collaborating with Trumbauer and other employees of the firm on creating and designing the new Gothic campus, Abele worked his own kind of magic, quietly ushering the weight of tradition into the age of electricity. Windows became bigger, finials and spires grew more graceful, archways came to life, and the buildings themselves reached upward. "When you look at Abele's buildings," one critic observed, "they float." From his office in downtown Philadelphia, Julian Abele hadn't just helped create a new university. He had created a prayer in stone.

The new field house would be one of the last buildings at Duke that Abele would design. Construction began in the spring of 1939 in order that the mortar on the outside walls could be laid before winter. Nine months and four hundred thousand dollars later, the new field house, which was officially called the Duke Indoor Stadium, was finished.

Set along the western edge of the campus in an area then known as

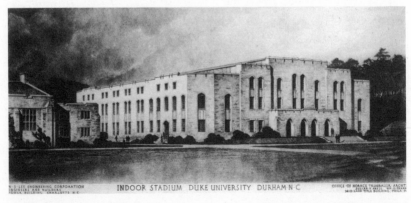

The Duke Indoor Stadium, later renamed in honor of Eddie Cameron. *(Duke University Archives)*

Maple Acres, the building wasn't, in truth, much to look at. Though its exterior blended in perfectly with the rusty browns and coppery tans and greenish grays of the other buildings, Abele had kept the outside practically free of decorative elements. With its flat external lines and narrow windows, the indoor stadium had all the charm of a National Guard armory.

Inside, it was another matter.

When the first visitors walked through the narrow doors and into the central expanse of the building itself, mouths popped open, heads tilted upward, and voices were stilled. For its time, the indoor stadium wasn't simply big. It was huge. Nine sets of massive steel girders, set two dozen feet apart, held aloft a roof that was nearly the size of a football field. Scores of incandescent lamps hung from the ceiling, flooding the basketball court with electric light, while daylight streamed in from more than four dozen windows set below the roofline. All-electric scoreboards, including a game clock that turned red during the last minute of play, sat at each end. Seemingly overnight, Duke didn't just have a beautiful brand-new home for the Blue Devils. They also had the largest basketball facility in the South.

But whether its primary creator ever saw it or not is a matter of speculation.

Despite rumors to the contrary—and the fact that Negroes, unless they were uniformed service workers, were far from welcome on campus— it is certain that Julian Abele made at least one visit to Duke during the early years of the construction of West Campus. On one trip to Durham, accompanied by Trumbauer designer William Frank, Abele was apparently denied a room at one of the white-owned hotels downtown. The truth of the matter was that Julian Abele had designed what would become one of the most revered athletic venues in the world. But as a colored man, he would never have been allowed inside to sit and watch a game—let alone attend the building's formal dedication on January 6, 1940.

One more thing was certain. By 1940, the winds of war were blowing overseas. Soon enough, they would be felt on campus as well.

CHAPTER 12

Blue Devil

By the fall of 1943, Duke had gone to war.

Even though the nearest fighting was almost five thousand miles away, the university had already practiced blackouts and air-raid drills, while barbed wire had been stretched across some of the athletic fields, which by then were serving as obstacle courses. On East Campus, female students rolled gauze bandages for the Red Cross, wrote letters to wounded GIs, and enrolled in new classes called Mathematics of Artillery Fire and Sea Power and Modern Navies. While the social life of the campus continued, it was tinged with a new reality. Homecoming floats, the Cotton Pickers Ball, and postgame bonfires had given way to the Ration Dance and the Navy Ball.

Each morning the sound of bugles, marching feet, and close-order drills echoed off the stone walls of West Campus as more than one thousand uniformed Navy and Marine recruits had descended upon Duke for specialized training. Remarkably, the enemy was on campus as well. Italian POWs worked as orderlies in the Duke hospital while battle-hardened members of the Afrika Korps, captured after Rommel's defeat at El Alamein, labored as members of the campus grounds crew — though not without a few maneuvers of their own. Ordered to trim the English ivy away from the windows and stonework on some of the Gothic buildings, the German POWs also stealthily cut the vines at ground level, after which they soon withered and turned brown.

"A little dig from the Krauts," one Duke student remembered.

But the war was there in other ways as well—in draft notices and hasty farewells, in military orders, and in the ever more common news reports published in the *Chronicle* and the *Durham Morning Herald* about former students who were already in the thick of the fighting. On the northern shore of Papua New Guinea, Daniel K. Edwards, class of '35, won the Distinguished Service Cross for "extraordinary heroism" in helping to repulse a Japanese counterattack. Off the beach at Anzio, Lieutenant George Patterson, class of '38, won the Silver Star after the PT boat he skippered was suddenly hit by German artillery fire. And Second Lieutenant Esther Hinshaw, who had graduated at the top of the class of 1941 in the School of Nursing, dodged disaster when the hospital ship she was riding on was attacked in the Mediterranean.

Others weren't so lucky.

Lieutenant Harold Kepnes, class of '34, a physician with the First Marine Division, was killed in action on Guadalcanal on November 3, 1942. Lieutenant Kenneth J. Murphy, class of '40, disappeared when his Lockheed F-4 Lightning never returned from a mission over Rabaul. And Naval Aviation Cadet Frederick Johntz, who graduated from Duke in 1937, died in a training accident at the naval air station in Corpus Christi, Texas, in late 1942. He was twenty-five.

"There is a great fight to be won," the 1943 edition of the *Chanticleer,* the school yearbook, had declared. "May we who are about to join those Duke graduates and our former classmates on the battlefronts of Asia, Africa, Europe, and the seven seas, maintain their same ideals of courage, honor, sacrifice, and love for Country and our honorable heritage." As it turned out, few knew this better than a tall, sandy-haired Army enlistee who could be seen from time to time strolling across the quadrangle on West Campus. What he did not yet know, however, was that his real fight was to start—not in some distant land but among the pines and oaks and spires and parapets that he knew better than practically anyone.

His name was David Smith Hubbell. On a campus that was well stocked with students named Carter, Clay, Cobb, Davis, Taylor, and other common Southern surnames, Hubbell blended right in as a son of Dixie through and through. Some of his forebears, such as the Montagues—whose beautiful handwritten letters his mother had read with her own eyes in the Virginia State Library in Richmond—had washed up on the shores of the commonwealth in the mid-1600s. Others had come to North Carolina in the years before the American Revolution or threaded their way through the gaps in the Appalachians to the grasslands of Kentucky. One of his great-uncles had been killed at Chancellorsville while another carried a lead bullet, delivered by a Yankee sharpshooter during the bloody fight at Spotsylvania, lodged inside his body for decades.

The son of a renowned professor of English and American literature, Dave Hubbell had practically grown up with Duke. At age seven he had been in the audience on the overcast Tuesday in June of 1928 when fifteen-year-old Doris Duke calmly scraped a trowelful of mortar onto the cornerstone of West Campus—just as the heavens opened up, scattering the black-robed faculty as though they were a flock of starlings. On Saturdays he would tag along with his father and older brother to mark the construction progress of the campus that, better than any storybook castle, took shape before his eyes. When he was eight, the Italian stonecutters, smoking pipes and humming arias by Verdi and Puccini, began shaping the Indiana limestone to be used on the chapel into vaults and buttresses, reredos and colonettes. They finished when Dave Hubbell turned thirteen.

There was magic at home as well.

There were baseball bats and bicycles, toy soldiers and tennis rackets, fried chicken and pot roasts for dinner, and outings in the family car. There were aunts and uncles and cousins to visit, movies to watch at the theaters downtown, and the sounds of *The Shadow* and *The Green Hornet* streaming out of the big floor-model console radio in the front parlor. Up in his bedroom on the second floor, his bookcase overflowed with books new and old, including *Smoky the Cowhorse* and *The House at Pooh Corner*, *Treasure Island* and *The Boy's King Arthur*, and books about Peter Pan and the Hardy Boys, the Swamp Fox and Stonewall Jackson.

Hubbell excelled as a student, and even at a young age homework had come easily—a by-product, perhaps, of having a parent who was a college professor. His dreams and aspirations flourished as well. While he had decided quite early on that he wanted to be a doctor when he grew up, he had also fallen in love with reading. And among his father's collection of novels and poetry, essays and plays, he discovered one writer to call his own.

At twelve years of age, Dave Hubbell purchased—with a needed infusion of cash from his mother's pocketbook—his very own multi-volume set of the complete works of Mark Twain. Bound in fake vellum, colored a mustardy yellow, with the individual titles stamped in imitation gold leaf, they were, nonetheless, a ticket to adventure. On lazy afternoons, on a patch of shaded grass in the backyard or stretched out on the love seat when the maid was gone or hidden beneath a flashlight-illuminated tent of covers after his bedtime, he floated down the muddy Mississippi, panned for gold in the foothills of the Sierra Nevadas, and jousted with knights in medieval England. "I'd read *Tom Sawyer* and *Huckleberry Finn* so many times that I could recite whole pages, word for word, from memory," he recalled.

He also inherited a certain worldview, especially when it came to the Southern past.

When David Hubbell's great-grandmother Mary Ann Carlton, a farmer's daughter from Beaver Creek, North Carolina, got married in 1849, she was given a slave—a young Negro boy—as a wedding

present. Decades later, long after the war and the Emancipation Procla-
mation, the ex-slave, riding in a horse-drawn buggy, would visit his
former mistress, sitting under the shade behind the house, talking ami-
cably, it was said, for hours on end. And while we don't know the exact
purpose of the visits, by the time Dave Hubbell was growing up they fit
the version of Southern history that was being taught in books and
newspaper articles, schoolhouses and Sunday schools, and across
kitchen tables all over Dixie. Slavery, it was said, hadn't been so bad.

"Usually, slaves were well treated in North Carolina. They were
more like members of the family," wrote the author of *North Carolina
Yesterday and Today,* a textbook published by the North Carolina
Department of Public Instruction. The Southern states, the new doc-
trine held, had a right to secede. The war, it was said, had been forced
upon the Southern people. "There was a great love between the blacks
and their masters," wrote Mary L. Williamson in *The Life of Gen.
Robert E. Lee, for Children, in Easy Words.* "For years, there had been a
feeling in the North that it was wrong to own slaves, and some of the
people began to hate the South and to try to crush it."

And once the war came, no one fought harder, or more brilliantly,
than the South. Dave Hubbell knew it all. Reading between the lines
in his books, or listening to the stories told by family members at the
dinner table, he had ridden with Jeb Stuart across Maryland and Pennsylvania, and he had flanked the Union right with Jackson at Chancellorsville. His heart had swelled with pride over the bravery of the North
Carolina troops at Manassas and Gettysburg, and he had felt the sor-
row of the furled flags in the spring of 1865.

He wasn't alone. It was a birthright offered to every Southern child.

Another youngster, growing up in another Southern college town,
knew it as well. "For every Southern boy fourteen years old, not once
but whenever he wants it, there is an instant when it's still not yet two
o'clock on that July afternoon in 1863," William Faulkner wrote. "The
brigades are in position behind the rail fence, the guns are laid and
ready in the woods and the furled flags are already loosened to break

out and Pickett himself with his long oiled ringlets and his hat in one hand probably and his sword in the other looking up the hill waiting for Longstreet to give the word and it's all in the balance, it hasn't happened yet, it hasn't even begun yet...."

Of course it had.

There was, of course, more to being a proper Southerner than venerating the past.

There were ways to say hello and ways to court, topics to be discussed in polite conversation and topics to be avoided. Backyard gardeners below the Mason-Dixon line knew that crepe myrtle needed little tending, that Sweet Betsy thrived in the shade, and that tea roses could weather even the hottest summers. A Southerner knew what Jeff Davis pie, Lane cake, Sally Lunn, spoon bread, and Brunswick stew were; that watermelon rind could be pickled; that the best way to flour your chicken was in a paper sack; and that the proper response, when sitting at the dinner table and handed a plate of hot biscuits, was to take two and butter them while they're hot.

But despite the best efforts of outsiders, particularly white Northerners, to comprehend the often puzzling ways of Dixie—especially when it came to relations between whites and Negroes—most attempts to do so fell decidedly flat. Northerners wondered how a land that produced Washington and Jefferson, some of the nation's greatest patriots, could also give us slavery, lynch mobs, and the poll tax. They wondered how a region that gave mankind the words "We hold these truths to be self-evident, that all men are created equal" could also give us Jim Crow railroad cars, *The Birth of a Nation,* and the all-white primary.

In truth, some Southerners couldn't understand it, either.

A reporter for the *Charlotte News* named Wilbur J. Cash decided to give it a go. For five long years he wrestled with trying to weave together all the contradictory threads of Southern life, from the great houses of colonial Virginia and the Lowcountry—"Here were silver and carriages

and courtliness and manners"—to Negro-baiting, venom-spewing dem-
agogues like "Pitchfork Ben" Tillman and Theodore G. Bilbo, the governor of Mississippi, who proposed deporting every colored person in
the South to Africa. It took Cash half a decade to write his four-
hundred-page masterpiece, *The Mind of the South,* which was published
in February of 1941 to rave reviews. Not only did he delve deeply into
Southern history and psychology, he also invented dazzling new ana-
lytical concepts, such as the savage ideal and the Proto-Dorian convention. "Anything written about the South henceforth must start where
he leaves off," *Time* magazine declared.

Four months later, in a Mexico City hotel room, Cash was found
hanging by his necktie, which had been attached to a hook on the back
of the bathroom door. The local authorities ruled the case a suicide,
though other people, including Josephus Daniels, the United States
ambassador to Mexico, were unconvinced. Only days earlier, Cash had
warned family members that he was being tailed by Nazi spies.

Not all Southerners, however, even those who regularly raised an
eyebrow at day-to-day Southern ways and means, were quite as long-
winded in their analysis as Cash was. One such critic was Carey Edwin
Goodwyn Sr., a Georgia-born and -bred colonel in the United States
Army, who, as he traveled from post to post throughout the 1920s and
1930s—from Virginia to Texas and Arizona to Hawaii, then back to
Virginia and Texas—was often called upon by his three young children to unravel the mysteries of life below the Mason-Dixon line.

"Southerners act the way they do," he'd say, "because they don't
know any better."

Despite segregation, colored people were a regular presence in Dave
Hubbell's world. Cooks and maids, whose last names he never learned,
washed the family's clothes, baked the chickens and shelled the peas,
pushed the carpet sweeper and dusted the sideboard, and set out the

cream-cheese-and-cucumber sandwiches for his mother's bridge parties. Sometimes the help would take some of the leftovers home with them, and come Christmas, his mother might slip them a ten-dollar bill or a bag filled with clothes. During the warm-weather months, Negro men in straw hats and khaki work suits stained with motor oil would descend on Pinecrest, Dogwood, Anderson, and the other oak- and hickory-canopied residential streets south of campus. Driving beat-up farm trucks and armed with a battery of shovels and rakes and hoes and lawn mowers, they would cut grass, trim hedges, dig flower gardens, and, come November, burn the reddish-brown leaves that carpeted the gravel driveways and littered the flagstone walks. Named Nate and Joe and Shorty, and sometimes accompanied by boys who were Dave's age, they said little as they went about their business, stopping from time to time to lift a dipperful of water to their lips from a galvanized aluminum pail.

In fact, if you actually looked, colored folk were everywhere.

There were nameless white-coated waiters and uniformed maids at the Washington Duke Hotel, sweat-drenched garbagemen who hauled the trash once a week, and the men's room attendant at the club who gave you hand towels, a fresh comb dipped in Barbicide, and a nostril-clearing splash of bay rum. Every mop and bucket in every office building, school, or factory building in Durham could claim a pair of colored hands, while there wasn't a ditch dug, a road paved, or a section of sewer pipe or water main laid without a Negro laborer taking part. Even at Duke they were there—cleaning the lavatories, washing the bedsheets, cooking and serving the hot lunches in the cafeteria, or silently walking a push broom down the corridors of the hospital.

They were there, but Hubbell didn't always see them.

For they lived in their world, and he lived in his.

Besides, there were more important things to think about. Basketball was one, and college was another. And in Dave Hubbell's world, the two would go together.

*　　*　　*

Picking a college had not been difficult. Hubbell would go to Duke.

His relationship with basketball was a little more complicated. Even though he was a graceful, natural athlete—one who would stand six feet three—Dave Hubbell had come to the game through a side door. Despite his height, he didn't play basketball as a high schooler. "I didn't bother going out for basketball because I knew I couldn't make the team," he later recalled.

He was right. For three years, between 1937 and 1940, Durham High School had the best basketball team in North Carolina. Led by Cedric Loftis, a guard who only had two fingers on his right hand, and six-foot-six-inch Horace "Bones" McKinney—a loose-screw crowd favorite who, while the ball was in play, used to sit on the opposing coach's lap or start selling programs in the stands—the Bulldogs won sixty-nine straight games. They didn't merely win three state

Duke Blue Devils, 1942–43. Dave Hubbell is in the back row at the far left. *(Duke University Archives)*

championships in a row, they crushed their in-state competition—beating Raleigh 57–6, Wilmington 57–11, and Pilot Mountain, a team that had won sixty games straight, 53–17—as well as freshman college teams. The Bulldogs also won a national title as well at the Eastern States Scholastic basketball tournament in Glens Falls, New York, where the team celebrated by going to a striptease show. "After all," McKinney later explained, "that's art."

At Duke, however, Hubbell got his chance. Not only did he make the freshman team—which apparently played the second game ever at the indoor stadium—he also, at the beginning of his sophomore year, won a place on the varsity squad, alternating between playing forward and serving as a backup center. It proved to be an exhilarating, up-and-down season, capped off by the Blue Devils beating South Carolina to win the 1941 Southern Conference championship. But for Hubbell it was also a crash course in basketball science led by Eddie Cameron. "We played man-to-man," Hubbell recalled. "We used a post position for the center to feed in, feed back, cut past. We used a lot of one guy moving to the basket, the ball moving cross-court, and then into the guy under the basket." And on defense, they tried to disrupt the other team by changing the tempo of the game.

Rebounding was a particular passion. "Hubbell, get the rebound!" the coach would call out, or he would shout, "Hubbell, where the hell were you?" Cameron had other quirks as well. He made his players wrap their ankles tightly before each game with cloth that was "like an Ace bandage, except that they were not elastic, they were just a kind of muslin," Hubbell recalled. Pregame meals were usually steak and eggs, "kind of a high-protein thing," plus potatoes and dessert. Cameron had his players drink his own magic elixir as well, which he made by combining TruAde, a noncarbonated orange-flavored soft drink, with a healthy dose of granulated Knox gelatin. "We had to mix it together in the locker room," Hubbell remembered. "It was pretty gooey and messy."

The season had other benefits as well. For the son of an English professor, it was the beginning of a new chapter in his life. By the close of

DAVID SMITH HUBBELL
K A, T Ψ Ω
Pre-Medical
121 Pinecrest Road
Durham, N. C.

Basketball; Lacrosse; Pre-Med. Society; Pegram Chemistry Club.

Dave Hubbell. *(Duke University Archives)*

his sophomore year, Hubbell was no longer just a bookish premed student or a date-happy fraternity boy. Underneath the incandescent lights of the indoor stadium, or out on the ball courts of the Southern Conference, Dave Hubbell was finding within himself a new persona. With beat-up sneakers, a letter sweater in his closet, and a game face that shone with confidence, he was discovering his path to manhood.

The following season, Hubbell's junior year, looked to be even better.

Cameron introduced a new fast break, while the ranks of the Blue Devils swelled with the arrival of Bob Gantt, Cedric Loftis, and Garland Loftis, three members of Durham High's championship team. Losing only two games during the regular season, Duke swept the field

in the Southern Conference tournament as well, downing N.C. State—
and the ex-Bulldogs' former teammate, Bones McKinney—by eleven
points in the title game. "The basketball team enjoyed the most successful season in the history of the school," crowed the *Chanticleer*.

But the war had arrived as well. And with it came change. Head football coach Wallace Wade announced that he was entering the Army. "My
boys were going in," he explained, "and I felt that we should stay together
as a team." In his absence, Eddie Cameron took over the football program, while the head coaching job for the basketball team was turned
over to one of Cameron's assistant coaches, Kenneth "Gerry" Gerard.

Though he had been born in Indiana, Gerard wasn't a through-
and-through basketball man. He had played football at the University
of Illinois and had come to Duke in 1931 to help run a new intramural
sports program on campus, which soon offered competition in more
than a dozen sports, ranging from tennis and horseshoes to touch football and boxing. But Gerard turned out to be a solid basketball coach
as well. During Hubbell's junior year, the Blue Devils won eighteen
games during the regular season, including hanging on to beat Temple
by one and clobbering the Tar Heels by nineteen. In the Southern
Conference tournament, by then held at the Raleigh Memorial Auditorium, Duke lost in the finals to the fast-breaking Colonials of George
Washington University.

As it turned out, however, the 1942–43 season would be Hubbell's
last as a Blue Devil.

For along with playing ball and belonging to a fraternity, he had hit
the books hard. Turning in his assignments on time, grinding out the
lab work, and, when necessary, pulling the occasional all-nighter, Hubbell had earned solid As in everything from organic chemistry to vector
analysis. And by taking courses each summer, he graduated from Duke
in three years. By the fall of 1943, Hubbell was still a student at Duke,
but he was a first-year student in the School of Medicine. Moreover, he
was also a cog in the nation's war effort—a cog, as it turned out, that
was moving very fast indeed.

CHAPTER 13

———

Medicine Ball

The war had come to the School of Medicine at Duke. And it had come quickly.

The morning after Pearl Harbor, all first-year medical students at Duke were informed that they would be finishing the program in three years, not four. Summer vacations and lengthy holiday breaks were thenceforth canceled. In addition to studying anatomy, biochemistry, physiology, and pharmacology, first-year medical students would have to shoulder classes in pathology, bacteriology, parasitology, and neuro-psychiatry. It didn't get any easier in the years that followed, and any student failing a class would be automatically inducted into the armed services.

The student body changed as well. Ninety percent of all incoming medical students would be in uniform, either as members of the Army Specialized Training Program or the Navy's V-12 program. Required to live in the dormitories and to occasionally take part in close-order drills ("We weren't very good at it," Hubbell recalled) and other military activities, the students would go on immediate active duty as military doctors upon graduation. In addition, there would be *more* medical students on campus than ever before, as the plan was that a new incoming class would be added every nine months.

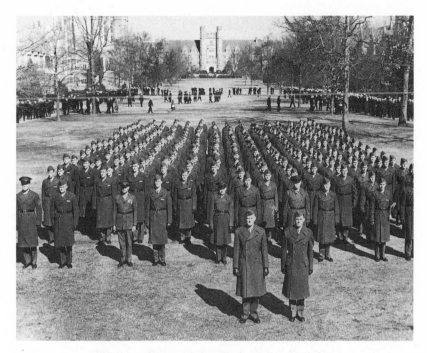

Military students at Duke. *(Duke University Archives)*

The Duke medical school was doing its part for the war effort, but there was an additional wrinkle. For not only had several members of the medical school faculty either enlisted or gone on active duty since the nation joined the fight, many of those who had planned on staying ended up going overseas anyway as part of the 65th General Hospital, a mobile Army hospital that was staffed by Duke doctors and nurses. The bottom line was that the School of Medicine had to train more doctors in more classes in less time than it ever had before—and it had to do it shorthanded. Somehow, it worked.

The architect of all this wizardry was a heavily jowled pipe-smoking genius named Wilburt Cornell Davison. Davison had gone to Princeton as an undergraduate, to Oxford as a Rhodes scholar, and to Johns Hopkins for medical school, and at the ripe old age of thirty-four he had been appointed the first dean of the School of Medicine at Duke. A commanding presence, with a physique that bore more than a passing resemblance to Teddy Roosevelt's, Davison was an intense, energetic man who had helped lay out the architectural plans for the medical school, hired its first faculty—stolen, primarily, from Johns Hopkins—and, on occasion, donned overalls and grabbed a trowel and anonymously helped the tobacco-chewing workmen erect its walls. A perennially busy ball of fire, Davison was also serving as a medical consultant to both the Army and Navy by 1943. He spent so much time on the train between Durham and Washington that he devised his own special traveling kit, which included sulfa powder, antihistamines, an inflatable rubber sitting ring, the latest issue of *Reader's Digest,* and a flask each of Scotch, bourbon, and brandy. Usually he took an overnight train, but the condition of the rail beds got so poor that sleep, which he desperately needed, became a near impossibility. "Only a capsule of Seconal made the trains endurable," he later wrote. "My friends called it my chemical warfare."

Davison's students, meanwhile, were almost equally tired—and busy. Not only did they have to grapple with the new, speeded-up course of study along with their military obligations, but because the Duke University Hospital was short-staffed, they also had to take on more and more clinical duties, including making rounds, monitoring vital signs, and consulting with patients. Even first-year medical students soon found themselves reading X-rays, lancing boils, and administering bismuth and arsenic injections to treat syphilis. "The patients thought that we were their doctors," one student later wrote. "One of them refused to have Dr. Odom do a trephination and air injection one morning until I okayed it."

There was so much to do, in fact, that medical students at Duke often fell asleep studying or caught catnaps while on duty. An OB nurse once discovered a student sound asleep in a patient's bed, while another was discovered—four hours after an appointment was scheduled to begin—dozing in the examination room as peacefully as a baby. Another medical student, in order to save time walking to and from class, simply gave up his dormitory room altogether and began sleeping on a stretcher in the obstetrics ward.

And yet somehow the students also found ways to fit some laughter into their day. An elaborate chalkboard drawing of the gastrointestinal system was used to rank fellow students—with weekly updates—on their proficiency at brownnosing the medical school professors. "The biggest ass kissers had their names bunched near the anus," Hubbell recalled, while the lesser types were stuck back in the ileocecal valve. Students told endless jokes about their professors, including their dean. One hand-drawn cartoon portrayed Davison talking to a similarly rotund, gray-haired member of the medical faculty. "Oh," read the caption, "I haven't seen it in years, either!" The handful of female medical students at Duke, meanwhile, were a favorite target of more than a few pranks—but they could dish it out as well. After looking over her male classmates for the first time, Dorothy Armstrong remarked, "I sure hope my eggs aren't fertile."

The medical students held picnics and cabin parties in the Duke Forest. Largely consisting of a fire, some hot dogs and marshmallows, some blankets, and, when possible, a date, they were an easy way to blow off steam and escape from the confines of the hospital and medical school. "There was a little smooching on the blankets," one participant remembered, "but things didn't go too far." There was also lots of singing. Some of the songs, such as "I've Been Working on the Railroad," "Down by the Riverside," and "Roll Me Over in the Clover," were sung by everyone, while loosely organized medical school singing groups, such as the Cadaver Quartet, also contributed their own compositions. "Arsphenamine, Arsphenamine," sung to the tune of the Maryland state song, was about the clap—"It started with a little scratch, now it's a mucus patch."

But Dave Hubbell outshone them all. "He had the most wonderful singing voice," recalled one of the nurses who used to attend the parties—"gorgeous." Possessed with a clear, deep tenor, he sang old songs and new ones, Appalachian ballads and nonsense songs.

But it was the slow songs—"America the Beautiful," "Swing Low, Sweet Chariot," and "I Come to the Garden Alone"—that, when Hubbell sang them, could silence even the most raucous party. And none more so than "Dixie." For when Hubbell sang it, in the autumn chill of the Duke Forest, eyes misted over and chests would swell—at least among the Southerners who were there. As he stood in the middle of the group, the light of the campfire shimmering in his hair, he sang with a voice of both hope and longing, the voice of a people who, although they did not know it yet, were slowly losing their way.

Then there was booze.

While some of the students tried to make their own beer, others stood in line at the ABC store to see what they could purchase. Since there was a nationwide whiskey shortage, the choices were rather slim. "Nothing but Four Roses," one student recalled. "And they had this awful fortified wine that was the big thing." Fortunately, however, the medical students had their own homemade concoction.

They called it Purple Jesus.

Its first ingredient was undenatured alcohol stolen from the supply cabinets in the Duke hospital. "One nurse that I knew," remembered Barbara Taylor, a nursing student at Duke during the early 1940s, "used to steal the bottles out of the supply cabinets in the OB ward. She'd strap the bottles to her thighs and smuggle them out under her skirt." The students would then slip into the staff kitchen after hours and commandeer one of the large electric coffee machines. Then they would fill the drip basket with a mixture of ripe, overripe, and slightly bruised fruit. Finally they would percolate their stolen alcohol, cut with a healthy dollop of Welch's grape juice, through the fruit, creating a heavenly, slightly sweet-smelling, purple elixir. One with the kick of a mule.

"It only took a little," a former student remembered.

One second-year student, after only a couple of shots, would start singing the Marine Corps hymn fortissimo no matter where he was. Shy student nurses suddenly found the courage to crash the dances at the USO club downtown, while buttoned-down types would slur their words, stand on tabletops, or collapse into fits of laughter. If you drank too much, you'd go blind. And if you *really* drank too much, it was said, then you'd find out why it was called what it was called in the first place.

There was also one other semi-official diversion.

Not every medical student — or even most of them — took part, but for those who did, it soon took on a life of its own. For in addition to being medical students and members of the armed services, Dave Hubbell and a handful of the others wore one other kind of uniform as well.

By the fall of 1943, each branch of the armed services — the Army, the Army Air Corps, the U.S. Coast Guard, and the Marines, as well as the Merchant Marine — was fielding its own military basketball teams. Some just played in camp or base leagues. Others, such as the Special Hospital Unit team, a crack outfit from Camp Rucker, Alabama, took the game with them — in their case to England, where they put on exhibition games for Allied soldiers awaiting the invasion of the Continent. Still others, such as the military squads out of Naval Air Station Livermore, Moffett Field, Treasure Island, and United States Coast Guard Base Alameda, in Northern California, scheduled games against leading college teams. Indeed, by late 1943, the "regular" college basketball season had largely become a thing of the past. Some schools dropped the sport for the duration of the war, while at many other campuses, varsity basketball teams played a mix of college and military games. During the 1943–44 season, the California Golden Bears at the University of California, Berkeley, played as many military teams as they did other college fives, while at the University of Arizona, the Wildcats did not schedule a single intercollegiate game but instead played exclusively against military and defense teams.

The Navy had led the way. Twenty-five years earlier, during World War I, naval authorities had used basketball as both a fitness activity and a morale builder. At Naval Station Great Lakes, outside Chicago, more than eight hundred sailors played in the base league during the winter of 1917–18, while the station's traveling team, the Bluejackets, ran through the Midwest like a souped-up roadster, beating Michigan by ten, Wisconsin by twenty-nine, and Bradley University by thirty-two.

When the winds of war began blowing in the late 1930s and early 1940s, the Navy turned to basketball once again as a training tool—especially for Navy fliers. "Basketball," read one official report, "is calculated to help produce efficient fighting pilots." Stressing the game's ability to help improve peripheral vision, sharpen left-hand motor skills, foster on-the-spot initiative, and develop the ability to judge speed and distance, those who designed training programs soon made basketball a fixture of naval preflight instruction. "The Navy needed a sport that would train men to meet the exacting rigors and needs of modern warfare," proclaimed a training manual produced by the Bureau of Aeronautics. "Basketball has an important job to do." Despite the bombast, the naval aviation authorities might have been on to something. The fast break, one former Navy pilot later recalled, helped him to visualize his squadron as it peeled off to engage Zeros over the Pacific.

Nor was that all. Not only did service leagues blossom on installations from Bainbridge Island to Pensacola, the Navy also took basketball with it overseas. Lieutenant Gerald R. Ford, the Michigan football star—and future president—who had trained at the United States Navy Pre-Flight School in Chapel Hill, used to play basketball in a makeshift court in the forward elevator well on board the USS *Monterey,* an aircraft carrier, between action in the Mariana Islands, Kwajalein, and the Ryukyus. Once the men went ashore, the game could come along as well. "One method of laying plane runways (grinding a few bags of cement into the dirt) will also prove helpful

United States Navy lieutenant Gerald Ford playing basketball on board the USS *Monterey*. The future president is at center left, shirtless, reaching for the ball. *(National Archives)*

when preparing the surface of an outdoor court," advised one wartime Navy basketball manual.

Regardless of the branch of service, the military squads were hardly pushovers. The Naval Station Great Lakes team not only won thirty-four games during the 1943–44 season, but according to the Converse-Dunkel ratings system—which ranked teams by margin of victory, with adjustments for home-court advantage—it was also the best team in the country, well ahead of Kentucky, Utah, and Ohio State. Naval

Station Norfolk went 31–2, while a military squad out of Saint Mary's College in Moraga, California, went undefeated. At Milligan College, a small Christian school in the mountains of eastern Tennessee that had been taken over by the Navy, the basketball team beat the Tar Heels on their home floor. And in Chapel Hill itself, more than a few basketball fans felt that the Cloudbusters—the squad at the pre-flight school at the University of North Carolina in Chapel Hill—with their razzle-dazzle offense and sky-blue satin warm-ups, were the best team in the state. Often stocked with former college players, the military teams could more than hold their own.

This was something the Duke Blue Devils soon discovered as well. Not only did they lose the second game of the 1943–44 season to the Cloudbusters by nineteen, eleven of their next fifteen games were scheduled against military teams—including those from Fort Bragg, the Coast Guard base in Charleston, the Marine Corps air station at Cherry Point, Columbia Army Air Base, and Naval Station Norfolk. As it turned out, the Blue Devils would also tangle with another team composed of servicemen—one that was practically next door.

According to the standards of a latter age, the 1943–44 squad of the Duke medical school basketball team never really existed. It had no coach, no colors, no nickname, and no true home court. The results of its games were rarely recorded in official score books, individual statistics for its players were never compiled, and even the number of games that the team played is unknown. The team belonged to no league, took part in no postseason collegiate or military championship tournaments, and received precious little attention in the press. Its players, each of whom—save one—were enlisted in either the Army or the Navy, were also full-time medical students at Duke. And if pushed, they probably could have told you as much about the symptoms of blastomycosis, the proper technique for administering Wassermann tests, or how to manually dilate a rectal stricture as they could the origins of the zone defense or how to properly execute a two- and three-post attack.

Most of them lived together as well, in a more or less phony fraternity of their own creation. The house that they'd rented at 202 Watts Street, in the crepe-myrtle-and-magnolia-heavy blocks just east of the women's campus, turned out to be a bedbug's paradise. To combat the problem, the students first got all new mattresses and bedding, but the bugs came back. Then they tried setting the legs of their iron bed frames in open cans filled with paint thinner, but that didn't work, either. Eventually they had to haul the bed frames out onto the driveway, douse them with kerosene, and set them on fire. That worked. "We didn't have any more problems with bedbugs in the house, except with a big stuffed chair in the living room," one of the students later recalled. "When somebody came to the house that we didn't like, we would always put them in that chair."

The team itself came out of earlier versions that had played in previous years in Duke's wildly popular intramural basketball program. "For a long time basketball at Duke University has set the standard for the entire South," gushed a writer in the *Chronicle*, the campus newspaper, about the campus intramural tournament. "This gigantic undertaking is expected to go a long way in promoting good basketball below the Mason-Dixon Line." Featuring more than fifty different teams and some four hundred players, the annual basketball jamboree at Duke was an intensive, no-holds-barred tournament—one in which medical school teams had excelled. Playing as the Cyclones, they went undefeated all season and won the 1942 tournament, which was watched by hundreds of fans crammed into the old gym.

By the beginning of the 1943–44 season, however, the intramural season at Duke was being undercut by the demands of the war, and the members of that season's medical school team began looking off campus for competition.

On the surface, their own basketball experience was, to say the least, mixed.

Dave Hubbell, of course, had been a Duke Blue Devil.

Dick Thistlethwaite was a dark-haired, dreamy-eyed, high-spirited lady-killer—and top-notch athlete—who had grown up along Monument Avenue in Richmond. The son of a football coach, Thistlethwaite had played three seasons of basketball at the University of Richmond, where, as the starting center during his junior and senior years, he helped lead the Spiders past Virginia, Virginia Tech, and North Carolina. He also captained the track team, for which he competed in pole vault, broad jump, and the hurdles, and he set the campus high jump record, edging the bar at six feet and seven-eighths inches. As a basketball player, he also had a dead-on set shot. "He could stand out there with what we would call three-pointers today and just swish them through," remembered a teammate. A "six-foot-three sharpshooter" is what Jack Horner, a Durham sportswriter, called him, adding that, even as a full-time medical student, Thistlethwaite "could make plenty of varsity squads in the Southern Conference." A Duke nurse who used to watch the medical school team play put it more succinctly: "Holy moly," she said. "That guy could shoot."

Dick Symmonds was from Memphis—the one in Missouri, that is. Lanky, long-necked, and bespectacled, he was a small-town doctor's son who was determined to follow in his father's footsteps. But at Central College, in Fayette, he was also a forward on the varsity basketball team. "Quick and fast, a very good forward," was how one former teammate described him. Playing in a gym the size of a shoe box, the Eagles not only won the Missouri College Athletic Union championship in 1943, they also went on to play in a postseason tournament in Kansas City that James Naismith had helped to establish.

Joe Walthall, a six-feet-two-inch guard from West Virginia, came from a family of basketball players, including a younger brother and a cousin who played college ball. But Joe topped them all. In the fall of 1942—seven months after West Virginia University had won the National Invitation Tournament in New York—he'd joined the Mountaineers as a walk-on. And he simply exploded as a player. Before the

1942–43 season was over, Walthall had set the school's single-season scoring record, tied the all-time single-game scoring record, and led the Mountaineers to within one point of a return trip to the NIT. At the end of his first and only college basketball season, the previously unknown star—a teacher's son from Princeton, West Virginia—was selected as a third-team All-American by *Sporting News* magazine.

From there, the experience level dropped—but not the enthusiasm.

Lloyd Taylor had played guard at Maryville, a small Presbyterian college outside Knoxville.

Homer Sieber, a Lutheran minister's son, hadn't played on the Roanoke College basketball team as an undergraduate. A hardworking student and the president of the junior class, he had, however, led the Kappa Alphas to the championship of the school's intramural basketball tournament.

Harry Wechsler had even less official on-court experience. Wechsler

Homer Sieber. *(Courtesy of Charlotte Mock Sieber)*

didn't have the chops to make it onto the McKeesport, Pennsylvania, high school varsity basketball squad, but he played on teams organized by a local synagogue. Bookish and an honor student, with hopes to one day become a doctor, he had planned on going to college in-state, at nearby Allegheny College, until an uncle advised him to look at Duke, where he ended up. Four years later he was set to go back home, to the University of Pittsburgh, for medical school. But when he learned that Pitt had already filled its quota of Jewish students, he stayed in Durham. And while he stood only five feet seven, he was a ball of energy on the basketball court.

The Duke medical school team claimed one other player as well.

Raised in Drumright, Oklahoma, a windswept oil town set in the cattle lands midway between Tulsa and Stillwater, Ed Johnson had played two years of basketball at Coffeyville Junior College, up in Kansas, and then a year at Phillips University in Enid. He was a year or two older than most of the others, and the war had brought him to Duke. But he was neither a medical student nor, for that matter, a student of any kind. What he was he had learned not to advertise.

Raised in a Disciples of Christ church, Johnson believed that war was a sin and that as a true follower of Jesus Christ he was morally obligated to follow the sixth commandment, "Thou shalt not kill." He was not alone. In scores of religious communities, small congregations, and so-called peace churches across the country, thousands of draft-age Mennonites, Quakers, Jehovah's Witnesses, members of Church of the Brethren, and German Baptists—as well as a smattering of Buddhists, Catholics, Muslims, and Jews—found themselves torn between their duties to God and to country. And while some young men went to prison for their pacifist beliefs, nearly twelve thousand entered the Civilian Public Service, an alternative program for conscientious objectors. Organized into work units and dispatched across the country, the COs—or conchies, as they were derisively called—worked in mental hospitals, planted trees, did farm work, took part in medical experiments, and served as firefighters in the national forests of the West. Johnson was one of them.

Originally assigned to a work camp outside Magnolia, Arkansas, where some of his fellow COs had been threatened with a lynching, he was eventually transferred to North Carolina, where he joined a group of COs that had been assigned to work as orderlies and attendants at the Duke hospital. "There weren't any special rules," Johnson later recalled. "Except in the beginning we were told by an administrator that we should pack our bags if we got out of bounds." They didn't. Happy to be out of Arkansas, Johnson and the others worked their tails off. They mopped floors, sorted linens and laundry, fed and bathed patients, took TPR—temperature, pulse, and respiration—followed orders from some nurses who despised them as slackers, and staffed the operating room on twelve-hour shifts, all for fifteen dollars a month, which was six dollars less than German POWs were paid for working at a nearby mental hospital.

But the COs didn't care. They organized their own Chinese-language study group, took walks in the Duke Forest, went to Sunday services in the chapel, and started rooting for the Blue Devils. And once he heard about it, Ed Johnson talked his way onto the medical school basketball team. Well schooled in the ball-control, defense-focused ways of Kansas and Oklahoma basketball—he had once scrimmaged against some of Hank Iba's Oklahoma A&M Aggies—Johnson, playing forward, quickly fit in.

The team was no fluke.

Beginning in the late fall of 1943, the medical students sliced their way through an assortment of church fives, high school squads, and textile-mill teams. "We played games usually on weekends or sometimes during the week," Dave Hubbell recalled. "Other times we'd get together and wouldn't know where we were going until somebody said, 'Well, we're playing down in Asheboro.'" Piling into a car, if one was available, or, more likely, walking, hitchhiking, or taking a bus to a collection of gymnasiums scattered across the region, they didn't play a set schedule—but when they did face another team, they played well. Unburdened, at least for a couple hours, of the stresses of school, the anatomy lab, and the hospital, they discovered that despite the fact that none of them had known any of the others before, they quickly developed a synergy all their own. "We found out what the other guys' strong points were," Hubbell remembered, "and we'd find somebody, pass to them, hand off." Out on the basketball court, they found a way to relax, and in doing so, their skills sharpened.

They also got an early test.

A few days before Christmas, an unexpected invitation made its way over to Dave Hubbell. Would the medical students like to play the Duke varsity team? The game, which was to be held one evening in the indoor stadium, was not to be publicized. The real purpose of the game, of course, was to give the Blue Devils a little clandestine competition during the holiday break. Hubbell had been a teammate of the Duke players until very recently, and he could provide a detailed scouting report on each of Gerry Gerard's players. He encouraged the matchup, the date for which was soon set.

The other medical students had been equally enthusiastic. That is, except for one of them. Not usually given to butterflies before a big game, fun-loving Dick Thistlethwaite suddenly had them by the armful. "Thistlethwaite became quite nervous before the game," Lloyd Taylor recalled. "He really was playing Duke University, and they're the conference leaders. And so he thought he'd have a little nip of brandy before we went to the game. He felt a little better, so he had a couple of more nips. He wasn't smashed when we got to the game, but he was feeling no pain."

Somehow, it worked. Buzzed on cheap wartime brandy, Thistlethwaite came out on fire. He nailed hook shots from ten feet, fed Hubbell and Walthall for breakaway layups, and fought his way for rebound after rebound. "He could not miss," Taylor remembered. "I don't know how many points that man scored that night, but he'd just throw it back over his head and it'd go into the basket." In the midnight quiet of the cavernous field house, surrounded by eight thousand empty seats, the Duke medical school basketball team didn't just beat the Blue Devils. They also beat the team that would win that season's Southern Conference Basketball Tournament championship. Come January, they would get even better.

CHAPTER 14

"He Can't Sit There"

If there were a lonelier place to spend Christmas, Aubrey Stanley didn't know about it. On the day after the last exams, the campus had all but emptied as practically the entire North Carolina College student body, bundled up in hats and overcoats, took off for the train station and the bus terminal in the brisk, sunshiny weather, grinning and chatting all the way. Some would ride in smoky railcars filled with colored soldiers and war workers all the way to Washington or Philadelphia, while others would squeeze in the back of Carolina Trailways buses bound for Farmville, Rocky Mount, or Ahoskie. But not the Eagles. During the break, with the basketball season firing up right after New Year's, McLendon had kept the team in Durham, where they tended the boilers, swept the sidewalks, performed odd jobs around campus, and practiced. Practiced. Practiced. Practiced.

For weeks Aubrey and his teammates had endured a rigorous daily practice schedule, complete with suicide drills and passing drills, ball-movement exercises and full-court scrimmages, usually at a breakneck pace. But during the break there were other drills as well—for fifty-foot bounce passes, filling the lanes, driving hard for a layup while shooting with the softest of releases, passing without changing speed. At the end of each practice, Aubrey and his teammates, each wearing two pairs of socks to prevent blisters, would collapse on the floor or on the benches in the locker room. But it didn't impress their coach. "Fatigue is purely a psychological phenomenon," McLendon would tell them.

They practiced at night as well. "Every evening but Sunday," Aubrey recalled. "We'd play three-on-three, full court. You only play to six points, but that could take a long time. And the losers had to stay on the floor. It was absolutely grueling." Plus McLendon seemed to notice *everything* and wasn't shy about offering direction when needed.

"Coach Mac could tell you which side of your jockstrap your balls were hanging on," as Pee Wee later put it.

In October McLendon had introduced an additional requirement, a forty-five-minute group run three mornings a week, out in the countryside just east of campus. While other college basketball teams across the country were doing deep knee bends or perfecting pregame layup drills, the Eagles, clad in gym shorts and T-shirts, huffed and puffed past cotton fields, rail lines, and tobacco barns.

There was a quiet, steel-trap logic behind McLendon's punishing workouts. Shorthanded to begin with, and likely losing more players to Uncle Sam as the 1943–44 basketball season unfolded, he no longer had the luxury of platooning his team. Instead, with hardly any reserves on the bench, it would be up to his starters to play, and win, each game. By having his players run cross-country in addition to their regular workouts, he hoped to give them what they would need for the long road ahead.

By the third week of January 1944, it was clear that all the hard work was paying off. While Big Dog was the unquestioned star of the Eagles, the other starters were a potent brew. Floyd Brown, the Phi Beta Kappa forward, was the team captain, while James "Boogie" Hardy, his fellow Indianan, played point guard. George Parks, a lanky Kentuckian whom McLendon had first spied at a filling station south of Lexington, traded center duties with Dog, while Aubrey, playing guard, was a highly talented work in progress. Other players would move in and out of the lineup, but that was McLendon's core. And it did not take long to see what they were made of.

The Eagles opened their season with a home game against a colored Army team then stationed at Camp Butner, the 389th Engineer General Service Regiment. Well stocked with former college players from Virginia Union, Kent State, and the University of Akron, the visitors were also undefeated, having won eight games in a row. But a late-first-half run by Boogie, Floyd Brown, and Howard Townsend—a local Durham athlete who was playing in what was both his first and last game as an Eagle before being inducted the following morning into the Navy—put North Carolina College ahead by eight at the break. In the second half, it was all Dog, who ended up scoring twenty points. The Eagles won, 44–36.

Eight days later, they faced another team from Camp Butner, the 930th Field Artillery, a former Illinois National Guard unit that could trace its roots back to an all-Negro militia formed in Chicago after the Civil War. Composed almost entirely of Northern enlistees, the members of the 930th hadn't taken kindly to the Jim Crow regulations at Camp Butner. "Our guys just would not buckle under," recalled Hondon Hargrove, a noncommissioned officer. When white soldiers, heading off on furloughs, were allowed to board Durham-bound buses before colored GIs, the men of the 930th tipped over two of the buses. "Henceforth," Hargrove added, "whites had their buses and blacks theirs—not the ideal situation, but at least guys got to town before it was time to return. I think we were grudgingly respected because the guys took certain stands."

In their game against the Eagles, played in the North Carolina College gym, the visitors from Illinois got clobbered. Big Dog scored twenty-two, while Smokey Davis—another first-time Eagle, soon to depart to the armed forces—had fourteen. But the big surprise of the matchup, which the Eagles won, 75–28, was Aubrey. Hit with rifle passes by Boogie on the break, and shaking free to get fed off the post from Dog, he knocked down twelve points.

It was a good start to the season. But it was also only the beginning.

One week later came the first road games. The team traveled in a jitney borrowed from one of Hayti's funeral homes.

McLendon had previously worked out a system for traveling to away games. If the trip was long enough, the team would pack bologna sandwiches or stop only at colored cafés. If any of his players needed to relieve himself, there was a plan for that, too. "Rabbit!" meant number one, and "Bear!" was number two. And if there was any trouble with whites, the coach would do the talking. Most of the time, he could quickly defuse any minor matter, such as a player boarding a bus or a train too quickly. But there was always the potential for something bigger, an incident that could suddenly grow dangerous. "The thing was that you could never lose your dignity in front of your players. That's the one thing you could never, ever, allow," McLendon later recalled.

But on the first road trip of the season, there were no such problems. After all, they were only going to Raleigh. Saint Augustine's College occupied a small cluster of buildings ten blocks east of the capitol. Sitting on a patch of land that had once been a plantation, the school had been founded two years after the Civil War ended. For years it seemed like the Saints had signed a long-term lease at the bottom of the Colored Intercollegiate Athletic Association rankings. The football team won no games in 1940, while the basketball team, which was winless in 1941, had fared little better. But after the war started and the school dropped football, the basketball team started winning. And as the 1943–44 season got under way, hope had blossomed on Raleigh's east side. The Saints were on the rise.

Still, the Eagles annihilated them. The game wasn't even close. Not only were the Saints unable to control the boards, they also had trouble even slowing down—much less stopping—the North Carolina College fast break. Playing inside the small Saint Augustine's gym before a packed but dumbfounded home crowd, the Eagles rained twelve-foot set shots, drove inside for layup after layup, and ran the Saints ragged up and down the floor. "Coach, they're getting faster and faster!" one Saint Augustine's player complained. The final score was 96–30.

McLendon, it appeared, was on to something. But not everyone was pleased. "The other coaches in the conference *hated* him," Pee Wee recalled. "You've got to remember that McLendon was in his twenties, and the other coaches were old, you know, in their forties and fifties. They didn't want to give Coach Mac respect for his innovative ideas because here was this new kid on the block making them look bad."

James Lytle, the Shaw basketball coach, was among them. At Shaw, the Raleigh university that had been founded by former slaves, Lytle had been both a star athlete and a dutiful student, graduating in 1925. Shortly thereafter he joined the faculty as a coach and a teacher. Highly competitive, despite the fact that he sometimes had trouble attracting top-level athletic talent to the small school, Lytle detested losing— especially to John McLendon. After getting waxed by the Eagles for three years in a row, Lytle had been bound and determined to ambush the speedy North Carolina College team on his home court. But rather than try to slow the Eagles down, something that Saint Augustine's had been unable to do, he decided instead to speed them up. And by Saturday night, January 22, 1944, Lytle had already set his plan in motion.

The basketball court at Shaw was located inside Tupper Memorial Hall, on the southern edge of the campus. Cramped and poorly ventilated, the building had been scheduled for renovations over the holiday break, many of which hadn't yet been completed. So rather than being able to change into their uniforms in a locker room, the Eagles instead had to squeeze into a bathroom that was barely big enough to hold them all. But an even bigger surprise waited for them when they walked into the gym itself.

It was the floor. Gleaming, glossy, and shining like a new dime, the work crew under Lytle's direction hadn't merely refinished the gymnasium floor over the Christmas break—stripping and sanding away the old varnish, painting new lines, and covering it with a brand-new coat of Seal-O-San—they'd also waxed it. And waxed it again. Buffed to a dazzling, mirrorlike finish, it was, John McLendon concluded when he first saw it, probably the prettiest gym floor he had ever seen. But as soon as he walked onto it, he also discovered that it was way too slippery. Someone, it was clear, was bound to get hurt. So the North Carolina College coach walked over to the Shaw bench.

"Jim, we ought not to play."

But the Shaw coach just smiled.

"What's the matter?" he replied. "You scared?"

Of course not, McLendon answered. It's the floor. He pushed, but he got nowhere.

"My team has got to play on it, too," Lytle added.

In fact, they had been — for days. In order to get his players acclimated to the deliberately overwaxed floor, he'd had them practice on it all week, walking them through lots of slow-paced, pass-oriented plays. Some of the Shaw players, it was later claimed, daubed a thin layer of pine tar on the soles of their sneakers to improve traction, while others practiced running flatfooted in order not to slide. By game day, the Bears had a solid feel for what lay beneath their feet.

The Eagles, of course, did not. Sticking to their run-and-gun, fast-break offense, the North Carolina College players slipped and fell all over the place, to the raucous delight of the home crowd. Passes went flying into the stands, surefire layups clanged off the front of the rim, and bodies went sprawling. Worse yet, near the end of the first half, Boogie got injured. "He came down on the break and tried to stop and kept going. Slid into the wall and hurt his ankle," McLendon recalled. By halftime, North Carolina College had — miraculously — crawled back into the game, but unless something changed, and changed quickly, the Eagles might be on the way to their first defeat. McLendon, for once, simply did not know what to do. Sitting on the floor of the cramped bathroom, the stale air reeking of sweat and ammonia, nobody said anything.

Then Floyd Brown had an idea. It was crazy, McLendon thought. Nuts, really. But it also might just work. Lytle, after all, didn't have to be the only fox in the henhouse.

McLendon kept his team in the bathroom for the entire break, and finally the referee came over.

"Aren't you going to warm up?"

"No," McLendon replied. "Not this time."

The referee gave him a long look.

"You're up to something."

Then, at the very last possible moment, just as the timekeeper was about to start the game clock, McLendon led his players out of the bathroom and onto the floor. And when they did, the stands erupted into hoots of laughter. The Eagles weren't wearing shoes or socks.

Immediately, Lytle popped up. They can't do that, he told the officials. It's against regulations.

Then it was McLendon who wouldn't budge. No, he said. It's not. There's no rule that says a player has to wear something on his feet. Here, he said, holding out his copy of the rule book. Go on, take a look.

Lytle wouldn't—but the officials did. They couldn't find anything, either. A few minutes later, the Eagles took to the floor in their bare feet.

It was all over in a heartbeat.

Finding their footing for the first time, the North Carolina College players exploded in the second half. "We ran 'em off the court," McLendon remembered, adding that the home crowd tried to stop them as well. "They threw peanut shells and everything," he said. "I mean, they covered the floor with orange peelings and peanuts, even threw baloney and hot dogs." It didn't matter. Aubrey scored fourteen points, Floyd sixteen, Boogie seventeen, while Big Dog piled in a career-high thirty-two. The final score was 87–44. A reporter for the *Norfolk Journal and Guide* dubbed McLendon's team the Shoeless Wonders.

That evening, after the happy, bumpy, ride back to Durham in the car from the funeral home, the Eagles went and rang the old bell by the administration building. Later that same night, Big Dog and Pee Wee snuck over to Minnie Hester's bootleg joint for a celebratory nightcap. Dog was in especially fine form, knocking back two-fingered shots of corn liquor, telling the small crowd of tobacco stemmers, day laborers, and cardsharps how, even barefoot, they'd left them Bears to watch the grass grow. He scored thirty-two points. Next time, it was gonna be forty-two.

Maybe fifty-two.

Wait and see.

News of the Eagles' growing accomplishments had even made its way across town. One morning while he was going over his playbook in his office in the gym, McLendon received a phone call out of the blue. It was from one of the trainers in the athletic department at Duke.

"We got some leftover practice uniforms, good quality," said the voice on the other end of the line. "Y'all want 'em?"

McLendon said yes.

The next afternoon, George Parks—who sometimes chauffeured for Dr. Shepard—drove McLendon over to Duke. Neither of them had been to the campus before, but they located the gymnasium without much trouble. As he said he would be, the trainer was waiting at the service entrance in the back with the uniforms. They chatted for a minute. Then, tilting his head toward the building just to the west, namely, the indoor stadium, McLendon asked, "Is that it?"

"Uh-huh. You boys want to take a peek inside?"

A minute later John McLendon was standing in the Southern version of basketball heaven. He had not come unprepared. As an undergraduate at Kansas he had spent hours at Hoch Auditorium, and during his one year at Iowa City, he had gotten to know the Iowa Field House, the cavernous home of the Hawkeyes. But this place, he knew on first glance, was someplace special. This was a place for champions.

Down on the court, a few of the Blue Devils had arrived early for practice and were horsing around with a couple of balls. McLendon watched for a moment until George Parks, who was nervous about Dr. Shepard's car being left unattended, suggested that maybe it was time to go. McLendon wheeled around and started walking back toward the door, but what he had seen would not go away quite so easily.

This was the kind of place, he would think to himself, where the Eagles ought to play.

Six days after the Shaw game, on the last Friday in January, John McLendon and his players walked out of the colored waiting room at the new Durham bus station and into the predawn chill, their breath illuminated by the streetlights. They had all risen in the pitch dark — with Pee Wee rapping on their doors — and groggily got dressed, shivering as they made their way to the terminal. Then, with each of them carrying a small traveling bag containing their uniforms, sneakers, a toothbrush, and a change of clothes, they waited to board a Carolina Trailways bus. Even though it was already standing room only, the driver let all the Eagles on. They walked to the rear, stowed their bags in the luggage racks above the seats, and grabbed hold of whatever they could. As the bus lurched onto Main Street, heading west, and drove past the Liggett & Myers cigarette plant, they began what would be one of their longest journeys together.

Southern bus terminal, 1943. *(Library of Congress)*

By midmorning they had made it to Winston-Salem. The landscape was different—the sky was bigger, and the land began to roll—but the northbound Greyhound bus they boarded inside the terminal was just as packed. Once again, McLendon and his players had to stand up in the back. But by then the coach of the Eagles was starting to worry. His team had already been on their feet for more than five hours. And that night, at eight o'clock, they had a game to play in West Virginia, against Bluefield State Teachers College. For despite the fact that the Eagles were in tip-top condition, nine hours of being on their feet was going to take a toll on his team. McLendon needed to rest his players, particularly his big men.

Finally he got his chance.

A few miles outside of Wytheville, Virginia, a seat suddenly opened up in the row dividing the white and colored sections of the bus. It was next to a young white mother—"a girl, really," McLendon remembered—holding a baby on her lap. And since there were no longer any white passengers standing, McLendon motioned for Big Dog to go and sit down.

"Excuse me, may I sit here?" Dog asked.

"Oh, yes, that's fine," the young mother said. "That's all right with me."

Big Dog sat down. A few minutes later he was playing with the baby.

Then the bus driver pulled over. They were in the Jefferson National Forest now. Great brown mountains, dusted with snow, rose up on either side of the highway, while below them, black water moved slowly through log-choked creeks rimmed with ice. The driver set the brake and walked toward the back of the bus.

"He can't sit there," he said, loud enough for everyone to hear.

McLendon immediately jumped in.

"Why not? It's a legal situation. What problem is it?"

"He just can't sit there."

But McLendon wasn't finished.

"Well, he can sit there legally, and I don't know how you're going to defend that."

None of the players said anything. Aubrey's heart was in his chest.

Then McLendon turned to the young woman.

"Do you mind him sitting there?"

"No," she said.

A few of the other white passengers began to stir. "What's the problem?" one of them asked.

The driver walked back to his seat, started the bus, and pulled back onto the highway.

But half a mile later, he pulled off again. "He couldn't stand it," McLendon recalled. "And I know they all carried guns. They kept them under the front seat."

Once again the driver walked to the back of the bus.

"He can't sit there."

"You're legally wrong, sir," McLendon replied. "And you won't be able to defend your position."

"I don't care nothing about that. He's not going to sit there. I'm not moving the bus until he gets up." The driver went back to the front seat. McLendon couldn't tell whether he had pulled out the revolver.

Then, nothing.

For three minutes, no one did or said anything. Aubrey was petrified.

Finally McLendon broke the stalemate.

"Ladies and gentlemen," he said to the other passengers. "We have a situation here that isn't right, isn't legal. But we do not want to detain you any further and keep you from arriving at your destinations on time." Then, to everyone's amazement—especially his players'—John McLendon led his team off the bus. The driver closed the door, put the bus into gear, and drove off down the highway. None of the Eagles said anything, but they exchanged wide-eyed, open-mouthed looks. Then, following their coach's lead, they all started walking along the side of the road, heading north. They would never, McLendon knew, make it to Bluefield in time and would forfeit the game. And the chances were good that they would all have to spend the night outdoors, which, given where they were, was a grim prospect indeed. But as the North Carolina College basketball players, holding their overnight bags, moved single file along US 52, with the last bits of sunshine blanketing the hillsides behind them, something else happened as well. For they were walking, for the first time in their lives, the walk of the free.

Half an hour later, as if McLendon knew it was coming, the Eagles flagged down a second bus. Not only was it nearly empty, but McLendon and his players also made it across the state line into West Virginia in time for the eight o'clock opening tip-off against Bluefield State Teachers College. The game wasn't even close. Despite being on their feet practically all the way from Durham, McLendon's players beat the Big Blue basketeers, 95–24. But there was a downside to the game as well, for two minutes into the first half, Big Dog tripped and fell while diving for a rebound, injuring his knee. After the game, McLendon could tell that Dog would need to sit out the next game. The Eagles would have to face West Virginia State without him.

McLendon was also finished, at least temporarily, with buses. The next morning the team gathered at the Bluefield railroad station and caught a train bound for Charleston. They were in the heart of coal country, and as the train wound its way past mining town after mining town, some of the players started to doze off. But an hour or so into the journey, McLendon noticed that Big Dog and Pee Wee were missing. He found them two cars back. Dog was preaching a sermon to a group of colored miners while Pee Wee passed the hat.

Let's not tell Dr. Shepard about this, shall we? he whispered in Dog's ear.

At Institute, West Virginia, that night, the Eagles faced West Virginia State, a middling team at best. But without Big Dog, the Eagles had a fight on their hands. Led by Floyd Brown, North Carolina

College won by six points, yet it was abundantly clear to all that, until Dog was back in the lineup, everyone was going to have to kick up his game a notch.

Sore knee or not, Big Dog maintained much of his usual routine.

A few nights after the West Virginia game, he, Pee Wee, and Billy Williams, a reserve forward who was soon to be entering the service, made a visit to Minnie Hester's. Dog was, once again, all talk, and the three of them ended up staying out later than usual. When they finally got up to go and walked outside, they discovered that it had been snowing. South Street, Lawson Street, and all the nearby yards and rooftops were covered with an inch or so of freshly fallen snow.

But by the time they got back to campus—the evening chill having gone a long way toward reviving them after the evening's liquid refreshments—Big Dog wouldn't let them go to bed. Instead he led them over to the maintenance shop. Doling out shovels and brooms, he had his two teammates help him shovel the snow off the sidewalks leading to the women's dormitory, all the way to the dining hall. Wearing only a light jacket, Pee Wee was soon chilled to the bone. But he didn't say anything.

He had learned long ago that once Dog got a notion into his head, there was no use trying to turn him around.

CHAPTER 15

Burgess

Across town, at Duke, the New Year had also ushered in change. For the medical school basketball team, it came in the form of a bleary-eyed newcomer smelling of cigarette smoke and wearing a wrinkled Army uniform who arrived at the Durham train station one evening just before Christmas. For three days straight he had been rattling across the country in stuffy railcars, some overheated, others underheated, their aisles clogged with sandwich wrappers, crying babies, and weary travelers. Sometimes standing for hours on end, other times crammed into a corner seat with his suitcase between his knees, he had ridden past frozen ranches and bleak mining towns, along the Platte River and across the Mississippi, past St. Louis and Cincinnati, and, finally, over the last of the mountains and into North Carolina. Bone-tired, bespectacled, and in need of a shave, he didn't look like much of a ballplayer. But then nothing about Jack Burgess was quite as it seemed.

Born in Wolf Point, Montana, a scratch of a town along the Missouri River, Burgess was the son of the town's only dentist and, as such, was a member of Wolf Point's tiny sliver of the well-to-do. A piano and a Victrola sat in the parlor, magazines from far-off Boston and New York arrived by post, and by the time he turned seven Jack had his own horse, an ornery black stallion that would try to step on his toes. The Burgess household also had its own outdoor basketball goal, the only one in town. Set in the backyard, it was an iron rim without a net nailed to a wooden backboard. Jack's dad, a Kansan, had played both in high school and for his dental-school team in Kansas City. Between fillings and extractions, he attempted to introduce his eldest son to the game's fundamentals, but the less advertised truth of the matter was that Jack really learned the game from someone else.

"The Indian kids taught me to play basketball," Burgess later recalled.

Wolf Point was the biggest town on the Fort Peck Indian Reservation. And every school day at noon, his Sioux and Assiniboine classmates would race over to play basketball in Jack's backyard until the one o'clock bell. With names like Yellow Robe and Blacktail, some were the direct descendants of the horsemen who had sent George Armstrong Custer and the Long Knives to their unexpected rendezvous with destiny. Now, dressed in jeans or bib overalls and flannel shirts, the reservation boys were absolutely crazy about basketball.

"And good, really good," Burgess added. "And big."

During the 1930s, not only did a Roosevelt County high school team—led by Philip Red Eagle and the three Bighorn brothers—win the Montana state championship, they also beat the Harlem Globetrotters, who stopped in Wolf Point on their way to the West Coast. During the long winter months, when the wind shrieked across the plains, the lunchtime roundball battles moved *inside* the Burgess family home. "When it'd get fifty below," Burgess recalled, "we had a hoop down in the basement of the house. The basement had, maybe, an eight-foot ceiling, and we could play down there."

By the time Jack hit the third grade, he was playing organized ball on a team that would play during halftime at the high school game. And while Dr. Burgess and his wife, like most whites in Wolf Point, wouldn't socialize with Indians, their son sure as hell did, running traps along the Missouri River bottomlands, hunting for jackrabbits near the creek, and listening to stories of how Wolf and Coyote had helped to bring summer, why otters had such thick fur, and how the Big Dipper came to live in the nighttime sky.

When Jack turned thirteen, his dad moved the family to Glasgow, Montana, to cash in on steady work during the building of the Fort Peck Dam.

"My dad," Burgess would later say, "made his grubstake."

Four years later the family moved again, this time to Missoula. Popular, determined, and a good student, Jack had flourished in his new hometown. He'd also grown into a hard-nosed, first-rate basketball player. "My forte was shutting down the other team's best shooter," he recalled. "Whoever their star was, I had to guard him." It was hard, demanding work, one that required brains as well as brawn. "The guys from Butte were the worst," he said. "Man, were they ever tough. Really, really tough." Jack's Missoula high school team played for the state championship his senior year, and though they lost to the Havre Blue Ponies, Burgess had carved a name for himself among Montana's small but impassioned basketball community. Not only did he make the all-state team his senior year, he also caught the eye of some of the nation's leading college coaches. Phog Allen, at Kansas, recruited him, as did Jack Gardner at Kansas State. In the end, however, he decided to stay home and attend the University of Montana. And while he'd already set his sights on becoming a physician, basketball was part of the picture as well.

Burgess played guard for the freshman team in 1940–41 and moved up to varsity the following year. The Grizzlies started the season poorly, losing their first seven games. Then, after trading wins in a two-game matchup with the University of Idaho, they went on a tear, winning thirteen games in a row, the longest winning streak in school history. Burgess played brilliantly, scoring little himself but successfully shutting down opponent after opponent—that is, until the Grizzlies faced the University of Wyoming.

Playing the Cowboys in Billings twelve days after Pearl Harbor,

The University of Montana Grizzlies basketball team, 1942. Jack Burgess is in the middle row, second from left. Joe Taylor is two players to the right in the same row. *(University of Montana)*

Burgess once again had the unenviable assignment of trying to guard Wyoming's star player. A rancher's son who had played his high school ball in Laramie, Kenny Sailors wasn't, at first glance, much to look at. Jug-eared and skinny, with downcast eyes and a pasty complexion, at five feet ten he wasn't even one of the tallest members of the Cowboy lineup. But with a basketball, Sailors was years ahead of his time. He had learned the game playing against his six-feet-five brother, Bud, on a hoop nailed to a windmill, their shoes scraping across the bare dirt. Not only did he develop a one-handed jump shot on his own, he could also turn on a dime, knife through zone defenses, and dribble the ball faster than anyone had ever seen before.

The matchup wasn't pretty. "God," Burgess recalled. "Kenny Sailors just faked me out of everything except my jockstrap."

Not only did Wyoming clobber the Grizzlies, but the following year, at Madison Square Garden in New York City, the Cowboys beat Georgetown, 46–34, to win the NCAA championship. Two nights later, at a special benefit game for the American Red Cross, Sailors led Wyoming past St. John's University, the new NIT champion, by five points in overtime. East Coast basketball writers had never seen anything like him.

Despite getting licked by one of the best basketball players in the country, Burgess had kept getting better and better. On defense he had learned when to feint and when to take a swipe at the ball, when to sag off and when to go full bore. On offense he'd taken the lessons he learned from playing in his backyard in Wolf Point and worked hard to perfect a repertoire of head fakes and stutter steps — little moves that would give him a split second to throw a shovel pass or make a quick drive to the basket for a layup. Rock-solid and grim-faced, with his eyeglasses taped to his temples, Jack Burgess became the kind of player that opponents soon learned not to take for granted.

Determined and energetic, he was endlessly patient. But give him an opening, and he was gone.

At the end of the 1942–43 season, the entire University of Montana basketball squad, following the patriotic example set by the football team, enlisted in the armed services. Burgess joined the Army, but he also had an ace in the hole. The family had a summer cabin up on Placid Lake, on the other side of the Blackfoot River, and one of their lakeside neighbors had a son, maybe three or four years older, who had gone to Duke for medical school. They encouraged Jack to apply as well, which he did. "When I left Missoula to go to Fort Lewis," Burgess recalled, "I had two pieces of paper in my pocket. One was an acceptance to Duke medical school for January forty-four, the other was a contract to go to Officer Candidate School." Forms were submitted, strings were pulled, and when Burgess left Fort Lewis in late 1943, he wasn't bound for Fort Benning. Instead he was headed to North Carolina.

*　　*　　*

It did not take long for Jack Burgess and the medical school basketball team to find each other. And once they did, they fit together hand in glove. It was Walthall to Burgess on the break, with a bounce pass to Hubbell or a lob to Thistlethwaite. Sometimes Burgess would hit Symmonds with a floater, or he'd feint right and then back-pivot left and hand off to a cutter. Other times he would hang around the post and then explode to the basket, banking in a layup. With each offensive set, he got to know his teammates better, learning their habits and predilections and what their eyes were telling him to do. And they learned the same about him. On the attack, he added an explosive quality, a gunslinger's quickness, that boosted the team's fast break.

All told, Burgess was nothing short of a revelation. Passes were stolen. Shots were blocked. Breaks were slowed. Textile-mill hotshots,

Jack Burgess. *(Courtesy of Jack Burgess)*

used to double-digit scoring, found themselves unable to shake the four-eyed phantom with the funny accent who seemed to know their every move. Easy buckets suddenly grew difficult, tough shots became impossible, and self-confidence took a nosedive. For the opposing factory fives, church teams, intramural squads, and military outfits, shooters became passers, game plans became upended, and winners became losers. All of a sudden it was Hubbell grabbing a miss and firing off a baseball pass to Walthall, already streaking past midcourt. Or it was Burgess with a steal off the dribble and a quick pass to Symmonds, breaking for the basket.

By mid-January, the medical school team had become a well-oiled machine. From the start they could score. But they could also do something else. For the newcomer from Montana hadn't just brought a bagful of defensive tricks, a speeded-up offense, or a rugged will to win. Though no one had missed him before, Jack Burgess had made the team complete. If they ever played the Blue Devils again, Thistlethwaite could pass on the brandy. The medical school team wasn't just good. They were ready for anyone.

The rest came easy. Burgess found a room on West Campus and quickly fell into the double-time cadence of life as both an Army private and a medical student. He fell in love with Duke, too—its glorious campus and the mild winter days bathed in sunlight—as well as with a redhaired Alabama beauty, a junior named Eugenia Wimberly. Nicknamed Spots, she was a daughter of upper-crust Birmingham society, a debutante who had a house in Forest Park, a daddy who was part owner of one of the largest agricultural-implement dealers in the South, and a fur coat hanging in her dorm room closet. Up to date on the Southern social calendar—the June Germans, in Rocky Mount; the North Carolina Debutante Ball, held in Raleigh Memorial Auditorium every September, at which nervous, white-gloved young women in pouffy gowns made their official entrance into Dixie high society—she was also a whole lot of fun. "Be it resolved," she wrote in a note prior to a trip to the beach, "I, Spots Wimberly, shall do my level best to make the most of this vacation while the sun shines."

Dressed in his long white lab coat or his Army uniform, Jack Burgess fit right in at Duke. Or at least he seemed to. "The darn rebels still don't admit that the North won the war," he wrote home to his folks back in Missoula one evening in January. "Oh well, I'm just glad that we from the West don't have to argue with these narrow minded people."

That part was easier said than done. Back in Missoula, Burgess had had a Negro teammate—"Joe Taylor, from Chicago," he later recalled. "He was big, rather slow, but his movements were smooth. Low-key; just a nice guy." A six-three guard, he was one of a handful of colored athletes whom the athletic department at the University of Montana recruited from Wendell Phillips High School, on the city's South Side—but he was the only one to play on the Grizzlies basketball team. After road games, Taylor and Burgess would room together. And after home games, Joe and the other basketball players would walk over to the Burgess house for chocolate milk and cinnamon rolls. He even came over for dinner a couple of times. "I'm not sure how my mother, whose people were from Texas, really felt about this," Burgess recalled, "but she didn't say anything."

But North Carolina wasn't Montana, and it didn't take long for the trouble to start.

If there was one place that first-year medical students got to know, and in a hurry, it was the cadaver room. There, beneath the glow of incandescent bulbs, theory became reality, textbook diagrams suddenly came to life, and the wonders of the human body emerged. The students were divided into groups of four, and each quartet shared one cadaver; for them, that was where the circulatory system sprang to life, where the rib cage became the vaults of a human cathedral, and where future surgeons first drew their scalpels through skin and muscle, ligaments and connective tissue. For five days a week, that was where first-year students were schooled in gross anatomy and histology by Johns Hopkins men and where they dissected bodies layer by layer, studying the cell structure of each under a microscope.

And on weekends and evenings, often seven nights a week, the anatomy lab was where the medical students, reeking of formaldehyde, labored over their cadavers—men and women, white and Negro, old and young—who were wheeled out on metal tables by a pair of colored orderlies. "You could never get rid of the smell," Lloyd Taylor recalled. "You'd wash your hands, but it was still there." Eventually, however, Taylor and his classmates spent so much time in the anatomy room that it all seemed normal. "A guy might leave a half-eaten sandwich on his dissection table then come back and finish it off a half an hour later."

One January afternoon Burgess was working late in the cadaver room, trying to find the answer to a question about the muscular system. While his classmates finished up, one by one, he was still removing tissue samples and making slides. Suddenly he noticed something he hadn't seen before. Whenever one of the students was finished with a cadaver, the orderly would wheel it back into one of two storage rooms. He couldn't believe he'd never noticed it before—the white cadavers all went into one room, and the colored cadavers went into the other.

After that it didn't take Jack Burgess long to start noticing a whole lot more.

There had been, of course, the signs at the train station. He'd seen them the night he arrived, and they'd made his stomach turn. Then he started seeing them everywhere.

WHITES ONLY.

COLORED ENTRANCE.

WHITE WAITING ROOM.

NEGROES SEAT FROM REAR.

But when he complained to his Southern classmates, they pushed him aside.

That's the way it is.

You don't know what you're talking about.

Leave it be.

Only there was more to it than that. "You weren't just a Yankee in those days," Burgess recalled. "You were a *damn* Yankee. Since I was from the West, I wasn't a Yankee, but it didn't matter. When I'd tell them that we didn't do all this out West, they'd get mad." He wasn't the only one. Across Duke, pockets of tension existed between Northern and Southern students, between the "yamndankees" and the Solid South. Most of the time it was unspoken, but when Southern honor was challenged, a response was called for. Beneath the surface of day-to-day warmth and hospitality, Burgess had discovered a layer of simmering resentment and wounded pride. He soon learned just how deep it could be.

One evening, at a medical school dance held at the Hope Valley Country Club, a trio of Northern students—"a bit on the liquid side," Burgess recalled—hatched a little surprise. When the band started to take its second break of the evening and the dance floor emptied, the threesome, chuckling to themselves, approached the still-live microphone and sang a song together. It was "Yankee Doodle."

"You could've heard a pin drop," Burgess recalled.

When they were finished, a couple hundred voices sang a different song in response: "Dixie."

No one laughed.

For Burgess, the whole affair was both shocking and distasteful. But as his displeasure hardened, his resolve grew. For behind his steely gaze, his flat nose, and his broad forehead, the truth of the matter was that when it came to race, Jack Burgess was a time bomb waiting to explode. Indeed, the fuse had already been lit.

Compared to the rest of the campus, the Duke hospital wasn't particularly memorable, at least from the outside. Viewed from the flagstone paths that ran alongside the main quadrangle or from the bus stop in front of the chapel, it might as well have been another classroom or administration building. But inside, beyond the waiting rooms and the front desk, was a bustling place like none other on campus, a theater of life and death, a miniature medical city that employed a workforce of more than six thousand, including surgeons, X-ray technicians, secretaries, night nurses, laundresses, dishwashers, dieticians, janitors, interns, and residents. There, Italian POWs folded and stacked patient linens while local Girl Scouts clad in heather-green uniforms, berets, and bright yellow scarves served as messengers.

"The hospital is a world of its own," wrote an unnamed reporter in the *Durham Herald-Sun.* On a typical day at the Duke hospital, babies were born, dozens of blood transfusions were given, a score of major surgeries were performed, a thousand laboratory tests were ordered, and more than three thousand meals were served. In a state where nearly one out of every four children died before the age of ten, where proper health care had long been unavailable or out of reach for many North Carolinians, here was a beacon of hope, one that ran night and day, seven days a week, all year long.

The patients flooded in. Nearly a thousand a day — in taxicabs and family cars, city buses and private ambulances — from every part of town. But most came from outside the city — more than seventy miles away, on average. They came from mill villages and one-horse towns and from sharecropper cabins and hardscrabble tobacco farms deep in the pines. There were gaunt-faced, malnourished children with spindly legs and yellow complexions; nervous middle-aged women in straw hats and cheap print dresses clutching their purses; and reed-thin men in overalls with years of work under an unrelenting sun etched on their faces. They came from every county in the state as well as all the way from Virginia and South Carolina. Rich and poor, from town and country, they all came to Duke.

Those who could afford it were sent to the Private Diagnostic Clinic — nicknamed the Gold Coast — where well-heeled patients were housed in private rooms. Others were dispatched to the pediatric wards, the physical therapy department, gastroenterology, the dermatological clinic, or obstetrics. But most went to the public dispensary, where for a one-dollar fee—or, for those who couldn't come up with that, a chicken, a side of bacon, or a basket of eggs or produce—an ailing family member could see a real doctor in a real hospital.

There, for Hubbell, Thistlethwaite, Walthall, and some of the others, young men who had grown up among the quiet comforts of the middle-class South, was where their larger medical education began. Making daily rounds, running diagnostic tests, writing workups and medical histories, and meeting one-on-one with patients was part of their hands-on medical training. There is where they met farm families suffering from pellagra, their hands and cheeks covered in angry red boils, or children stunted by rickets, their legs bowed like a wishbone. There is where they came face-to-face with TB and typhoid, diphtheria and Gilchrist's disease. There they learned that polio was more prevalent in the summer and that measles, as the old-timers claimed, smelled like freshly plucked chicken feathers.

Twice a week, in a crowded basement clinic, they gave bismuth and arsenic injections to dozens of men and women infected with syphilis. Friday and Saturday nights, when thousands of military recruits from Camp Butner swarmed into town, were the busiest—a nonstop parade of busted jaws and broken bones. There, beneath the incandescent lamps of the Duke hospital, was where the medical students became intimately acquainted with the diseases of the poor and the uneducated, the forgotten and the careless, the wanton and the unlucky.

"It opened your eyes," Dave Hubbell recalled. And one ward in particular opened them even more.

Tucked away on one of the upper floors, the Negro wing at the Duke hospital wasn't very big. There was a small central ward occupied by both men and women as well as a handful of private rooms. The hospital didn't go looking for Negro patients, and white ambulance and taxi drivers were known to bypass Duke in order to drive injured or sick colored passengers—even those on the brink of death—to Lincoln Hospital in Hayti. But the relatively few Negro patients who were admitted were attended to by white nurses and doctors. Only the orderlies were colored.

"Once I caused a ruckus when I cleaned off the bedside table of a woman patient in the Negro ward. I'd thrown away her dipstick for her snuff. To me it looked just like a twig," Barbara Taylor, a former nurse, recalled. While some of the nurses loved playing with the colored babies down in pediatrics, others dreaded having any contact at all with Negro patients, calling them niggers behind their backs. There had been some incidents along the color line as well, including one that Jack Burgess had caught wind of shortly after he arrived on campus.

A medical student had been directed to run a set of urine tests for a patient in the colored ward, one who was suspected of having diabetes. Rather than run the tests, however, the student simply filled in some made-up numbers on the patient's chart. But the student was caught red-handed by a nurse, who then told her supervisor. Eventually the student was hauled into Dean Davison's office. After the young man admitted the wrongdoing, Davison asked him if he had anything to say in his defense. He did.

"It was only a nigger."

Davison expelled him.

For Burgess's classmates, the episode was an object lesson—on fairness, on Davison, and on how, at Duke, they were all held to a higher standard. The good guys won. Case dismissed. But a few weeks later, Burgess got his own firsthand view of race relations at the hospital.

It happened on a Monday, when a group of first-year medical students, including Burgess, and one of their professors were making their regular morning rounds in the hospital. Moving from bed to bed, the students would take turns presenting their patients to the professor and their classmates. The faculty member, usually with the chart in hand, would often ask questions, sometimes of the patient but more often of the presenting student. The patients, of course, be they a six-year-old with a busted elbow or a grandmother battling TB, would be greeted courteously, but the rounds themselves were professional, no-nonsense affairs, designed to move quickly and efficiently.

When Burgess's turn came to present, the group was in the colored ward.

"Good morning, Mrs. Smith," he said.

The patient was an elderly Negro woman. Burgess then presented the facts of her case, discussed the changes on her chart, and described the results of her treatment thus far. Hers was a fairly routine case, and a couple of minutes later the group was back out in the corridor. But no one started moving toward the next ward. Instead, the professor and most of the other students—the Southern ones, at least—lit into Burgess.

"What the hell you doing calling her *Mrs.?*"

"Don't do that again."

"Call 'em by their first names."

"Don't never call a nigger Mr. or Mrs., you hear?"

But when Burgess tried to protest, they cut him off.

"That's the way we do it *here.* You got that, Jack?"

Burgess, face flushed, the blood pounding in his temples, didn't say anything else, and the group soon moved on. But inside he was enraged. It was also the last straw. For as he walked along the linoleum floor of the hospital hallway, Jack Burgess, a twenty-one-year-old Montanan who was two thousand miles away from home, decided that he had seen and heard enough. From that moment on, he declared his own private war, a war on Jim Crow.

What he didn't know was that he wasn't alone.

Ever since the first green infantry recruits arrived at Camp Butner, the sprawling Army training base that had been carved out of the shortleaf pine and tobacco country fifteen miles northeast of town, Durham had felt different. Military buses ran back and forth regularly from the base to downtown, and on any given weekend as many as four thousand GIs with cash in their pockets and between twenty-four and forty-eight hours to kill showed up in town, lining up outside the movie theaters and the sandwich shops, the USO clubs and the ABC stores. And while some of the soldiers used their time in town to eat a decent meal, hear a talk at the library, go to church, or send something home to their sweethearts, others had a different goal. So many prostitutes started doing business in Durham, in fact, that the United States Public Health Service set up a two-hundred-bed venereal disease treatment center on the east side of town.

The majority of the local merchants, of course, threw open their doors to the troops who were stationed at Camp Butner—as did bootleggers, shoe shiners, luncheonette waitresses, and chamber of commerce types. But for many in town, the soldiers also brought trouble. More than a few whites were unnerved by seeing Negroes in uniform, while some of the downtown shopkeepers complained that colored soldiers had attempted to try on clothes in the department stores and, even worse, had been "uppity" to some of the clerks. Most of the troublemakers, it was agreed, were undoubtedly from up North, where such insolent behavior was tolerated. But that didn't make it any easier to take.

White soldiers, however, had been causing problems as well. Some had tried to eat in Negro-owned and -patronized cafés. Others, also undoubtedly Northerners, had tried to sit in the colored sections at the movie theaters. And at colored-only nights at the armory, when white spectators could pay seventy-five cents to sit in the stands and watch the jitterbugging down below, some white GIs and their dates had even jumped onto the dance floor and started dancing. By the time the police arrived, the white dancers had vanished into the night. The lawmen didn't like it, not at all. But they couldn't arrest what they couldn't see.

The Durham police weren't the only ones watching. Meeting regularly in one another's homes, or perhaps in a machine shop after hours or in a willow grove on a warm night, a group of local white men had also had their ears to the ground for some time, keeping tabs on trouble-makers and looking out for hot spots. They had heard rumors that colored people were buying up ice picks and guns and hatching plans to take over when all the white men had been drafted and sent overseas.

Most of the time these men worked quietly and efficiently, passing on what they had learned to friends and allies downtown. But when they needed to they could take matters into their own hands — just as their fathers and grandfathers had done before them. Posing as delivery-men, they would knock on doors to bring a message instead of a package. Other times, smelling of whiskey and kerosene, their robes billowing in the breeze, they would leave another kind of message, lit with a wooden match, on a front lawn at night. And for extreme cases, there were extreme measures. A ride in the country. Car doors closing around a circle of headlights. Bullwhips cracking.

The war had kept them busy, busier than ever. Not only did they have to contend with the local rabble-rousers, who were more brazen than ever, they also had to contend with all the outsiders — those who were out to destroy them, the South, and their way of life. It wasn't hard to figure out who most of the enemies were and where they lived. Most of the time the men could tell just by the way people looked. Even so, there were always some surprises, individuals whom even sea-soned members of the local Klan would never have guessed would be right there in Durham.

CHAPTER 16

A Knock at the Door

Ernst Manasse wasn't the type to draw attention to himself. Standing five feet six, a bit on the slim side, with black hair and blue eyes, he had, in fact, spent years of his life trying not to be noticed. In truth nothing suited him better than to lose himself in a book or to construct, in his mind, a possible solution to a vexing philosophical issue. An authority on Plato, he had published learned treatises on the *Sophist* and the *Politicus,* could speak half a dozen languages — some, admittedly, far better than others — and he never felt more at home than when he held a book in his hands. But as the only white faculty member at the North Carolina College for Negroes, his fate was to stand out. Indeed, on most days, Manasse was the only white person in Hayti.

Serving as the one-man German department, he taught both elementary and intermediate language classes on top of specialized courses on Goethe, Lessing, and Schiller. He also taught Latin and philosophy. Big Dog and Pee Wee adored him. And while they didn't pay any more attention in his class than they did in any of the others, they loved to hear Manasse talk, especially as he turned his *w*'s into *v*'s and his *v*'s into *f*'s. After class they would sometimes hang out in his office and shoot the breeze. Pee Wee, in particular, was interested in learning how to say various cusswords and obscene phrases in German, an interest that Manasse, a wry smile tilting below his cocked eyebrows, was happy to indulge. But behind the smile there was something else. For Ernst Manasse wasn't simply the only white teacher at North Carolina College. What he was, in fact, was a walking miracle.

In 1933, the year that Adolf Hitler seized power in Germany, Manasse had been a graduate student at Heidelberg University, one of the most prestigious schools in Europe. Within months, however, all Jewish faculty members had been fired, and Nazi student groups had begun harassing anyone suspected of being critical of the Führer, while hundreds of books—including the writings of Albert Einstein and Sigmund Freud as well as novels by Thomas Mann and Ernest Hemingway—had been publicly burned on the ancient cobblestones of the Universitätsplatz. Even though he was a Jew, Manasse still managed to earn his doctorate. But there were no jobs, and no future, for someone like him in Germany's new order.

For two long, darkening years he improvised. He scratched up stray bits of fellowship money, finagled a brief research trip to Italy, and tutored a fifteen-year-old Jewish girl whose parents, fearing for her safety, had withdrawn her from the public schools. But when his own father, a well-liked farm-implements dealer in Pomerania, died in 1935, Ernst Manasse could see the writing on the wall. Not only did storm troopers appear outside the funeral home, they also approached the handful of Polish farmers who had come to pay their respects.

"Why are you here?" they asked. "The death of a Jew is nothing to be sorry about."

It was time to leave Germany. Miraculously, that's just what Manasse did.

Manasse was hired to teach at the Landschulheim Florenz, a school for German Jewish refugee children housed in the Villa Pazzi, just outside of Florence, Italy, and for three glorious years his nightmare turned into a dream. The villa itself was a wonder, with centuries-old oil paintings, views of the Tuscan hills, and gardens filled with palm trees,

Ernst Manasse. *(Ancestry.com)*

thickets of wild roses, and lemon trees planted in giant clay urns. Even more entrancing was an attractive young art teacher from Berlin, Marianne Bernhard. Ernst and Marianne fell in love and were married in the ancient town hall in Florence, and, on January 1, 1938, Marianne gave birth to the couple's first child, a son named George.

Then the nightmare returned.

While Benito Mussolini, the lantern-jawed dictator of Italy, wasn't particularly anti-Semitic, when his staunchest ally, Hitler, visited Italy that spring, certain allowances had to be made. In Florence that included the temporary arrest of all of the male teachers at the Landschulheim— as well as Marianne and the baby. Then when Ernst and Marianne were released, they learned that they could no longer reside in Italy. Either they had to find another country to accept them or be deported back to Germany. Desperate, and with little money, the family decided to take different routes. Marianne was able to get visas so that she and the baby could join relatives in Brazil. Ernst was able to secure a brief appointment at Ridley Hall, Cambridge. But that did not last, either. Time was running out.

Finally, on September 15, 1939, exactly two weeks after Germany had invaded Poland and the war began, a twin-engine passenger plane en route to Florida from Havana touched down on the concrete runway of the Miami Municipal Airport. One of its passengers was a tired man with dark hair and blue eyes carrying a wallet stuffed with 560 American dollars. Inside the terminal, the immigration officer who typed up the manifest noted that Ernst Manasse could read and write and that his destination was the North Carolina College for Negroes.

It was Dr. Shepard who saved him.

Shepard had not, however, acted alone. Spurred on by humanitarian organizations and the federal government, more than ten Negro colleges and universities offered jobs to two dozen refugee scholars, mostly Jews, who had fled Nazi persecution. Not only were these men and women frequently the first white faculty members at most of the schools, the teaching positions also literally saved some of their lives. "It is almost certain," Manasse later wrote, "if I had not found a refuge at that time, I would have been arrested, deported to a Nazi concentration camp, tortured and eventually killed." Despite the fact that North Carolina College had been hit hard by both the Depression and the wartime draft, Shepard found room on the faculty for a German Jew who spoke little English and arrived in Durham with little more than the clothes on his back.

It was an audacious experiment. While students and faculty alike had to get used to the presence on campus of someone who was white—and a foreigner to boot—Manasse, too, would make his first personal contact ever with people of a different color. Moreover, he would have to straddle two different worlds. At the end of the day, when his colleagues at the college walked home to their houses and apartments in Hayti, Manasse rode a city bus north, to an all-white neighborhood near Duke, sitting alone near the front of the bus while colored riders sat in the back. Life improved immeasurably when Marianne and little George arrived in December, having taken a steamer from Rio to New York, the tickets for which Ernst bought with the last of his funds. Reunited and alive, they spent the New Year, and George's second birthday, in a cramped apartment on Minerva Avenue.

Ernst had found the room through the help of a local Jewish family, who also sent over some food, writing materials, and household items. But not being religious, Manasse had only limited contact with members of Durham's Beth El Synagogue, preferring to spend whatever off time he had reading and writing. He was a scholar at heart.

One afternoon a colleague at North Carolina College gave Manasse a ride home in his car. Ernst invited the fellow professor in for a cup of coffee. But that was not the end of it. "I was called to come to the rental office," Manasse later recalled. "The neighbors had complained that I had a Negro visitor who was not working at my house." A month and a half later, it happened again. "I was called again and told the neighbors wouldn't stand for this." This time, however, the rental manager added his own warning. If it happened again, he said, he'd shoot.

Three years later the Manasses had moved to another cramped apartment in another subdivided house. The house itself was a huge, boxlike affair, with a big front porch overlooking 6th Street, only a short walk from the women's campus at Duke. Inside, books and papers spilled out of the too-small bookshelves and rested on top of the dresser and the dinner table as well as on the lumpy secondhand love seat and on the kitchen counter. Back in Berlin, Marianne had grown up in a household with its own cook, and as a result she could barely boil an egg. Her housekeeping skills were similarly limited, but it didn't really matter. For her art brightened the walls: sketches and pencil portraits, still lifes and studies for oil paintings, a lemon-yellow Tuscan sun hovering in a cloudless Carolina sky. Five-year-old George, meanwhile, had started school, while a younger brother, two-year-old Gabriel, spent much of his time napping. Even though the family still had precious little money, they were beginning to find their way in their new land. America had saved them.

But there were some things about their new country that Ernst and Marianne simply could not accept. As Jewish refugees from Germany, they were all too familiar with the bitter wages of hatred and prejudice — signs that told you where you could and could not go, stores and restaurants you could not enter, laws that hemmed you in. They had these in North Carolina as well as Germany, except that in North Carolina they were intended for other people. It did not matter. For Marianne and Ernst, segregation was an evil that needed to end. They soon learned that others, particularly at North Carolina College, felt the same way.

One of them was Ernst's fellow North Carolina College professor John Hope Franklin. At age twenty-nine, the Oklahoma-born Negro historian, educated at Fisk University and Harvard, was already carving out a name for himself. "Someday you will be able to tell people that you work at *John Hope Franklin's* college," he said teasingly to Dr. Shepard. Funny, worldly, and sharp as a tack, Franklin was also a bitter foe of segregation. After Pearl Harbor he had attempted to enlist in a program for Navy officers only to be told that because he was colored he'd never get in. "Oh, I'm sorry. I thought there was some kind of national emergency," he informed the white naval officer who met with him. After that Franklin vowed that he would never serve in a Jim Crow military — and he never did.

Ten years and four thousand miles away from Heidelberg, at a small college in North Carolina, Ernst had finally found someone he could talk with. There were others, too, including those on the other side of the color line. For slowly but surely Ernst had also gotten to know a number of local white professors, mainly philosophers at Duke and the University of North Carolina, who shared his intellectual interests. Most of their conversations revolved around Plato, Socrates, and more modern philosophers, such as Dewey, but he also discovered that some of them were quite interested in North Carolina College, in his colleagues there, and in their views on race relations. After that, with Marianne's enthusiastic support, he would bring the two groups together in their apartment. It was an audacious—and dangerous—plan. Not only did it violate the very spirit of segregation, he and Marianne would also run the risk of being discovered and turned in by the other tenants.

It did not matter. True to their word, Ernst and Marianne began hosting small gatherings of like-minded professors, white and Negro, from North Carolina College, Duke, and the University of North Carolina inside their apartment on 6th Street. Held over coffee and plates of store-bought bread and jam, these were collegial affairs—ones that could never happen, because of Jim Crow, on their own campuses. Yet despite the fact that they had no set agenda and were composed, in the main, of polite discussions of arcane matters, the gatherings had a breathtaking quality, one felt by everyone present. In the heart of Dixie, a new world was stirring to life.

By the winter of 1943–44, small groups of students at both Duke and North Carolina College had also decided that it was time for a change. Ignoring college administrators and the ways of most of their fellow undergraduates, they not only gave themselves permission to violate the spirit and letter of segregation laws but also to act on their own. Who were these campus radicals? Nothing less than Naismith's old outfit.

While its name would, in later years, conjure up images of over-chlorinated indoor pools, cheap lodging, and summer camps, the Young Men's Christian Association was for many decades also an on-campus student organization. By the beginning of the war, YMCA chapters could be found at most colleges and universities across the country. At Duke, the campus chapter did volunteer work at the hospital, launched study groups on the role of religion in student life, and hosted mixers for incoming freshmen. But its biggest service project took place in the Durham neighborhood known as Edgemont, or Smoky Hollow. There, in the shadow of the redbrick walls of the then-shuttered Durham Hosiery Mill No. 1, was one of the city's grimmest neighborhoods, a broken landscape haunted by prostitution, violence, and despair. At the Edgemont Community Center, the student volunteers worked with neighborhood children, organizing basketball games and four-square tournaments among the sons and daughters of Durham's white poor.

But the young men also grappled with race as well. Concluding that segregation was a sin against God, these volunteers looked toward the future. Back in November, four of the members of the YMCA cabinet had attended a national conference focusing on how, once the war finally ended, the Christian church should be reconstructed. "The Duke delegates returned with a particular interest in the racial problem," wrote John Powell, the chapter president. Then in January, Powell attended a second meeting, in Ohio, with a similar theme. "Probably one of the most interesting conferences that I shall ever have the opportunity to attend," he later wrote. "Students attended from all over the world and from every race and religion." Fired up, he came back determined to act — not when the war was over, but right then.

Quietly, Powell and the others contacted their counterparts across town, at the YMCA chapter at North Carolina College. Between them a proposal was floated for a joint vespers service at North Carolina College on a Sunday night. It was a bold idea, one that they would have to keep secret from Dr. Shepard. By February it had turned into a reality, as the YMCA members from Duke drove across town for the service — held, without fanfare, at the campus in Hayti. Meeting secretly, they would defy segregation, creating a place where Jim Crow wasn't on the list of invitees.

"It was dangerous," Powell later recalled. "We had to lie down in the cars."

It was also a success. After the first service came another, and another after that. Then one Sunday evening, during the idle chatter that always cropped up after the last amen of the last prayer in the formal service, the subject of basketball came up, laced with more than a little school pride. Floyd Brown and George Parks, after all, were members of the North Carolina College chapter. And although the Blue Devils had been struggling, one of the Duke students knew all about the medical school team.

Nobody can keep up with those guys.

Oh, yeah? The Eagles are undefeated. They could.

Mouths dropped open, eyebrows lifted, heads tilted. Then someone said it.

Well, how about we find out?

To make it work, however, they would need some help. And while Dr. Shepard would have to be kept in the dark once again, there was one faculty member at North Carolina College whose participation and approval would be necessary.

To survive life in the South, John McLendon had made a few rules.

Number one was to never voluntarily segregate himself.

"If there was an event somewhere, and you had to sit in a certain place, and if I didn't have to go, I wouldn't. I wasn't going to help them make me a second-class citizen."

Number two was that you could never lose your dignity. Ever.

Especially in front of your players.

"You had to die first. And I was prepared to do so. Because if you didn't, you couldn't ask them to be men anymore."

The most dangerous activity was traveling. "Coaching in the South was like coaching in a minefield. You don't know when you are going to meet someone who's crazy," he later said. Still, you had to have rules, you had to have a code, and you had to live by it.

That is, you had to do those things most of the time.

For even though McLendon wouldn't order food at the downtown lunch counters or shop at any of the department stores or take Alice and the kids to the county fair, he did once break his own promise to himself. Not long after he'd first arrived in Durham, the movie version of Emily Brontë's novel, *Wuthering Heights,* came to town. McLendon had read—and loved—the book, and the temptation was just too hard to resist. So one balmy spring night just before the war started, he walked downtown, alone, to the Center Theater, purchased a ticket, and walked through the door marked COLORED ENTRANCE. Sitting by himself in the nearly empty balcony, with the projector rattling and the silvery images flickering against his face, he lost himself for an hour and a half in the tragic world of Heathcliff and Catherine and the wild, windswept Yorkshire moors.

But playing a game against a white team from Duke was another matter.

Standing in McLendon's corner office in the gymnasium one weekday afternoon, the student representative of the North Carolina College chapter of the YMCA slowly made his case. We've already been meeting with some of them on Sunday nights, he said, and there haven't been any problems. And this team is supposed to be good, really good. They're in medical school now, but they all used to play college ball. We figured that it would be a good thing for everyone if they played our Eagles.

But McLendon wouldn't hear of it. For one thing, there had been a second episode with Duke that had left a sour taste in his mouth. Not long after he and George Parks had picked up the practice uniforms, someone in the Duke athletic department invited McLendon to come and watch a home basketball game at the indoor stadium—and not from just any seat but from the Duke bench. The invitation itself was cloaked in more than a little smugness—as a reward for your accomplishment, it seemed to say, you can come and see how the game is *really* played—but McLendon ignored that aspect of the invitation. He had not been in a field house anywhere near that size since leaving

Iowa City, and he wanted to see the Blue Devils play. But when McLendon learned that he would have to wear a white jacket, like the one a waiter might wear, he didn't even bother to respond. There was no sense in trying to deal with people like that.

Even more important, McLendon and his players had been lucky that the episode on the bus to West Virginia hadn't gotten out of hand. He or Big Dog or any of the others might have gotten thrown in jail or killed. And they had all been fortunate that the news of what did happen had not made it, it seemed, to Dr. Shepard's office. For if he had found out, Shepard would have fired him on the spot.

There was something else, too. Late one afternoon a few days after the West Virginia trip, McLendon had noticed a Durham police car slow down as it passed in front of his home on Fayetteville Street, just off campus. At first he didn't pay it any mind, but a week later it happened again. Even more troubling, one of his neighbors, who worked at the Mutual, told McLendon that a police officer had stopped him on the sidewalk after work one day and asked him who lived in every house on the block between George and Nelson Streets, including the McLendons. The officer wrote it all down on a pad of paper. McLendon hadn't told Alice about any of it. After all, it might have been nothing. But deep in his gut, he didn't think so.

No, McLendon told the young man standing in his office, it was just too dangerous. Anything could happen.

The Eagles would not play.

Had McLendon needed more proof of why playing such a game was a bad idea, he could have asked Ernst Manasse.

The gatherings Ernst and Marianne hosted at the house on 6th Street had not gone over well with the neighbors. There had been complaints to the landlord, pointed comments on the stairs, sneers, and frowns. Marianne had tried her best, despite her upper-class Berlin ways, to smooth things over, but she didn't make much headway. Then everything grew quiet. It seemed the storm had passed.

One evening, while Ernst labored over a stack of volumes by Max Weber and Marianne got the boys ready for bed, a knock came at their door.

Deliverymen. Only they didn't leave a package or a parcel, an envelope or a piece of furniture. Instead they had a message. It was a message from the Klan.

You have yourself another meeting here, they said, we'll burn the whole *god*damn house down.

You *in* it.

Five thousand miles from Heidelberg, on a quiet residential street in the heart of North Carolina, a nightmare was stirring back to life.

Back on the other side of town, a few days later.

It was well past midnight in the old dormitory at North Carolina College. Pee Wee was sacked out on the spare bed in Big Dog's room, unable to fall asleep. The taste of Minnie Hester's corn liquor still lingered on his tongue, while the jukebox sounds of Blind Boy Fuller and Duke Ellington echoed in his brain. Outside, the wind whispered through the bare branches. In the distance, an automobile went by. Finally he spoke.

Hey, Dog.

No answer. Sheets rustled, bedsprings creaked.

Hey, you, Dog man.

Uh-huh.

Küssen Sie meinen Esel.

CHAPTER 17

"You Could See It in Their Eyes"

On February 5, a bright, fair Saturday, with temperatures climbing into the midfifties, the Eagles traveled by jitney to face North Carolina A&T. Played in the Greensboro school's gymnatorateria — a combined gymnasium, auditorium, and cafeteria — the contest wasn't close. The Eagles were on fire, even with Big Dog still out: McLendon's players clobbered the Aggies by nineteen points. Five nights later, playing at home on a dreary, rain-swept evening, the night air creeping beneath sweaters and overcoats, they upended the visiting Hampton Institute Pirates by fifteen. Twenty-four hours later, with Dog back in the lineup, North Carolina College faced Bluefield State in a return engagement in Durham. This time, the Eagles won by *fifty*, defeating the visiting West Virginians, 76–26.

McLendon, it was clear, *was* on to something. During an era when the fast break was still in its relative infancy, the Eagles were moving the ball from one end of the court to the other as quickly as McLendon had pushed them to in practice — in less than five seconds. At a time when full-court pressing defenses were largely unknown, the North Carolina College team, like a bad dream, regularly challenged opponents' in-bounds passes and harried their ball handlers. And to other teams' astonishment, they never seemed to get tired. During an age when most conditioning programs for basketball didn't go much further than jump-rope exercises, dribbling drills, and a steak dinner the night before the game, the Eagles were running mile after mile every week. Operating under the radar at a little-known college in the South, John McLendon had unlocked some of the game's big secrets.

And his players had bought into it. Spurred on by Floyd Brown, the Phi Beta Kappa team captain from Indiana, they had found their places in their young coach's brilliant if unorthodox system. In particular, Boogie, the other Hoosier, by then playing point guard, had noticeably blossomed. Looking more like a wrestler than a basketball player, with heavily muscled legs and a low center of gravity, Boogie could suddenly explode down the court. Plus he'd fully embraced McLendon's "freelance" offensive strategy. But it was Floyd Brown who was the closest thing that the team had to a floor leader. For while the Eagles had a number of set plays that they ran, more often than not what guided them was Brown's fast-paced probing of the other team's

North Carolina College Eagles, 1943–44. Left to right: John McLendon, George Parks, George "Crazy Horse" Samuel, Billy Williams, James "Boogie" Hardy, Aubrey Stanley, Floyd Brown, Henry "Big Dog" Thomas, Edward "Pee Wee" Boyd. *(Courtesy of the North Carolina Central University Archives, Records and History Center—James E. Shepard Memorial Library, Durham, NC)*

defense. "Everybody has to key off what he does," McLendon recalled. "If he dribbles this way, everybody's going to react in a certain way, whether he passes to one guy or cuts in front of him or if he cuts back to the post. That's the play. Everybody knows it."

Even Big Dog had flourished under McLendon's direction. A lethal weapon on the court—manhandling defenders, grabbing rebounds, and effortlessly swatting away passes as though they were June bugs—he nonetheless often marched to his own tune. One night at Minnie Hester's, he began boasting so much about the number of points he had scored in the previous game and how many more he would score in the next one that a pile of well-worn dollar bills soon appeared on one of the bootlegger's tabletops, pulled from pants pockets and hatbands. Dog, to his credit, won the bet, but not without shooting the ball practically every time it came his way. "I'd always wondered just why he was so *active* that day," McLendon later admitted. In another game, Big Dog took to the floor with a chaw of tobacco tucked inside his right cheek, an escapade that worked well—until he was submarined by the opposing center and swallowed a mouthful of juice.

Despite his hijinks, Dog, like the others, had signed up for the McLendon school of basketball. Unused to facing a seemingly free-form offensive onslaught like that unleashed by the Eagles, their opponents often found it difficult to get their own offenses in gear, in no small part because McLendon's players stealthily switched between zone and man-to-man defense. "If the score was even on the scoreboard," McLendon said, "we'd play one offense. But if a guy made a free throw and the score became uneven, we'd play another." Not only did most of North Carolina College's opponents tire quickly—not just from the frantic pace set by the Eagles but also because they couldn't rest, even for a minute, on offense—the superior physical condition of the Eagles also gave them an added psychological edge. Late in a game, whenever a time-out was called or play was stopped, McLendon had his players *run* to the bench.

"It would just kill the other team," he added. "You could see it in their eyes."

*   *   *

McLendon was an innovator, but he also adhered to Naismith's ideals. For despite his devastating, go-straight-for-the-jugular approach, he was also a firm believer in fair play, in following the rules, and, most important, in the game itself. As word of the Eagles' triumphs began to make its way across Hayti, more and more Negro spectators began to show up for the games—not just students, though they now came in droves, but also maids, cigarette-factory workers, and men and women who dug ditches, cleaned kitchens, and swept floors. McLendon printed up some tickets and handed them out for free to local youngsters—whom he dubbed the Eagles Knothole Club—so they could come and see the games. In the third year of what was already a bloody world war with no clear end in sight, the North Carolina College basketball team was something that folks in Hayti could cheer about.

McLendon also established some strict new guidelines for fan behavior. The gymnasium, he announced, would be known as the House of Good Sportsmanship. At home games there would be nothing unseemly: no booing or profanity, no hooting or catcalls when an opponent was at the free-throw line. While visiting teams would try their best to beat them, the Eagles and their fans would treat them with nothing but respect. Somewhere, James Naismith—who had died three and a half years earlier—was smiling.

Meanwhile, as the North Carolina College juggernaut began to pick up steam, the Eagles found themselves subjected not only to odd-ball defenses and far-fetched game plans but also to cheap shots, questionable fouls, homer refs, and petty chicanery. On one campus, their sleeping accommodations the night before the game were cots set up in a boiler room. On another, students blew whistles and rattled noise-makers outside their windows well past midnight, hoping to keep them from getting a good night's sleep. None of it worked. But there was another opponent as well, one that McLendon knew he could never beat.

The draft had played havoc with McLendon's plans for the season. Not only had the previous year's star, Rocky Roberson, gone into the service, but by mid-February the Eagles had lost two other teammates to the military as well. Nervous about having enough players, especially should one of his starters foul out or get sick, McLendon had gone through the small undergraduate male student population at the college with a fine-tooth comb, looking for any kind of athletic talent. He'd even briefly given one of Dr. Shepard's cousins, Sam, a spot on the team.

For Aubrey, this meant playing an even bigger role on the team than anyone, including Aubrey himself, had imagined. Though he was still the butt of most jokes—Pee Wee, announcing the players at home games, never failed to raise a few laughs by shouting "*Stinky* Stanley from Beaufort, North Carolina," over the public address system—he was by then both a starter and a key member of the Eagles lineup. He had knocked down a dozen points against one of the military teams from Camp Butner, fourteen against Shaw, ten in the A&T game, and another dozen against Hampton. While his grades weren't anything to write Aunt Lillie about, he was starting to feel at home on campus as well. He had even been asked to pledge one of the fraternities, and if he could have scraped up enough money for dues he had planned on doing so—until he was talking with McLendon one morning on a sidewalk near the dining hall. As they were chatting, a group of pledges walked by, barking like dogs under the watchful gaze of a couple of fraternity brothers.

"Look at those guys," McLendon said quietly, more to himself than to Aubrey, while shaking his head.

That was all it took. After that Aubrey didn't think about fraternities anymore.

On Valentine's Day the Eagles were scheduled to play a home game against Johnson C. Smith, the colored Presbyterian university in

Charlotte, whose basketball team had lost only one game all season. The contest turned out to be a dogfight. Led by some skillful ballhandling, the Golden Bulls took an early lead, but by halftime, the Eagles—keyed by Floyd Brown's tough defense and by the strong play of George Parks, then playing forward—went ahead by four. But even though McLendon's team eventually won by ten points, the victory wasn't entirely a happy one. For the Johnson C. Smith game was also the last for Anthony "Smokey" Davis, the forward from Southport, North Carolina, a deep-sea fishing port along the Intracoastal Waterway, south of Wilmington. The following week, Davis was set to enter the Marines.

From then on, McLendon would be, for all intents and purposes, down to his starters. He could no longer platoon his players, and with every foul, and every twist of an ankle, disaster beckoned.

Big Dog. Boogie. Floyd Brown. George Parks. Aubrey. He called them his Iron Five. And for the rest of the season, they would have to play practically every minute of every game.

There were two exceptions. The first was Billy Williams, a walk-on from Durham. "He was a good student," Pee Wee recalled. "Brilliant, really." And while he rarely lit up the basketball court, he had other appeals—especially to Big Dog and Pee Wee. "He always had money," Pee Wee remembered. "His mama worked for Eddie Cameron, while Billy had a job as the manager at a dry cleaner's on Fayetteville Street. All the money he wasn't making he was stealing. And a lot of that money ended up in Big Dog's pockets. Mine, too."

The other exception was a world unto himself. The name on his draft card was George Lindsey Samuel Jr. He had been born and raised in Hayti. Tall and handsome, with an athlete's build, by the time he was twenty, in 1942, Samuel was working for a white-owned construction company that was helping to build Camp Butner. But when a chance to attend North Carolina College suddenly materialized one year later, he leaped at it. Even though he had not played basketball at Hillside High in Hayti, it wasn't long before McLendon had talked him into trying out for the Eagles. McLendon even boasted that Samuel was a real "discovery."

The truth was a bit more complicated. While he did score eight points in the second game against Bluefield, helping to sub for a still-ailing Big Dog, George Samuel was very much a rarely played member of the Eagles. But as a person he was hard to ignore. Nicknamed Horse, he rocked back and forth across the line that divided the rational from the unbalanced. On some days he was as normal as he could be. On others he appeared to be as mad as a March hare. Sometimes he spoke only nonsense. One day he showed up for school wearing all his clothes inside out.

For a while Horse walked around campus with an imaginary dog, which he liked to take with him down to the small concession stand located in the basement of the administration building. Run by a blind couple who counted change by touch, it sold sandwiches and candy bars, ice-cold bottles of Yoo-Hoo and Coca-Cola. "Here, boy," Horse would say. "Stay." Then he would walk away. A few minutes later he'd be back. "C'mon, boy," he'd say. "Let's go." Upstairs in the dean's office there were already whispers about psychologists, psychiatrists, and perhaps the state hospital in Goldsboro.

Big Dog didn't buy it. "Dog thought it was all a big act," Pee Wee later recalled. "He thought that Horse was acting crazy just so he could get out of having to work." Pee Wee wasn't so sure.

He did, however, give him a new name, thanks to Dr. Manasse.

Verrückt Pferd.

Crazy Horse.

Despite being down to five starters, McLendon's team neither faltered nor ran out of gas. Instead they took off. On Friday, February 18, North Carolina College beat Saint Augustine's at home, 119–34. Not only did they set a national collegiate scoring record—and become the nation's highest-scoring college basketball team—they also caught the eye of the *Pittsburgh Courier,* the *New York Amsterdam News,* and other colored newspapers across the country. The next night, with American flags and red, white, and blue bunting brightening the gymnasium as part of a "salute to the armed forces" homecoming ceremony, McLendon's players crushed the Shaw Bears by forty-three.

The rest kept coming easy. A week after the Saint Augustine's game, North Carolina College beat Johnson C. Smith for a second time, on the road in Charlotte. Then, on February 28, they defeated A&T at home to win the CIAA title. Aubrey was the high scorer.

Operating out of a shoe-box-size gymnasium in the middle of North Carolina, at a school that few of their fellow countrymen had heard of, John McLendon's players hadn't simply won a conference championship or run through their regular season without a single loss. For the lucky few who saw them play, they had also opened the door to a new kind of basketball. And soon they would take it out of the South.

CHAPTER 18

———

New York

New York hadn't always been a basketball town. In its heart of hearts, the city was still a full-fledged member of the great baseball nation, a three-team megalopolis where the citizens still fawned over Ruth and Gehrig, where Saturday's pitching lineup was the hot topic at office watercoolers and in stuffy IRT subway cars, and where hearts still raced, whether at the Polo Grounds or Yankee Stadium or Ebbets Field or huddled in front of Red Barber's voice on the radio, at the crack of a thirty-two-ounce bat cut from a solid piece of Pennsylvania ash. For its first few decades, basketball, when New Yorkers paid any attention to it at all, lingered somewhere back in the pack of third-string sports, behind football and boxing but ahead of steeplechase and rowing. Even the most famous basketball team in the world at the time, the Harlem Globetrotters, was actually from Illinois.

But Naismith's game had made inroads. Practically every high school, junior high, and elementary school in the five boroughs of New York had either a basketball team or, at the very least, some form of a basketball court, even if it was only the corner of an undersize patch of asphalt that served as a playground. Most of the city's colleges fielded their own teams, and amateur leagues had blossomed at athletic clubs and YMCAs. Equally important, the game had been embraced by the children of various ethnic groups, especially Jewish immigrants from Russia and the Balkans. For them basketball became a badge of their Americanness, a red-white-and-blue symbol of their open-armed embrace of their new home.

In 1934, however, the fortunes of basketball in New York City took a dramatic new turn.

The author of this metamorphosis was a twenty-nine-year-old sportswriter and budding athletic promoter named Ned Irish. Three years earlier, when bread lines had begun to appear across the city, he had helped organize a series of benefit games to raise money for mayor Jimmy Walker's unemployment relief fund. Not only were the games a success, Irish also became convinced that there was a larger market for basketball in the city—even during the Depression. Eventually he was able to convince the management at Madison Square Garden to give it a try. Irish's plan was straightforward, and—equally important—it involved very little overhead. On six nights during the 1934–35 basketball season, two local New York City college teams would play against two teams from somewhere else in the country. Not only would, say, New York University and St. John's fans want to see their teams play in the Garden, college teams from Kentucky and Purdue and Notre Dame would also leap at the chance to play in New York.

Soon known as basketball doubleheaders, Ned Irish's brainchild—which was first announced at the White Horse Tavern, a West Village watering hole frequented by writers and longshoremen—was an immediate hit. Local students and alumni bought enough tickets to make the games profitable, and as some of the country's highest-ranking teams began appearing at the Garden, word got out that if one wanted to see the best basketball in the world, the place to be was at Madison Square Garden. Moreover, as top-flight teams such as Kansas, Oklahoma A&M, and Stanford began appearing at the Garden, bringing with them their own particular styles of play, the doubleheaders became a roundball graduate school for local players and coaches. In the pretelevision era, when you had to *go* to a game to actually see how another team played, Ned Irish's big idea helped raise the level of New York City basketball immeasurably.

The games themselves, meanwhile, were entertainment all their own. Not only did New Yorkers marvel at the play of the Western teams, fistfights and bench-clearing brawls were also far from unknown among the local fives and their devoted and most assuredly vocal followers. And as the fame of the doubleheaders grew year after year, getting invited to play in New York—and winning while you were there—became a top priority for schools across the country. Frank Keaney, the Rhode Island coach, even placed smudge pots in the gym to help get his players prepared for the smoke-filled Garden air.

But Irish and his friends at the Metropolitan Basketball Writers Association weren't done. At a luncheon at the Hotel Lincoln on February 2, 1938, they announced plans for a national collegiate championship tournament to be held six weeks later, over a seven-day period in March, at Madison Square Garden. Although it was officially known as the National Invitation Tournament, it was called by many the New York Invitational. The inaugural version was little more than an extended, winner-take-all version of a pair of doubleheaders, with Temple defeating Colorado, 60–36, to win the first NIT. Whether the Owls were the best team in the country wasn't all that important. The genie had been let out of the bottle, and the country was on its way to a national college basketball championship.

The following year, however, another horse joined the race.

Unwilling to let Ned Irish and his New Yorkers steal the limelight, the National Collegiate Athletic Association debuted its own tournament, the opening rounds of which were held in Philadelphia and San Francisco. In the championship game, which was to be played at the Northwestern University field house outside Chicago, Ohio State, the Big Ten champion, was the odds-on favorite over largely unheralded Oregon. But Howard Hobson, the coach of the Ducks, had purposely scheduled a long road trip during the regular season, all the way to New York and back, which exposed his players to different styles of play. It paid off, and Oregon won the first NCAA tournament, beating the Buckeyes by thirteen.

While the nation still struggled with the Depression and the world drifted toward war, college basketball had quietly gone national.

But not everyone was invited. For even though a handful of non-white ballplayers found their way out onto the floor at Madison Square Garden and into various postseason tournaments, in the new wartime college basketball world Negro teams did not. For despite the fact that there were clearly some extremely talented teams at the colored colleges—in an exhibition game in New York in 1939, for example, Virginia Union defeated an all-star lineup from Long Island University, who went on to win that year's NIT—the Negro colleges would not be allowed to take part in the early years of either the NIT or the NCAA tournament. Whether this was intended to appease the Southern white schools or not, it was abundantly clear that in the bright new world of postseason college basketball that was being created in the late 1930s there was no place for the likes of John McLendon and his Eagles. Like the Negro Leagues teams in baseball, the colored basketball teams had no way to know how they stacked up against the white teams.

By the time the Colonial pulled into the vast, echoing beehive that was Pennsylvania Station, Aubrey Stanley's eyes had grown used to wonder. At Union Station in Washington, he had walked outside with the others into the frigid air and gazed up at the dome of the Capitol, brilliant white in the midday sunshine, while flags snapped in the wind above him. Then came Baltimore and Wilmington, Delaware, the back lots and row houses of Philadelphia, and the last, slow crawl past the Meadowlands, with the spire of the Empire State Building hovering like a church steeple above a single line of New Jersey hills. But nothing had quite prepared him for the shock that was New York.

For a week and a half, ever since they had defeated A&T and

clinched the Colored Intercollegiate Athletic Association championship, Aubrey and his teammates had been preparing for this. For ten days McLendon had run them through extra practices and quick-time drills, timing their runs through the blustery, unpredictable weather that moved into Durham at the beginning of the spring. Then, on the second Thursday in March, the North Carolina College Eagles arrived in New York City to play, that Friday, for the 1944 National Negro College Basketball Championship.

Colored basketball tournaments weren't new. National high school championship tournaments had been held for years, as had invitational tourneys hosted by Negro fraternal orders. Serious efforts to determine which colored college had the best basketball team in the country had been percolating for years, especially since the Negro schools had been Jim-Crowed out of the doubleheaders, the NIT, and the NCAAs.

In the spring of 1941, the first national Negro college championship basketball tournament was held in Cincinnati. A shoestring affair that featured six teams playing as many as four games in one day—as well as at least one team sleeping in the stairwell of a local armory after they got booted from their hotel—the tournament was nonetheless a success. But when the news from Pearl Harbor arrived eight and a half months later, plans for a follow-up were scuttled. Finally, in 1944, the National Negro College Championship tournament was revived.

This time, there would be just one game. Travel was too difficult and unpredictable for a larger field of competitors. But if the tournament schedule reflected wartime conditions, the venue did not.

Stretching along 7th Avenue all the way from 137th to 138th Streets, the Renaissance Ballroom and Casino was one of Harlem's hometown jewels. The site of prizefights and formal dress balls, political conventions and theatrical productions, it featured a soaring ceiling, underground gambling parlors, and a massive wooden dance floor that shook beneath the feet of hundreds of smiling, sweating, churning dancers, busting moves to the sounds of Cab Calloway, Fletcher Henderson, and Count Basie and His Barons of Rhythm.

Part of the largest Negro-owned and -operated entertainment center in America when it first opened in 1923, it had also been the home court of the Renaissance Big Five, Harlem's legendary barnstorming basketball team of the 1920s and 1930s. The Rens won the first-ever world professional basketball championship, and their home games at the Ballroom were raucous, live-wire affairs, with street toughs and hepcats in the cheap seats showering obscenities on the referees, the opposing team, and the well-heeled patrons who sat down below. There, using the same portable goals that the Rens used, John McLendon's Eagles would try to win their first national championship, playing against the Lincoln University Lions, from Pennsylvania. "The arrangement committee," noted the *New York Age*, a Harlem newspaper, "hand picked these teams knowing the contestants will give a game comparable to any in the strictly LILY WHITE tournaments being staged at Madison Square Garden."

Standing alongside the wall in a crowded bar on Lenox Avenue, holding what he thought was his second Coca-Cola of the evening between his palms, Aubrey Stanley still couldn't believe it all. First there had been the dizzying looks upward from the sidewalks outside Penn Station at buildings that seemed to sway in the bright March sky. Then the clattering subway ride uptown on a 7th Avenue express, the local stops whooshing by, changing at 96th Street for the Lenox–Bronx Park Express, and spilling out four stops later into the heart of the Negro capital of America. There, alongside tenement after tenement, their brick and stone facades laced with iron fire escapes, storefront Pentecostal and Holiness churches rubbed shoulders with fruit markets and butcher shops, while street-corner orators, their breath as white as ghosts, spoke of Jews and Jesus, communists, the CIO, Adam Clayton Powell, and Father Divine. There, in neighborhoods called Sugar Hill and Strivers' Row, were more colored people than Aubrey had ever seen before. It was all at once thrilling, frightening, exciting. And the next

James "Boogie" Hardy. *(Courtesy of the North Carolina Central University Archives, Records and History Center—James E. Shepard Memorial Library, Durham, NC)*

night, beneath the lights of the Renaissance Ballroom, he would play in the biggest game of his life.

For a week and a half, Negro newspapers had been building up the championship match between North Carolina College and Lincoln University, a small colored college outside Philadelphia. But it was the Eagles who received the lion's share of attention. "Johnnie McLendon's Tar Heels are always good, but this year's looks like a banner crop," gushed one New York paper. "At present they are the class of eastern colleges, if not the country." Floyd Brown, announced one story, was "a coach's dream." But it was Big Dog who stole the spotlight. "He is a superb ball handler," the *Norfolk Journal and Guide* wrote. "His marksmanship is as unorthodox as it is sensational." And while the Lincoln Lions were credited for having a sturdy, serviceable team, you didn't need a crib sheet to tell which way the wind was blowing.

"The wise money is with the Eagles," wrote one New York columnist.

For Aubrey, in a steamy bar on Lenox Avenue, that all lay ahead. Thinking about it later, he came to conclusion that he should have realized it was Big Dog who did all the ordering that night, which might explain why the Coca-Colas in Harlem didn't taste the same as they did back in Beaufort. By the time he and Big Dog and Pee Wee hit the ice-cold air outside the bar and started wobbling down the sidewalk toward their room in the Harlem branch of the YMCA, over on 135th Street, he finally put two and two together. But it didn't matter. Between the blurry neon signs and the gauzy streetlamps, the tilting buildings and the swerving, moving sidewalk, all he could do was smile.

Stinky Stanley was in New York City. And he had come to play.

Pee Wee woke up feeling like he had a mouthful of socks. Dog and Aubrey didn't fare much better. After a quick breakfast in their rooms at the Y, a morning scrimmage, and a shower, they started to regain their bearings. In the team meeting, McLendon went over what little scouting information he had been able to turn up about the Lincoln Lions—no real standouts, but all quite talented and quick—then he gave voice to what was on everyone's mind. This evening, he said, we'll have a chance to do something no North Carolina team has ever done before.

A little after six o'clock, the Eagles made the two-and-a-half-block walk together to the Renaissance, with the last bitter winds of March, mixed with a few stray snow flurries, whipping their pant cuffs and pounding against their overcoats and faces. Around them, Harlem was beginning to stir.

Even though tip-off wasn't until half past eight, the ballroom was already filling. Men in dark suits and women in fur-trimmed coats clustered near the bar or lingered in small groups, talking quietly by the folding chairs that had been set up alongside the court. The calm did not last. By game time, the Renaissance was standing room only. And once the ball was in play, it didn't take long for the Eagles to realize that they were going to have their hands full.

Led by Rudy Johnson, a speedy forward from Baltimore, and Bill Hoffler, a rangy center from the Virginia Tidewater region who started grabbing rebounds on both ends of the court, the Lions were no pushovers. The Lincoln ballplayers not only were able to slow down the Eagles' transition game, they also responded with their own high-speed offense. Equally daunting, the Lincoln bench seemed to be just as good as North Carolina College's own starting five. Without a dominant star, Lincoln was especially tough to defend against. Midway through the first half, the Lions were up by six points.

The architect of their attack was a thirty-five-year-old Cuban American named Manuel Rivero. Born in Havana, he had come at the age of nine to the United States, where he was raised by a single mother who worked as a servant at the Cuban consulate. Athletic and bright, Rivero became one of the first colored athletes to play football and baseball at Columbia University, where he also earned a master's degree. After a brief career as a third baseman in the Negro Leagues, Rivero was hired by Lincoln, where he coached every sport the school offered. And while his 1944 Lions basketball team may have been short a single, game-changing athlete, they excelled at hard-hitting, unselfish play.

The Eagles, meanwhile, didn't seem to be themselves. Whether it was the huge, noisy, overflow crowd, the weird lighting, or the odd floor, which felt dead beneath their feet, they stumbled through the first half. Their passing was ragged, and Boogie and Aubrey were off their game, launching shots from well outside their normal range that clanged off the rim or bounced off the backboard into the hands of the Lions. Equally troubling, their defense was off as well. They began by playing zone, only to get burned inside by the Lions. But when they switched to man-to-man, they kept mixing up their assignments. During the first half, only Big Dog played up to form, hammering in shots from inside and, when he was fouled, making his free throws. But it wasn't enough. The Lions led by twelve points at the half.

McLendon didn't know what to do. His Iron Five seemed to be made of tin.

The second half started a bit more promisingly.

While the crowd showered the Eagles with hoots, catcalls, and four-letter words, Floyd Brown finally started to shine. Dog continued to battle down low, and Aubrey and Boogie then began to peel off give-and-go's and quick pull-up jump shots. And even though they still struggled on defense, the North Carolina College players were finding their game.

Then disaster struck. Midway through the half, Big Dog fouled out. Only he didn't. Perhaps still feeling the effects of the previous night's escapades, or rattled by the earsplitting rants of the spectators sitting right behind the scorer's table, Pee Wee had mistakenly given Dog one more foul than he actually had, and Dog had to leave the game. Down by eleven points, with only ten more minutes left to play, it was clear to most of the spectators inside the Renaissance that the game, for all practical purposes, was over. Without their star player, who had scored more than half their points, McLendon's team didn't have a prayer.

But the Eagles suddenly caught fire, even with Crazy Horse inserted into the lineup. Not only did they start finding the basket, they found their legs as well. All the suicides, all those miles they'd run out in the countryside east of campus, all the workouts and extra practices began to pay off. While the Lions, who had kept the tempo fast all game long, began to fade, the Eagles took over. And possession after possession, McLendon's players kept slicing away the Lincoln lead, from eleven to nine, from nine to seven, from seven to five. Even the chorus of hipsters and hepcats, buzzed on reefer and sitting in the balcony, had switched sides and were yelling, more loudly than ever, for the North

Carolinians. The tide had turned. The Eagles were going to win. By the time the Lions' lead was cut to three, even McLendon knew it was going to happen.

Then it was all over.

The referee, who was keeping track of time on his wristwatch, suddenly announced that the clock had run out. Immediately McLendon jumped up. There were, he knew, at least four more minutes of playing time left, something that Pee Wee, by then as sober and attentive as a choir director, signaled was true. But the Renaissance Ballroom and Casino was not the House of Good Sportsmanship, and the bookies and bagmen who lingered along the edges of the court, silently exchanging knowing looks and tight-lipped smiles, had had a much different agenda.

"The game was fixed," McLendon later claimed.

His protests went nowhere.

Lincoln won.

Game over.

Early the following afternoon, the Eagles rode out by train to Orange, New Jersey, where, in a rented hall in an Italian neighborhood, they played a game against the Triangles, a colored semiprofessional team. The contest was a rough one. Big Dog played fierce on defense, throwing elbows and grabbing rebounds, but he couldn't find his shot, nor could most of the others, still stunned by what had happened the night before. Fortunately, George Parks, the lanky Kentuckian, scored a career-high nineteen points, leading North Carolina College to victory by six. That night, back in Manhattan, the team had a spaghetti dinner. After another round with Dog and Pee Wee, most of Aubrey's dinner ended up in the gutter along Lenox Avenue.

The next morning, a Sunday, dawned brisk and clear. A west wind coming up off the river pushed bits of paper and other trash along the sidewalks on 135th Street, while more than one hundred blocks to the south, the large American flag flying over Pennsylvania Station fluttered in the breeze. New Yorkers would awaken to headlines that morning telling them that Soviet armies had broken out along a one-hundred-mile front in the Ukraine, and that crews of American B-25 bombers, flying in less than ideal weather, had successfully bombed the Littoria rail yards on the northern edge of Rome. Three years into the costliest war in the nation's history, the country was ready for the final chapter to begin. But in New York and all along the Eastern Seaboard that morning, the unspoken and most welcome news, ushered in by clear skies and rising temperatures, was that spring, at last, was clearly on its way.

The Eagles didn't do much talking that day.

Floyd Brown, as usual, was curled up with a book, while Dog and Pee Wee quietly played bid whist as the New Jersey countryside rolled past the train's windows. McLendon, deep in thought, kept to himself, while the others—the ones who weren't asleep—talked about New York and Harlem and what they'd tell the others at school of all that they had seen. Nobody, however, wanted to talk about the game.

For Aubrey it was a day of contrasts. When they rolled into D.C. and transferred to the Jim Crow cars at Union Station, he felt like he was going back to another country—his homeland, to be certain, but the change was undeniable. The weather, of course, was noticeably warmer. Near Richmond, the first green leaves were already coming out on the willows, and bright patches of forsythia and lilies of the valley could be spotted along the back fences and side yards of the farms and little towns they passed along the way. But there was another change as well, one that returned as a familiar tightening in his chest. For despite all the madness in New York, there had also been a kind of freedom there. And Aubrey had gotten a taste of it.

Finally, somewhere south of Petersburg, Virginia, McLendon called a team meeting.

We can't worry none about what happened, he told his players. We can't be bothered by missed shots and called fouls and who should have been guarding whom. That's all over now. What's done is done.

Huddled together at the end of the railroad car, the Virginia countryside streaming past, none of the Eagles said anything; they simply nodded.

Besides, McLendon added, we've got some things to work on.

And while none of the players knew it yet, their season wasn't quite over after all.

CHAPTER 19

The Secret Game

Sunday, March 19, 1944.

A few minutes past ten o'clock, Dave Hubbell eased the borrowed Packard onto Campus Drive and headed east. The morning was bright and fresh, with the last few traces of Saturday's rain drying quickly atop the asphalt. After weeks of rumor and innuendo, spring had finally arrived in full force across North Carolina. The maples and cherry trees were in bloom, and backyard gardeners started lingering near the seed racks in hardware stores while the first of the warm-weather aviators, the vesper sparrows and yellowthroats, had winged in from Florida on their way north.

Inside the car, nobody was doing much talking. Wearing light jackets and holding their gym bags on their laps, the players were jammed knee to knee in both the front seat and the backseat. There would be no ducking, no lying down on the floor of the car this time. If they were seen, they were seen. Luckily, aside from a few stragglers late for church, the downtown streets were empty. Just before they crossed the Southern Railway tracks, near the tobacco warehouses, somebody mentioned that they hadn't brought a ball. But once they crossed over into Colored Town, all conversation ended. There weren't any cars here, either — especially no police cars — just empty chairs set out on front porches, a stray dog slowly nosing its way along the sidewalk, and the faint sounds of a choir coming from the big brick church along the way.

That was just fine with them. They weren't looking for company.

Jack Burgess had been in from the get-go.

"Yeah, you bet," he'd told the fellows from the Duke Y chapter. "Let's do it." Persuading his new teammates was another matter. A couple of the guys—Wechsler, from Pennsylvania, and Johnson, the CO from Oklahoma—were open, even enthusiastic, about playing a colored team. But the Southerners were dead set against it. We don't do stuff like that down here, they told him. Burgess kept pushing, but he had trouble making any headway.

As it turned out, however, there were circumstances that were tilting his way. Because of the military draft, which was whisking away more Duke undergraduates than ever before, the 1944 campus intramural basketball tournament had been suddenly canceled. Not only would the medical school team be unable to defend its title, the disappearance of the tournament also left them decidedly short on games. This was no minor matter, for in truth they longed to compete. "We were a bunch of guys who *needed* to play basketball," Lloyd Taylor said. In order to play at all, they were having to hustle up some competition on their own, playing against military teams and textile-mill outfits in local high school gyms. It wasn't much, but it was something.

As Burgess needled and probed, attempting to get the Southerners to change their minds, he tried everything. He pulled his teammates aside, one by one, and reminded them that he'd played against colored players before—hell, he'd even had a colored teammate—and that it was no big deal. He talked about how they'd all treated Negro patients in the hospital. And he talked about how great a team they had and how they could play against anyone. He didn't get anywhere. Naw, they told him, things just weren't done like that down here.

Finally Burgess found a chink in their armor. It was something he

Scheduled In State This

Medical Students Play Benefit Game Tonight

Caught between classes, these Duke Medical School students will don their basketball togs here tonight for a polio benefit game with Erwin Auditorium in the Durham High School gymnasium. Left to right, front row, they are Homer Seibert, Harry Wechsler, Dick Symmons and Jack Burgess; back row, Dick Thistlethwaite, Dave Hubbell, Ed Johnson and John McCoy. The med quint is unbeaten in league competition and meets Erwin Auditorium for the first time this season. A preliminary sends Duke Hospital Nurses against Watts Hospital Nurses, starting at 7:30 o'clock.

Duke medical school basketball team, 1946. Front row: Homer Sieber, Harry Wechsler, Dick Symmonds, Jack Burgess. Back row: Dick Thistlethwaite, Dave Hubbell, Ed Johnson, John McCoy. *(Durham Herald-Sun)*

had earned the right to speak about because he had already battled alongside them out on the hardwood of half a dozen or more local gyms and ball courts against GIs and mill workers and other teams they had run up against. It was also the one sore point that white Southerners, still stung by the ancient defeats along Cemetery Ridge and at Appomattox, carried with them in the long, haunted decades that followed the war.

"Are you guys chicken?" he asked.

Jack Burgess had challenged their pride and, with it, their honor. This was no small matter to a group of young men reared in the land of Lee and Jackson. No longer was this only about how things were done in Dixie. It was about whether they had the guts to play. It was a question that the Southerners on the team simply could not ignore.

It was Hubbell who finally broke.

"Well," he finally said one afternoon in the gym, "maybe we just ought to go and find out who is better."

The others quickly agreed. The way forward had been found.

But pride and honor hadn't been the only reasons. For behind their decision to cross the color line was something else as well.

Located only a short bus ride north of Durham on what had once been a cluster of tobacco farms and rolling forest, what was officially known as the Camp Butner Military Reservation was a world unto itself. Scores of two-story wooden barracks housed more than thirty thousand military recruits. There, fresh-faced eighteen-year-olds who had been studying twelfth-grade English nine months earlier, twenty-five-year-old truck drivers and apprentice butchers, nervous young fathers and out-of-place country bumpkins would be molded into crack infantrymen. Camp Butner had its own obstacle courses and a full-size mock German village for what turned out to be nearly round-the-clock training drills, as well as commissaries and post exchanges, three swimming pools, five churches, and a handful of movie theaters.

The enemy was there, too. Hundreds of grim-faced veterans of Field Marshal Erwin Rommel's vaunted Afrika Korps, who had clashed with the British Eighth Army across the Libyan desert, would be housed at Butner, where they would be sent out on work crews to pick cotton, harvest peanuts, or work in tobacco warehouses. While some maintained their loyalty to Hitler to the end, others started up a black-market business with the colored tenant farmers and day laborers they worked alongside, trading soap powder for cash. Italian POWs were housed at Camp Butner, too, as well as thousands of non-Germans—Poles and Russians, Danes, and even Mongolians—who had been forcibly conscripted into the German army. When the first film footage of the liberated concentration camps was shown on the base, more than a thousand of the German prisoners voluntarily burned their uniforms.

Stretching across more than ten acres, Camp Butner was also home to one of the largest convalescent and general hospitals ever built by the United States Army. Anchored by a central administration building, the massive medical complex included more than fifty separate buildings, some linked by corridors that stretched for more than a thousand feet. The hospital had its own power plant and warehouses and hundreds and hundreds of hospital beds. At the front entrance, ringed by azalea bushes and daffodil beds, was a statue of a kneeling woman, a visitor from antiquity, pouring water from a clay jar into a large circular fountain. There, soldiers embarking for overseas would toss in pennies for good luck. So, too, did the wives and mothers of the men in the wards, mouthing silent prayers that their sons and husbands might one day be put back together again. This was the side of the war that didn't show up in newsreels.

Here, in row after row of hospital beds, were young men who could not see anymore, men who had lost both their legs, men whose lives had been irreparably shattered in combat. Here were burn victims and psychiatric cases, the shattered remnants of the once-green troops who had borne the brunt of the German counterattack along the Kasserine Pass in Tunisia or faced the machine guns and the eighty-eights at Anzio. Here were airmen whose shot-up B-17s, returning from daylight raids over Schweinfurt and Düsseldorf, had pancaked onto English runways before bursting into flames. Here was the real cost of the war, right here in North Carolina—the one the public rarely saw.

But the Duke medical students saw it all.

While their visits weren't frequent, perhaps once a month, they were sobering. "You'd see all these GIs, all these guys who were just about your age," Dave Hubbell later remembered. "It was a grim reminder of what was going on overseas." Not only was the severity of some of the cases unnerving, so was the sheer number of patients. "One time we went by bed after bed of GIs with trench foot, all of them with toes needing to be amputated. You just couldn't believe how many there were," he recalled. Other students were haunted by the burn victims, their facial features nearly obliterated, or by the foul stench of gangrene. These were days the medical students could not forget.

"On the bus rides home, nobody did too much talking," Lloyd Taylor recalled.

The visits to Camp Butner also reinforced a truth that they all by then knew deep in their guts, a lesson that wasn't in any of their textbooks or lecture notes. They had learned it in the ghost light of the surgical amphitheater, where sometimes even the strongest patients failed to pull through. They had seen it in the common wards and private rooms at the Duke hospital, in eyes that had lost their sparkle, skin that no longer held a healthy glow, and in numbers that were headed in the wrong direction on a patient's chart. They had learned it as well in the bright blue pen strokes of a mother's handwriting or the carefully folded newspaper clippings tucked inside a letter from home, informing the soldiers of classmates and neighbors who were reported missing and presumed dead on Guadalcanal, in Sicily, or in the nightmare skies over Germany. And they had learned it at Camp Butner.

Unlike most people their age, they had learned that they, too, were living on borrowed time.

Everyone in the car that Sunday morning knew this: one day in the not-too-distant future, each of them would find himself in harm's way, in an Army field hospital or a naval infirmary on the other side of the world. And one day after that, if they were lucky, they might find themselves on the tourist deck of a crowded troopship, headed for home.

But those days were not today. And right now, on this Sunday in March, there were chances to take, honor to defend, a ball game to play.

Dave Hubbell turned the car into the campus of North Carolina College and found the gymnasium. Then he killed the engine and stuck the key in his shoe. With the others, some of whom had pulled their jackets up over their heads in an effort to disguise themselves, Hubbell walked directly toward the small, copper-colored Negro man who was holding a clipboard and, it was clear, waiting for them.

"The man who let us into the gym locked the door behind us," Jack

Burgess recalled. Then the man led them to a small locker room smell-ing of old socks and cleaning fluid, where they changed into their uni-forms. When they were finished he walked them onto the basketball court. Aside from the other team—along with a referee, a young man sitting at the scorer's table, and a small girl sitting all alone in the stands, all of whom were colored—the gymnasium was completely empty.

The feeling was both eerie and uncomfortable, and most of the medical students wondered to themselves whether they had made a ter-rible mistake by coming there. Then a funny thing happened. Harry Wechsler, the walk-on from Pennsylvania who had played neither high school nor college ball and was by far the least experienced member of the Duke team, calmly walked up to the referee and, to the amazement of his silent teammates, asked which way they were going. The ref pointed to the goal at the west end. A couple of minutes later, the offi-cial blew his whistle, and the game was on.

John McLendon had not slept well the night before.

He had tossed and turned, got up and sat at the kitchen table, and wrestled, unsuccessfully, with the question of whether or not he had made the right call. If Dr. Shepard found out, he'd get fired—there was no question about that. And if the Durham cops, or the Klan, caught wind of what was going down, there was no telling what the consequences might be. They could all get arrested, beaten, or worse. His basketball career could end in a heartbeat. He had even fussed with himself about telling Alice, and when he finally did, her silence confirmed his nervousness. She was right, of course. Anything could happen. It was too late to worry about that. But the larger truth of the matter was that the two of them were already drifting apart, and he knew it. He also knew that he was to blame. He had given his all to do what he had done with the Eagles, and, as a result, he had not been an ideal husband. Basketball had consumed him.

The team was as well prepared as he could make them—of that he was confident. Despite what had happened in New York, and despite the fact that he was down, really, to his starters, this was the best outfit he had ever had. But when the team from Duke came to play, he would find out what that *really* meant. Even though he had watched the Jayhawks play again and again back in Lawrence, he was not immune to the lingering doubts that haunted colored coaches in those days. "There was always a little part of you that wondered whether you could really compete with them—white teams—or not. And until you did, there was no way to know," McLendon later recalled. As crazy as it might seem to later generations, most Negro basketball players during the 1940s had no way to know whether they could play as well as white players could—they'd never had the chance to find out on the court. The following day, the Eagles would find out.

Maybe, McLendon thought to himself before drifting off to sleep, he would take one of the kids with him. Alice might like that.

All morning on Sunday, Aubrey Stanley could feel his heart in his throat.

He could feel it on the short walk from the dormitory. He could feel it when he heard the car door slam. And he could feel it when the white players first walked into the gym.

His entire life, Aubrey had been warned to keep away from whites when you could, and when you couldn't, to watch what you said and did. What was more, you never knew when even the most innocent situation could turn ugly. Back in Beaufort one time, his church choir had set out on a trip to sing at a revival meeting in the next county. But along the way, one of the cars had a flat tire in a small village. While two of the deacons, with their coats off and their sleeves rolled up, were changing the tire, a young white boy, maybe five or six years old, rode up on his bicycle and stopped to watch what was going on. After a few minutes he looked at the deacons, then at the other choir members fanning themselves in the morning heat, and said, "This ain't no nigger town." Then he spat on the ground and rode away.

The truth was, danger was everywhere. Coach McLendon had even told them about a North Carolina College student, a young man who a few years earlier had been accused of looking improperly at a white woman downtown. "The police charged him with 'ogling,' which was a capital offense," McLendon had told them. If the student had been arrested, he could have ended up in the electric chair. "We had to sneak him out of town on a night train. He never came back to Durham again." Even in New York Aubrey had been nervous, especially in the subway and at Penn Station. The truth was, he had been taught all his life to avoid white folks, and never, ever, to touch one if you could help it.

Now he would be guarding one.

Aubrey picked the fellow with the glasses.

Big Dog wasn't worried.

As the only member of the Eagles to have ever played against whites before, he knew there were plenty of talented ones. Some of his teammates back in Farrell were tough as shoe leather, while during his brief stay in Toledo he saw enough of Bob Gerber, the Rockets' scoring machine, to know that talent came in all colors. Only that was up North. Here he hadn't given the guys from Duke a second thought, and in the dorm the night before he had boasted to his teammates how they were going to teach those crackers a lesson. Despite the bitter loss to Lincoln in New York and his struggles in New Jersey the next day, he was confident both in himself and in his teammates. But as soon as Dog saw the Duke team's backcourt in action—with their sly screens and no-look passes—his bravado suddenly evaporated.

Hot *damn,* he thought. These guys can *play.*

After the opening tip, the Eagles got off to a ragged start. Despite all they had endured that season, from the blistering workouts and their all-but-disappearing bench to crooked officiating and pistol-packing bus drivers, nothing had prepared them for this. And it showed.

Early on, the team from Duke went up by four.

Boogie and Aubrey both dropped routine passes, easy shots fell wide off the mark, and overanxious rebounding sent the ball out of bounds. Even the always cool Floyd Brown seemed lost as he brought the ball up the court after another score by the visitors. Instead of pushing the ball up quickly and firing a bounce pass to one of the wings, he kept glancing over at McLendon, looking for a called play. George Parks look confused, while Boogie even bounced the ball off his shoe.

The problem with the North Carolina College players, however, went beyond early jitters. Schooled by McLendon in his relentless pressure defense, and well experienced in the rough-and-tumble play of the Colored Intercollegiate Athletic Association, the Eagles opened the game by sagging off the Duke players, avoiding physical contact. Given the extra real estate, the visitors exploded to the basket, driving in for a layup or a quick pass or pulling up for a six-foot jumper. On their own floor, the Eagles were playing hands-off.

Duke by eight.

The exception was Big Dog. Double-teamed by their two big men, his was a game of pushes and shoves, sweaty arms and swiveling hips. He had faced this all season long, from their first game with the colored soldiers from Camp Butner all the way to his less-than-spectacular showing against the Orange Triangles. As usual, he was all fight. And while he had his hands full, Dog was holding his own.

But if the Eagles were going to beat these guys, he was going to need some help from the others.

McLendon knew that, too. Sitting on the home bench with his daughter, Querida, in the row behind him, McLendon said nothing. But inside he was dying. His players were behaving like islands. Worried about themselves and what they each could or could not do, they had broken the string that wove them all together, the one that had produced the greatest team that he had ever seen, much less coached.

They weren't playing like his team now. The Eagles were getting stomped.

This wasn't the outcome that McLendon had been waiting for. This wasn't the news that every colored college basketball coach in America, whose teams couldn't play in the NCAA tournament or in the NIT or in the doubleheaders at Madison Square Garden, wanted to hear—that even the best colored players just weren't as good as white players were. This wasn't the news that John McLendon wanted to hear, but out on the floor of the House of Good Sportsmanship, that was the message that was being sent.

Duke by ten.

Burgess had exploded from the start. Though these colored guys *looked* like players, he had reminded himself, you never could tell. No one who laid eyes on Kenny Sailors for the first time would have thought that the Wyoming guard was anything special, much less an All-American. The same with the Bighorn brothers back in Wolf Point. You could never know how good the other guy was until he showed himself out on the floor. But as soon as Burgess tested his own man, a short—and dark—guard wearing number 21, his concerns evaporated. Feinting right, then driving left, Burgess threaded a pass to Joe Walthall, making a backdoor cut while their big center got blocked by Thistlethwaite. This, the Montanan thought to himself, was going to be a good morning.

Burgess wasn't the only confident medical school player. Despite being taught all their lives that whites could never, ever, exist on the same societal level as Negroes, the Southerners on the team had adjusted much more easily to playing against a colored team than anyone might have imagined. Losing themselves in the game play, and being used to telling colored people what to do, they quickly took command. Dick Symmonds was his normal self from the start, while Dave Hubbell, more cerebral than impulsive, broke down the home team's defensive tendencies early on. While he and Thistlethwaite managed to pull down more than their share of rebounds on both ends of the court, they had their hands full with the colored center. It was a good thing, Hubbell decided, that they weren't all like him.

Still, it was going their way.

Midway through the first half, the medical students were up by a dozen.

Then it happened.

Near the end of the first half, a hard shove sent Big Dog crashing into one of the Duke players, knocking them both onto the floor with a loud, sickening sound. It was the kind of collision that, in a neighborhood pickup game, often resulted in a fight. And in Dog's case, he had already seen plenty. Back home in Farrell, there had always been fights after school, and sometimes fistfights would erupt on the football field. The thing was, you never wanted to go looking for one. But if someone was trying to push you around and wouldn't stop, you *had* to confront him. And once you had committed yourself, you had to go hard, and you had to go all the way. You also knew that the other guy knew this, too.

Dog cussed under his breath and pushed himself up by his palms, keeping an eye on the Duke center, who was slowly getting up, a small trickle of blood staining the right side of his chin. Big Dog would have his hands full with that one. But first there was another matter to attend to, as two of the Duke players were already moving his way, quietly curling their hands into fists. In an instant, the atmosphere inside the gymnasium turned menacing. The game, it seemed, was about to turn into a race riot.

Then the strangest thing happened, something the players would remember long after the game had finished and everyone had headed home.

The referee blew his whistle and marched over and grabbed the ball.

No foul was called. As the players got back into position, the tension quietly lifted. The game continued, just continued; all in a day's work. Pee Wee, sitting at the scorer's bench, couldn't believe it.

Game on. The Eagles were still behind.

Something, however, had changed. A subtle shift had taken place.

McLendon noticed it first. Dog's shoulders suddenly seemed more relaxed. Floyd Brown began to bring the ball up more quickly. And Boogie started to physically push back against the Duke players, breaking through screens, sticking a hand on their backs, and getting away with his usual assortment of hand checks, hip bumps, and ball slaps whenever he thought the referee wasn't looking. Even George Parks, the backup center on the North Carolina College team, started blocking out more aggressively. It was if the hard no-call had released something that had been trapped inside the Eagles, turning them into something they hadn't been all day. For the first time that morning, McLendon decided, his players were starting to play like themselves.

All, that is, except for Aubrey. Nervous to begin with, Aubrey, almost automatically, had been chilled to the bone by the near fight. It didn't matter that Coach was there or that his teammates were there or that they were within the confines of the college. Back in Beaufort, Aubrey had been taught time and time again to avoid any and all trouble with whites because, in the end, they held all the cards, whether you could see them or not. When he was younger he had been told that the body of a colored man had once been found lying in the weeds alongside the railroad tracks outside of Morehead City. The county authorities said that he was only a hobo and that he'd probably gotten drunk and had gone to sleep too close to the tracks. But the Negroes knew better. They said his throat had been slit. Now, even playing deep into a game against a group of strange whites, Aubrey still kept his distance.

Yet without him, the Eagles were slowly climbing back into the game. Urged on by Big Dog—C'mon, Boog!—Hardy had begun shaking loose of his man just long enough to hit Dog breaking for the basket or to peel off a quick give-and-go with Floyd Brown. At the other end of the court, North Carolina College was pressuring every Duke shot, and Big Dog and Parks were finally pulling down their share of rebounds. The Eagles had stanched the bleeding. But if they were going to cut into the other team's lead, McLendon was going to need some kind of miracle. And he was going to need it soon.

Crazy Horse heard them first.

Sitting all alone on the Eagles bench, lost in his own thoughts, he had heard the knocking, faint and distant, beyond the usual noises of the game—the ball bouncing, sneakers squeaking, and the players shouting plays to one another. With it, he thought, came the brief metallic rattling of the knob to a locked door being quickly turned one way and then another. None of it lasted very long. But someone was trying to get inside the gym. That Horse knew for certain.

Before he had a chance to consider who it was and what they wanted, he saw them. The first one appeared, suddenly, like a black sun, along the bottom pane of one of the far windows. Then, a few minutes later, came another, then another after that. Horse couldn't recognize any faces, but he could tell that they were all cupping their hands alongside their temples. By reducing the glare, they were trying to better see just what on earth was going on inside the gym on a Sunday morning.

McLendon had done his best to keep the game quiet. He had not, of course, informed Dr. Shepard or any of the other teachers, and he'd asked the referee, whom he paid out of his own pocket, to keep the matter strictly to himself. McLendon had asked the same of his players, but there were some things that he simply could not control. Hardly any of the faculty members—and of course none of the students—at North Carolina College owned automobiles in those days, and the appearance of a strange car, a late-model Packard at that, parked by the gym was enough to stir up some curiosity all by itself. But Big Dog had done some publicity work on his own. Despite McLendon's admonitions, Dog had not been able to resist making some cryptic comments in the dining hall the night before about "something big" taking place in the gym in the morning. When pressed to explain, he had suddenly turned close-mouthed.

You'll find out, was all he had said.

That had been enough. By late in the first half, word had started to spread on campus that something was indeed going on over at the gymnasium. But when the first handful of North Carolina College students arrived to investigate, they discovered to their surprise that all the doors were locked. They rattled the doorknobs and pounded on the glass, but nothing happened. Hearing the sounds of a ball bouncing and sneakers squeaking, a few of the braver ones finally shimmied themselves up onto the window ledges and, cupping their eyes against the glare of the late morning sun, looked inside.

They could not believe what they saw. Nor were they alone. For as the morning wore on, more and more heads began to appear in the windows, wide-eyed witnesses to an unimaginable, brave new world.

The Duke medical school team led by eight at the half.

Playing their game, they had easily switched back and forth between what passed as called plays and their more usual freelance approach. Led by either Burgess or Joe Walthall, theirs was a cat-and-mouse affair of cuts and dribble drives, weaves and screens, a search for that precise moment when, for a split second, one of the players on the other team lost his man or bit hard on a ball fake. Patient, almost scientific, it was a game of opportunity. And while Hubbell and the others did not take lots of shots, they hit a high percentage of those they did take. As the players sprawled out in the visiting team's locker room during halftime, the talk drifted, as it usually did, toward sandbagging.

Man, you see the one I got?

You can have mine if you want.

All y'all is crazy. Twenty-two is quicker than a hot knife through butter.

But beneath the chatter ran a chorus of confidence. They had this one, and they knew it.

The same could not be said next door. Most of the time, McLendon knew what he was going to tell his team at halftime well before a first half ended. He would always have a list of player-specific suggestions to go through, tendencies he'd noted, little things that could be exploited. But psychology played a big role in his halftime pep talks as well. In truth the talks were always easier on the road. There you could always appeal to the players' sense of justice, how they needed to overcome shady officiating and abusive fans, how in the face of adversity they needed to stand tall. It was trickier at home. Most of the time the team was plenty keyed up to begin with. If you pushed the defending-our-home-court angle too hard, their emotions might get in the way of sound play. But nothing had prepared McLendon for this.

So he took a chance.

Reasoning that all his players needed no reminders that they, in effect, were playing for every Negro team in America, he turned his halftime talk into a coaching clinic: Boogie, he said, the dark-haired one almost always fakes right twice, then spins left, when he's got the ball in the key. Floyd, try driving low on Eyeglasses, then pop up for a lob to Dog. McLendon talked switching defense and pressuring their inbounder and trying to do a better job getting their break going in the second half. What was a dangerous, emotion-laden experiment had been transformed, within the walls of the home locker room, into little more than a regular-season game.

Inside, of course, McLendon was overflowing with anxiety. But this was something that you could never, ever show. Calmly, he walked the team out onto the court and then, this time, joined Querida up in the stands. It was up to them now. A few minutes later, after a brief shoot-around, the referee blew his whistle, and the second half began.

Twenty minutes to go.

Epiphanies don't run on timetables. They aren't printed on calendars or maps. They travel on their own schedule and arrive when and where they are supposed to—be it on a rocky patch of road near Damascus, beneath an English apple tree, or in a raft on an ink-black night on the Mississippi. Aubrey Stanley's came on the North Carolina College gymnasium floor about two minutes into the second half.

During the previous seven months, ever since he had arrived at the college, he had gone more places and done more new things, it seemed, than he had during the rest of his entire life. In Beaufort, Aubrey had never met anyone like Coach McLendon—or Big Dog or Pee Wee or Dr. Shepard or most of his classmates. His own mother had barely been outside of Carteret County, while he had seen the Capitol in Washington, looked up at the Empire State Building, ridden in a subway, and traveled, by Greyhound, into the heart of the Appalachians. His world was bigger now. Though he did not know it yet, Aubrey was no longer the same young man who had arrived at the Durham bus station half a year earlier. He had changed.

Perhaps his biggest change would be the one that happened out on the floor of the gymnasium that Sunday morning.

"All of a sudden, it hit me," he later recalled. "These guys weren't supermen," he realized. "They weren't some master race or machines or something like that. They were just a bunch of guys. Like us."

It happened in a heartbeat. On the surface, Aubrey did not look any different from the way he did before. But on the inside, he would never be the same again. His transformation was just what the Eagles needed. No longer an island, no longer holding back from throwing his body into the game, not frozen by what could happen if the wrong people found out about the game that morning, Aubrey had an explosion of his own. Fresh off his insight, he started driving straight at the other team's center and forwards, hooking in layups and stealing the ball right off the dribble on defense. Fed the ball by Boogie at the top of the free-throw circle, he shook his man and whipped a behind-the-back pass to Floyd Brown along the baseline. Driving between two defenders, he kissed a layup off the right side of the backboard, then slapped the ball out of the hands of one of the Duke guards near the midcourt line when they brought it up and scored two more. With Dog rooting him on—Over here, Stinky!—and the others watching in open-mouthed amazement, Aubrey launched an offensive the likes of which they had never seen before.

Three minutes later, the game was tied.

But Aubrey was only getting warmed up. And whatever he had, it was contagious. Inspired by his fearlessness, Aubrey's teammates stepped up their own play as well. Now it was Floyd Brown and Boogie flashing to the wings, skirting along the edge of the end line, launching one-handed jumpers or driving ahead for a reverse layup. Now it was Big Dog snatching loose balls, manhandling defenders, and firing off half-court baseball passes to Boogie or Aubrey on the break. Pee Wee, sitting all by himself at the scorer's table, had never been so busy.

Ten minutes to go.

The Eagles by ten.

For the Duke medical school team, what began so promisingly in the first half quickly fell apart in the second. Suddenly all their regular plays—the give-and-go's to Hubbell or Symmonds, the backdoor cuts around Thistlethwaite, Burgess popping back for a Kenny Sailors–style one-hander—began to sputter and stall. Routine passes were stolen midair. Rebounds started falling into the wrong hands. And try as they might, they just couldn't move the ball downcourt quickly enough. Even worse, close-in shots by Hubbell and Symmonds were rattling out, while Jack Burgess, who with his collection of feints and stutter steps had handled his man with ease for the first twenty-odd minutes of the game, found himself getting scorched on nearly every possession. Comfortably ahead at halftime, the medical students had their hands full in the second half.

Only there was something else bothering the team as well. For what the Duke players simply could not fathom was that as the half wore on, their opponents only seemed to go faster. They had never faced a team like this. Never. Ever. Even the ref got winded.

Who the hell are these guys? Burgess wondered.

Then, gritting his teeth and giving a quick nod to the others, Jack Burgess took the handoff below the Duke basket and started driving toward the midcourt line. This wasn't over, he thought to himself. Not now. Not yet. Burgess made a quick shovel pass to Symmonds near the top of the key, exploded past his man, and drove toward the basket.

Only it *was* over.

The second half ended in a blur. "They shellacked us," Dave Hubbell recalled. The Eagles had gone on such a run of unanswered points, played so true to the form they'd established and built on all season, that the final score was North Carolina College 88, Duke medical school 44.

The South's first integrated college basketball game was history.

No one expected what happened after that.

After a water break, and after the teams spent a few minutes catching their breath, Aubrey walked back out on the court alone, picked up a ball, and began shooting fifteen-foot set shots. A dozen or so shots later, Burgess joined him, feeding Aubrey the rebounds at first, then, as the two players began to talk, trading shots while their teammates watched. One by one, some of the others drifted down as well. Finally even Dog and Thistlethwaite, the two big men, who each had been stretched out on a bleacher, came down. Then George Parks had an idea.

You all want to play again?

Everyone agreed. Only this time, it was different.

Mixing their players together, with white and colored players on each side, the two teams played a game of shirts and skins. This time it was Burgess feeding Big Dog in the low post, Hubbell kicking out to Aubrey on the break, and Boogie sending perfect, high-arcing lobs to Thistlethwaite beneath the basket. With the early afternoon sunlight slanting in from the north windows of the gymnasium, this was a contest that wasn't being played for honor or glory. It wasn't about opening doors or righting old wrongs. This, until the first team made twenty-one, was a battle staged for stakes no higher than the love of the game itself.

"It was just God's children horsing around with a basketball," George Parks said.

McLendon, however, had missed the beginning. Off with Pee Wee in his office, where they'd tallied up the team and individual player statistics for both the Eagles and the visitors from Duke, he had been completely oblivious to the second game until he emerged several minutes later. Rather than stop the game that was then in progress, McLendon took a moment, watching, then walked up into the stands. Sitting down next to Querida, he soon had a bird's-eye view of what was going on. What he saw amazed him.

For what was going on was much more than a simple game of shirts and skins. Negro and white, Northern and Southern, textbook plays and school-yard moves: there, all jumbled together like a child's wooden puzzle, were bits and pieces of Phog Allen and Hank Luisetti, of hotshot Indiana farm boys and colored stars whose fame never reached outside the pages of the *Journal and Guide* or the *Pittsburgh Courier*. There were plays that he could diagram in his sleep and moves that he had only read about, made by teams that he would never see. There was even old Naismith, watching those kids in that dusty playground back in Lawrence, getting to the heart of it all. For down on the court, in fits and starts, a whole new kind of game was stirring to life.

Down on the floor of the North Carolina College gymnasium, in the House of Good Sportsmanship, it was all coming together, adding up to nothing less than the future of basketball.

McLendon wasn't the only one who had been amazed.

For as the day had worn on, more and more North Carolina College students, in groups of twos and threes, had steadily made their way over to the locked gymnasium, hoping to find out what was going on inside. "Man, they were *everywhere*. Standing on buckets and chairs and ladders. There must've been fifty or sixty of them out there," Pee Wee recalled. The first ones who had come, standing on the window ledges and peering down onto the gymnasium floor, had been shocked by what they had seen, a *white* team playing against their Eagles. But the late arrivals, the ones who came during the second game, were in for an even bigger surprise. For this was an even bigger violation of Dixie's racial code.

"I'm pretty sure Floyd Brown's team won," Aubrey later recalled.

No one remembered the score. But anyone who saw either game, whether from inside or outside the gym, would never forget the sight. On a spring Sunday in North Carolina, in a locked gymnasium, Jim Crow had not been invited. The only lines on the court were made of paint.

The day was not over yet.

Enlisting the help of Lillian Davis, the school dietician, McLendon had quietly arranged for a postgame reception for the two teams to be held in the men's dormitory. Cookies and punch and even a few ice-cold bottles of Pepsi-Cola were set out, while the players for both schools, back in their street clothes, had an informal bull session. Much of the talk, not surprisingly, centered around basketball, particularly the Eagles' season and their misadventures in New York. The North Carolina College players were especially interested in hearing from Dave Hubbell what it was like to play basketball at Duke. But other subjects were kicked around as well, including what kinds of classes everyone was taking, and what it took, schoolwise, to become a doctor. It was all pretty lighthearted, and the Duke students lingered much, much longer than anyone had planned. Afterward they took a tour of the dormitory. Everyone, it seemed, had a good time.

Well, almost everyone. Because in order to use the men's dorm, Miss Davis had to inform Mrs. Washington, the dormitory matron, who had hurried over from church, clutching her Bible as well as her handbag. During the tour, she didn't say much. "She made a point of telling us that she made all of the boys wear bathrobes whenever they were out in the hall," Dave Hubbell remembered. But aside from that, she spent most of the get-together keeping an eagle eye on Big Dog and Pee Wee, a sour expression firmly fixed on her face.

It was nearly dark and starting to rain by the time the Duke students got up to leave.

The Packard pulled away into traffic that stayed light on the way home. Not a police car in sight.

Together, the two teams had pulled it off.

Or at least they thought they had.

For what they did not know was that among the people looking through the windows of the gymnasium earlier that afternoon, there was one who wasn't merely watching. He was also taking notes.

CHAPTER 20

———

"Did You Hear About…"

The next day, Monday, March 20, 1944, dawned cool and overcast. In the *Durham Morning Herald*, wire-service bulletins reported that more than one thousand British and American bombers, flying in rapidly changing weather conditions, had attacked Nazi munitions factories, airdromes, and rail yards in Germany, Austria, and occupied France. Along the bomb-shattered moonscape near Monte Cassino in Italy, military dispatches announced that New Zealand and Gurkha infantrymen were flushing out the last of the German defenders, while in Romania, the Red Army had crossed the Dniester River along a thirty-one-mile front, pushing ever closer to Bucharest. Four thousand miles away, in Burma, the Associated Press reported that Lieutenant General Joseph Stilwell's combined Chinese and American troops were digging in and that a major Japanese counteroffensive was expected within days. In German-occupied Greece, meanwhile, the SS had launched an intensive new campaign to identify and arrest any Jews they had missed in previous roundups. The new detainees were informed that they would be temporarily relocated to a special work camp. Instead they were loaded onto boxcars and taken to Auschwitz.

It would be one of the deadliest years in human history.

In basketball news, both the NIT and NCAA tournament would

be kicking into high gear that week, with no less than seven double-headers at Madison Square Garden and at Municipal Auditorium in Kansas City. Dartmouth, DePaul, St. John's, and Kentucky were considered to be the front-runners. Nobody gave much of a chance to the University of Utah, a freshman-heavy team that had played against only three college teams during the regular season. Instead they won the sixth NCAA championship tournament and, after that, defeated the NIT champion, St. John's, in a benefit game for the American Red Cross.

There were no newspaper reports of what had happened in the North Carolina College gymnasium on Sunday. Nor were there any the following day or the day after that.

Louis Austin, the editor of the *Carolina Times,* didn't give a plugged nickel about sports. Whether talking on the phone in his office on Fayetteville Street, sitting at the dinner table at home, or following the leads for a story on the sidewalks of Hayti, he had other things on his mind. There were too many other things to do, too many battles to fight, and too much white hypocrisy to expose. Colored men were still getting murdered by bloodthirsty mobs, Negro women were getting disrespected on public transportation, and despite all its high-and-mighty pronouncements about the war being fought for democracy and the Four Freedoms, the government of the United States had a Jim Crow head, Jim Crow hands, and a Jim Crow heart. But Austin also knew that in order to tell those stories in the pages of the *Carolina Times,* he needed to sell some papers. And if covering Negro athletics helped him meet his own circulation benchmarks, then he had no problem whatsoever setting aside some column inches, and sometimes even a couple of pages, for sports news in each issue. By reading reports sandwiched between outrage and church news, his readers could keep abreast of CIAA title races, how many rounds it took Joe Louis to finish off his latest challenger, and whom the Eagles played next.

But by early 1944, Austin also faced a problem that was familiar to newspaper publishers across the country—namely, that most of the stringers who reported on sporting events for him were by then in uniform. To replace them he had patched together a loose network of replacements, part-time reporters who telephoned in scores or wrote up accounts of football and basketball games. While all of them were pretty green, some were noticeably better than others.

One in particular was outstanding. Though he was only nineteen, Lin Holloway had an ear for news. In fact he'd grown up surrounded by it. His father owned the Bull City Barber Shop, while his mother worked across town at Duke. If there was a hot scoop floating around town, it was more than likely passed—along with biscuits, cornbread, butter beans, and Brunswick stew—around the family dinner table at their home in the East End. A good writer with an inquiring mind and a lively, nonchalant style, Holloway had been snatched up by Austin when he was still a student at North Carolina College. At the *Carolina Times* he was both the sports editor and the author of "Around the Town," a column that covered everything from football games to entertainment news.

It hadn't taken Holloway long to smoke out that something was going on at the gym the day before. Perched up on one of the window ledges, furiously writing in his reporter's notebook, he had seen enough on Sunday to know that he had one hell of a story. Not only would Austin love it, it would also definitely get picked up by the colored wire services. Not just a front-page story, it might also be the scoop of a lifetime. But even though he was still a teenager, Lin Holloway knew that if the story ran, there would be a price to pay—and he knew who would pay it. For when the next edition of the *Carolina Times* came out, a copy would make its way over from the newspaper department of the state library to the state board of education. A couple of phone calls later, Dr. Shepard would summon Coach McLendon into his office and fire him on the spot.

"He would have to," Pee Wee later recalled. "Dr. Shepard wouldn't have had a choice."

It was too high a price. Holloway tore up his notes and didn't say anything to his boss. As far as the *Carolina Times* was concerned, the game never happened.

Over at Duke, the medical students had mostly kept the plans for the game to themselves, and now that it was over and they had been beaten, there was little incentive for talking about it. Inside each man, however, it was another matter—especially for the Southerners. It wasn't just that they had been whipped by a colored team. That part was obvious. But it was also the rest of the day—spending time on the campus and in the dormitory, talking to the players and, especially, their coach, who had gone to Kansas and knew Phog Allen and even Naismith. What's more, he seemed to know what you were thinking before you said it. These weren't the kind of Negroes they were used to.

"Oh, I wonder if I told you that we played basketball against a Negro college team," Jack Burgess wrote to his folks back in Montana. "Well we did and we sure had fun and I especially had a good time for most of the fellows playing with me were Southerners and boy they were none too hot on it at first and when the evening was over most of them had changed their views quite a lot on the negro problem."

It was a start. Here, on a spring Sunday, was the beginning of something new.

At North Carolina College, though, the contest briefly took on a life of its own. Stories of what had happened quietly made the rounds in the dormitories, bringing soft whistles of wonderment, while practically anyone who had been involved experienced a brief moment of glory. For the next few days, Pee Wee discovered that it wasn't quite so hard to bum a smoke at the College Inn, while Aubrey suddenly found himself returning the hellos of female classmates who never seemed to have noticed him before. Even Crazy Horse basked in the glow of a newfound esteem.

As the spring of 1944 ended, word of the game leaked out here and there in Durham. Not many people found out, and not everyone believed what they heard, but the game was no longer an ironclad secret. News of what had happened did make the rounds at Minnie Hester's, where it elicited wry smiles and grunts of approval, and it hovered, briefly, over the dinner table at the Holloways'. At Duke, some of the nurses were cut in on the secret, as were a handful of fellow medical students and roommates. And after the college basketball season ended, rumors of the game circulated along the local basketball grapevine.

"Did you hear about..." was how it'd usually begin.

Talk of the game also made its way down the road to Chapel Hill, where members of the Cloudbusters, the top notch Navy pre-flight team at the University of North Carolina, also heard that there was some newfangled kind of ball being played at some colored college in Durham. As a result, all summer long, carloads of white basketball players from UNC quietly drove over to North Carolina College, looking for a pickup game in the gym. Impressed by what they faced, some of the Cloudbusters, during the next couple of years, would begin taking bits and pieces of McLendon's techniques back home with them to New York, Philadelphia, and other cities.

And finally, word of the game seemed to have made it to the Durham draft board. In early June, right after graduation, McLendon was informed that his exemption from the draft—based, in part, on the fact that he taught swimming, lifesaving, and first aid at North Carolina College—had been canceled. Ten days later he found himself on a bus bound for Fort Bragg, the sprawling US Army base outside Fayetteville, in the eastern part of the state. His coaching days were over, at least for the time being. Although he was still in his twenties, part of him felt like an old man among the other recruits, many of whom were still in their teens.

Near the end of his first week in uniform, on a burning hot afternoon, McLendon was ordered to report to one of the large Quonset huts located near a Negro mess hall. Inside the sweltering building

Forty-First Engineers, Fort Bragg, North Carolina. *(National Archives)*

were scores of colored soldiers, packed in all the way to the back. When McLendon walked inside, a white officer handed him a tattered, grade-school spelling book and informed him that he was to teach these men how to read. McLendon nodded, but inside he was stupefied. He had never done anything remotely like this.

As he stepped up onto the makeshift stage, however, and looked out upon the sea of silent, eager faces, an unexpected calmness swept over him. Walking over to the portable chalkboard, the former basketball coach hesitated a moment. Then, raising his right hand in the stale air, with the eyes of scores of former sharecroppers, trash haulers, kitchen help, and day laborers intently following his every move, John McLendon slowly began to write A, B, C, D on the board. Later, while the sun pitched over the horizon, flooding the hut with a pinkish glow, he began to sound out the soldiers' first written words.

d-o-g. Dog.

c-a-t. Cat.

m-a-n. *Man.*

It did not last.

In the middle of that very night, while he slept in his bunk in the barracks, McLendon suddenly awoke to a strange hand shaking his shoulder. The hand belonged to a white corporal, who gruffly whispered for him to get dressed and gather his belongings. Once they were outside, in the damp night air, the corporal stopped and turned toward McLendon, facing him straight on.

"Just *who* in the hell do you know?" he said.

A few hours—and signatures—later, McLendon was a civilian again. They had him on a bus back to Durham by dawn.

As the midsummer sun rose behind him, flooding the countryside with copper and gold, John McLendon found himself wishing that his players were with him. He would have liked that. And there was something else he would have liked as well. For by then he knew what he should have said to that white corporal.

"Shepard," he'd have told him. "Dr. James E. Shepard."

News of McLendon's return to North Carolina College was welcome back in Hayti—or at least it should have been. For by the end of the summer of 1944, one local story had swept up the attention of practically every colored person in Durham.

It had begun on July 8.

By the time the number 5 bus rounded the curve and began making the long climb up the hill toward Fayetteville Street, the windows of the Lucky Strike plant were ablaze with the last fire of the summer sunset. There was still plenty of light left, and even though it would be a good half hour before most of the downtown cafés switched on their electric signs, the driver of the bus, a nervous, rail-thin thirty-six-year-old man named Lee Council, could already feel the darkness creeping up the back of his neck. Later on, in court, it would come out that he had already been reprimanded not once but twice that year for drinking on the job. But none of his passengers that evening, not even the deaf and mute girl who seemed to have noticed everything else, could say for sure whether the driver had liquor on his breath. What was known for certain, however, was that on the evening in question Lee Council had a nickel-plated .38-caliber revolver holstered along his right thigh, there for the world to see.

All day long the number 5 had rattled back and forth across town. Beginning in Hayti, the Negro district, it had rumbled past the colored shops along Fayetteville Street and the shanties and tobacco warehouses off Pettigrew. Crossing the Southern Railroad tracks, it then rolled downtown, stopping near the banks and department stores on Main Street. At Five Points, the bus turned north, through the elm- and magnolia-lined streets where the city's white gentry lived, before coming to a halt at Watts Hospital, on the edge of town. There the driver would turn the bus around and begin retracing his route. All day long, with whites sitting up front and colored in back, the number 5 passed in and out of Durham's separate but adjacent worlds, hauling tobacco stemmers and housewives, maids and mill workers, and soldiers and airmen on three-day passes.

The early evening was quiet. The day shift at the cigarette plants had ended, and the Saturday shoppers, clutching their parcels and fanning themselves in the sweltering heat, had already gone home. The nighttime crowd, the people who lined up outside the air-conditioned Carolina Theatre or swayed to the dance bands down at the armory, was still to come. After them, though, would come the people whom Lee Council dreaded the most: the drunks and the delinquents, jacked up on bootleg whiskey and looking for a fight. Bus drivers in Durham weren't armed for nothing.

On this day, though, the trouble began in Colored Town. An old man, probably a janitor, got on by the Negro college, and a young couple boarded near the colored hotel. All the new riders moved quietly to the rear of the bus. But five blocks later, at the corner of Ramsey and Pettigrew, a Negro woman, her young son, and a colored soldier climbed on board. After dropping their coins in the fare box, these riders all sat down at the *front* of the bus, on the bench seat opposite the driver. At first Lee Council didn't say anything. By state law, whites were to sit in the front and colored in the back, but there weren't any white passengers yet. When the bus crossed the tracks and turned onto Main Street, however, he told them to move. They weren't in Hayti anymore.

The woman and her son quickly moved to the back of the bus. But the soldier, Private Booker T. Spicely, who was stationed at Camp Butner just outside of town, did not. After hesitating for a moment, he moved only partway back, muttering—it was said—something about a 4-F, someone who was judged to be physically or mentally unfit for military service. Three blocks later, at Five Points, when a group of white passengers got on board, the driver angrily ordered the soldier to move all the way back. Private Spicely, however, did not move at all. Instead he started talking with two white soldiers who had sat down nearby.

"I don't see why I have to move back," he told them. "In Pennsylvania, we pay our fare and sit where we please."

The soldiers agreed. The driver did not.

"Shut up or get off the bus," he said.

"I thought I was fighting a war for democracy," Spicely replied. "But it looks like it doesn't work that way down here."

"I don't care what you say or like," the driver said. "If you don't like it, come and get me."

Hurtling through the tunnel of trees along Gregson Street, with the sound of the cicadas rising and falling through the open windows, the precisely ordered world of the number 5 bus was about to explode.

Twenty-nine years old, Booker Thomas Spicely was a cook turned military truck driver. And while he stood more than six feet tall and weighed close to one hundred and eighty-five pounds, he knew, as the bus neared the end of the line, that the stakes had become very high. So did the driver, Lee Council.

"If you want anything," the driver said, "come up front and get it."

"You come back here," the soldier shot back, "if you want to see me."

"Come up here. I've got something that will cool you off."

But when the bus pulled to a halt along Club Boulevard, near Walltown, the small Negro neighborhood that bordered the hospital, Private Spicely suddenly changed his tone. "If I done you any harm, bus driver, I beg your pardon," he said. "I didn't mean any harm with what I said."

The soldier walked off the bus and onto the sidewalk.

Lee Council followed him. Then he raised the .38 and pulled the trigger.

The first bullet smashed through the soldier's rib cage and lodged in his chest. When Spicely doubled up and began to turn away, the driver fired again, hitting the soldier in the back. Hearing the shots, neighbors poured out of nearby houses. And while someone quickly called the police, no one bothered to run across the street to the hospital. It was for whites only.

A few minutes later, a police cruiser pulled up, and the two officers knelt down beside the soldier and loosened his shirt and tie. Then, as Lee Council got back on board the number 5 bus and began driving back to the carbarn, Private Spicely looked up at the darkening North Carolina sky, slowly bleeding to death on the warm, soft grass.

The trial began on a Wednesday, nine and a half weeks later. Lee Council wore a silk necktie and a pin-striped suit. Charged with second-degree murder, he sat quietly at the defense table. Across the aisle, three private attorneys, one white and two Negro, who had been hired by the friends and family of the deceased, sat next to the state prosecutor. The judge in the case, Luther Hamilton, was an experienced jurist and had already been praised in the local press for his integrity and unwavering sense of fairness. "Fortunately," the *Durham Morning Herald* declared, "we live in a city where justice may be guaranteed." Despite the heat and the fact that the trial was held during working hours, the courtroom was packed.

It took all day to select the jury. As with practically every criminal trial held in the South in those days, the jury pool was composed entirely of white men. In the end, four mechanics were selected as jurors, along with three farmers, two men who worked at a local knitting mill, a night watchman, a used car salesman, and a florist. Judge Hamilton admonished the twelve not to discuss the case with anyone. The next day, however, the morning papers published each of their names. That way everyone in town would know exactly who they were — and how they voted.

Eighteen witnesses gave testimony.

Carrie Jackson recalled how Private Spicely had boarded the number 5 bus with her. "He helped my little boy put a watermelon on the bus," she said. Two white Army corporals, both of whom were also stationed at Camp Butner, testified to the conversation between the bus driver and the soldier, while other eyewitnesses, both white and colored, filled in pertinent details. Mary Anne Williams, the deaf and mute girl, described the actual shooting in sign language, while an interpreter read aloud her remarks to the judge and jury. Patrolman R. H. Barnhill, one of the first two police officers to arrive at the scene, attested to the powder burns on Private Spicely's uniform, while a white physician testified to the cause of death. "There were two jagged wounds in his body, one on the left side and one near the stomach," the doctor said. "One bullet went through the man's Army dog tag."

The third day of the trial opened with closing arguments. The prosecution recounted, step by step, the events of the fateful evening and appealed to the jury's innate sense of justice. "He that ruleth over men must be just ruling in the fear of God," said one of the prosecuting attorneys, quoting 2 Samuel, chapter 23. The defense focused, instead, on the North Carolina statute that prohibited mixed seating on public transportation, a copy of which had been posted in plain sight on the number 5 bus. "It is only by the unruly and unlawful," the lead defense counsel declared, "that this law is disobeyed."

After a ten-minute recess, Judge Hamilton spoke to the jurors for nearly one and a half hours, carefully explaining to them both their duties and responsibilities. "The law of North Carolina is supreme," he said. "Justice recognizes no creed, races or social standings. Equal justice must be done for all." Then, after carefully reviewing all the evidence that had been presented in court, Judge Hamilton added, "The bus driver is empowered to eject from the bus anyone causing trouble, but he does not have the right to take the life of a violator. It is up to you, gentlemen, to determine whether Council's life was endangered to the extent that he was forced to use his weapon as he did."

It did not take long for the jury to decide.

After twenty-eight minutes of deliberation, they found the driver to be not guilty.

When Lee Council heard the verdict, he let out a big sigh of relief and smiled. As the Negro observers filed quietly out of the room, groups of whites came up to the driver and shook his hand. But the prosecuting attorneys remained seated. "It was as if they had not heard," a reporter later wrote, "while hearing."

The jury's message was loud and clear: there would be no more crossing of the color line. And if you did you took your life into your own hands. The world might be changing, but segregation wasn't.

CHAPTER 21

Look Away

The Eagles were never all together again.

Boogie took off for Chicago, while George Parks rode a Greyhound bus all the way out to Los Angeles. Some ended up in uniform, others didn't, but most of them shared one thing in common. In one way or another, they were finished with the South.

For Big Dog, the game against the team from Duke marked, in a way, the beginning of the end of his Durham days. He played one more year at North Carolina College, a war-shadowed season during which the Eagles lost only two games, both to Morgan State, who won the CIAA basketball title for the first time in more than a decade. Dog played like a gladiator in the first contest, scoring twenty-five points, but he failed to connect in the second, forcing McLendon to frequently replace him, one reporter wrote, with "waves of green reserves." But there was also something else hovering nearby, a dark cloud that sapped his strength and dulled his spirit. In the team photograph for the 1944–45 season, the old devil-may-care Dog was no longer there. In his place was a tired young man with a forced smile and worry lines etched beneath his eyes.

He had reason to worry. There had been a young woman, it was said, from the mountains. A student at North Carolina College, she had, like others, fallen under his spell. But one day during basketball season, she had a message for Dog. Her period had stopped. It didn't matter that she wasn't showing yet. Shepard would find out. It was all over, and Dog knew it.

And so, one morning before the end of the spring quarter, Big Dog packed a bag, went downtown to the train station, and bought a one-way ticket to New York. For a couple of years, he played semi-professional basketball in New Jersey with the all-colored Orange Triangles, whom the Eagles had played after they lost to Lincoln in the Renaissance Ballroom. He earned a few brief mentions in the sports columns of the Harlem papers, only to once again slip from view. He kept up with Pee Wee, though, and once, back in the early 1960s, even came down to Durham for a weekend visit, driving a Cadillac.

"It was just like old times," Pee Wee remembered. "I never laughed so hard in my life."

Later Pee Wee learned that there were car dealerships in the North where Negroes could rent fancy automobiles for visits back home. "Dog always said that he was going to come back one day, but he never did." Pee Wee, meanwhile, stayed in Durham, and much to the displeasure of his future father-in-law he and his Ruth got married and started a family. Pee Wee also had a long career in recreation, working with young people, and following the fortunes of the Eagles. He kept up with McLendon, too. "Mac was the greatest man I ever met," Pee Wee later said.

Crazy Horse stayed as well.

But his world continued to unravel. His family had tried one doctor, then another and another. But as the months went by, Horse's behavior grew more and more irrational. McLendon tried to help, too. When his former player expressed an interest in his days as an Eagle, McLendon lent him a box of materials about the 1943–44 season. But that didn't work, either, and Horse was taken to the hospital one morning for psychiatric observation. Big Dog had been wrong. Horse hadn't been faking anything.

McLendon rushed over to the small rented room off Dunstan Avenue where Horse had been living, but by the time he got there it was too late. Everything that McLendon had lent him—his playbook, the mimeographed game rosters, and, most important of all, the official game registers and score sheets—was gone. The landlord told him that he would ask the other tenants if they knew anything about any books or papers, but nothing ever came of it.

Aubrey lingered longer than most.

He played three more years at North Carolina College, blossoming into a dazzling guard with a golden shot. But during the summers he didn't go back to Beaufort. "I was looking around to find a way to put some money in the pot," he later recalled. "And friends of mine had been doing the resort circuit." With the help of a classmate, he headed up to Rhode Island, where he got a part-time job waiting tables at the Ocean House, a fabled resort in Watch Hill. On their days off, Aubrey and some of the other members of the all-colored waitstaff started playing pickup games against other teams, including whites. A couple of times they'd even pooled their tip money to go into New York, playing back-to-back games in Brooklyn and Harlem. Aubrey had also gotten to know the owner and manager of Ocean House, who offered him a full-time position.

Inside, however, the wheels were turning. Then one day it was his turn. Not long after the close of the 1947 basketball season, Aubrey left as well, riding two Trailways and one Greyhound all the way to New York City, to a new life in a new home. He never graduated. The truth was, Aubrey was done with school, done with signs, done with segregation. Though he was a Tar Heel born and bred, there was no place in North Carolina for someone like him. Not anymore.

Aubrey had lost his place.

*   *   *

The former Duke players, meanwhile, found theirs.

There had been talk, for a time, of playing a second game against North Carolina College, but it never happened. Yet even though Burgess and some of the others would probably have welcomed a return engagement and a chance to get even, the Duke chapter of the YMCA had already set its sights elsewhere. Anticipating the birth of a new kind of American society in the postwar world, some of the members began to call for Duke to begin to accept Negro students. It would be a long fight.

After their game against the Eagles, the Duke medical school basketball team lasted two more seasons. Led by Hubbell, Walthall, and Burgess, they pummeled a hodgepodge of military teams, factory clubs, and, once again, intramural outfits. In late January of 1946, they even got their photograph in the *Durham Morning Herald.* As they stood for the photograph clad in their surgical whites, theirs were the smiles of the dawn of the postwar age, the faces of young men who made it through the war all in one piece. By then, of course, regular peacetime college sports had returned to the nation's campuses. College basketball teams no longer played games against military teams, who, as it turned out, were soon forgotten. Many colleges and universities, however, had taken the lessons of basketball's wartime popularity to heart. At many schools where the student population was augmented by large numbers of war veterans studying on the GI Bill, there was talk of bigger field houses.

To a man the Duke med school players went on to long, successful careers in medicine, some especially so. Dick Symmonds ended up at the Mayo Clinic, where he became a renowned authority on abdominal surgery. Dick Thistlethwaite became a White House surgeon during the Gerald Ford administration and was one of the doctors who operated on Betty Ford's breast cancer. Their hurry-up wartime training under Dean Davison had served them well.

After a brief stint in Lexington, Kentucky—where a friendly

janitor let him sneak into the Alumni Gymnasium in order to watch Adolph Rupp run basketball practice with the Wildcats—Jack Burgess finally went home to Montana. He got married, set up a family practice in Helena, and, together with his wife, Donna, started a family. Though his politics, unlike those of his decidedly eco-friendly children, grew more conservative as the years went on, he became the gruff and much-beloved patriarch of a large family. And while he remained true to the University of Montana Grizzlies, he was a Duke fan as well.

"Tell Coach K that I still have a year of eligibility yet," he once told a reporter.

Burgess died in 2003.

Dave Hubbell outlasted nearly all of them. He ended up in St. Petersburg, Florida, where he became a well-known and well-respected thoracic surgeon. Not surprisingly, he was a devoted fan of the Blue Devils, but another passion from his youth followed him as well. Over the years he put together an impressive collection of first editions of Mark Twain, including his personal favorite, a pristine copy of *The Adventures of Huckleberry Finn*. And while he never joined the front lines of the civil rights movement, some of the lessons of the game against North Carolina College weren't lost. During the 1960s Hubbell quietly helped to desegregate a medical dinner by taking a black doctor with him as his guest, while in later decades his regular tennis partner was African American. "It had an impact on my thinking," he later said of the game.

Not all of them, however, told the whole story. After Harry Wechsler passed away in 1996, his daughter, Laura, could never quite understand what her father had done. "Daddy always talked about playing basketball, but we could never figure out what it meant," she said. "He did, though, have this gold basketball charm with '1944' engraved on it. We were never sure what it was all about."

Although a second secret game never happened, something else did.

Late one fall night, eight months or so after the game, the driver of a Durham city bus got into a heated argument with one of his white passengers over the color line. "They pay their money just like anyone else," the passenger, a Duke medical student, argued, just as the bus rolled to a stop in front of the Duke chapel.

"Why the heck can't they sit where they want? Why—"

The bus driver had heard enough.

Setting the parking brake, he pulled a large knife from his back pocket and unsheathed the blade. Then he took off after the student, who had bolted out the back door. According to an eyewitness, the driver kept up a brief pursuit but eventually had to call off the chase. On the war-darkened campus, it was too difficult for the driver to see clearly, and the student managed to slip into the shadows.

In time, of course, they would all be forgotten. In an age of monster slams and multimillion-dollar shoe contracts, of integrated professional leagues, year-round conditioning, and even eighteen-year-olds who became household names all over the country, there was little room for stories about military basketball squads or about teams and coaches that never made it to the Big Dance.

But for those who actually saw the players of the war years, the memories would not so easily fade.

One winter Sunday afternoon in the 1990s, more than four decades after his days at North Carolina College, Aubrey Stanley met a friend in a quiet corner bar in Harlem. By all outward appearances, Aubrey was a New Yorker, with a home in Queens and a long career working at the Morgan General Mail Facility of the United States Post Office in midtown Manhattan. Inside, however, he was still a North Carolinian, and he was already working on a campaign to convince his wife, Bertie, that they should move back to Beaufort. "Things are different now," he'd tell her. "They've changed there, too." Bertie was skeptical, and the issue would remain unresolved. In his immediate future would be first one visit, then many others, to the Memorial Sloan Kettering Cancer Center. Aubrey would never live back home in North Carolina again.

But for the time being, those concerns still lay ahead. His friend, who had worked as a businessman, confided that he was thinking about changing his career, while the conversation, as those of old men are likely to do, changed seamlessly from sports to spouses to grandchildren. Outside it was starting to snow, but within the quiet warmth of the bar the two men slowly nursed their Seven and Sevens and reminisced about the past. During the course of the chat, another patron — a stranger, also black, about Aubrey's age — dropped by their table and introduced himself, and Aubrey did the same.

"*Aubrey* Stanley," the stranger said. "Man, that sure do sound familiar."

But after a few unsuccessful attempts to make a connection, the man bade them good-bye and headed out the door.

Forty-five minutes later, he was back. His cap and shoulders were dusted with snow.

"I walked all the way home, fifteen blocks," he told them. "But I couldn't get it out of my mind. Then it hit me. Now I know who you are. You're *Stinky*. Stinky Stanley. Man, nobody could play like you." Then he was off once more.

For Aubrey it was better than the thousand cheers that he never had a chance to hear at Madison Square Garden, better than the newspaper stories that were never written, the stories that were never told, maybe better than anything. Decades after he'd played, sitting with a friend on a snowy New York afternoon, he received a validation of all he and his teammates had done, all the games they had played, in the days of long ago.

Even back when he was still an Eagle, he could tell that change was in the air.

The game he had known was already changing.

*　　*　　*

Boogie hadn't planned on staying long in Indiana. Just a quick mid-summer visit to Gary to see his family before taking a new job in the fall. His younger brother Richard was working a regular shift at National Tube, while his mom and stepdad were still living in the same house he had lived in as a child, next to the Pilgrim Baptist Church. By then the house was cramped with cousins and boarders. One Saturday afternoon when he was home, dressed in jeans, a T-shirt, and sneakers, Boogie went looking for a basketball game. Before, when he was in his teens, he would simply walk to his alma mater, Theodore Roosevelt High School. Boogie had a talent for persuasion, and he could almost always coax the janitor or maybe one of the coaches to let him and his buddies inside.

"Boogie was half saint and half con man," Pee Wee once said.

But Boogie's old high school gym was no longer the place to be. For by the last, anxious summers of the war, if you wanted a game of basketball, a *real* game, you headed over to the Delaney Community, the new Negro housing project just west of the park, which had opened in 1940. There, on a concrete-slab outdoor court, was where the action was.

Three hours to the south, in Indianapolis, it was the same story.

While the Tigers of Crispus Attucks High School were still the pride of the Negro community, a new kind of basketball fever had taken root there as well. Ground zero was Lockefield Gardens, a massive, 748-unit housing project that the federal government had constructed on the site of an aging slum on the city's northwest side. Unusually spacious, with ample lawns and sidewalks connecting the new tan-and-brown brick buildings and rents hovering near twenty dollars a month, the Hoosier capital's first housing project was the prime destination of hundreds and hundreds of colored families from Alabama, Mississippi, and Tennessee who had ridden the rails and bus lines north on one-way tickets and a prayer, hoping to find jobs in the defense plants.

But it was also in Lockefield Gardens, on a set of outdoor basketball courts that would soon be known as the Dust Bowl, that their teenage sons would stage their daylong roundball battles, scuffing their cheap, war-issue sneakers across both concrete and hard-packed dirt. In the evenings, after quitting time, some of the men would join them, playing until you couldn't see the ball anymore. Back home, in the South, there were plenty of places to play baseball, along with creeks to fish and woods to go hunting in. But in Indianapolis, practically in the shadow of the Soldiers and Sailors Monument, it was all basketball.

It was the same down in Shelbyville, a prosperous furniture town thirty miles to the southeast, past the corn country that stretched along both sides of State Road 29. The colored population in Shelbyville had never grown large enough to necessitate the building of a separate, all-Negro high school. But Booker T. Washington Elementary School, a dilapidated, gymless structure that had been condemned thirty years earlier, had one of the few outdoor basketball courts in town. There, on August nights and frigid, ice-blown January weekends, the sons of Shelbyville's small colored population were beginning to create their own spin on the Hoosier State's civic religion.

One afternoon the previous fall, two former Shelbyville High School stars, one who was on leave from the Navy, challenged a couple of the local youngsters—including a tall but baby-faced fourteen-year-old named Bill Garrett—to a game of two-on-two. The two older men no doubt thought they would make quick work of the youngsters, but early in the game, Garrett shot past his man and, spinning like a ballet dancer, laid in a quick one-handed reverse layup. A couple of minutes later, while being blocked out for a rebound, Garrett simply leaped higher than his opponent, and, coming over the top, snatched the ball out of his hands.

"Damn," one of the men said.

"Guess we been away a while," his partner replied.

The same thing was happening all over the country.

From South San Francisco to Chicago, from D.C. to New York, a whole new generation of Negro youth, most of them recent migrants from Dixie, had taken to basketball as never before. Lost in the shadow of the war, they had no coaches, no uniforms, and no team names. No reporters recorded the results of their all-day hoops battles, no statisticians compiled their shooting percentages. But on concrete-slab courts set among modest duplexes and four-unit apartment buildings, or on scraggly, weed-rimmed Negro school yards and playgrounds, they had become basketball's artists, innovators, and mad scientists. Armed with the new, inexpensive, all-rubber balls that had just begun to show up in dime stores and hardware shops, they played an unorthodox, inventive game that was focused, most of all, on who had the ball.

"It was art," recalled Chet Walker, who grew up playing basketball in a housing project in Benton Harbor, Michigan. "It was theater."

For some the game was a way to make a name for themselves in a strange new land. For others it would be a way to survive. And for a few it would be a way out.

John McLendon stayed at North Carolina College for eight more seasons, winning games, conference championships, and the lasting esteem of his fellow residents of Hayti. The Eagles' home games became so popular, in fact, that fans started to come to the gymnasium hours ahead of the game, camping out in the stands with paper sacks filled with sandwiches and fried chicken. Word of what McLendon was doing at North Carolina College had finally spread beyond the confines of the Colored Intercollegiate Athletic Association. In the spring of 1950, one of his players, a guard from Kansas City named Harold Hunter, was one of the first three Negro ballplayers to sign a contract with a new professional basketball league. In truth, however, nobody knew whether the new league, which called itself the National Basketball Association, would survive or not.

McLendon's marriage to Alice, meanwhile, did not.

Nor, in the end, did his job.

After Dr. Shepard passed away in 1947, leadership at the college shifted, and priorities changed. During the spring of 1952, under pressure from the state, the new president of North Carolina College announced that all athletic scholarships would be canceled. McLendon objected, and students planned a sit-down strike, but there was, in fact, little he could do. By the end of the summer, McLendon had resigned.

What followed was a rich and eventful career. In 1954, after a brief stint at the Hampton Institute, McLendon landed at Tennessee State, whose president, Walter S. Davis, was unlike any college administrator he had ever met — or would ever meet. Shortly after arriving in Nashville, McLendon was called into Davis's office.

"You've got to win, but I want you to know that I'll help you any way that I can," Davis said.

McLendon thanked him, then mentioned something about doing the best he could.

The Tennessee State president shook his head.

"You don't understand. You've *got* to win. If you don't, you're gone."

Fortunately, win was exactly what McLendon did. Not only did the Tigers capture four Mid-Eastern Athletic Conference tournament titles, they also won the 1957 National Association of Intercollegiate Athletics basketball tournament, becoming the first Negro college to win an integrated postseason championship tournament. Occurring the same spring that an all-white University of North Carolina team defeated the Kansas Jayhawks, led by Negro sensation Wilt Chamberlain, for that year's NCAA crown, the NAIA championship was potent evidence that as far as basketball was concerned, the old racial order was slowly dissolving. Southern politicians would still cling to all-white schools, neighborhoods, and lists of registered voters for a few years yet, but on the basketball court, it was increasingly becoming all about the game.

McLendon, not surprisingly, was a barrier buster all his own. At Kentucky State, where he coached for three seasons after leaving Nashville, McLendon was the first colored coach to successfully recruit, and play, a white player at a Negro college. At Cleveland State in 1965, he became the first black head coach at a predominantly white institution. On behalf of the Department of State, he also took teams of young American basketball players on tours overseas. In one memorable contest, his players were so much larger and more athletic than their opponents that during one hectic fast break, McLendon's point guard, rather than dribble around a defender, leaped over him instead. In 1968 he became a member of the coaching staff for the US Olympic basketball team at the Mexico City summer games. A year later he had a brief tenure as the head coach of the Denver Rockets in the American Basketball Association.

But being ahead of your time has downsides as well. For during his prime as a basketball coach, most doors had been closed to him. Then, as more and more of the nation's most talented black high school players began playing for predominantly white schools, the competitive level of basketball played at historically black schools began to decline. Despite his genius, in the last decades of his working career there weren't a lot of secure, top-level opportunities for John McLendon in the new world of college basketball, a world he had helped to create.

McLendon died of pancreatic cancer in 1999. And while a handful of national newspapers ran an obituary, the truth of the matter was that when McLendon left the earth, he was far more forgotten than remembered—though he was not forgotten by all.

Fifteen years earlier, in 1984, when Georgetown won its first NCAA championship, Hoyas coach John Thompson was approached by a television reporter.

"How does it feel to be the first black coach to win a national basketball championship?"

"I don't know," Thompson replied. "You'll have to ask John McLendon."

During the last years of his life, McLendon had no time for regrets. Along with teaching classes on sports history at Cleveland State, he

maintained an active and regular schedule as a leader of coaching clin-
ics. Most were held at out-of-the-way recreation centers or in low-
ceilinged church basements. Many were a long way from Ohio. And
while he rarely received anything more than gas money, McLendon
would also rarely turn an invitation down.

Once, two and a half years before he died, he even drove his aging
Dodge Caravan all the way to Springfield, Massachusetts. In a neighborhood gymnasium located not far from where James Naismith had invented
basketball, McLendon put on a free clinic for a group of local ten-year-
olds—white, African American, and Hispanic, girls as well as boys—
demonstrating for them the seven kinds of layups and the five kinds of
passes. "You don't have to watch it," he gently informed one anxious child
trying to master the art of the dribble. "It'll come back to you." But to the
parents sitting on the sidelines, McLendon's message was far larger.

"Principles," he declared without even a hint of self-consciousness,
"are timeless."

Some of the parents fidgeted in their seats, while others returned
blank looks to the elderly figure dressed in workout clothes. "Now, who
is this man, again?" one mother whispered to another. "I don't know,"
came the reply. "I think he used to play in the NBA or something."
Soon, however, the majority of the parents had quit paying attention
altogether. Most were reading or talking on their cell phones.

It did not matter. For out on the gymnasium floor, surrounded by a
dozen young faces, John McLendon had an audience all his own. Listening intently to everything he said and watching his every move,
they, too, soon forgot about where their parents were or how long it
would be before they had a snack or when they were going home.
Together with the old man, they had become lost.

Lost in a game.

Dr. Shepard never mentioned the secret game. If he knew about it—
and there was very little on campus he did not know about—he said

nothing. Either way, however, the campus that he presided over for so long, like the South itself, was changing. And eight months after the game, in the fall of 1944, he got a foreshadowing of what that new world would be like.

A man of practical inclination, Shepard had long relished bringing well-known speakers to campus, white as well as Negro. Not only would they generate publicity and expose his students to important perspectives of some of the leading men of both the South and the nation, it was also a way for him to expand his contacts, raise money, and, in particular, protect the funding he had already carefully secured. So along with writers and statesmen and religious leaders, Shepard made sure that white North Carolina politicians regularly spoke to the student body at North Carolina College.

Clyde Roark Hoey was one. With his snow-white hair, striped trousers, high-topped shoes, and an ever-present red carnation pinned to the left lapel of his swallowtailed walking coat, Hoey would have looked at home in a Currier and Ives print or maybe a Thomas Nast cartoon. The son of a captain in the Confederate army, he had left school at age twelve to take a job in a Cleveland County print shop. Five years later he bought his own newspaper, and four years after that, in 1899, he was elected to the state legislature. A teetotaler who drank as many as a dozen bottles of Coca-Cola every day, he was the epitome of an old-school Southern politician, a yellow dog Democrat who once declared that the Lord would never lead him into the Republican Party. A spellbinding orator—"When he got through you weren't sure what he said, but it was beautiful," one confidant remarked, while another observed, "He just took the Bible and wrapped the American flag right around it"—he was wildly popular among North Carolina voters. A former state legislator and US congressman, he was elected governor in 1936. Eight years later, in 1944, he was elected to the United States Senate, carrying ninety-seven of the state's one hundred counties.

Not long after that, he spoke at North Carolina College.

Held in the B. N. Duke Auditorium, Hoey's address was attended by the entire student body. "You had to go," one undergraduate recalled. "Every seat had a number on it, and you were assigned to a particular one. If you didn't show up, Dr. Shepard would know." For Shepard, this was a tremendously important day, one that was ripe with promise. As governor, Hoey had steered precious state funds toward North Carolina College. As an incoming United States senator, he could open even more doors. Hoey, for his part, had spoken in the auditorium before. Indeed, six years earlier, he had helped dedicate the building. This time, it would be different. For as the former governor began his address, something extraordinary happened.

It had to do with the word *Negro*. Hoey pronounced it "Nigra." And whenever he did, students began rubbing the soles of their shoes on the auditorium floor. At first it was just a few. But by the fourth or fifth time, the scraping and rubbing filled the auditorium and began to drown out the speaker. Dr. Shepard furiously bolted upright in his chair and glared out at the students, but the scuffing did not stop. And as the senator-elect droned on about Nigra schools and Nigra leaders and Nigra progress, there could still be heard the sound of shoe leather being scraped across the auditorium floor, like the first whisperings of a rising wind.

EPILOGUE

B ig Dog shall have the last word.

Before he left town for good, Dog had one last piece of business to attend to.

It was a year after the game. The evening started as it usually did, with Dog and Pee Wee paying a visit to Minnie Hester's joint. "Minnie's was hopping!" Pee Wee later recalled. There were tobacco stemmers and maids rubbing shoulders with mill workers and salesmen for the Mutual. It being the spring of 1945, the mood inside was upbeat. Jobs were plentiful, Hitler and Tojo were on the run, and you could even find a bottle of genuine bonded bourbon every once in a while. Better times, it seemed, were just around the corner. And though each was about to lose his running buddy, both Dog and Pee Wee kept the conversation light and easy. "Man, they gonna have you in jail before the week is over," Pee Wee said teasingly to Dog, who was leaving Durham early the following morning.

When they finally left Minnie's and started to make their way back to campus, however, Big Dog once again led Pee Wee on a detour to the maintenance shop. But this time, instead of shovels and brooms, they stole a couple of paintbrushes, a flat-head screwdriver, and a can of green paint. Then they headed over to the main gate of the college, along Fayetteville Street, where they popped open the can of paint, grabbed their paintbrushes, and got to work. A few minutes later, the school had a new name. For a world that had always told them who they were, what they could do, and where they should be, Big Dog and Pee Wee had some news. From that moment on, they would decide that for themselves.

Instead of NORTH CAROLINA COLLEGE FOR NEGROES, the sign on the gate now read, simply,

NORTH CAROLINA COLLEGE

Late the following afternoon, well after Dog had caught his train, the Spanish instructor at the college, Mr. Holmes, discovered a speck of green paint on one of Pee Wee's sneakers. But they never found the paint or the paintbrushes, and Pee Wee denied everything. Even though it was only a couple of weeks until graduation, many on the faculty felt that Dr. Shepard should have expelled him on the spot. But in deference to Pee Wee's mother, who worked at the colored orphanage in Oxford and whom Dr. Shepard had long admired, Pee Wee was only kicked out of the dormitory.

Until it all blew over, McLendon let him sleep in the gym.

Afterword

The Ghosts of Jim Crow

One October afternoon more than half a century after the primary events in this book took place, I set out across a stretch of southern Virginia countryside, driving along the back roads of Amelia and Nottoway Counties. Even though I wasn't far, mileagewise, from the western suburbs of Richmond and Petersburg, with their apartment complexes and fast-food restaurants, this was still farm country, as it had been for more than three hundred years. Indeed, it was also part of the oldest America. Slaves from Angola, Benin, and Senegambia had once worked the same fields that whooshed by the car windows at fifty-five miles per hour, as did farm laborers, servant girls, and apprentices from Bristol, Cornwall, and London. Word of the great declaration in Philadelphia had once traveled along these same fields and woods, as did the news from Long Island, Trenton, and Yorktown. And it was just west of here, in a brick farmhouse along the old Richmond–Lynchburg highway, where Generals Grant and Lee put an end to the first, and longest, chapter in the nation's racial drama. Along these same roads had once walked bluecoats and graycoats as well as newly freed slaves, looking ahead toward an uncertain future.

I pulled into a rural mini-mart, set off by itself among fields of corn and soybeans. Inside, a couple of hunters were comparing wing-shooting techniques while a static-heavy broadcast of an NFL game faded in and out from a beat-up portable radio on the counter. I paid for a fill-up, squeegeed a fine layer of dirt off the windshield, and was on my way again, just another anonymous traveler on an autumn afternoon. The roads themselves—shining beneath a bright blue October sky, dotted with only a handful of small clouds—were practically empty. And with the oaks and elms still holding their leaves in this last bit of Indian summer, the day had a timeless, eternal feel to it.

It should have.

After all, I was looking for a grave.

In Blackstone, an old colonial stagecoach stop, I turned off the main road by the Pizza Hut and worked my way east, stopping to read a Commonwealth of Virginia historical marker about an African American training school set up in the early 1900s. A couple of minutes later, I reached the entrance to the Greenview Cemetery, marked by two redbrick columns, each topped with a handmade crucifix made from sections of two-inch lead pipe, painted white. An empty twelve-pack of Coors Light and a couple of bald tires rested nearby on the pine-needled forest floor. I parked my car and got out. Aside from a knot of sparrows chattering nearby and a light breeze pushing through the tall stands of oaks and pines, I was all alone.

It took a while to find.

Walking past decades-old mausoleums, now cracked with age, brand-new laser-cut granite monuments, and homemade grave markers, with bits of colored glass pressed into their hand-poured concrete, I finally spied a solitary government-issue military headstone, tilting slightly forward, next to a small palmetto plant. Time had taken a toll on its marble surface, which had grown powdery and rough, while the edges were streaked with mold. But its inscription was still legible.

†

BOOKER T. SPICELY

V<small>IRGINIA</small>

PVT

3712 Q.M. Truck Co.

World War II

December 1, 1909

July 22, 1944

He had not died a forgotten man. Not here.

Not in Durham, either.

For weeks after the trial, printed stickers that simply read REMEM-BER appeared in shop windows and on front doors across Hayti, while Louis Austin vented his rage in the pages of the *Carolina Times*. The white bus driver, Austin declared, might have gotten away with the murder of a Negro, but he would be "the last one." Meetings were convened, letters were written, and a new spirit of defiance made its presence clear. But there was something beyond these actions as well. For even though Booker Spicely may have only been in Durham once or twice, a deeper connection had been forged. *He* had taken the bullets that could have been meant for *them*. Though his body was laid to rest beneath the pines and oaks of his native Nottoway County, part of him would live on in Hayti. He was theirs now as well.

I stood there for a few minutes, listening to the wind in the pines, when something that George Eliot had once written came to mind. "That things are not so ill with you and me as they might have been," she wrote near the end of *Middlemarch,* "is half owing to the number who lived faithfully a hidden life, and rest in unvisited tombs." It seemed to fit. Like Big Dog and Aubrey, Burgess and Hubbell, Ernst and Marianne Manasse, Shepard and Austin, and even McLendon himself, they were all part of their own lost generation, men and women who had paved the way for bigger changes and helped create a new America. Booker Spicely was theirs, too. And ours.

But did anyone still remember?

Did anyone still care?

For if the secret game was a shining moment in the history of the segregated South and a forgotten story worth telling, then the murder of Private Spicely was the other side of the coin, a tragedy that was also worth telling but one, I feared, that was already becoming forgotten.

As I turned to walk away, something caught my eye. Partially hidden at the base of the marker was a sun-bleached artificial flower, its plastic-covered metal stalk, now a dull olive drab, nestled among the grass and lichen. It wasn't much. But it was there.

On the way to the car, however, it suddenly struck me that my journey wasn't over yet.

Out of the blue, I realized there was another place I needed to see.

A place that, until that moment, I would have never visited on my own.

But now I had to.

Simple and unadorned, Martha's Chapel sits alongside a gently winding two-lane state road out in the country, some thirteen miles south of Durham, just across the Chatham County line. Painted white, with clear glass windows, a boxlike tower, and a plain green roof, it is a Southern country church at heart, more Greek temple than cathedral. Though the church was founded more than two centuries earlier by a former circuit-riding minister, it has kept up with the times. The church website advertises Martha's Chapel as an ideal place for weddings— boasting of "the elegance and romance your special Wedding Day deserves"—while the accompanying set of photographs from one ceremony shows a handful of African Americans sprinkled among the white wedding guests. On the late Tuesday afternoon when I visited, however, the church was empty. A handful of cattle regarded me from their side of a nearby fence, but beyond that I was once again all by myself. I parked my car and walked over to the cemetery in the back.

Here, the headstones hinted at larger stories.

Stillborns and octogenarians; a woman born in 1793; a man named after President Wilson; children who lived less than one week. There

was also the grave of a Confederate soldier: PVT PASCHALL MULHOL-
LAND, CO E, 5 NC INF. And threading through them all were family
names as old as this part of North Carolina.

Morgan. Horton.

Family plots spanning decades, even centuries.

Fearrington.

Weathered obelisks with old-fashioned hand-cut lettering, fading
fast.

Mangum.

Large central markers with small satellite stones that simply read
MOTHER or FATHER.

Council.

After that it didn't take long to find what I was looking for.

A low granite slab, set horizontally, it simply read HERMAN LEE
COUNCIL, FEB. 4, 1908–JAN. 24, 1982.

The second of five children born to a farmer, he had been a mill
hand as a young man, working for scant wages among the spindles and
lung-choking dust at the Erwin Cotton Mill No. 6 in Durham. When
Lee Council got married, at age twenty-nine, he and his wife had to
live with her parents in a clapboard house on the city's north side. But
when the war came—and with it, a manpower shortage—he got his
chance and was hired as a bus driver by the Duke Power Company,
who operated the city's bus lines. With a wife and four children, he
considered it a path out, a way ahead.

The murder, and the trial, ended that.

By 1947 Lee Council was back in the mills, working as a cleaner for
Golden Belt Manufacturing, makers of tobacco bags. That didn't last,
either. And for the next decade he bounced from job to job. He tried to
make it as a salesman for Royal Crown Cola, drove a bus in Chapel
Hill, returned briefly to Erwin Mills, and worked as a floor checker for
a company that sanded and installed flooring. None of them panned
out. Neither did his marriage. He got divorced at age sixty-three. He
died in a nursing home eleven years later.

"That thing," one of his relatives once told me, "ruined his life."

Perhaps.

He had, after all, killed an unarmed man in cold blood—and gotten away with it.

But there was another truth about Lee Council, one that I tried to make sense of as I stood uncomfortably by his grave. Because in the end he had been a victim of segregation as well. Jim Crow had laid its malodorous hand on his shoulder, too. It had poisoned his mind, blinded his eyes, filled his ears and mouth with salt, and, for one murderous moment, crushed his humanity.

And like it or not, he was one of ours, too.

"We must love our enemies," Martin Luther King Jr. once said, quoting Scripture. "The darkness of racial injustice," he added, "will be dispelled only by the light of forgiving love."

Standing in the small Southern graveyard, I thought it seemed like an awfully tall order.

What would forgiveness look like?

Who deserved to have it?

And where, in a rapidly changing America, did one even begin?

I stood for a few minutes longer, hoping to hear an answer.

But as I walked back toward the car, with the October sunset shimmering through the stand of pines behind the church graveyard, the only sound I could hear was that of the late afternoon traffic, commuters from Raleigh and Durham and Chapel Hill, rushing along the two-lane state highway, trying to get home before dark.

Acknowledgments

It can take an army to write a book. Mine was pretty big.

Here are some of the folks who helped along the way.

The first, of course, was John McLendon. We met, fittingly enough, at the Basketball Hall of Fame in Springfield, Massachusetts, only a few blocks from where James Naismith first tried out his new game. But it was in Cleveland Heights, Ohio, sitting at the kitchen table of the home he shared with his wife, Joanne, that he first told me about the secret game. And it is because of his earnestness, his deep passion that the past be preserved, and his unmatched generosity of time and spirit that this book exists. He was a true giant, and it was an honor to have known him. Thanks, Coach.

Equally important were those who either took part in — or helped to create the conditions for — the secret game, as well as their families and their friends. Not only did they agree to talk with me about a long-buried piece of their past, but they patiently explained how basketball was played during the Depression and World War II, spoke openly of their experiences in the 1920s, 1930s, and 1940s, and painted an intimate portrait of their day-to-day lives in segregated America. They spent endless hours with me on the phone, dutifully answered letters, invited me into their homes — and walked straight into my heart. Thank you Aubrey and Bertie Stanley, Pee Wee and Ruth Boyd, Jack and Donna Burgess, Dave and Barbara Hubbell, Lloyd and Barbara Taylor, Dick Symmonds, George Parks, and Ed Johnson. Thank you as well to Charlotte Sieber, Helene Wechsler, Laura Broff, Clavis Ballard,

Skip Thomas, William "Buckethead" Harris, Larry B. Harris, and the family of Dick Thistlethwaite.

There were others. John Hope and Aurelia Franklin, George and Mary Stewart Manasse, Alex Rivera, Leroy T. Walker, William Styron, Bob Seymour, Robert Durden, Floyd K. Hill Jr., Milta Fulford, Laura "Sissy" Smith, Inez Jackson, Harry Boatner, Bobby Hammond, Rudy Hammond, Johnie Bloodsaw, and Helmut Stern all helped to make this book, as did dozens of North Carolina College and Duke alumni from the 1930s and 1940s, including Edith Stanford, Sam Shepard, Mabel Wright, Hubert Robinson, Bill Malone, Rosemary Johnson, Clifford Jenkins, Roy D. Moore, Ethel Lineburger, Carter Smith, John L. Powell, Mahon Elliott, Roy Bell, James Allan Knight, and Art Jaffey.

Thanks are in order as well for all of the former basketball coaches and players who not only took time for interviews, but also helped me better understand how basketball was played in decades past, including John Wooden, Frank McGuire, Pete Newell, Aubrey Bonham, Clarence E. "Big House" Gaines, Dean Smith, Arthur Lloyd Johnson, K. C. Jones, Hal Perry, and Bill Esposito. I also owe a debt of thanks to the late Ian Naismith, and to the Naismith Museum in Almonte, Ontario.

I've also benefited from the generosity, professionalism, and care of archivists, librarians, historians, and sports information officers from Montana to New Jersey to North Carolina. Andre' D. Vann and Brooklyn McMillon at the North Carolina Central University Archives provided essential help and information, as did Valerie Gillispie, Amy McDonald, and Bill King at the Duke University Archives, and Jolie Braun at the Duke University Medical Center Archives. Hats off as well to all the talented people at the Southern Historical Collection and the Wilson Special Collections Library at the University of North Carolina at Chapel Hill, the Durham County Library, the State Archives of North Carolina, the Spencer Research Library at the University of Kansas; to Cheryl Smoot of the Stey-Nevant Public Library in Farrell, Pennsylvania; and to Joanne Retone, Verna Smith, and Joanne Lloyd of the Farrell Area High School.

This book also owes its creation to all of the friends who, over the course of years and years, lent vital support in more ways than one. Thank you Hilary and Ethel Lipsitz, Jean Stephens, Bill and Nancy Ellsworth, Debbie and Louis Stalsitz, Larry and Nell Goodwyn, Michele Giguere, Patty and Gary Himes, John Fawley, Alice O'Connor, Jim and Melanie Pearson, Jane Vessels, Barbara Griffith, Rachel Mason, Charlie Hill, Cliff and Linda Cronk, Lane Tapley and Steph Munro, Kathy Hoblitt, Sue Dorn, Mike Reddy, John Sauerman, Steve Yarbrough, George and Harriet Bodner, Constance Strawn, John Van Meter, Linda Eklund, Dana Tapper and John Akin, and Bill and Kathy Tuttle. My deepest thanks as well to the Reverend Dr. Fairfax F. Fair and the wonderful staff and congregation at the First Presbyterian Church in Ann Arbor, Michigan.

Although it was written in three different states, the truth of the matter is that *The Secret Game* is a product of North Carolina. It was at the Duke Oral History Program and at the Southern Oral History Program at the University of North Carolina that, as a graduate student in my twenties, I first learned the skills necessary to write this book. It was in a rented office in an old house on Rosemary Street in Chapel Hill that I finally reached David Hubbell on the phone, the first member of the Duke medical school team that I made contact with. It was in North Carolina libraries, living rooms, and front porches, and along North Carolina highways, that this book, written by a two-time North Carolinian, came to life. And it was in Durham where the writing began in earnest. So thank you, all you talented and thoughtful North Carolinians who have supported this book over the years, including Bill Chafe, Raymond Gavins, Wesley Hogan, Tim Tyson, Lynn Richardson, Bridget Booher, Bob Bliwise, and my dear friends Dan Whittle and Jane Harwell, upon whose seven-foot American chestnut dining-room table in Carrboro significant portions of this book were written.

In Portland, Oregon, thanks are in order for that city's astonishing community of writers, including John Strawn, Larry Colton, Ellen Heltzel, and Kim Stafford. I'm also grateful for the top-shelf work done by Carol Studenmund, Jonas Hinckley, and Leah White at LNS Captioning in Portland, who transcribed my taped interviews.

In Ann Arbor, I've benefited from the help and support of another great team of writers, including Victoria Johnson, Jim Tobin, John Bacon, Randy Milgrom, and Jennifer Conlin. At the University of Michigan, special thanks are in order for the incredible staff at the Hatcher Graduate Library, perhaps the greatest library that a writer could ever want, to Kelsey Kennedy, John Wei, Felix Feng, Steve Gradwohl, Stephanie Clark, Mitch Rosenwasser, Carrie Fediuk, and to the superb students, staff, and faculty in the Department of Afroamerican and African Studies. Ruth Miller of the Greenhills School helped to translate some key documents written in German.

In New York, a tip of the hat to Wayne Lawson, Neil Amdur, and Heather Mitchell.

Whoever said that the golden age of editing is dead never met John Parsley, my editor at Little, Brown. I can't thank you enough, John, for all that you've done. The same can be said for Michael Pietsch, Reagan Arthur, Heather Fain, Morgan Moroney, Ben Allen, Malin von Euler-Hogan, and all the spectacular people at Little, Brown and Company and at Hachette Book Group, as well as for my world-class copyeditor, Barbara Clark. Thanks for making dreams come true. Ditto for David Larabell, my literary agent extraordinaire, for David Black and the great folks at the David Black Agency, and for the indomitable Jeff Jacobs at the Creative Artists Agency.

Two to go.

The first is to my oldest friend, Lee Elementary School classmate, and fellow writer, Craig Ryan, and to his wonderful wife, Kathy Narramore. You guys are simply the tops. Thank you for coming along for the ride.

Finally, the biggest thank-yous belong to my spectacular wife and kids, who have lived with this story for a long time. This book is theirs too. Trust me on this.

Betsy, I couldn't have done it without you. P.S. We sold the book.

Johnny and Will, thanks for putting up with all those weekends that I was gone.

Oh yes, one more.

Cameron, our Welsh Corgi, assisted my writing production by waking me up at 5:57 a.m. every single morning of the week for the past three years. Thanks.

Sort of.

Notes

CHAPTER 1: *Aubrey*

The primary source materials for this chapter are the taped interviews, letters, and notes from telephone conversations that I conducted with Aubrey Stanley, both in Durham and in Queens, New York. Aubrey's wife, Bertie Stanley, and their children also provided substantial information, as did his half brother Floyd K. Hill Jr., his childhood classmate Milta Fulford, and his cousins Laura "Sissy" Smith and Inez Jackson, whom I interviewed in Beaufort and Morehead City. Through their generosity and precise memory for detail, I was able to construct a map—both spatial and psychological—of Aubrey's childhood world in Beaufort during the 1930s and early 1940s.

To re-create Aubrey's bus journey, I used period street and road maps, combined with Carolina Trailways bus timetables from 1941 to 1945—which I purchased on eBay for twenty-five dollars—as well as other books and printed materials, including two Federal Writers' Project guides, *North Carolina: A Guide to the Old North State* and *Raleigh, Capital of North Carolina;* back issues of *The State: A Weekly Survey of North Carolina* from 1943 to 1945; *North Carolina: Today and Tomorrow,* an extensive geography issued by the North Carolina Department of Conservation and Development in 1936; Catherine W. Bishir and Michael T. Southern's *A Guide to the Historic Architecture of Eastern North Carolina;* and period travel brochures such as *Kinston, North Carolina: Key City of Eastern North Carolina,* published by the Kinston chamber of commerce in the 1940s. Then, one sunny fall day, armed with my half-century-old maps and bus schedules, I retraced Aubrey's journey from Beaufort to Durham, hour by hour and mile by mile.

The history and geography of Beaufort and the surrounding region is documented in Jean Bruyere Kell's *The Old Port Town,* Bland Simpson and Ann Cary Simpson's *Into the Sound Country,* (Mrs.) Fred Hill's *Historic Carteret County, North Carolina, 1663–1975,* Pat Eula Davis and Kathleen Hill Hamilton's *The Heritage of Carteret County,* Paul Branch's *Fort Macon,* and in the Carteret County sections of Bill Sharpe's *North Carolina: A Description by Counties* and *A New Geography of North Carolina.* To reconstruct the atmosphere of the area just prior to and during the first months of World War II, I utilized back issues of the *Beaufort News,* especially the Carolina Coast Defense Edition of July 3, 1941.

For a compelling window into African American life and aspirations during the period, particularly in North Carolina and Virginia, see back issues of the *Norfolk Journal and Guide,* easily the most insightful, best-written and -reported, and most influential black newspaper in the region—if not in the South as a whole. And while they focused on other areas, three classic sociological studies of African American life in the South—Charles S. Johnson's *Growing Up in the Black Belt,* E. Franklin Frazier's *Negro Youth at the Crossways,* and John Dollard's *Caste and Class in a Southern Town*—all contained useful insights, as did John Temple Graves's "The Southern Negro and the War Crisis," *Virginia Quarterly Review* 18, no. 4 (Autumn 1942), 500–517. The description of Scotland Neck, where Aubrey's aunt Lillie hailed from, comes from *North Carolina: A Guide to the Old North State,* 309–10.

For descriptions of local flora and fauna, I relied upon Elizabeth Jean Wilson's *A Guide to Salt Marsh Plants Common to North Carolina,* Karl E. Graetz's *Seacoast Plants of the Carolinas,* Gene Silberhorn's *Common Plants of the Mid-Atlantic Coast,* B. W. Wells's *The Natural Gardens of North Carolina,* Jack L. Griggs's *All the Water Birds: Atlantic and Gulf Coasts,* L. S. Caine's *Game Fish of the South, and How to Catch Them* from 1935, and Robert J. Goldstein's *Coastal Fishing in the Carolinas.* Also helpful was naturalist Edwin Way Teale's majestic *North with the Spring,* his account of his seventeen-thousand-mile journey along the Eastern Seaboard, including a stop in Beaufort, taken during 1947.

Menhaden—the fish itself, menhaden fishing, and the local fish industry—is well described in Barbara Garrity-Blake's *The Fish Factory,* John Frye's *The Men All Singing,* Harden F. Taylor's *Survey of Marine Fisheries of North Carolina,* the Smithsonian Institution's *A Review of the American Menhaden,* and the US House of Representatives' 1942 hearings on HR 6885, "A Bill to Aid in the Prosecution of the War Effort by Providing for the Temporary Suspension of the Operation of State Laws Imposing Restrictions with Respect to Menhaden Fishing." For the *Parkins* tragedy, see the *Raleigh News & Observer,* December 20, 1942.

On the U-boat war along the North Carolina coast, see Michael Gannon's *Operation Drumbeat,* Roderick M. Farb's *Shipwrecks,* and L. VanLoan Naisawald's *In Some Foreign Field.* Travelers who make the long journey to Ocracoke Island may visit the tiny British cemetery where the remains of four crewmen of the HMS *Bedfordshire* are buried. A weathered bronze plaque at the cemetery quotes Rupert Brooke's 1914 poem "The Soldier":

> *If I should die, think only this of me:*
> *That there's some corner of a foreign field*
> *That is for ever England.*

A wind-battered Union Jack, loyally replaced from time to time by Ocracokers, still flies, to this day, over the graves.

The early years of basketball in North Carolina are discussed in Ken Rapoport's *Tar Heel: North Carolina Basketball* and Jim L. Sumner's *A History of Sports in*

North Carolina. James Naismith himself described the theft of the first typewritten copy of the rules of basketball—by Frank Mahan, who, guiltily, later returned them—in his 1941 book, *Basketball: Its Origin and Development*, 55–60. On Mahan, see William S. Powell, ed., *Dictionary of North Carolina Biography* 4, 202–3; *The Association Seminar* 14, no. 9 (June 1906), 334–35; and the 1900 federal census record for "Frank Mahon," Lynn City, Essex County, Massachusetts. On the variety and deeper meanings of basketball in the Tar Heel State, see Tom Brayboy and Bruce Barton, *Playing Before an Overflow Crowd: The Story of Indian Basketball in Robeson, North Carolina, and Adjoining Counties;* Mac C. Kirkpatrick and Thomas K. Perry, *The Southern Textile Basketball Tournament: A History, 1921–1997;* and especially Fred Hobson's wonderfully poetic *Off the Rim: Basketball and Other Religions in a Carolina Childhood*. Finally, sportswriter and journalist Al Featherston has been a penetrating chronicler over the decades of basketball along Tobacco Road. See especially his most insightful essay "North Carolina: The Basketball State" in the *Duke Basketball Report*, June 11, 2011.

CHAPTER 2: *Negroes with LaSalles*

The biography of James E. Shepard has yet to be written. In the meantime, the most complete sources readily available are to be found in the James E. Shepard Papers, 1905–1990, which are housed in the James E. Shepard Memorial Library at North Carolina Central University. Many items in the collection are available online at www.lib.unc.edu, and a number of them reveal much about Shepard's worldview. See, for example, his undated speech-essay "If I Were Young Again"; *The True Solution*, a circa-1907 pamphlet; and two radio addresses from the 1930s, "God Bless Old North Carolina" and "The Spirit of North Carolina." Also of value are documents pertaining to Shepard available on Ancestry.com, including his December 15, 1906, application for a US passport.

Accounts of the voyages of the *Romanic* and the *Neckar,* the two steamships that carried the American delegation to the World's Fifth Sunday School Convention in Rome, May 20–23, 1907, as well as the text of Shepard's address, can be found in Philip E. Howard's *Sunday-Schools the World Around,* 9–37, 300–306. J. A. Whitted's *Biographical Sketch of the Life and Work of the Late Rev. Augustus Shepard, D.D.,* a 1912 biography of Shepard's father, is also a key early source. On Charles Manly, see the entry in William S. Powell, *Dictionary of North Carolina Biography,* available online at docsouth.unc.edu. The history of Raleigh during Shepard's years there can be found in the Federal Writers' Program 1942 guidebook, *Raleigh: Capital of North Carolina.*

Also useful is Vicki Leverne Suggs's "The Production of Political Discourse: Annual Radio Addresses of Black College Presidents During the 1930s and 1940s," PhD dissertation, Georgia State University, 2008; Charles W. Eagles's profile, "James Edward Shepard," available online at ncpedia.org; and various brief biographical sketches, including "James Edward Shepard," *Journal of Negro History,* January 1948, 118–19; George W. Reid, "James Edward Shepard," in Rayford

Logan and Michael R. Winston, *Dictionary of American Negro Biography*, 553–55; and Sarah C. Theusen, "James Edward Shepard," in Henry Louis Gates Jr. and Evelyn Brooks Higginbotham, eds., *African American National Biography*, 171–73. My interviews with former North Carolina College students and professors, including John Hope Franklin, also proved to be of great value in plumbing the character of North Carolina College's visionary founder.

For the challenging conditions faced by black North Carolinians during the late nineteenth and early twentieth centuries, see Leon F. Litwack, *Trouble in Mind*; Steven Hahn, *A Nation Under Our Feet*; Jeffrey J. Crowe, Paul D. Escott, and Flora J. Hatley, *A History of African Americans in North Carolina*; Helen Edmonds, *The Negro and Fusion Politics in North Carolina, 1894–1901*; and David S. Cecelski and Timothy B. Tyson, eds., *Democracy Betrayed*. Lynching in North Carolina is described in Vann R. Newkirk's *Lynching in North Carolina*, Claude A. Clegg III's *Troubled Ground*, J. Timothy Cole's *The Forest City Lynching of 1900*, and, most powerfully, in James Allen and Hilton Als's *Without Sanctuary*, which includes a lithographed photographic postcard from the 1906 lynching in Salisbury.

For African American life in Washington, D.C., during Shepard's sojourn there, see *The Black Washingtonians: The Anacostia Museum Illustrated Chronology*, Sandra Fitzpatrick and Maria R. Goodwin's *The Guide to Black Washington*, Constance McLaughlin Green's *Washington: Capital City, 1879–1950*, and Marya Annette McQuirter's *African American Heritage Trail, Washington, D.C.* Shepard's early political activism is touched upon in Jeffrey J. Crow, "'Fusion, Confusion, and Negroism': Schisms Among Negro Republicans in the North Carolina Election of 1896," *North Carolina Historical Review* 53, no. 4 (October 1976).

A comprehensive history of North Carolina Central University—formerly the North Carolina College for Negroes—does not yet exist. For an overview of the school's founding and history, see the online centennial edition of the *Campus Echo*, the North Carolina Central University student newspaper, May 15, 2010, at www .campusecho.com. My interviews with former North Carolina College students— especially the late Brooklyn T. McMillon—and faculty were invaluable in resurrecting campus life during the 1930s and 1940s.

Efforts by Shepard to keep his school solvent are discussed in Jean Bradley Anderson's *Durham County*, 259–60, and in Augustus M. Burns III's "Graduate Education for Blacks in North Carolina, 1930–1951," *Journal of Southern History* 46, no. 2 (May 1980), 195–218, while the quote on his skill as a politician is from Charles W. Eagles's 1994 profile of Shepard, available online at ncpedia.org. On the Hocutt episode, see Richard Kluger's *Simple Justice*, 157–58; Gilbert Ware's "*Hocutt*: Genesis of *Brown*," *Journal of Negro Education* 52, no. 3 (Summer 1983), 227–33; and Kimberley Johnson's *Reforming Jim Crow*, 156. On the effort by Pauli Murray to enter the law school at Chapel Hill and her run-in with Shepard, see *Pauli Murray*, 114–29, and the *Daily Tar Heel*, January 5, 7, 10, and 11, 1939.

Shepard may have fired her, but Zora Neale Hurston managed to have the last word. In two articles she wrote for *The American Mercury* magazine in 1943 and

1945—which were later reprinted in the *Negro Digest*—she pointedly mentioned an African American college in the South that had "very little else besides its FOUNDER." She also mentioned Shepard by name, adding, "A pharmacist heads up higher education for Negroes in North Carolina." See Hurston, "The 'Pet Negro' System," *American Mercury* 56, no. 223 (May 1943), 593–600, and "The Rise of the Begging Joints," *American Mercury* 60, no. 255 (March 1945), 288–94. Hurston's brief tenure at North Carolina College is discussed in Robert E. Hemenway, *Zora Neale Hurston*, 253–56; Valerie Boyd, *Wrapped in Rainbows*, 327–41; and Georgann Eubanks, *Literary Trails of the North Carolina Piedmont*, 379–81.

Key sources on African American businesses in Durham, and on Hayti's upper crust, include W. E. B. DuBois, "The Upbuilding of Black Durham," *World's Work*, January 1912, 334–38; Walter B. Weare, *Black Business in the New South*, on North Carolina Mutual; Mary E. Mebane's memoir of growing up in and around Durham, *Mary, Wayfarer*; Andre D. Vann and Beverly Washington Jones, *Durham's Hayti*, a photographic history; E. Franklin Frazier, "Durham: Capital of the Black Middle Class," in Alain Locke, ed., *The New Negro: An Interpretation*; Hugh Penn Brinton, "The Negro in Durham: A Study of Adjustment to Town Life," PhD dissertation, University of North Carolina, 1930; Thomas W. Holland, "Negro Capitalists," *Southern Workman* 55, no. 12 (December 1926), 536–40; C. C. Spaulding, "Business in Negro Durham," *Southern Workman* 66, no. 12 (December 1937), 364–68; C. C. Spaulding, "Business Is My Business," *Negro Digest* 1, no. 4 (February 1943), 32–33; and extant issues of the *Carolina Times*. Leslie Brown's *Upbuilding Black Durham: Gender, Class, and Black Community Development in the Jim Crow South* (2008) is a detailed analysis of the rise of Hayti. White Rock Baptist and Saint Joseph's AME, Durham's two most prominent African American churches, are discussed in Anderson, *Durham County*, and in Joel A. Kostyu and Frank A. Kostyu, *Durham: A Pictorial History*, 141–44.

Spaulding's quote on segregation can be found in Harry J. Walker, "Changes in Race Accommodation in a Southern Community," 160, a first-rate University of Chicago doctoral dissertation from 1945 that is also a key source on Hayti during World War II.

Louis Austin, the crusading editor of the *Carolina Times*, has yet to receive his due. A master's thesis—Harold Kent Boyd, "Louis Austin and the *Carolina Times*," North Carolina College, 1966—is now apparently lost, as are issues of the *Carolina Times* from part of 1943 and all of 1944, which were burned in a fire. Still, readers can get a solid appreciation of him by reading, on microfilm, those back issues of the *Carolina Times* that do exist, which can be found online at the North Carolina Digital Heritage Center website, digitalnc.org. Other sources on Austin include Walker, "Changes in Race Accommodation in a Southern Community"; Jerry Gershenhorn, "Double V in North Carolina: The *Carolina Times* and the Struggle for Racial Equality During World War II," *Journalism History* 32, no. 3 (Fall 2006); Gershenhorn's biographical entry, "Louis Ernest Austin," in Gates and Higginbotham, eds., *African American National Biography* 1, 202–3; and Henry Lewis Suggs, *The Black*

Press in the South, 1865–1979, 267–69. Pauli Murray's description of Austin is from *Pauli Murray,* 124.

Austin's Federal Bureau of Investigation file—which I obtained through a Freedom of Information Act (FOIA) request from the FBI—contains much helpful information, including quotes from editorials and articles from the *Carolina Times* that were later destroyed by fire. The Bureau, who concluded that Austin was not a communist but a potentially dangerous racial "agitator," investigated his business affairs and draft status, interviewed a number of his acquaintances, and placed him on a security index list from 1943 to 1946.

The Dorris Lyons episode was reported in the *Carolina Times* on April 3 and June 12, 1943, and in the *Durham Morning Herald* on June 2, 4, and 5, 1943. The quotes from the policeman, the politician, and the citizen are from Walker, "Changes in Race Accommodation in a Southern Community," 279, 290, 310. The riot involving black GIs and white policemen outside the liquor store on Fayetteville Street is described in the *Carolina Times,* April 10, 1943, while the beating of Thomas "Skeet" Allen by white Durham police officers is detailed in the April 17, 1943, edition, which also includes a sworn affidavit by Allen, who was subsequently given a six-month jail sentence. See Robert A. Hill, *The FBI's RACON: Racial Conditions in the United States During World War II,* 281–83.

CHAPTER 3: *Big Dog*

Henry "Big Dog" Thomas also has no biographer. But like Dr. Shepard, he made a lasting impression on those who knew him, and as a result I was able to reconstruct significant portions of his early life and career through a combination of oral-history interviews and the occasional written record. Ancestry.com, which has utterly transformed genealogical research—and is quickly doing the same to traditional historical investigation—offers bits and pieces of Dog's slender paper trail online, including old Farrell High School yearbooks and entries in the federal manuscript censuses of 1930 and 1940. Another website, pahoops.org, features rosters of the Pennsylvania all-state basketball teams over the decades.

For Big Dog's years in Farrell, I've relied heavily on the recollections of four octogenarians who knew him and were gracious enough to allow me to interview them: Harry A. Boatner Sr., Bobby Hammond, Rudy Hammond, and Mrs. Johnie Bloodsaw. Helen Mitchell, who grew up next to Dog on Hamilton Avenue—his childhood home, at 1110 Hamilton Avenue, is still standing—also shared some important memories. Other helpful sources in Farrell included Big Dog's school census cards and high school transcript, copies of the Farrell High School yearbook, *The Reflector,* city directories from the 1920s through the 1940s, Paul A. Komar's *Farrell Golden Jubilee, 1901–1951,* and Roland Barksdale-Hall's *Farrell,* a first-rate history in Arcadia Publishing's Images of America series.

In tracing Dog's "lost years," I relied on his old classmates from Farrell and Durham for clues and then went looking. I eventually picked up his trail in Jefferson City, Missouri, during the fall of 1939, when he enrolled as a freshman at Lincoln

University. For Big Dog's year in Missouri, see *Archives of 1940*, the Lincoln University yearbook for the 1939–40 school year. On Pittsburgh's Pennsylvania Railroad terminal, also known as Union Station, see *Pennsylvania: A Guide to the Keystone State* (1940), 302; the historical essay accompanying the Pittsburgh entry at www .greatamericanstations.com; and Marilynne Pitz, "Let's Tip Our Cap to Pullman Porters," *Pittsburgh Post-Gazette*, February 20, 2011, available at www.post-gazette .com. Some tantalizing possibilities exist as to where else Dog may have lived, including New England, but his full story is not yet known.

For the remarkable story of Lincoln University's founders, the soldiers and officers of the Sixty-Second and Sixty-Fifth Regiments of the US Colored Troops, see Lorenzo Greene, Antonio F. Holland, and Gary Kremer, "The Role of the Negro in Missouri History, 1719–1970," from the official manual of the state of Missouri, 1973–1974, available online at law.wustl.edu; Richard Baxter Foster, *Lincoln Institute, Jefferson City, Missouri: Full History of Its Conception, Struggles, and Triumph;* Cole County Historical Society, "Richard Baxter Foster," at www.colecohistsoc.org; "62nd & 65th Regiments United States Infantry, Co-founders of Lincoln Institute, Later, Lincoln University," at www.buffalosoldier.net; Osborne County Hall of Fame, "Richard Baxter Foster — 1997 Inductee"; and Adam Arenson, *The Great Heart of the Republic: St. Louis and the Cultural Civil War,* 169–74.

For coverage of the 1941 North Carolina College football season, see *Durham Herald,* October 28 and November 5, 1941; *Norfolk Journal and Guide,* November 8 and December 13, 1941; and the NCCN football vertical files in the North Carolina Central University Archives, James E. Shepard Library. Big Dog's eligibility troubles are documented in *The 1942 Bulletin of the Colored Intercollegiate Athletic Association,* 21–24, while both John McLendon and Pee Wee Boyd, in their interviews with me, shared their memories of the Johnson C. Smith game. On Burghardt, see "Half of Legend Dies in Maryland," *Carolina Times,* August 15, 1981; and Mark Shields, "A Personal Anecdote in Defense of Ronald Reagan," *Oak Ridge Now,* November 28, 2010.

Regarding the early history of African American students at white colleges and universities, see Robert Bruce Slater, "The Blacks Who First Entered the World of White Higher Education," *Journal of Blacks in Higher Education* 4 (Summer 1994), 47–56, and Gregory Bond, "The Strange Career of William Henry Lewis," in David K. Wiggins, *Out of the Shadows: A Biographical History of African American Athletes,* 38–57. On the 1934 Willis Ward–Michigan–Georgia Tech incident, see Tyran Kai Steward, "Jim Crow in the Big House: The Benching of Willis Ward and the Rise of Segregation in the North," and *Time,* October 29, 1934.

On the rise of basketball at the University of Toledo during the 1940s, see Barbara Floyd, *The Tower's Lengthening Shadow: 125 Years of the University of Toledo,* 7–15; University of Toledo Basketball Media Guide, 2012–2013; "African Americans in Toledo Sports," www.toledosattic.org; University of Toledo *Blockhouse* yearbooks, 1941–45; David L. Porter, ed., *Basketball: A Biographical Dictionary,* 11–12; "W. Harold Anderson," Naismith Basketball Hall of Fame 1991 yearbook, 102;

"Harold Anderson," bgsusports.com; "Bob Gerber," www.utrockets.com; "Toledo Boasts Crack Quintet of Freshmen," *Stars and Stripes,* March 4, 1943; Marty Ford Pieratt, *First Black Red: The Story of Chuck Harmon, the First African American to Play for the Cincinnati Reds,* 125–27; "Chuck Harmon," Negro Leagues Baseball eMuseum, www.coe.ksu.edu; and Robert W. Peterson, *Cages to Jump Shots: Pro Basketball's Early Years,* 128–29.

For Big Dog's brief sojourn at the University of Toledo, see "Toledo Grid Squad Has 3 Sepia Players," *Afro-American,* October 6, 1942; Dan Burley's "Confidentially Yours" column of October 31, 1942, *New York Amsterdam Star-News,* 14; and the 1943 University of Toledo *Blockhouse* yearbook. Much helpful information also came via my telephone interviews with former University of Toledo athletes Chuck Harmon on January 28, 2013, and Dallas Zuber on January 29, 2013.

On Burl Friddle, see Phillip Ellett, *The Franklin Wonder Five: A Complete History of the Legendary Basketball Team;* biographical entry for Friddle at www.hoops hall.com; and "Burl Friddle: Led TU's 'Friddle's Freshmen' to 1943 NIT Finals in New York," *Toledo Blade,* October 13, 1978. Both Chuck Harmon and Dallas Zuber, who played under Friddle, also shared their memories of their former coach.

CHAPTER 4: *"Nobody Wanted to Mess with Him"*

In Michael Eric Dyson's penetrating 2011 essay on Shelby Foote in *American Homer: Reflections on Shelby Foote and His Classic* The Civil War: A Narrative, he relates a little-known passage about how one of our greatest chroniclers of war was moved by the life and career of the nation's martyred thirty-fifth president. "What we felt about Kennedy cannot be expressed with facts," Foote said. "It was a feeling and that is going to be very difficult for future generations. They may be able to quote what some of us had to say about him, but that is not enough either." In a similar way, the impact of the news of the surprise attack on Pearl Harbor, for those Americans who were alive at the time, is difficult to convey. More shocking at the time than 9/11 or the assassinations of either JFK or Martin Luther King Jr., it was *the* defining event for multiple generations of Americans, many of whom would also witness V-E Day, V-J Day, and the death of President Franklin D. Roosevelt. To have known grown-ups who were adults on December 7, 1941 — such as my parents, my aunts and uncles, and practically every other adult who raised me, from teachers and ministers to baseball coaches and Scout leaders—was to know how just two words, *Pearl Harbor,* could cause conversations to pause, brows to furrow, and faraway looks to appear in their eyes.

On the British warships leaving Mobile Bay in 1815, see William S. Coker, "The Last Battle of the War of 1812: New Orleans. No, Fort Bowyer!," *Alabama Historical Quarterly* 43, no. 1 (Spring 1981), 43–63.

On the American home front during World War II, good places to begin are Geoffrey Perrett, *Days of Sadness, Years of Triumph: The American People, 1939–1945;* John Morton Blum, *V Was for Victory: Politics and American Culture During World War II;* and Ronald Takaki, *Double Victory: A Multicultural History of*

America in World War II. The immense technological impact of World War II is still being measured. Malcolm Gladwell's TED lecture from July of 2011, on "The Strange Case of the Norden Bombsight," is captivating and illuminating and can be found at www.ted.com/talks/malcom_gladwell.html. A recent comprehensive volume on the B-17 is Frederick A. Johnsen, *B-17 Flying Fortress: The Symbol of Second World War Air Power.* For the pipelines that helped win the war, see Jerrell Dean Palmer and John G. Johnson, "Big Inch and Little Inch," *Handbook of Texas Online,* www.tshaonline.org. On the inventor of the LCVP (Landing Craft, Vehicle, Personnel), or Higgins boat, former president Dwight Eisenhower once remarked, "Andrew Higgins is the man who won the war for us." But before Higgins came a Shanghai-based intelligence officer in the US Marines who quietly took photographs—which the Marine Corps brass promptly ignored—of the retractable-ramp boats used by Japanese troops when they invaded China. For his story, see Richard Goldstein, "Victor H. Krulak, Marine Behind U.S. Landing Craft, Dies at 95," *New York Times,* January 4, 2009.

Despite their significant role in the Allied victory, a comprehensive history of the Seabees during World War II has yet to be written. Journalist William Bradford Huie's *Can Do!,* despite being colored by the pressing propaganda needs in place in 1944, is still a valuable source. Other helpful texts include the US Bureau of Yards and Docks, *Building the Navy's Bases in World War II: History of the Bureau of Yards and Docks and the Civil Engineer Corps, 1940–1946,* chapter 6, "The Seabees"; Edmund L. Castillo, *The Seabees of World War II;* "Seabee History: Formation of the Seabees and World War II," at www.history.navy.mil; and numerous battalion histories, most published at the end of the war, including *Danger: Fighting Men at Work* (Twenty-Seventh Battalion) and *The 55th Seabees, 1942–45.* Gina L. Nichols's *The Seabees at Gulfport,* 9–38, features a number of World War II photographs of the advance-base depot, including three of the Eightieth Naval Construction Battalion.

For an overview of the history of African American Seabees during World War II, see *The Negro in the Navy,* a 1947 first-draft narrative prepared by the Historical Section of the Bureau of Naval Personnel, and a brief history, *80th Naval Construction Battalion: Historical Information,* is available online from the US Navy Seabee Museum at www.history.navy.mil/museums/seabee_museum.htm. But for the most revealing inside look at the experience of black Seabees during the war, see the NAACP Papers, part 9, series B—Armed Forces' Legal Files, 1940–1950. The Henry Thomas case is mentioned in a series of letters written by Daniel E. Byrd, president of the New Orleans NAACP chapter, which can be located in the Legal File for U.S. Navy, Seabees, 80th Construction Battalion, 1943, NAACP Papers. Pee Wee Boyd, in my interview with him on June 13, 1997, first alerted me to this key episode in Big Dog's life.

Big Dog appears in a handful of documents dating from his second stay at North Carolina College, including *A Decade of Greatness, 1937–1947,* a booklet celebrating John McLendon's coaching career at North Carolina College; copies of *The Maroon and Gray,* the school yearbook; the vertical files for NCCN basketball, located in the North Carolina Central University Archives, James E. Shepard Library; and the World War II servicemen newsletters, 1943–44, located in the James E. Shepard Papers, also in the North Carolina Central University Archives. But my primary sources for Big Dog's years in Durham are the oral-history interviews I conducted with his former coach, teammates, and classmates at North Carolina College, including John B. McLendon Jr., Edward and Ruth Boyd, Aubrey Stanley, George Parks, Alex Rivera, Brooklyn McMillon, Edith Stanford, Mabel Wright, Hubert Robinson, Bill Malone, Sam Shepard, Rosemary Johnson, Clifford Jenkins, Roy D. Moore, Ethel Lineburger, Carter Smith, and LeRoy T. Walker.

For Edward "Pee Wee" Boyd Jr., my primary sources were the multiple interviews I conducted with him—and his wife, Ruth Boyd—over the years, usually while sitting at the kitchen table at their home in Durham, with the Golf Channel quietly murmuring in the background. Although both Ruth and Pee Wee are now deceased, their openness during those sessions continues to astonish me. Other valuable sources on Pee Wee include interviews with John B. McLendon Jr. and Aubrey Stanley as well as various official records in the North Carolina Central University Archives.

Silas Green's tent show is described in Lynn Abbott and Doug Seroff's *Ragged but Right,* 306–55 and 379–82, and by Eleanor J. Baker in Charles Reagan Wilson and William Ferris, eds., *Encyclopedia of Southern Culture* 1, 381–83. Handcrafted letterpress reproductions of original Silas Green posters are still produced in Nashville, Tennessee, by Hatch Show Print, which printed the originals. "Silas Green from New Orleans, best damn show you *ever* seen!" as Pee Wee used to say.

Aubrey Stanley discussed his years at North Carolina College in detail during our November 25, 1995, interview and in subsequent telephone conversations. On freshman hazing, see also "Notice to All Men of the Freshmen Class," an undated typescript sent by the Lettermen's Club, in the North Carolina Central University Archives.

CHAPTER 5: *Fathers and Sons*

My primary sources for the life of John B. McLendon Jr. are the recorded interviews, letters, telephone conversations, and face-to-face conversations that we had over a five-and-a-half-year period, beginning when I first met him at the Naismith Memorial Basketball Hall of Fame in Springfield, Massachusetts, in early 1994 and ending a few weeks before his death in the fall of 1999. It is out of this work—double-checked, whenever possible, against written sources and interviews with other individuals—that I have reconstructed my portrait of this remarkable American hero.

For those wanting to learn more about McLendon, particularly his post–North Carolina College life and career, the place to begin is Milton S. Katz's superb biography, *Breaking Through: John B. McLendon, Basketball Legend and Civil Rights Pioneer.*

Some researchers believe that the 1918 influenza pandemic had its origins among American soldiers stationed at Fort Riley, Kansas. See *Contagion: Historical*

Views of Diseases and Epidemics, "Spanish Influenza in North America, 1918–1919," Harvard University Library Open Collections, ocp.hul.harvard.edu. On McLendon's parents, Effie Katherine Hunn and John Blanche McLendon Sr., see the 1910 and 1920 federal census, Hiawatha, Kansas, manuscript schedules; Julie Robinson, "Soul of Kansas: Blacks Found Hope in Post-War Kansas," *Topeka Capital-Journal,* October 8, 2011, cjonline.com; and Katz, *Breaking Through,* 1–2. Although she is listed on the federal census as "mulatto," Effie Hunn was "a full-blooded Delaware Indian," according to Katz. I am indebted to Clavis Ballard, grandnephew of Effie Hunn, for helping me better understand the Hunn family saga.

In reconstructing McLendon's early years in Colorado, I utilized the Hunn family entries in the 1920 federal census for Model and Tabasco Coal Camp, Las Animas County, Colorado, as well as *Colorado: A Guide to the Highest State,* 191–94, 326–28, 377, published by the Writers' Program of the Works Progress Administration in the state of Colorado.

In Kansas City, Kansas, the McLendons lived at 342 Haskell Avenue. And while John's family home was left untouched—his father carried a .45-caliber revolver—violence against African Americans in Kansas City was far from uncommon. Sources used for McLendon's Kansas City years include Kansas City, Kansas, and Kansas City, Missouri, city directories, 1911–32; Charles E. Coulter, *"Take Up the Black Man's Burden": Kansas City's African American Communities, 1865–1939,* especially 1–17, 60–68; Rattlebone Hollow, "History of Our Public Schools," Wyandotte County, Kansas, 1844–2012, www.kckps.org; *Kansas: A Guide to the Sunflower State,* 205–19, published by the Federal Writers' Project of the Works Progress Administration for the state of Kansas; Sumner High School class of 1932 fiftieth anniversary booklet, available online from the Kansas City, Kansas, public library; and *Missouri: A Guide to the "Show Me" State,* 247–53, published by the Writers' Program of the Works Progress Administration in the State of Missouri.

In the end, McLendon did make it onto a basketball team—that of the Sumner High School branch at Kansas City Junior College. The team went 17–0 that year, but McLendon's role was that of a rarely used substitute. "First time I got into a game," he later recalled, "I threw the ball clear over the backboard. I looked over at the coach, and he yelled at me, 'Keep playing!' I thought he was going to take me out." But he added, "I could always say that I was on a championship team."

For such a towering figure in modern athletics, James Naismith remains curiously one-dimensional, or virtually unknown, in the popular mind. Only a handful of pictures of him ever appear in print; recordings of his voice—if they exist—remain unheard; while his essential nature seems as anonymous as the four-cent US postage stamp issued on the centenary of his birth: a hand, a basketball, and a hoop, alongside which appears NAISMITH 1861–1961. His earthiness, humor, inventiveness, humanitarianism, and pathos, meanwhile, have all been largely forgotten.

Two prominent exceptions, both of which capture his complex vitality, are Bernice Larson Webb's *The Basketball Man: James Naismith,* an expansive biography filled with significant personal detail, and Rob Rains and Hellen Carpenter's *James*

Naismith: The Man Who Invented Basketball, a new biography cowritten by Naismith's granddaughter, which makes good use of a cache of previously unused family materials. Both feature detailed accounts of the central themes and incidents in Naismith's life, including the invention of basketball. Other helpful sources include Jack G. Hammig, "A Historical Sketch of Dr. James Naismith," master's thesis, University of Kansas, 1962; John Dewar, "The Life and Professional Contributions of James Naismith," EdD dissertation, Florida State University, 1965; "James Naismith's Life and Legacy: Celebrating 150 Years," a joint online exhibition created by McGill University, Springfield College, and the University of Kansas, at lib.ku.edu; and the biographical materials available online from the Naismith Museum at the Mill of Kintail, Almonte, Ontario, at www.naismithmuseum.com.

The most complete accounts of Naismith's childhood and youth are Webb, *The Basketball Man,* 1–22, and Rains and Carpenter, *James Naismith,* 1–16. On McGill University and Montreal during his time there, see Karl Baedeker, *The Dominion of Canada, with Newfoundland and an Excursion to Alaska: Handbook for Travellers* (1894), 19–30; Edgar Andrew Collard, *Montreal: The Days That Are No More,* 299–307; John Kalbfleisch, "Montreal's Last Streetcar Rolled Down the Tracks 49 Years Ago," *The Gazette* (Montreal), August 31, 2008; photographs of the McGill campus from the 1890s at www.mccord-museum.qc.ca; and Tamara Myers, *Caught: Montreal's Modern Girls and the Law, 1869–1945,* 44–45, 59–64.

James Naismith describes the rugby-profanity incident in his *Basketball,* 22–23. On Naismith's athletic career during his years in Montreal, see Webb, *The Basketball Man,* 22–45, and Rains and Carpenter, *James Naismith,* 19–28.

The early decades of Springfield College are recounted in Laurence Locke Doggett, *Man and a School: Pioneering Higher Education at Springfield College* (1943), which is also the source for the dimensions of the wooden boxes that Naismith asked James Stebbins for—as related by T. Duncan Patton, who played in the first game; see page 71. According to Naismith's card in the naturalization index for the western district of Missouri, 1848–1990, available at Ancestry.com, he arrived in Springfield on September 15, 1890.

Naismith himself credited duck-on-a-rock, a childhood game, as one of the inspirations for basketball—which he describes in his *Basketball: Its Origin and Development,* posthumously published in 1941—and there is little reason to doubt his version. That said, Naismith's invention also occurred during an era when, coincidentally, new archaeological information was being revealed about an ancient Mesoamerican ball game played by the Aztecs, Mayans, and scores of other indigenous peoples in South, Central, and North America.

Indeed, some thirty years ago, at a small antiquarian bookshop a block west of the Plaza in Santa Fe, New Mexico, I ran across an English translation of Lucien Biart's *The Aztecs: Their History, Manners, and Customs.* Published in Chicago in 1887, four years before Naismith's act of origination—and costing more than I could afford, but I bought it anyway—the book described the ancient American game, which was played in an "immense quadrilateral" with a rubber ball of "great elasticity." But even by today's standards, when hundreds of millions of dollars are wagered on the Final Four, the outcome of the old game was hardly inconsequential. "In the middle of the enclosure stood two stones," Biart wrote, "like our mill-stones, with a hole in the centre a little larger than the ball. The player whose ball went through one of these holes—a rare feat—won not only the game, but the clothing of all the people present." See also Vernon L. Scarborough and David R. Wilcox, *The Mesoamerican Ballgame;* Theodore Stern, *The Rubber-Ball Games of the Americas;* George E. Stuart, "City of Kings and Commoners," *National Geographic* 176, no. 4 (October 1989), 488–505; and Scott Ellsworth, "Hoops! Were the Aztecs and the Mayas in on the First Jump Ball?," *New York Times,* May 29, 1994.

Naismith's original thirteen rules for basketball were first published in the Springfield College newspaper; see *The Triangle* 1, no. 10 (January 15, 1892), 144–47. On the early, central role played by the YMCA in disseminating basketball, both in the United States and abroad, see Naismith, *Basketball,* 111–60; Webb, *The Basketball Man,* 67–76; and Genzaburo Ishikawa, "First Time I Met the Basketball," http://tailchaser.halfmoon.jp/genzaburo/10.html. Laurence Doggett's *Man and a School* also contains helpful information on how the YMCA and Springfield College graduates helped spread basketball around the globe, including Doggett's observations from Cairo, made during a mid-1930s world tour; see pages 12, 72–73, 276, and 289.

Basketball has a long history among American Indians. Henry Kallenberg's description of introducing the game to the Lakota Sioux is recorded in Naismith, *Basketball,* 137–40, as is Naismith's own experience observing Native American ballplayers at the Haskell Institute. For a penetrating portrait of basketball in contemporary Indian country, see Larry Colton, *Counting Coup: A True Story of Basketball and Honor on the Little Big Horn.*

On rule changes and the development of new equipment for basketball during its first half century, see Naismith, *Basketball,* 87–109; Greg Brown, ed., *The Complete Book of Basketball,* vii–10; Joe Hutton and Vern B. Hoffman, *Basketball,* 20–43; and Zander Hollander, *The Modern Encyclopedia of Basketball,* rev. ed., 6–8. "Chuck Taylor remains the most famous name in sports that no one knows anything about," wrote Abraham Aamidor in his 2006 biography, *Chuck Taylor, All Star: The True Story Behind the Man Behind the Most Famous Athletic Shoe in History,* 3. Aamidor's book is the place to begin. Converse's All-Star basketball shoes, however, preceded Taylor, and despite some changes in design over the years, they have remained remarkably close to the earliest versions. See "The Perfect Fit" advertisement in the *Athletic Journal* 4, no. 1 (September 1923), 25.

On Maude Evelyn Sherman, see Webb, *The Basketball Man,* 51–53, 86–91, and her profile at Ancestry.com. Naismith's post-1891 Springfield career, his years in Denver, and the move to Lawrence are discussed in Webb, *The Basketball Man,* 86–107, and Rains and Carpenter, *James Naismith,* 60–72.

Women and girls played basketball from the beginning, and Senda Berenson, a faculty member at Smith College, played an important role early on. Indeed, at a number of the nation's colleges and universities, women's basketball teams were organized before men's teams. See, especially, Senda Berenson, ed., *Basket Ball for Women* (1905); chapter 9, "The Development of Girls' Basketball," in Naismith, *Basketball*, 161–70; and Ralph Melnick, *Senda Berenson: The Unlikely Founder of Women's Basketball*, especially 1–10. On women playing the game at KU prior to Naismith's arrival, see Nancy Nygard Pilon, "Women's Athletics at the University of Kansas during the Progressive Era," PhD dissertation, University of Kansas, 2008, 39–40, and Rains and Carpenter, *James Naismith*, 72–73.

On the first decade of Jayhawks basketball, see Harold C. Evans, "Some Notes on College Basketball in Kansas," *Kansas Historical Quarterly* 11, no. 28 (May 1942), 199–215; Robert Taft, *The Years on Mount Oread*, 64–67; Max L. Rife, "Basketball in Its Early Years at the University of Kansas, 1898–1925," master's thesis, University of Kansas, 1967; and John Hendel, *Kansas Jayhawks: History-Making Basketball*, 2–11.

CHAPTER 6: *Lawrence*

Blair Kerkhoff's *Phog Allen: The Father of Basketball Coaching* (1996), the first book-length biography, is the place to begin to assess the impact of Forrest C. Allen on the development of college basketball. Allen's own books—ghostwritten, it seems, by his wife, Bessie Milton Allen—are also key, not only in revealing Allen's broad interests and expertise but also for getting a sense of his outsize, larger-than-life personality: *My Basket-ball Bible* (1924), *Better Basketball: Techniques, Tactics and Tales* (1937), and *Coach "Phog" Allen's Sports Stories for You and Youth* (1947). Helpful sources available at Ancestry.com include the Allen family public tree; individual profiles and attached source citations for George Pogue Allen (1829–83), William T. Allen (1850–1937), Mary Elexene Perry (1863–1952), Forrest C. Allen (1885–1974), and Bessie Evalina Milton (1887–1970); the William Kyle Poage family history note attached to William Kyle Poage Allen; and the World War I draft registration card for Forrest Clare Allen, dated September 11, 1918. On Bess Wallace and Harry Truman, Allen's childhood neighbors in Independence, see Margaret Truman, *Bess W. Truman*, 1–10; oral-history interview of Mary Paxton Keely by James R. Fuchs, July 12, 1966, transcript available at www.trumanlibrary.org; and Alfred Steinberg, *The Man from Missouri: The Life and Times of Harry S. Truman*, 24–26. For the Buffalo Germans, see Robert W. Peterson, *Cages to Jump Shots: Pro Basketball's Early Years*, 56–65; Robert D. Bole and Alfred C. Lawrence, *From Peachbaskets to Slamdunks: A Story of Professional Basketball*, 14–19; and Annette R. Hoffmann, "The Buffalo Germans and the 1904 Olympic Tournament in St. Louis," *Journal of Olympic History* 11, no. 3 (September 2003), 19–21. On the March 1905 series with the Kansas City Athletic Club, see Kerkhoff, *Phog Allen*, 10–16.

For Allen's years at KU prior to World War II, see Kerkhoff, *Phog Allen*, 19–164; Hendel, *Kansas Jayhawks*, 6–44; Max L. Rife, "Basketball in Its Early Years at the University of Kansas," master's thesis, University of Kansas, 1951, 1–2, 19–40, 61–99; and Clifford S. Griffin, *The University of Kansas: A History*, 429, 661–67. Allen's "Ailments of Basketball," *Athletic Journal* 5, no. 5 (January 1925), 16–17, 52, is a good example of his concise yet comprehensive early magazine articles. The gargling story comes from Aram Goudsouzian, "'Can Basketball Survive Chamberlain?': The Kansas Years of Wilt the Stilt," *Kansas History* 28, no. 3 (Autumn 2005), 150–73. On Hoch Auditorium, see Taft, *The Years on Mount Oread,* 134–36; and Griffin, *The University of Kansas,* 428–29.

Goal-Hi, Allen's backboardless basketball game, was tested in Lawrence during the summer of 1939. And while materials shortages caused by the war soon sank production, decades-old Goal-Hi baskets—and similar freestanding basketball goals produced by other manufacturers, such as Pole-Goal, produced by Rawlings—can still be occasionally seen on the playgrounds of aging elementary and junior high schools across the United States. On Goal-Hi itself, see Kerkhoff, *Phog Allen,* 85–90; "New Game Developed by Noted Basketball Authority," *Athletic Journal* 20, no. 4 (December 1939), 36–40; and Goal-Hi advertisements in *Athletic Journal* 20, no. 6 (February 1940), 44, and *Athletic Journal* 20, no. 7 (March 1940), 48.

No other early college basketball coach could lay claim to as many influential former players as Phog Allen could, whose personal Jayhawks roster included Dutch Lonborg, Paul Endacott, Ralph Miller, Dean Smith, and Wilt Chamberlain. Of all of Allen's former players, however, none cast a longer shadow than Kansas-born and -bred Adolph Rupp, the legendary University of Kentucky basketball coach, who won 875 games, four NCAA championships, one NIT title, and an Olympic gold medal. On Rupp's Kansas roots and his Austro-German forebears, see Dave Kindred, *Basketball: The Dream Game in Kentucky,* 81–83; and the individual profiles and family trees for his parents, Heinrich Rupp (1863–1910) and Anna Lichti (1865–1954), at Ancestry.com. The free-throw drills and the use of washable paint on the gymnasium floor are from an oral-history interview of John McLendon conducted on June 9, 1997.

Phog Allen's role in creating, in Lawrence, the first-ever true college basketball town cannot be overemphasized. Well before the student bodies at Duke, North Carolina, Kentucky, Indiana, Louisville, Arizona, Connecticut, and UCLA were swept away by basketball fever, with all its attendant highs and crushing lows, Kansas students were already seasoned vets. Indeed, even before Wilt Chamberlain arrived in Lawrence, a KU chemistry professor wrote, "As for important events of University life, the most important in the lives of these youngsters were the basketball victories of 1952." See Taft, *The Years on Mount Oread,* 188.

Key sources on Naismith's years at Kansas prior to the mid-1930s include Webb, *The Basketball Man,* 103–267; Rains and Carpenter, *James Naismith,* 70–150; and Edward Pinkowski, *Forgotten Fathers,* 95–96.

CHAPTER 7: *"That's How You Do It!"*

The best available source on the experiences of African American students at the University of Kansas prior to the 1960s is Kristine M. McCusker's "'The Forgotten Years' of America's Civil Rights Movement: The University of Kansas, 1939–1971" (master's thesis, University of Kansas, 1994), a groundbreaking piece of historical research. A portion of it can be found in *Kansas History* 17, no. 1 (Spring 1994), 26–37. Also of value is Bill Mayer's "Jayhawk Pioneers Deserving," August 14, 2009, www2.kusports.com. On race relations in Lawrence, see Brent M. S. Campney, " 'Hold the Line': The Defense of Jim Crow in Lawrence, Kansas, 1945–1961," *Kansas History* 33, no. 1 (Spring 2010), 22–41; Rusty L. Monhollon, "Taking the Plunge: Race, Rights, and the Politics of Desegregation in Lawrence, Kansas, 1960," *Kansas History* 20 (Autumn 1997), 138–59; and Paul E. Wilson, *A Time to Lose: Representing Kansas in* Brown v. Board of Education, 54–58. The 1882 lynching is mentioned in Genevieve Yost's "History of Lynchings in Kansas," *Kansas Historical Quarterly* 2, no. 2 (May 1933), 182–219, and Campney, " 'Hold the Line,' " 25.

Race relations in Kansas have long resisted easy categorization. "Scholars now basically agree that Kansas defies classification as either 'Northern' nor 'Southern' in its racial views," wrote James N. Leiker in "Race Relations in the Sunflower State," *Kansas History* 15 (Autumn 2002), 214–36. Or, as John McLendon once said, "Kansas is great. It's great except for the crazy stuff." With these caveats in mind, useful sources on late nineteenth and early twentieth century race relations in Kansas include the section on "Race, Ethnicity, and Class in Kansas and the West" in Rita G. Napier, "Rethinking the Past, Reimagining the Future," *Kansas History* 24, no. 3 (August 2001), 240–47; James N. Leiker, "Imagining the Free State: a 150-Year History of a Contested Image," *Kansas History* 34 (Spring 2011), 40–49; Brent M. S. Campney, " 'This is Not Dixie': The Imagined South, the Kansas Free State Narrative, and the Rhetoric of Racist Violence," *Southern Spaces,* June 6, 2007, www.southernspaces.org; Cheryl Brown Henderson, "Lucinda Todd and the Invisible Petitioners of *Brown v. Board of Education of Topeka, Kansas,*" in Quintard Taylor and Shirley Ann Wilson Moore, eds., *African American Women Confront the West, 1600–2000,* 312–27; Richard Kluger, *Simple Justice: The History of* Brown v. Board of Education *and Black America's Struggle for Equality,* 368–96; and Wilson, *A Time to Lose,* 27–50.

My primary source on John McLendon's years at KU was John McLendon himself, both in lengthy oral-history interviews and in correspondence, numerous telephone conversations, and face-to-face question-and-answer sessions over a period of four and a half years—as well as the typescript of his *Tales of the Hardwood,* an unfinished autobiography. Arthur Lloyd Johnson, who was born and raised in Lawrence and who briefly attended KU, was also a key informant. I interviewed Mr. Johnson, later a legendary high school basketball coach in Kentucky, at his home in Louisville on June 27, 1992.

Kristine McCusker paints a dark portrait of Phog Allen's role in barring African Americans from KU athletic teams, especially when it came to the creation and maintenance of the so-called gentleman's agreement among the Big Six. See her " 'The Forgotten Years,' " 5–6, 28, 32–34. I have relied more heavily on the memories of both McLendon and Arthur Lloyd Johnson—"I'm a bitter motherfucker," Johnson, then age seventy-seven, informed me in 1992 while describing the racism prevalent in Lawrence during his youth. That said, important questions remain. The

Jayhawks basketball team, it should be noted, did not have its first African American player, LaVannes Squires, from Wichita, until the 1951–52 season.

Certainly one would like to know far more about William Holland, who was Phog Allen's neighbor on the 800 block of Louisiana Avenue in Lawrence. Born in Macon County, Tennessee, around 1847, he in all likelihood was a runaway slave. He enlisted in Company E, Fortieth U.S. Colored Troops, in Gallatin, Tennessee, on February 16, 1865, under the name of Andrew J. Dixon, signing his enlistment papers with an *X* and listing his occupation as "farmer." By 1880, during the Exoduster era, he was living in Lawrence, listing his occupation as "laborer." He died in Leavenworth on October 31, 1926. Sources on Holland, all available online at Ancestry.com, include US Colored Troops military service records, 1865–1961, for Andrew J. Dixon, 40th USCT; US federal census manuscript data for Thomas and Julia Holland, Lawrence, Kansas, 1880–1930; Kansas State Collection, 1885–1925; US Civil War pension index: general index to pension files, 1861–1934; and US burial registers, military posts, and national cemeteries, 1862–1960.

McLendon, however, remembered the Holland family as important figures in shaping the racial views of Allen, who, it should be recalled, was the descendant of Southern migrants to Missouri. "The interesting thing about Phog is that he had this black neighbor that he knew," McLendon told me. "I mean, there's a difference...If Phog had been someone who didn't know any black people, and then all of a sudden he knows one, then he can say, 'Well, you're different.' But he did know someone. It breaks through all the static of the culture and all that."

On a similar note, Naismith's familiarity with African Americans—prior to meeting John McLendon—is somewhat unclear. "While the Naismith family did employ a black woman, known as Auntie Silvers, to help with household chores and childcare," Bob Rains and Hellen Carpenter wrote, "Naismith viewed her as another member of the family and never as a servant. He also would not allow his children to view her as less than equal" (*James Naismith*, 144). Efforts to identify this woman, however, have not been thus far successful. Susie Silvers, listed as a "colored servant," appears in both the 1900–1901 Lawrence city directory and the 1900 federal census, while Fanny Silvers, listed as a "mulatto housekeeper," appears in the 1905 Kansas state census. In addition, an Eliza Silvers, a "col'd cook," and a Mary Silvers, who appears to have been an African American live-in servant, also appear in period sources. See Hoye's *City Directory of Lawrence, Kansas, 1896; Chittenden's 1900–1901 Lawrence City Directory; Green & Foley's Lawrence City Directory, 1888;* Kansas State Census Collection, 1855–1925; and the 1900 US federal census schedules for Lawrence, Kansas—all accessible online at Ancestry.com.

On KU's black Greeks and the segregated spring dance, see McCusker, "'The Forgotten Years,'" 21–38, and Richard M. Breaux, "Nooses, Sheets, and Blackface: White Racial Anxiety and Black Student Presence at Six Midwest Flagship Universities, 1882–1937," in Marybeth Gasman and Roger L. Geiger, eds., *Higher Education for African Americans Before the Civil Rights Era, 1900–1964,* Perspectives on the History of Higher Education 29 (2012).

On the swim test and the segregation of the pool in Robinson Gymnasium, see Taft, *The Years on Mount Oread,* 86, 201; McCusker, "'The Forgotten Years,'" 22, 28; and Katz, *Breaking Through,* 17–18.

On Naismith's 1936 voyage to Europe, see the list of United States citizens arriving from Cherbourg on the SS *Aquitania,* New York City, August 26, 1936, at Ancestry.com; Rains and Carpenter, *James Naismith,* 155–57; and Webb, *The Basketball Man,* 277–78.

CHAPTER 8: *Berlin, 1936*

Writers, journalists, and historians have not ignored the Berlin Olympics.

Important sources include Armin Fuhrer, *Hitlers Spiele: Olympia 1936 in Berlin* (2011); David Clay Large, *Nazi Games: The Olympics of 1936* (2007); Richard Mandell, *The Nazi Olympics* (1971); Guy Walters, *Berlin Games: How the Nazis Stole the Olympic Dream* (2006); Christopher Hilton, *Hitler's Olympics: The 1936 Olympic Games* (2006); and Arnd Kruger and William Murray, *The Nazi Olympics: Sport, Politics, and Appeasement in the 1930s* (2003).

The single most helpful source on the 1936 games, however, is *The XIth Olympic Games, Berlin, 1936,* written and published by the Organisationskomitee für Die XI. Olympiade Berlin 1936. Even though it is the "official report" of the games and thus not overly objective, it is so exhaustive that it is simply invaluable. See, especially, volume 1, pages 129–40 (on buildings and grounds); 283–86 (on timing and épée hit registering); 289–92 (on landscaping); 293–97 (on meteorological service and weather); 335–50 (on radio and television); 380–88 (on railways); 454–59 (on the decoration of Berlin); and volume 2, pages 1074–83, the report on the basketball competition.

Also quite helpful in capturing 1930s Berlin, though covering slightly different periods, are two compelling first-rate books—Erik Larson's *In the Garden of Beasts: Love, Terror, and an American Family in Hitler's Berlin* (2011) and Roger Moorhouse's *Berlin at War* (2010)—as well as what turned out to be one of the last of the great red-covered Baedekers: *Germany: A Handbook for Railway Travellers and Motorists* (1936), especially pages xxv–xxxix and 1–24. Other helpful sources include Jason Lutes's remarkable graphic novels *Berlin: City of Stones* (2000) and *Berlin: City of Smoke* (2008) as well as Robert Siodmak's haunting 1930 silent film, *People on Sunday,* available as a restored edition from the Criterion Collection.

The American basketball experience during the 1936 games has been admirably chronicled by Carson Cunningham in his *American Hoops: U.S. Men's Olympic Basketball from Berlin to Beijing,* 1–28. See also Walter Richter, ed., *Die Olympischen Spiele 1936 in Berlin und Garmisch-Partenkirchen* 2, 132–33. On Naismith's journey to, and experience during, the games, see Webb, *The Basketball Man,* 277–87, and Rains and Carpenter, *James Naismith,* 155–62. On the initial imbroglio concerning Naismith's presence in Berlin, see "Naismith Ignored," *Montreal Gazette,* August 8, 1936. W. H. Mifflin's letter concerning his conversation with Naismith appears in the *Kansas Alumni Magazine* 83, September 1984, 18. The theft of the

American basketball team's uniforms is noted in Mandel, *The Nazi Olympics,* 197. Brief footage of the Italian basketball team performing a layup drill appears in Leni Riefenstahl's landmark documentary film *Olympia.* Go to the 5:37 mark in part 2, "The Festival of Beauty." And while the location of the scene is unclear—perhaps the Olympic Village—Riefenstahl's signature clouds appear.

William Shirer's short but penetrating writings on the games appear in his *Berlin Diary,* 64–66.

Life in prewar Nazi Germany, and the concurrent rise in anti-Semitic actions, has been extensively documented. For further study, good places to begin are the websites maintained by the United States Holocaust Memorial Museum, www.ushmm.org, and Yad Vashem, the Holocaust Martyrs' and Heroes' Remembrance Authority, www.yadvashem.org; Richard Evans's historical trilogy, *The Coming of the Third Reich* (2000), *The Third Reich in Power* (2005), and *The Third Reich at War* (2008); and *The Holocaust Chronicle* (2000), a 700-plus-page illustrated history. On Jewish life in the German capital, see Andreas Nachama, Julius H. Schoeps, and Hermann Simon, eds., *Jews in Berlin* (2001). On the Judenboykott of April 1933, see the interview with Henry Guterman, "All Jewish Shops Were Boycotted," in the British Library's *Voices of the Holocaust,* www.bl.uk/learning; and Christoph Kreutzmüller, "The 'Boycott' of April 1, 1933," Berliner Themenjahr, 2013: Diversity Destroyed, www.berlin.de, and *Ausverkauf: Die Vernichtung der Jüdischen Gewerbetätigkeit in Berlin, 1930–1945* (2012). On the Nazi laws, see "Anti-Jewish Legislation in Prewar Germany," US Holocaust Memorial Museum, www.ushmm.org.

For a chilling inside view of rising anti-Semitism in the Third Reich, see Otto Dov Kulka and Eberhard Jackel, eds., *The Jews in the Secret Nazi Reports on Popular Opinion in Germany, 1933–1945.* The incident involving Elisabeth Bergner appears on page 36, while the ice cream boycott is mentioned on page 138. On conditions in the Third Reich leading up to Kristallnacht, I am also indebted to ninety-three-year-old Helmut Stern, whom I interviewed in Ann Arbor on July 4, 2013. Born and raised in Hannover, he was arrested and held by the Gestapo for a week but was able to escape to the United States in September of 1938.

My primary source of information on Otto and Lili Bernhard and their two daughters, Gabriela Johanna Bernhard and Marianne Emilie Luise Bernhard, comes from Marianne's son, George Manasse of Durham, North Carolina. Equally key were numerous documents available on Ancestry.com, including New York's incoming passenger lists, for Otto Bernhard (1936, 1942, 1943) and Gabriela Johanna Bernhard (1939); Otto Bernhard's petition for naturalization in New York City, March 14, 1949; Marianne Manasse's declaration of intention for citizenship, Greensboro, North Carolina, April 13, 1940; and *Amtliches Fernsprechbuch für Berlin und Umgegend, April 1935,* a telephone directory. Also see *Jüdisches Adressbuch für Gross-Berlin: Ausgabe 1931* (1994), 30. A list of Bernhards from Berlin who were murdered during the Holocaust can be found in *Gedenkbuch Berlins: Der Jüdischen Opfer des Nationalsozialismus* (1995), 107–8. On Ford, see Simon Reich, "The Ford Motor Company and the Third Reich," *Dimensions* 13, no. 2, available online at the

Anti-Defamation League's Braun Holocaust Institute website, archive.adl.org/braun, as well as Reich's *The Fruits of Fascism: Postwar Prosperity in Historical Perspective,* 107–46.

The Museum of Modern Art's *German Expressionism: Works from the Collection,* an online exhibition available at www.moma.org, is a comprehensive introduction to the vibrant art scene that flourished in pre-Nazi Germany, a subject that has attracted the attention of Peter Gay, Walter Laqueur, Otto Friedrich, and other noted scholars and writers. My own introduction came—when I was an eighteen-year-old freshman at Reed College—at the hands of Ottomar Rudolf, a former member of the Hitler Youth who had served in the Wehrmacht on the eastern front and then in the US Army Signal Corps during the Korean War. A thoughtful and humane professor of literature and a gifted teacher, he instilled in his students an appreciation for the high-wire act that artists must perform, especially in a society where their voices are not always welcome. See his 2012 memoir, *I Remember: A Boy's Years in Nazi Germany.*

For an introduction to the complex issues surrounding Jewish emigration from Germany prior to Kristallnacht, in November of 1938, see "German Jewish Refugees, 1933–1939," *Holocaust Encyclopedia,* US Holocaust Memorial Museum, www.ushmm.org; and Aubrey Boag, "They Expected the Worst—They Did Not Expect the Unthinkable: Jewish Emigration from Germany, 1933–1941" (2007), a first-rate essay by an undergraduate history major at the University of California at Santa Barbara, available at www.history.ucsb.edu. On the June 1935 attacks on Jews and "Jewish-looking" people on the Kurfürstendamm, see Large, *Nazi Games,* 81. "Nobody came to their aid," one witness later observed, "because everyone is afraid of being arrested."

The Heimatschein für den Aufenthalt im Ausland, Berlin, 24 Marz 1936, for Fraulein Marianne Emilie Luise Bernhard was courtesy of George Manasse. The daily weather report from the Berlin-Tempelhof weather station for March 24, 1936, can be accessed at www.tutiempo.net. I also consulted "Germany and Its Approaches," a fold-out map appearing in *National Geographic Magazine* 86, no. 1 (July 1944).

CHAPTER 9: *Racehorse Basketball*

My primary sources for McLendon's year at the University of Iowa and his being hired by Dr. Shepard at the North Carolina College for Negroes were our February 16, 1995, and June 8, 1997, interviews as well as McLendon's unfinished autobiography, *Tales of the Hardwood,* which I read in typescript. See also Katz, *Breaking Through,* 22–25; Terry Todd, "A Pioneer of Physical Training: C. H. McCloy," *Iron Game History* 1, no. 6 (August 1991); the McCloy bibliography in George B. Pearson and Jacqueline K. Whalin, *Reference Index of the Research Quarterly: Health, Physical Education, Recreation, 1930–1960,* 63–64; and "Half a Legend Dies in Maryland," the *Carolina Times,* August 15, 1981.

On Alice Hultz, McLendon's first wife, see the following records, available on Ancestry.com: entries for Alice Hultz, Joseph Laspy, and Zuella Laspy, Kansas state census for 1925, Lawrence, Douglas County; the entry for Joseph and Zuella Laspy, *Calnon's Lawrence City Directory, 1929–30;* the entry for Alice E. Laspy, 1930 US federal census, Lawrence; and the entry for John and Alice McLendon, 1940 US federal census, Durham, North Carolina. Before going to Iowa, McLendon had done some practice teaching at Lincoln Elementary School and at Lawrence Memorial, where he also coached the school's *Negro* basketball team. The school had a white team as well.

While at North Carolina College, McLendon also taught swimming to local African American Boy Scout leaders. In 1943, not only did Durham have *ten* black Boy Scout troops, there was also an "interracial activities" chairman. See "Negro Scoutmasters and Commissioners Will Meet Tonight," *Durham Morning Herald,* July 6, 1943, 12.

The elimination of the center jump was, arguably, the single most important rule change during basketball's first century—although one of its desired effects did not come to pass. "One of the major reasons for the jump elimination was the advantage of unusually tall centers," Herman L. Masin, the editor of *Scholastic Coach* magazine, wrote on June 2, 1947, to John Wooden, who was writing his master's thesis at Indiana State. "Yet, since the rule was put into effect, we seem to have more 'goon' centers than ever before." On the history of the rule change, see John Robert Wooden, "A Study of the Effect of the Abolition of the Center Jump on the Height of Outstanding College Basketball Players," master's thesis, Indiana State Teachers College, 1947, 1–5, 30–34; "Basketball Rule Change Is Asked, Center Jump May Be Eliminated," *Bend Bulletin,* April 3, 1935; Roger Robison, "The Campaign to Eliminate the Center Jump: 1930–1937; Cause and Effect," library.la84.org/Sports Library/NASSH_Proceedings/NP2007/np2007v.pdf; and Wilho Frigard, "Effect of the Elimination of the Center Jump on the Game of Basketball," *Research Quarterly* 10, no. 2 (1939), 150–53.

On the desirable characteristics of pre–fast break basketball players, see J. M. (Sam) Barry, *Basketball: Individual Play and Team Play,* 14; Mark A. Peterman, *Secrets of Winning Basketball,* 15–24; G. N. Messer, *How to Play Basket Ball* (Spalding's Athletic Library, Group 7, no. 193), 28–32; and *Basketball Hints: How to Play, Championship Play, Training Advice, 1937–38.* "The best method for advancing the ball is by Short Passing," the authors of *Basketball Hints* advised, adding, "However, all players should be able to dribble in case of emergency."

On Bill Reinhart, see Gordon Oliver, "Fast Break Hoops: Coach Bill Reinhart and the Nephew Who Wanted to Preserve His Memory," *Oregon Quarterly* 90, no. 3 (Spring 2011), www.oregonquarterly.com; Thomas J. Whalen, *Dynasty's End: Bill Russell and the 1968–69 World Champion Boston Celtics,* 23, 43–44; David Holt, "GW's Greatest Hoops Teams Played in the '50s," *The GW Hatchet,* November 23, 1998, www.gwhatchet.com; Ronald L. Mendell, *Who's Who in Basketball,* 191; and US federal census returns for William Jennings Bryan Reinhart—Jamesport, Missouri (1900), and Salem, Oregon (1910). Charles "Chic" Hess's *Prof Blood and the Wonder Teams: The True Story of Basketball's First Great Coach* (2003) is not only the first comprehensive biography of one of the game's most colorful characters but also a riveting portrait of basketball in the 1920s. Also see Richard Cowen, "'Prof' a Character, Winner," northjersey.com, October 13, 2009; Catherine M. Derrick, "Ernest Artel 'Prof' Blood," in Porter, *Basketball: A Biographical Dictionary,* 46; and US federal census return, 1880, Fitchburg, Massachusetts; New Hampshire marriage and divorce records, 1659–1947, for Ernest A. Blood and Margaret Thomas, Nashua, New Hampshire, 1901; and Somerville directory (1901), 43, the last three items all available at Ancestry.com. On John Roosma, see West Point Association of Graduates, "Colonel John Sieba Roosma, Class of 1926," www.westpointaog.org; and "Col. John Roosma Dead at 83; Basketball Star at West Point," *New York Times,* November 14, 1983.

William V. Woodward's *Keaney—If You Don't Love to Play, Pivot and Go Home* (1991) is the most detailed biography to date on Frank W. Keaney, the founding father of Rhode Island basketball. See also "Ram Legends: Frank Keaney," University of Rhode Island Men's Basketball Media Guide, 2006–2007, 86–92; Maury Klein, "Keaney Invented the Fast Break and Rhode Island Made the Big Time," *Sports Illustrated,* November 27, 1978; Jack Cavanagh, "A Shot to Remember," *Sports Illustrated,* March 18, 1996; William Woodward, *Runnin' Rams: University of Rhode Island Basketball,* 7–39; "Frank Keaney Dead at 83," *Nashua (NH) Telegraph,* October 11, 1967; and Massachusetts birth records, 1840–1915, for Frank William Keating, 1900 US federal census return for Cambridge, ward 4, Massachusetts, and Keaney family tree, the last three at Ancestry.com.

John McLendon later expressed the core of his fast-break coaching philosophy in his 1965 book, *Fast Break Basketball: Fundamentals and Fine Points,* especially pages 3–26. Also see Doug Merlino, "Fast Break Basketball: How a Black Coach Revolutionized the Game," April 22, 2011, www.bleacherreport.com, an excerpt from his book *The Crossover: A Brief History of Basketball and Race, from James Naismith to LeBron James* (2011); Eric Angevine, "Everybody into the Pool: How the Inventor of Basketball and the Father of the Fast Break Beat Segregation in the 1930s," *The Classical,* February 8, 2012, theclassical.org; Katz, *Breaking Through,* 29–30; and Pamela Grundy, *Learning to Win: Sports, Education, and Social Change in Twentieth-Century North Carolina,* 181–83.

The definitive creation story for the fast break may never be fully known. "Inventions and/or innovations in the game are difficult to trace back to their origins," Chic Hess observed in *Prof Blood and the Wonder Teams.* "They often evolved in different places and piece by piece over a period of time" (397). That said, McLendon's contributions were both revolutionary and fundamental—a fact that even the then nearly all-white Basketball Hall of Fame recognized when it selected McLendon as its first African American contributor in 1978. They also took place, as McLendon himself expressed it, "before visibility," that is, in the era before whites paid attention to what was happening, athletically, at black colleges and universities. Moreover, as time marches on, McLendon's impact on how basketball is played is, finally, being more fully recognized. "As it is," as Doug Merlino wrote in 2011, "every coach from Jerry Tarkanian to Brad Stevens has a little of McLendon's DNA in his system." I am also indebted to a number of former college coaches who, in interviews with me, helped to unravel the development of the game through the decades: Aubrey Bonham, Capitola, California, July 9, 1987; Pete Newell, Inglewood, California, October 21, 1990; John Wooden, Encino, California, January 3, 1995; and Forrest Anderson, Oklahoma City, November 14, 1990.

For some 1930s examples of recommended practice drills, conditioning programs, and diet and pregame meals for basketball players, see Charles C. Murphy, *Basketball*, 79–91; Lon W. Jourdet and Kenneth A. Hashagen, *Modern Basketball*, 117–57; and Allen, *Better Basketball*, 65–76. For McLendon's fast-break drills, a later version can be found in his *Fast Break Basketball*, 97–116, 159–96. According to McLendon, Rocky Roberson's scoring feat also made it onto Bill Stern's *Colgate Sports Newsreel*, the popular NBC radio network program.

CHAPTER 10: *Hoosiers*

"Basketball may have been invented in Massachusetts," basketball coaching legend Bob Knight once remarked, "but it was made for Indiana."

Fortunately, the Hoosier State's basketball heritage has been well documented and analyzed over the years, and four works are essential: Phillip M. Hoose, *Hoosiers: The Fabulous Basketball Life of Indiana*, by far the best overview; Herb Schwomeyer, *Hoosier Hysteria: A History of Indiana High School Basketball*, a labor of love; Troy D. Paino, "The End of Nostalgia: A Cultural History of Indiana High School Basketball During the Progressive Era," a remarkable unpublished 1997 PhD dissertation from Michigan State University; and "Ain't God Good to Indiana!," John R. Tunis's chapter on Indiana basketball in his insightful 1958 book, *The American Way of Sport*. Other critical sources include Kyle Neddenriep, *Historic Hoosier Gyms: Discovering Bygone Basketball Landmarks;* William Gildea, *Where the Game Matters Most: A Last Championship Season in Indiana High School Basketball;* Jeff Washburn, *Tales from Indiana High School Basketball;* Bob Adams, *Hoosier High School Basketball;* Greg L. Guffey, *The Greatest Basketball Story Ever Told;* Norman Jones, *Growing UP in Indiana: The Culture & Hoosier Hysteria Revisited;* and, of course, the movie *Hoosiers,* David Anspaugh and Angelo Pizzo's deeply resonant 1986 re-creation of the epic 1954 Indiana state basketball championship won by tiny Milan, population 1,150, whose star player, Bobby Plump, still got telephone calls—decades later, from out of the blue—on whether the clock had expired when he launched the shot heard 'round Indiana.

On the early history, and rise, of basketball in the Hoosier State, see Hoose, *Hoosiers,* 87–117; Paino, "The End of Nostalgia," 1–192; Schwomeyer, *Hoosier Hysteria,* 11–44, 532–36; Gildea, *Where the Game Matters Most,* 7–13; Todd Gould, *Pioneers of the Hardwood: Indiana and the Birth of Professional Basketball,* xiii–29; Tunis, *The American Way of Sport,* 79–98; and Greg Guffey, *The Golden Age of Indiana High School Basketball,* 1–18. The hog bladder anecdote is from Jason Hiner, *Mac's Boys: Branch McCracken and the Legendary 1953 Hurryin' Hoosiers,* 57, while

Schwomeyer's *Hoosier Hysteria* remains the go-to history of the state championship tournament. The cheer is from Donald E. Hamilton, *Hoosier Temples: A Pictorial History of Indiana's High School Basketball Gyms,* 22. Also relevant are David G. Martin, "Gymnasium or Coliseum? Basketball, Education, and Community Impulse in Indiana During the Early Twentieth Century," in William J. Reese, ed., *Hoosier Schools: Past and Present,* 121–44, and Robert S. Lynd, *Middletown: A Study in Contemporary American Culture,* 284, 485. On the Indiana style of basketball, see Paino, "The End of Nostalgia," 2–5; Hiner, *Mac's Boys,* 22–26; and Branch McCracken, *Indiana Basketball.*

Kenneth Stampp's classic 1949 study, *Indiana Politics During the Civil War,* still provides valuable insights into the Hoosier State's split political personality. Helpful sources on Indiana and Indianans during the War Between the States include Alan D. Gaff, *On Many a Bloody Field: Four Years in the Iron Brigade;* Nancy Niblack Baxter, *Gallant Fourteenth: The Story of an Indiana Regiment;* William Thomas Venner, *Hoosiers' Honor: The Iron Brigade's 19th Indiana Regiment;* Nicole Etcheson, "The Most Desperate Battle Ever Fought," *New York Times,* September 18, 2012; Jennifer L. Weber, *Copperheads: The Rise and Fall of Lincoln's Opponents in the North,* 17, 80, 104–5; Stephen E. Towne, "The War Comes Home to Indiana," *New York Times,* March 13, 2013; and Ben Pitman, ed., *The Trials for Treason at Indianapolis, Disclosing the Plans for Establishing a North-Western Confederacy* (1865).

Leonard J. Moore's *Citizen Klansmen: The Ku Klux Klan in Indiana, 1921–1928* is a first-rate modern analysis. On the Klan basketball tournament, see *The Fiery Cross* — the Klan newspaper published in Indianapolis — March 24, April 4, and April 11, 1924. Arthur Trester's 1927 ban on Negro and Catholic schools in the state basketball tournament is discussed in Hoose, *Hoosiers,* x, 143–53, and in Aram Goudsouzian, " 'Ba-ad, Ba-a-ad Tigers': Crispus Attucks Basketball and Black Indianapolis in the 1950s," *Indiana Magazine of History* 96, no. 1 (May 2000), 7–8. "When Attucks opened its doors in 1927," Goudsouzian wrote, "the klan led a parade past the school. The procession took an hour to pass."

Indiana's Catholic high schools were banned from taking part in the state basketball tournament from 1927 to 1942. Not only did the Hoosier State's Catholic schools create their own state tournament, Indianapolis Cathedral and Fort Wayne Central also won national Catholic high school championships in 1933, 1939, and 1940. Indeed, the quality of basketball in Indiana was of such a high level that the Indiana School for the Deaf won the Central State Deaf Championship five times between 1927 and 1940 and won the National Deaf Championship in 1935 and 1940. See Schwomeyer, *Hoosier Hysteria,* 395–404, and the Seal-O-San advertisement, featuring Fort Wayne's Central Catholic's 1939 championship team, in the February 1940 issue of the *Athletic Journal.*

McLendon discussed his recruiting techniques, especially in Indiana, in our June 9, 1997, interview. On North Vernon, Indiana, and Slam and Slim, see North Vernon historic photographs, Jennings County Public Library, North Vernon, Indiana; Writers' Program, Indiana, *Indiana: A Guide to the Hoosier State,* 363–68;

North Vernon High School class of 1936, freepages.genealogy.rootsweb.ancestry .com; US federal census schedules, 1930 and 1940, for North Vernon, Indiana, and 1920 federal census schedules for Center, Indiana; family trees for Levi Colbert (1887–1927) and Norbert Bolden Downing (1916–77), Ancestry.com; "Giant Eagle Guard Sets Scoring Record in CIAA," *Norfolk Journal and Guide,* November 16, 1941; "N.C. State Favored to Win Tournament in Cincinnati, Ohio," *Pittsburgh Courier,* March 22, 1941; "It Pays to Be Tall," newspaper photograph, *Afro-American,* January 25, 1941; "2 CIAA Teams Enter National Cage Meet," *Afro-American,* March 15, 1941; "Basketball Press Book," North Carolina College for Negroes, 1946, typescript; and on the average height of American men and women from 1710 to 1970, see Richard H. Steckel, "A History of the Standard of Living in the United States," Economic History Association encyclopedia, July 21, 2002, eh.net/encyclopedia.

For details about Gary, Indiana, see Raymond A. Mohl and Neil Betten, *Steel City: Urban and Ethnic Patterns in Gary, Indiana, 1906–1950,* especially chapter 3, "Jim Crow in the Steel City," 48–90; Alex Poinsett, *Black Power Gary Style: The Making of Mayor Richard Gordon Hatcher,* 26–38; and Writers' Program, Indiana, *Indiana,* 163–79. On James "Boogie" Hardy, Floyd "Cootie" Brown, and John "Big" Brown, see "A Decade of Greatness, 1937–1947," a booklet commemorating McLendon's years at North Carolina College, and "Official Basketball Program, N.C. College vs. Tuskegee, January 27, 1941"; John B. McLendon Jr., "Great Moments in North Carolina Basketball History," a typescript; and Charles A. Ray, North Carolina College News Bureau, "John McLendon Starts Tenth Year in CIAA Basketball at NC College," a press release, all in the North Carolina Central University Archives.

Even though many of them were slow by later standards, the logic of the fast break, once the center jump was eliminated, was powerful, and the tactic rapidly spread far and wide. "The fast break is the most useful offense today," wrote Alexander J. Hogarty in "Basketball, the Changing Game," an article that appeared in *Athletic Journal* 20, no. 1 (September 1939), 38–39. At the time, Dr. Hogarty was coaching basketball in Ecuador.

CHAPTER 11: *City of Stone*

On the history of Duke University—as well as on the lives and philanthropy of the Duke family—the work of Robert F. Durden is essential: *The Dukes of Durham,. 1865–1929* (1975), *The Launching of Duke University, 1924–1949* (1993), *Lasting Legacy to the Carolinas: The Duke Endowment, 1924–1994* (1998), *Bold Entrepreneur: A Life of James B. Duke* (2003), and *Electrifying the Piedmont Carolinas: The Duke Power Company, 1904–1997* (2008). Also of great value is *If Gargoyles Could Talk: Sketches of Duke University* (1997), by former university archivist William E. King.

Aldous Huxley wrote about his visit to Duke for *Time and Tide,* a weekly British magazine, during the summer of 1937. His article, "Notes on the Way, July 3, 1937," was reprinted in the *Aldous Huxley Annual* 4 (December 2004), 26–31.

William Blackburn's *The Architecture of Duke University,* published in 1937, is a model of expository English prose; the quotes are from pages 7–8 and 15. A larger-than-life teacher of literature and writing, Blackburn helped to mold the early work of William Styron, Reynolds Price, Anne Tyler, Fred Chappell, Mac Hyman, and James Applewhite. See also *One and Twenty: Duke Narrative and Verse, 1924–1945* (1945), an anthology of the work of some of Blackburn's students, including "Autumn" and the "Long Dark Road," two early pieces by Styron. The quote on Duke looking like a great university is by Tallman Trask III. It can be found on the website of the Office of the University Architect. On the Duke chapel, see Blackburn, *The Architecture of Duke University,* 17–69.

Late one beer-soaked evening in the spring of 1977, I traipsed along with the high-spirited brother of a romantic interest across the nearly deserted main quadrangle of West Campus to the front entrance of the chapel, where, the young man had discovered, the statue of Lee was loose. "Let's swipe it," he said, lifting the statue a couple of inches off the metal bar it rested on. "C'mon, gimme a hand." Fortunately, however—with images of shattered concrete and the sounds of handcuffs clicking running through my brain—I was able to talk him out of it. His sister and I didn't get far, either.

An illustration of the Omicron Delta Kappa robes can be found in the 1944 *Chanticleer.*

On the Harvard Glee Club incident, see "A Program of Choral Music," Duke University Chapel, April 3, 1941, concert program, Dorothy Newsom Rankin Papers, Duke University Archives; "Glee Clubs Open Cycle of Services" and C. F. Sanborn, "Rubbish in Our Back Yard," April 4, 1941, and "Duke's Mixture," April 8, 1941, *Duke Chronicle;* Harvard Glee Club yearbook photograph, 1943, Harvard University Library Visual Information Access, viacs.hul.harvard.edu; and Ted Gup, "Southern Discomfort: With Quiet Grace, Two Black Men Change the Heart of Harvard in 1941," *Boston Globe,* December 12, 2004, www.boston.com.

On regional ambivalence toward Duke, see William Styron, *Sophie's Choice,* 30.

Hilary Lipsitz, now of New York City, heard the blue-toned limerick about Duke while growing up in Ahoskie, North Carolina, in Hertford County. There were also additional stanzas. "It was quite dirty," he added.

On the story of how Duke's teams became the Blue Devils, see King, *If Gargoyles Could Talk,* 85–86. Irving Berlin's "The Blue Devils of France" was featured in the Ziegfeld Follies of 1918. A copy of the sheet music can be found at the web page for the Levy Sheet Music Collection at Johns Hopkins University, https://jscholarship.library.jhu.edu, while a rousing piano version may be heard at www.pitt-payne.com.

The Edmund M. Cameron Records, 1929–1972, held in the David M. Rubenstein Rare Book and Manuscript Library at Duke, relate primarily to his career at Duke. Sources on his early years include 1870 US federal census data for Peter Cameron, Bloss Township, Tioga County, Pennsylvania; 1910 US census data for Alexander P. Cameron, Ward 1, Irwin, Westmoreland County, Pennsylvania; genealogical profiles for Christina Marr Pollack (1835–1917), Peter Cameron (1828–96), May Betsy Roberts (1863–1923), Alexander Pollock Cameron (1859–1930), and Edmund McCullough Cameron (1902–88), available at Ancestry.com; World War II draft card for Edmund McCullough Cameron, 1942; *An Outline History of Tioga and Bradford Counties in Pennsylvania, Chemung, Steuben, Tioga, Tompkins and Schuyler in New York,* 3–18; Westmoreland Coal Company, "Our Legacy," www.westmore land.com; *The Calyx,* 1924 yearbook, Washington and Lee University; Les Harvath, "Duke's Blue Devils Have Strong Ties to Western PA," *Pittsburgh Tribune,* March 11, 2011, triblive.com; and "Edmund M. Cameron, 1902–1988: The Man and the Stadium," library.duke.edu/uarchives.

Anyone researching the history of Duke basketball is indebted to the fine work of John Roth, whose *The Encyclopedia of Duke Basketball* is a model of careful research, colorful writing, and an author's dedication to his subject matter. His entries on Bill Werber, Chalky Councilor, Boley Farley, and Joe Croson were key to my understanding of the beginning of the Eddie Cameron era at Duke. "Bill Werber: Duke's Oldest Living Sports Hero," by Al Featherston, which appeared on June 16, 2008, at www.goduke.com, was also of help, as were Richard Goldstein, "Bill Werber, Infielder Who Played with Ruth, Is Dead at 100," *New York Times,* January 24, 2009; the family tree profile for William Murray Werber (1908–2009) at Ancestry.com; and Werber and Rogers, *Memories of a Ballplayer.* Finally, the contributions of journalist Bill Brill to documenting the history of Duke basketball can't be easily minimized. In addition to his award-winning articles, also see his *Duke Basketball: An Illustrated History* and *An Illustrated History of Duke Basketball: A Legacy of Achievement.*

On the Southern Conference, its basketball tournament, Duke's early efforts, and the tournament's original home, see "New College Body Planned in South," *New York Times,* December 12, 1920; "The History of the Southern Conference," www.soconsports.com; 1929 *Chanticleer,* Duke yearbook, 172–76; "Kentucky-Duke All-Time Series History" and "Kentucky vs. Duke: Monday, March 3, 1930," both at www.bigbluehistory.net; and the historic postcards and other images of the Atlanta Auditorium and Armory available online at www.atlantatimemachine.com.

On the Duke gymnasium—later named Card Gym—the home of the Blue Devils from 1930 to 1938, see Lewis Bowling, *Duke Basketball: A Pictorial History,* 17–23; Bryan, *Duke University: An Architectural Tour,* 84–88; "Above the Rim Places," Duke Libraries website, library.duke.edu/uarchives; and Blackburn, *The Architecture of Duke University,* 67. The 1933 Duke yearbook, the *Chanticleer,* in a master stroke of understatement, referred to the 1933 home game against Carolina as having "an overflow crowd." See also Roth, *The Encyclopedia of Duke Basketball,* 5, 212.

The key source on the Duke Indoor Stadium—later renamed in honor of Eddie Cameron—is Hazel Landwehr, *Home Court: Fifty Years of Cameron Indoor Stadium* (1989). Also see "Duke Will Build South's Largest Stadium," *Durham Herald,* April 5, 1939; "Duke's Indoor Stadium to Cost Over Third of a Million," *Durham Herald,*

May 17, 1939; "Duke to Open Gymnasium Jan. 6," *Durham Herald-Sun,* December 10, 1939; Ben Cohen, "Seventy Years in Cameron," *Duke Chronicle,* March 17, 2010; "Duke (Cameron) Indoor Stadium," www.opendurham.org; "Duke University Indoor Stadium, Exterior, Architectural Rendering," University of Pennsylvania Archives Digital Image Collection, library.upenn.edu/dla/archives; and the "Cameron Indoor Stadium" entries in the *Duke Basketball Yearbook* since at least the 1980s. Sybil Cameron Schiffi attested to her belief in the matchbook story in the Les Harvath article that appeared in the *Pittsburgh Tribune,* March 11, 2011, triblive .com. For the 1938 Duke football season and the 1939 Rose Bowl, see Bowling, *Wallace Wade,* 225–48, and the 2013 Duke Football Media Guide, 92, 101–7.

Although his achievements as an architect are finally beginning to be recognized, Julian Abele is still in need of a biographer. In the meantime, important sources on his life and work include Susan E. Tifft, "Out of the Shadows," *Smithsonian,* February 2005; William E. King, "The Discovery of an Architect: Duke University and Julian F. Abele," *Southern Cultures* 15, no. 1 (Spring 2009), 6–21; and Dreck Spurlock Wilson, "Julian Francis Abele (1881–1950)," in *African American Architects: A Biographical Dictionary, 1865–1945,* 1–4. Also see "Julian Abele, Architect: Hidden in the Shadows," Duke Libraries, library.duke.edu; "Julian Francis Abele," University of Pennsylvania Archives, www.archives.upenn.edu; "Julian F. Abele, Architect," Free Library of Philadelphia, www.freelibrary.org; "Julian Abele," www.opendurham.org; "Julian Francis Abele (1881–1950): Published Biographical References" and "Julian Francis Abele," Philadelphia Architects and Buildings database, www.philadelphiabuildings.org; James G. Spady, *Julian Abele and the Architecture of Bon Vivant,* Black History Museum Committee, 1982; Bryan, *Duke University: An Architectural Tour,* 13–15; and David Sokol, "Peter Cook: On Lines and Shadows," Architonic: Resource for Architecture and Design, www.archi tonic.com.

Ancestry.com is also a vital source on Julian Abele. Documents pertaining to Abele's life available online include a passport application for Julian F. Abele, September 18, 1908; US federal census entries, 1910–1940; incoming New York City passenger lists for the SS *Ultonia,* May 26, 1914, the SS *Fort St. George,* June 29, 1925, and the SS *France,* October 24, 1928; petition for naturalization for Marguerite Abele—Julian's French wife—February 9, 1926; World War II draft registration card, April 27, 1942; and the family tree profiles for Julian Abele, Charles Sylvester Abele (1841–93), Marguerite Eugeni Anna Bulle (1900–1971), and Jozef Kowalewski (1906–85).

On Horace Trumbauer and the work of his firm, see Frederick Platt, "Horace Trumbauer: A Life in Architecture," *Pennsylvania Magazine of History and Biography* 125, no. 4 (October 2001), 315–49; "Horace Trumbauer (1868–1938)," Philadelphia Architects and Buildings, www.brynmawr.edu; Oliver H. Bair Funeral Home records index for the estate of Horace Trumbauer and the Horace Trumbauer family tree profile, both at Ancestry.com; Michael C. Kathrens, *American Splendor: The Residential Architecture of Horace Trumbauer* (2012); and Rachel Hildebrandt and the Old York Road Historical Society, *The Philadelphia Area Architecture of Horace Trumbauer* (2009).

CHAPTER 12: *Blue Devil*

Robert Durden's *The Launching of Duke University,* especially chapters 8–14, contains the most thorough portrait of Duke during the war years. I've also benefited greatly from my in-person interviews, telephone interviews, and correspondence with Duke alumni from the early 1940s—all of whom have been generous with their time and knowledge—as well as from numerous conversations over the years with Jane Vessels, senior editor at *National Geographic,* who first studied this era as a Duke undergraduate. Other sources include the *Chanticleer,* Duke University yearbooks, 1939–44; Alice M. Baldwin, "The Woman's College as I Remember It: A Memoir," April 1959, typescript, Duke University Archives; Jessica Burchell, "Do Clothes Make the Woman? The Duke Dress Code," and untitled essays by Rosanne Jones and Alexandra Misretta, all prepared for Professor Jean O'Barr's class, "Education 146: Gender at Duke"; and several articles in the *Durham Morning Herald:* "Air Raid Courses Completed by 57 at Duke University," December 19, 1942; "Co-eds to Mix with Servicemen at Duke," July 7, 1943; "Military and Civilian Classes at Duke University to Stage Their First Sessions Tonight," July 1, 1943; "1,600 Begin Military Careers on Duke Campus This Morning," July 6, 1943; and "Another Navy V-12 Group Reaches Duke," November 2, 1943.

The Italian and German POWs who worked at Duke were likely housed at Camp Butner. On Axis prisoners of war in North Carolina, see Robert D. Billinger, *Nazi POWs in the Tar Heel State,* especially pages 51–69 and 108; Billinger, "Enemies and Friends," *Tar Heel Junior Historian,* Spring 2008, ncpedia.org; "Prisoners of War in North Carolina," *North Carolina History: A Digital Textbook,* www.learnnc.org; and Louis E. Keefer, *Italian Prisoners of War in America, 1942–1946,* 90, 92.

On Duke alumni fighting in World War II, see "Alumni in the Service," the *Chanticleer,* 1943, 19–24 (Edwards, Patterson, Murphy, Hinshaw); "3 Duke University Men Are Reported as War Casualties," *Durham Herald-Sun,* December 20, 1942 (Kepnes, Johntz); and "Remarks by Secretary Eric K. Shinseki, War Memorial Dedication at Duke University, October 23, 2009," US Department of Veterans Affairs, www.va.gov (Kepnes). On Edwards and the bitter combat in New Guinea also see George H. Johnston, *The Toughest Fighting in the World,* 142–240, and *New Guinea Diary,* 203–7; Robert L. Eichelberger and Milton MacKaye, "Our Bloody Jungle Road to Tokyo," *Saturday Evening Post,* August 13, 1944, 17–19, 104–11; and "Urbana Force During the Battle of Buna," The 32d "Red Arrow" Veteran Association, www.32d-division.org. The death of Kepnes was also recorded in "American Jewish War Service: From December 7, 1941 to June 30, 1943" in the *American Jewish Year Book* 45, 1943–1944, 417, and in *The History of the Medical Department of the United States Navy in World War II* 2, 3 (Navmed P-5021). For Murphy, see also the entries "1/Lt MURPHY, Kenneth J" and "Lockheed F-4-1-LO Lightning

41-2137" at the Project Priam website, www.projectpriam.com (no longer available). On Johntz, see the World War II draft card for Frederick Fones Johntz, Winston-Salem, North Carolina, and the Texas death index listing for Frederick F. Johntz, December 14, 1942, Nueces County, Texas, both at Ancestry.com.

The war—in letters received from friends and loved ones who were away, through the physical presence of someone who had witnessed it firsthand, or in newspaper stories with ties to Duke—was present on campus in other ways as well. See "Duke Alumnus Dog Is Veteran Flier," *Durham Morning Herald,* October 3, 1943; and two lengthy articles in the *Durham Herald-Sun,* "Duke Graduate Describes Life in Jap Prisons," February 6, 1944, and "Flying Tiger at Duke Was Last American Out of Rangoon," February 20, 1944.

The quote from the 1943 Duke yearbook, the *Chanticleer,* appears on page 6.

My primary source on the life of Dave Hubbell was the man himself, especially our taped interviews together. I also gleaned information from our numerous telephone calls, letters, and face-to-face meetings over the years. On his early American ancestors, see the letter from Nell Downing Norton to Rosalie Allen Furman, January 23, 1942, available at freepages.history.rootsweb.ancestry.com; Jay B. Hubbell, "The South in American Literature," in *South and Southwest: Literary Essays and Reminiscences,* 49–50; "James Eller Genealogy," www.surnameguide.com; 1860 US federal census return for Thomas Carlton, Wilkes County, North Carolina; profiles for Mary Ann Carlton (1830–1924) and Thomas Carlton (1790–1877) at Ancestry .com; and J. B. Hubbell, *Lives of Franklin Eller and John Carlton Eller,* 11–12.

On Jay B. Hubbell and his wife, Lucinda Smith Hubbell, see Rayburn S. Moore, "Jay B. Hubbell: A Memorial Tribute," *Southern Literary Journal* 12, no. 1 (Fall 1979), 92–95; profiles for Jay Broadus Hubbell and Lucinda Ada Smith, Smith Maddox Parrish family tree, Ancestry.com; US federal census return, 1920, for William Jordon Joseph Smith, Precinct 8, Dallas, Texas; Goldie Capers Smith, *The Creative Arts in Texas: A Handbook of Biography,* 80–81; online finding aid for the Jay B. Hubbell Papers, 1816–1998, Rubenstein Library, Duke University, and the web page for the Jay B. Hubbell Center for American Literary Historiography at Duke, both at library.duke.edu.

On the laying of the cornerstone for Duke's West Campus, see Durden, *The Launching of Duke University, 1924–1949,* plate 15, and "University Cornerstones" at the Duke University Libraries website, library.duke.edu. Longtime Duke archivist William E. King discussed the Italian stone carvers in his essay "Construction Laborers Unsung Campus Heroes" in his *If Gargoyles Could Talk,* 94–96.

The quote from Jule B. Warren, *North Carolina, Yesterday and Today,* can be found on page 188. Those from Mary L. Williamson, *The Life of Gen. Robert E. Lee,* are on pages 39–40 of the 1895 edition. The William Faulkner quotation is from *Intruder in the Dust,* pages 430–31 in the Library of America edition of his *Novels, 1942–1954.*

The origins and nature of Southern distinctiveness has long caught the attention and energies of a chorus of first-class essayists, travel writers, journalists, novelists, social scientists, and historians, including Alexis de Tocqueville, H. L. Mencken, C. Vann Woodward, John Hope Franklin, Robert Penn Warren, Carl Degler, and others. More recent contributions include Larry J. Griffin, "Southern Distinctiveness, Yet Again, or, Why America Still Needs the South," *Southern Cultures* 6, no. 3 (Fall 2000), 47–72, and Frederick F. Siegel, *The Roots of Southern Distinctiveness: Tobacco and Society in Danville, Virginia, 1780–1865.* On Southern manners, gardening, and foodways of the 1930s and 1940s, see "History and Manners" in Charles Reagan Wilson and William Ferris, eds., *Encyclopedia of Southern Culture;* Elizabeth Lawrence, *A Southern Garden,* 21, 79–83, 131; and a trio of period cookbooks, Harriet Ross Colquitt's *The Savannah Cook Book: A Collection of Old Fashioned Receipts From Colonial Kitchens* (1933), Marion W. Flexner's *Dixie Dishes* (1941), and the Junior League of Charleston's *Charleston Receipts* (1950). For a fascinating window into the origins of codes of conduct upheld by middle-and upper-class white Southerners, see Robert F. Pace, *Halls of Honor: College Men in the Old South* (2004).

On W. J. Cash and his remarkable book, *The Mind of the South* (1941), see Joseph L. Morrison, *W. J. Cash: Southern Prophet;* Bruce Clayton, *W. J. Cash: A Life;* Paul D. Escott, *W. J. Cash and the Minds of the South;* and Charles W. Eagles, ed., *The Mind of the South: Fifty Years Later.* Cash himself, by the way, wasn't overly impressed with the elites of Hayti and other leading African American businessmen of the South. "Most of these Negro Babbitts," he wrote, "were a good deal more interested in exploiting their race than in attempting to improve its general condition" (*The Mind of the South,* 316).

Major Goodwyn might have moved farther up the Army chain of command during the 1920s and 1930s had he gone along with the prevailing view in the War Department, which held that the nation's next foe would be the Soviet Union. Goodwyn believed, instead, that we would fight Germany and Japan. The quotation was shared by his son, Larry.

Surprisingly, a comprehensive history of African American maids, household cooks, laundresses, and yardmen in the South during segregation has yet to be written. On female domestic workers, see "More Slavery at the South, by a Negro Nurse" (1921), available online at the University of North Carolina's Documenting the American South website, docsouth.unc.edu; Susan Tucker, *Telling Memories Among Southern Women: Domestic Workers and Their Employers in the Segregated South* (1988); and Rebecca Sharpless, *Cooking in Other Women's Kitchens: Domestic Workers in the South, 1865–1960* (2010).

My primary sources for information about Dave Hubbell's career as a Duke basketball player were my interviews with the man himself, supplemented by correspondence and telephone conversations. Also helpful were wartime copies of the *Chanticleer,* John Roth's *The Encyclopedia of Duke Basketball,* and Duke basketball media guides.

On the victory-smitten Durham High School basketball teams of the late 1930s and early 1940s, see Bones McKinney and Garland Atkins, *Bones: Honk Your Horn If You Love Basketball*—one of the funniest roundball books ever—33–49, and Jim

Sumner, *Tales from the Blue Devil Locker Room: A Collection of the Greatest Duke Basketball Stories Ever Told*, 11–12.

TruAde, soft drink with a legendary following in Virginia, North Carolina, and South Carolina, apparently first appeared on the market in 1938. See "Soda and Carbonated Beverage Trademarks, 1940s," www.bottlebooks.com, and "Soda Pop of the Week: TruAde Noncarbonated Orange," www.retroplanet.com. The 1942 Rose Bowl and Wallace Wade's decision to reenter the armed forces are discussed in Bowling, *Wallace Wade*, 261–87. On Gerry Gerard, see Brill and Cohen, *An Illustrated History of Duke Basketball*, 40–44; *Duke Basketball Yearbook, 1995–1996*, 194–95; and copies of the 1935 *Chanticleer*, 232–34; the 1943 *Chanticleer*, 274–78, 294–97; and the 1944 *Chanticleer*, 246–49.

CHAPTER 13: *Medicine Ball*

Sources on the Duke medical school and the Duke hospital prior to and during the war years include bulletins of the Duke University School of Medicine, 1940 through 1944–45; the fiftieth anniversary edition of the Duke medical school yearbook, *Aesculapian, 1930–1980;* Durden, *The Launching of Duke University, 1924–1949*, 347–79; James Gifford, *The Evolution of a Medical Center: A History of Medicine at Duke University to 1941* (1972); Walter E. Campbell, *Foundations for Excellence: 75 Years of Duke Medicine* (2006); *The First Twenty Years: A History of the Duke University Schools of Medicine, Nursing and Health Services, and Duke Hospital, 1930–1950* (1952); and Deryl Hart, *The First Forty Years at Duke in Surgery and the P.D.C.* (1971). My interviews with war-era Duke medical students were key in re-creating the pressures they faced, as was a typescript of *The Sentinal Pile*, the class of 1946 yearbook.

On the larger-than-life Wilburt Davison, see Jay M. Arena and John P. McGovern, eds., *Davison of Duke: His Reminiscences* (1980); W. C. Davison, *The Duke University Medical Center (1892–1960)*, another volume of reminiscences; "Festschrift in Honor of Wilburt Cornell Davison," *American Journal of Diseases of Children* 124, no. 3 (September 1972), 332–81; and William G. Anlyan, *Metamorphoses: Memoirs of a Life in Medicine*, 37–38.

In ways that would both amaze and befuddle later generations, the college students of the 1940s — and earlier — would regularly sing together at parties and get-togethers. Not only were the words to most of the songs known by all, it was also an opportunity for individuals to show off their vocal talents. By the 1950s, however, the practice was on the decline, only to essentially disappear a decade later. Dave Hubbell believes he know why. "The transistor radio killed it," he told me at his home in St. Petersburg, Florida, one afternoon in 1997. "When transistor radios became available, kids stopped singing."

The wartime whiskey shortage — and, below the Mason-Dixon line, "whiskey" meant bourbon — was no small thing in the South. "Sometimes you could buy a bottle of whiskey," Hubbell remembered, "as long as you also bought a bottle of something else, usually rum." The Distilled Spirits Institute, a trade group, even took out a full-page advertisement entitled "A Frank Statement on the Whiskey Shortage" in the *Durham Morning Herald* on December 2, 1943. The classic Southern take on whiskey, however, was written by a Carolina man, the novelist Walker Percy, who attended medical school in New York. In his luminously poetic essay "Bourbon," Percy recalls a 1935 Duke-Carolina football game that he went to armed with a hinged-top hip flask and a stunningly beautiful blind date. "Her clothes are the color of fall leaves and her face turns up like a flower," he wrote. "Will she have a drink? No. But that's all right. The taste of the Bourbon (Cream of Kentucky) and the smell of her fuse with the brilliant Carolina fall and the sounds of the crowd and the hit of the linemen in a single synesthesia." Originally appearing in the December 1975 issue of *Esquire* magazine, the essay is reprinted in Percy's *Signposts in a Strange Land*, 102–7.

On Purple Jesus, see Arena and McGovern, *Davison of Duke*, 123; *The Sentinal Pile*; and interviews with Dave Hubbell, Lloyd and Barbara Taylor, and Jack Burgess. Ed "Pee Wee" Boyd told me he thought that an African American hospital employee at Duke might have taught the students how to make it.

Key sources on military basketball teams—and on basketball itself—during World War II include: *Converse Basketball Year Book 1943–1944;* Seymour Smith, Jack Rimer, and Dick Triptow, *A Tribute to Armed Forces Basketball, 1941–1969;* Mokray, *Ronald Encyclopedia of Basketball,* a key reference guide for pre-1960s basketball; and John R. Tunis, "Sports in Wartime," *New Republic,* April 3, 1944, 466–68. An impressive array of photographs of both men's and women's basketball teams at Camp Rucker, Alabama, appears in chapter 3, "The Fields of Friendly Strife," in James L. Noles Jr.'s *Camp Rucker During World War II,* 41–56. On the Milligan College team, see James G. Schneider, *The Navy V-12 Program: Leadership for a Lifetime,* 267; "Jack Lee Reitz," *Enid News and Eagle,* May 2, 2013; telephone interview with Bill Allen, former Milligan player and legendary Tulsa high school basketball coach—and, of all things, my onetime Sunday School teacher.

While most military sports teams were segregated, a handful—if that—appear not to have been. Pioneering research on this and related subjects has been undertaken by contributors to two first-rate websites, those of the Association for Professional Basketball Research and the Black Fives. See, for example, Jon Scott, "Larry Doby, Chuck Harmon and Great Lakes Naval Station," October 3, 2007, www.apbr.org, and "Vintage All-Black U.S. Military Basketball Teams," May 28, 2009, www.blackfives.com.

Francis Buzzell's *The Great Lakes Naval Training Station: A History* surveys the World War I–era basketball program, while Donald William Rominger Jr.'s "The Impact of the United States Government's Sports and Physical Training Policy on Organized Athletics During World War II," a 1976 doctoral dissertation from Oklahoma State University, details the Navy's influence on collegiate sports during World War II. The quotes from the Training Division, Bureau of Aeronautics, US Navy, are from *Basketball,* a Naval Aviation Physical Training Manual published in 1943 by the United States Naval Institute, 7–11.

Dave Hubbell, Dick Symmonds, Lloyd Taylor, Ed Johnson, and Jack Burgess were not only players on the Duke medical school basketball team: in their interviews, letters, and phone conversations they comprised the most important sources for reconstructing the team's brief but eventful career. Also of great assistance were my conversations and correspondence with numerous team players' family members, including Barbara Taylor, Donna Burgess, Charlotte Sieber, Jeane Thistlethwaite, Helene Wechsler, Laura Broff, and the entire Montana branch of the wonderful and most welcoming Burgess family.

On the Duke intramural Basketball Jamboree and the experiences of the medical school teams, see the Duke *Chronicle,* February 19, March 9, and December 17, 1943, and January 7, 21, 28, and March 10, 1944; Lucile K. Boyden, "War Recreation Program Is Pushed at Duke University," *Durham Morning Herald,* September 3, 1943; the *Chanticleer,* 1942, 354–55, and 1943, 294–97; and "Duke De-emphasizing Spring Sports for Navy Build-Up," *Durham Morning Herald,* March 10, 1944. The Duke medical school team also made a few brief appearances in the Durham newspapers, primarily in the form of box scores. See, for example, *Durham Morning Herald,* January 12 and February 2, 1944. A photograph of the 1946 team, however, captioned MEDICAL STUDENTS PLAY BENEFIT GAME TONIGHT, appeared in the *Durham Morning Herald,* January 28, 1946. Undated clippings about the medical school basketball team were given to me by Dick Symmonds.

On James Richard Thistlethwaite, see "Thistlethwaite, Named Successor to Dobson, to Visit Campus," March 16, 1934, and "Wheeler, Thistlethwaite, Kellison Elected New Captains," May 22, 1942, both in the *Richmond Collegian;* 1940 federal census data for Glenn F. Thistlethwaite, Lee Ward, Richmond; *The Monticello,* 1939 yearbook for Thomas Jefferson High School, Richmond; *The Web,* 1941, 1942, and 1943, University of Richmond yearbooks; "Richmond Cagers Led by Father and Son," *Sarasota Herald-Tribune,* December 9, 1941; the University of Richmond Basketball Media Guide, 1995–1996; and "Polio Twin Bill Offers Naturals," an undated column from Jack Horner's Sports Corner in my possession.

Richard Earl Symmonds: correspondence and telephone interviews; 1940 US census data for Emmett E. Symmonds, Jefferson Township, Memphis City, Scotland County, Missouri; and the 1941 and 1943 editions of *The Ragout,* the yearbook for Central College, Fayette, Missouri.

Lloyd M. Taylor: correspondence, oral-history interviews, and telephone interviews with Lloyd and Barbara Taylor, Great Falls, Montana. On Maryville College, see Samuel Tyndale Wilson, *A Century of Maryville College, 1819–1919* (1916), and James B. Jones Jr., "Maryville College: An Early Leader in the Struggle for Biracial Education in Tennessee, 1819–1901," Tennessee History Resource Page, www.geocities.ws.

Joseph Emmett Walthall III: family history profiles for Clara Kathryn Grimm, Joseph Emmett Walthall Jr., and Joseph Emmett Walthall III, available at Ancestry .com; *The Monticola,* 1942 and 1943, University of West Virginia yearbooks; basketball player profiles for Joe Walthall, Jim Walthall, and Randy Walthall at wvustats .com; Sandy Wells, "1942 WVU National Title Team Had Heart," *Charleston*

Gazette, March 10, 2012; and George Hohmann, "Remembrance of 1942 NIT Championship Tournament," *Charleston Daily Mail,* April 2, 2010.

Homer A. Sieber: correspondence and telephone interviews with Dr. Charlotte Mock Sieber; 1930 US federal census entry for John Luther Sieber, Highland Ward, Roanoke City, Virginia; 1940 US federal census entry for Homer Alden Sieber, Jefferson Ward, Roanoke; and the 1942 *Rawenoch,* the Roanoke College yearbook.

Harry L. Wechsler: correspondence and telephone conversations with Helene Wechsler and Laura Broff; US federal census data for Harold A. Wechsler, Third Ward, McKeesport, Pennsylvania, 1930, and Fourth Ward, McKeesport, 1940; the 1940 and 1942 *Yough-A-Mon,* the McKeesport High School yearbook; and *Polk's McKeesport City Directory,* 1939.

Edgar Johnson: correspondence and telephone interviews with Edgar W. Johnson; 1940 US federal census, Ward 7, Coffeyville, Kansas. The Civilian Public Service Story, a website dedicated to preserving and telling the story of the CPS, offers much information on World War II–era conscientious objectors. In addition to posting profiles of individual CPS workers, it features brief historical essays, period photographs, and overviews of the camps and work units at civilianpublicservice .org. On the CPS camp in Magnolia, Arkansas, and its basketball team, see "CPS Unit Number 007-01," civilianpublicservice.org; Guy Lancaster, "Camp Magnolia, *The Encyclopedia of Arkansas History and Culture,* www.encyclopediaofarkansas .net; and James F. Willis, *Southern Arkansas University: The Mulerider School's Centennial History,* 158. Leslie Eisan's *Pathways of Peace: A History of the Civilian Public Service Program Administered by the Brethren Service Committee,* 165–69, contains a profile of recreation at Brethren-administered CPS camps; on pages 90–91 is an excerpt from an unpublished journal of a conscientious objector based at Camp Magnolia.

William Stafford, who later became one of the most important American poets of the twentieth century, was also a CO at Magnolia. A Kansas native and a 1937 KU graduate, he had been part of a small group of white and African American students who quietly desegregated dining tables at the student union. For the near lynching in McNeil, see William Stafford, *Down in My Heart,* 13–22, and Kim Stafford, *Early Morning: Remembering My Father, William Stafford,* 41–45, and e-mail correspondence from Kim Stafford, October 2013. On the protests at KU, see William Stafford, *You Must Revise Your Life,* 10–11.

On conscientious objectors at Duke during World War II, see "Plans Under Way to Work Conscientious Objectors at Duke," *Durham Morning Herald,* October 14, 1942; "Duke Hospital Project," *World Peace Newsletter,* December 22, 1942, 3, in the Robert L. Blake Papers, 1943–1988, Duke University Medical Center Archives; Louis E. Swanson and James F. Gifford Jr., "Conscientious Objection and Clinical Care: A History of Civilian Public Service Camp No. 61 at Duke University, 1942–1946," *North Carolina Medical Journal* 46, no. 7 (July 1985), 418–22; "CPS Unit Number 061-01," civilianpublicservice.org; and Civilian Public Service Camp #61 Collection, Duke University Medical Center Archives.

Lloyd Taylor and Dave Hubbell are the primary sources for the Duke medical school–Duke Blue Devils basketball game, for which no written records are known to exist. According to Bones McKinney, the Duke varsity played against the Durham High School team in an unpublicized game a few years earlier; see McKinney, *Bones*, 40–41. "It's true that we didn't have much of a crowd that night," he added. "We didn't get much of a write-up in the paper either. In fact, you had to look between the classifieds and the hemorrhoid remedy ads to find us."

CHAPTER 14: *"He Can't Sit There"*

Because of a paucity of records, caused in part by wartime conditions, reconstructing the 1943–44 North Carolina College basketball season required some detective work, especially regarding the number of games that the Eagles played. See "Schedule—1944" in "North Carolina College 'Eagles' vs. 1319th Engineers," a mimeographed game roster in the "N.C.C.U. Sports, 1944," vertical file, and the "N.C.C.U. Sports, Schedules, 1941–42, 1944–49," vertical file in the Shepard Library, North Carolina Central University; and J. L. Whitehead, comp., *The 1944 Bulletin of the Colored Intercollegiate Athletic Association*, 25–26. See also "NCCN Opens Season Friday," January 5; "17 Tilts Listed for Eagle Five," January 6; "Negro College Eagles to End Home Season," February 28; and "Eagle Cagers Face Two Eastern Teams," March 9, 1944, *Durham Morning Herald;* various individual game summaries reported in the *Durham Morning Herald*, the *Durham Sun*, and the combined Sunday morning edition, the *Durham Herald-Sun*, as well as in the *Norfolk Journal and Guide*, 1943–1944; "A Decade of Greatness, 1937–1947," a pamphlet celebrating John McLendon's tenure as the North Carolina College basketball coach; and North Carolina Central University, Men and Women's Basketball Media Guide, 1994–1995, 38.

Similarly, determining who played on the 1943–44 North Carolina College basketball team and when is not an exact science, largely because of the military draft. George Parks, who also served as an occasional chauffeur for Dr. Shepard, was a key member of the team. A Kentuckian, he later had a long career as an attorney in Los Angeles. On Parks, see *National Registry of Who's Who*, 1999 ed., 577; I also relied on undated clippings, correspondence, and telephone interviews with Parks. George Lindsey Samuel Jr., a.k.a. Crazy Horse, was also a vital component of the squad, as were William "Billy" Williams and Smokey Davis. Other players that season included Howard "Skeeter" Townsend, Joe "Buke" Williams, Sam Shepard, and Arthur Marshal "Gip" Gibson.

Individual histories of most African American military units have not been written. Steven D. Smith and James A. Zeidler, eds., *A Historic Context for the African American Military Experience*, a 1998 report commissioned by the Cultural Resources Research Center at the US Army Construction Engineering Research Laboratory, is a helpful overview. See especially Robert F. Jefferson, "African Americans in the U.S. Army During World War II," and Steven D. Smith, Keith Krawczynski, and Robert F. Jefferson, "Victory and Context: Recognition of African

American Contributions to American History," the latter of which includes a roster of World War II–era military units, including the 1319th Engineer General Service Regiment. For the game with the 1319th, see "Eagles Record 44–36 Victory," *Durham Morning Herald,* January 8, 1944.

On the origins of the 930th Field Artillery, see Eleanor L. Hannah, *Manhood, Citizenship, and the National Guard: Illinois, 1870–1917,* 11–12; Christopher Robert Reed, *Black Chicago's First Century,* vol. 1, *1833–1900,* 220–21; and the historical overview of the Eighth Infantry, Illinois National Guard, at www.8thinfantry.org. An interview with Hondon Hargrove can be found in Mary Penick Motley, ed., *The Invisible Soldier: The Experience of the Black Soldier, World War II,* 319–26. For the 390th's game with North Carolina College, see "Eagles Take Contest with Butner Quintet," *Durham Herald-Sun,* January 16, 1944.

The terms "rabbit" and "bear" come from an interview with Arthur Lloyd Johnson conducted in Louisville, Kentucky, on June 27, 1992.

Brief mentions of the two games that the Eagles played in Raleigh appeared in the *Durham Morning Herald:* "Eagles Preparing for 2 Court Scraps," January 19, and "Eagles to Invade Raleigh for Two Games," January 21, 1944.

On Saint Augustine's College, see "The Negro in North Carolina and the South: His Fifty-Five Years of Freedom and What He Has Done," a commencement address by Walter Clark, *St. Augustine's Record* 25, no. 5 (1920), and Sarah and A. Elizabeth Delany, *Having Our Say: The Delany Sisters' First 100 Years,* 37–93. For the founding and early years of Shaw University, see J. A. Whitted, *A History of the Negro Baptists of North Carolina,* 146–65; "December 1865 — Henry Martin Tupper and the Founding of Shaw University," University of North Carolina, University Libraries, www.lib.unc.edu; Shaw University Archives website, www.shawu .edu/archives; and "Shaw University: The First Historically Black University in the South," Documenting the American South, docsouth.unc.edu.

James Ellis Lytle Jr. (1901–87), the sleepy-eyed but crafty coach of the Shaw Bears, was a force on the Raleigh campus for a half century. See "James Lytle," North Carolina Sports Hall of Fame, www.ncshof.com; "James E. Lytle, Jr. Appointed to Provide Physical Education Program," *New York Age,* November 20, 1943; North Carolina House Resolution Honoring the Shaw Women's Basketball Team, 2012, www.ncleg.net; 1880 US federal census, Marshville Township, Union County, North Carolina, entry for Isham Lytle; 1920 US federal census, Marshville Township, Union County, North Carolina, entry for James E. Lytle; 1930 US federal census, Third Ward, Raleigh, entries for Shaw University; World War II draft registration card for James Ellis Lytle Jr.; and North Carolina death indexes, 1997–2004, at Ancestry.com.

My primary sources on the "barefoot game" were my interviews with John McLendon, Aubrey Stanley, and Edward "Pee Wee" Boyd as well as "'Shoeless Wonders' of North Carolina Aided by Strategy," a brief account that appeared in the January 29, 1944, edition of the *Norfolk Journal and Guide.* In "Eagles Take Contest from Bears Easily," a report on the game that appeared in the January 23, 1944, edition of the *Durham Morning Herald,* the unnamed—"Special"—reporter referred to North Carolina College's opponents as "the tricky Shaw team."

In reconstructing the Eagles' road trip to West Virginia in January of 1944, I used both oral and printed sources. The recollections of John McLendon, Aubrey Stanley, and Edward "Pee Wee" Boyd were key, as were the contributions of various local history experts along the route, including Linda Evans at the Greensboro Historical Museum; Fam Brownlee and Damien Miller at the Forsyth County Public Library in Winston-Salem; James Leedy, the archivist at Bluefield State College; and the staff at the Craft Memorial Library in Bluefield, West Virginia. Interstate bus timetables from the 1940s were used to reconstruct the route, which was then plotted on both period and modern maps, including the 1944 North Carolina highway map published by the North Carolina State Highway and Public Works Commission; the 1944 official state highway map for Virginia; a 1940s Texaco road map of Delaware, Maryland, Virginia, West Virginia, and North Carolina; period railroad maps of North Carolina, Virginia, and West Virginia, published by C. S. Hammond and Co., New York; The 2013 *Rand McNally Road Atlas;* DeLorme's *North Carolina Atlas & Gazetteer* and *Virginia Atlas and Gazetteer;* and ADC's *Raleigh and Durham Street Atlas.* In early 2013, I retraced the route taken by the Eagles, traveling as much as possible on the roads that were used in 1944.

Another set of key sources for reconstructing the bus trip were the Federal Writers' Project guides for the three states: *North Carolina: A Guide to the Old North State* (1939), *Virginia: A Guide to the Old Dominion* (1940), and *West Virginia: A Guide to the Mountain State* (1941). Other helpful sources included Michael Hill, ed., *Guide to North Carolina Highway Historical Markers,* 10th ed. (2007); Virginia Writers' Program, *The Negro in Virginia* (1940); 1940s photographs of the train station in Bluefield, West Virginia, from the James N. Gillum Archives, Norfolk and Western Historical Society, nwhs.org; and an undated, circa-1942 copy of *The Bluefieldian* in the Bluefield State College Archives.

In July of 1944, six months after the Virginia bus incident involving the Eagles, an African American defense plant worker named Irene Morgan boarded a Trailways bus in Baltimore. Morgan, who was going to visit her mother in Gloucester County, Virginia, refused to yield her seat to a white passenger, and she was arrested. But after she refused to pay a ten-dollar fine for violating a Virginia statute mandating segregated seating in public transportation, the legal affairs division of the NAACP took up her case. In 1946, the US Supreme Court, in *Morgan v. Commonwealth of Virginia,* ruled in her favor and declared that segregated seating on interstate bus lines was unconstitutional. See Raymond Arsenault, *Freedom Riders: 1961 and the Struggle for Racial Justice,* 11–21, and Richard Goldstein, "Irene Morgan Kirkaldy, 90, Rights Pioneer, Dies," *New York Times,* August 13, 2007.

McLendon's standoff with the bus driver reflected both a growing sense within the African American community that segregation laws were, in fact, illegal and perhaps the knowledge that African American plaintiffs, especially in North Carolina, had had some success in the courts over segregation issues on public carriers, as in *State v. Harris,* 213 N.C. 758, 197 S.E. 594 (1938), and *Harris v. Queen City Coach Co.,* 220 N.C. 67 (1941). See "The Hour Will Come," *Carolina Times,* December 4, 1943, and North Carolina Advisory Committee to the US Commission on Civil Rights, 1959–1962, *Equal Protection of the Laws of North Carolina,* 211–18. On a 1942 complaint filed against the Southern Railway, see Anthony Lewis, "Abroad at Home; 'Imposing on Them a Badge of Inferiority,'" *New York Times,* January 22, 2000.

On the games against Bluefield State and West Virginia State, as well as Big Dog's knee injury, see "Big Blue Basketeers Play North Carolina," *Bluefield Daily Telegraph,* January 28, 1944; "Eagles' Cage Star Is Doubtful Starter," February 3, 1944, and "North Carolina College Cage Club Faces Hampton Five Here Tonight," February 10, 1944, *Durham Morning Herald;* "Thomas May Be Lost to Carolina for Entire Season," *Norfolk Journal and Guide,* February 12, 1944; and Whitehead, *The 1944 Bulletin of the Colored Intercollegiate Athletic Association,* 25–28.

On Minnie Hester and her "drink house," see Christina Greene, *Our Separate Ways: Women and the Black Freedom Movement in Durham, North Carolina,* 28–29, 247n107, and the 1940 US federal census entry for Minnie Hester, Ward 3, Durham, North Carolina.

CHAPTER 15: *Burgess*

My primary source on Jack Burgess was Jack Burgess himself, as revealed in lengthy interviews, telephone conversations, and correspondence, including a box of letters that he sent to his parents when he was away during World War II. On the Burgess family history, see the 1895 Kansas state census for James R. and Sara A. Burgess, Jackson Township, Riley County, Kansas; 1900 US census entry for Frank Milton Benton, Wamego Township, Pottawatomie County, Kansas; World War I draft registration card for John Ralph Burgess, Butte, Montana; 1930 US census entry for John Ralph Burgess, school district 45, Wolf Point, Roosevelt County, Montana; 1940 US census entry for John R. and Esther Burgess, Precinct 8, Missoula, Montana; and family tree entries for Anna May Clark, Homer Erasmus Benton, Esther Ann Taylor, John R. Burgess, and Esther Ann Benton, available at Ancestry.com.

On Wolf Point, see Federal Writers' Project's *Montana: A State Guide Book,* 228.

On the Bighorn brothers—Alpheus, Leonard, and Ernest—and Philip Red Eagle, see the Montana Indian Athletic Hall of Fame website, www.montanaindian athletichof.org. Three good sources on Assiniboine stories are Robert H. Lowie, *The Assiniboine* (1910), 201–2; Assiniboine Elders Board, *How the Summer Season Came* (1981); and Jerome Fourstar, *How the Morning and Evening Stars Came to Be* (1978).

The very first issue of *LIFE* magazine, published on November 23, 1936, featured a cover story on the building of the Fort Peck Dam, with photographs by Margaret Bourke-White. Seventy-five years later, in a remarkable act of public self-criticism, the editors at *LIFE* revisited their coverage and filled in pieces of their story that were not so rosy. See *LIFE 75 Years: The Very Best of LIFE* (2011), which includes a reprint of the first issue.

On Jack Burgess's career at the University of Montana—then called Montana State University at Missoula—see athletic record ledgers for varsity basketball, 1940–44, University of Montana basketball office, Missoula; *The Sentinel*, 1942, University of Montana yearbook; *Montana: 1995–96 Grizzly Basketball Guide;* family history profile for George P. "Jiggs" Dahlberg, Ancestry.com; and R. L. Polk & Co., Butte city directory, 1925. John Christgau's *The Origins of the Jump: Eight Men Who Shook the World of Basketball* not only features a profile of Kenny Sailors but is also a terrific, first-class book on basketball. Also see Adolph H. Grundman, "Kenneth Lloyd 'Kenny' Sailors," in Porter, *Basketball: A Biographical Directory*, 417–18; Louis Effrat, "Wyoming Downs Georgetown to Capture N.C.A.A. Basketball Title," *New York Times*, March 31, 1943; and "American Red Cross Benefit," in Brenner, *College Basketball's National Championships*, 599–600.

The development and functioning of the School of Medicine at Duke, and that of the Duke hospital, are inextricably linked, a fact that is well borne out in Walter E. Campbell's first-rate history, *Foundations for Excellence: 75 Years of Duke Medicine* (2006). Other helpful sources on the medical school and hospital at Duke both prior to and during the war years include Gifford, *The Evolution of a Medical Center* (1972); Arena and McGovern, *Davison of Duke* (1980); Davison, *The Duke University Medical Center* (ca. 1966); Deryl Hart, *The First Forty Years at Duke in Surgery and the P.D.C.* (1971); *The First Twenty Years: A History of the Duke University Schools of Medicine, Nursing and Health Services, and Duke Hospital, 1930–1950* (1952); and "Vast Hospital at Duke University Is a World of Its Own," *Durham Herald-Sun*, May 21, 1944. My interviews with Barbara Taylor, Lloyd Taylor, Dave Hubbell, and Jack Burgess were crucial in reconstructing the inner workings of the Duke hospital. They also told me the story of the medical student who was expelled by Davison. On the status of health care in North Carolina during the early 1940s, see the final report of the North Carolina Hospital and Medical Care Commission, 1945.

The North Carolina state legislature passed a law in 1903 mandating that cadavers used in medical research be segregated. See North Carolina Advisory Committee to the US Commission on Civil Rights, 1959–1962, *Equal Protection of the Laws of North Carolina*, 225. At the public dispensary in the Duke hospital during the early 1940s, white patients were allowed to register forty-five minutes earlier than African Americans. See the bulletin of the Duke University School of Medicine, 1940, 28–30. Historian Spencie Love, in her groundbreaking and diligently researched book, *One Blood: The Death and Resurrection of Charles R. Drew*, recounts the story of Maltheus Avery, a black World War II veteran, who in 1950 died at Lincoln Hospital in Durham after being refused admission at Duke hospital; see 217–57.

Generally speaking, Durham's daily newspapers refrained from reporting stories about soldiers—white or black—crossing the color line during the war. My primary sources on incidents in which they did were my interviews with John McLendon, Edward "Pee Wee" Boyd, Ruth Boyd, Jack Burgess, Robert Seymour, Ed Johnson, John Hope Franklin, and other wartime residents of Durham.

"Servicemen's Guide to Durham, North Carolina: Home City of Camp Butner," a wartime brochure prepared by the Service Division, Works Progress Administration, State of North Carolina, was distributed free to GIs by the Durham Chamber of Commerce. On Camp Butner, see Anderson, *Durham County*, 383–86; Sarah McCulloh Lemmon, *North Carolina's Role in World War II*, 13; Campbell, *Foundations for Excellence*, 103–4; and an interview with Captain Hondon Hargrove, 597th Field Artillery Battalion, in Mary Penick Motley, ed., *The Invisible Soldier: The Experience of the Black Soldier, World War II*, 319–26.

While national Ku Klux Klan organizations faltered during the early 1940s, local chapters remained active throughout the South, including in Durham. See Arthur F. Raper and Ira De A. Reid, "The South Adjusts—Downward," *Phylon* 1, no. 1 (1940), 6–27; David Cunningham, *Klansville, U.S.A.: The Rise and Fall of the Civil Rights–Era Ku Klux Klan*, 16–31, 43–73, 239; Civil Rights Congress, *We Charge Genocide: The Historic Petition to the United Nations for Relief from a Crime of the United States Government Against the Negro People*, 17–20, 147–49, 158–60, 189–92, 201–16; Arnold S. Rice, *The Ku Klux Klan in American Politics*, 107–18; Michael Newton and Judy Ann Newton, *The Ku Klux Klan: An Encyclopedia*, 125, 189, 430–33, 458–59, 519; Chester L. Quarles, *The Ku Klux Klan and Related American Racialist and Antisemitic Organizations*, 77–88; Hill, *The FBI's RACON*, 140–41, 272, 276–83, 345, 572–73; and James Shumaker, "The Rise and Fall of the Ku Klux Klan," *Durham Morning Herald*, October 5, 1952.

On the Klan in Durham, see Anderson, *Durham County*, 303–5, 532n31; Leonard Rogoff, *Homelands: Southern Jewish Identity in Durham and Chapel Hill, North Carolina*, 132–33; Elin N. Evans, *The Provincials: A Personal History of Jews in the South*, 216–17; Osha Gray Davidson, *The Best of Enemies: Race and Redemption in the New South* (1996); "The Secret Game," ABC News *Nightline*, 1997; and interviews with Edward "Pee Wee" Boyd, Ruth Boyd, and Alex Rivera. Pauli Murray's efforts to gain admission into the University of North Carolina in 1938–39 caused her Aunt Pauline—who had been acquainted with Klan terror in Durham and Orange Counties as a schoolgirl—to rekindle old fears. "When I telephoned Aunt Pauline after receiving her letter," Murray later wrote, "I found that she was terrified of the possibility that aroused whites might burn our house down." See Murray, *Pauli Murray: The Autobiography of a Black Activist, Feminist, Lawyer, Priest, and Poet*, 46–47, 199–220.

CHAPTER 16: *A Knock at the Door*

On Ernst Moritz Manasse (1908–97), I relied on interviews with his son George Manasse; his daughter-in-law, Mary Stewart Manasse; his North Carolina College colleagues John Hope Franklin and John McLendon; and interviews with Edward "Pee Wee" Boyd, Alex Rivera, and other former students and acquaintances. The

North Carolina Central University Archives also contain helpful materials, including Manasse's faculty record cards; copies of some of his professional articles; "Dr. James E. Shepard—The Humanitarian," a speech by Dr. Ernst M. Manasse; "German Refugee Will Teach," an undated newspaper clipping; and miscellaneous biographical materials. Other sources on Manasse include Ernie Suggs, "Jewish Refugee Recalls Tenure at NCCU," June 13, 1993, and "Scholar, NCCU Prof Manasse dies at 88," May 14, 1997, both in the *Durham Herald-Sun;* a World War II draft card for Ernst Moritz Manasse; and a petition for naturalization, US District Court, Greensboro, North Carolina, September 15, 1939.

For information on Heidelberg in 1933, see Norbert Giovannini, "Heidelberg," in Julius H. Schoeps and Werner Tress, *Orte der Bücherverbrennungen in Deutschland, 1933,* 477–93; Werner Tress, *"Wider den undeutschen Geist": Bücherverbrennung 1933* (2003); Clemens Zimmermann, "Die Bücherverbrennung am 17. Mai 1933 in Heidelberg: Studenten und Politik am Ende der Weimarer Republik," in Joachim-Felix Leonhard, ed., *Bücherverbrennung: Zensur, Verbot, Vernichtung unter dem Nationalsozialismus in Heidelberg,* 55–84; US Holocaust Memorial Museum, online entry on "1933 Book Burnings," www.ushmm.org; Alice Gallin, *Midwives to Nazism: University Professors in Weimar Germany, 1925–1933,* 48–105; Steven P. Remy, *The Heidelberg Myth: The Nazification and Denazification of a German University,* 14–29; Max Weinrich, *Hitler's Professors: The Part of Scholarship in Germany's Crimes Against the Jewish People* (1946, reprinted 1996); and Arye Carmon, "The Impact of the Nazi Racial Decrees on the University of Heidelberg," *Yad Vashem Studies* 11 (1976), 131–41, available online at the Shoah Resource Center, www.yadvashem.org.

Manasse vividly described the Jewish cemetery in Dramburg, Pomerania, Germany—now Drawsko Pomorskie, Poland—in his essay "The Jewish Graveyard," *Southern Review* 22, no. 2 (April 1986), 296–307. See also "Jewish Cemetery in Drawsko Pomorskie" at the Virtual Shtetl website, www.sztetl.org.pl.

The most comprehensive source on Landschulheim Florenz—and on Ernst and Marianne's years in Italy—is A.W.L.M. (pseud.), comp., *Dial 22-0756 Pronto: Villa Pazzi, Memories of Landschulheim Florenz, 1933–1938,* especially Ernst Moritz Manasse, "Recollections Concerning the Landschulheim Florenz," 99–112. Also see Klaus Voigt, *Zuflucht auf Widerruf: Exil in Italien, 1933–1945* 1, 198–213, 396–97, 525–29, 611; and Henry Kahane, "A Linguist's Vita as Historiography," in Konrad Koerner, ed., *First Person Singular II: Autobiographies by North American Scholars in the Language Sciences,* 188–204.

Manasse's September 1939 arrival in the United States is recorded on US Department of Labor, Immigration and Naturalization Service, form 548, Index to Alien Arrivals by Airplane at Miami, Florida, 1930–1942, Record Group 85, National Archives. Marianne and George arrived permanently in the United States two months later, on December 10, 1939, aboard the SS *Brazil,* sailing from Santos, Brazil. See List or Manifest of Alien Passengers for the United States Immigrant Inspector at Port of Arrival, New York City, list 8, November and December 1939;

and US Department of Labor, Immigrant Identification Card for Georg Manasse, December 11, 1939. Norman E. Pendergraft's article "Marianne Manasse (1911–1984), Art Historian and Painter" is a brief introduction to her vivid, expressionistic paintings, now held in museums, libraries, and private collections in North Carolina.

On Manasse's early years at North Carolina College, see Ernst M. Manasse, "Dr. James E. Shepard—The Humanitarian," undated speech typescript, North Carolina Central University Archives, James E. Shepard Library; Gabrielle Simon Edgcomb, *From Swastika to Jim Crow: Refugee Scholars at Black Colleges,* xiii–xiv, 66–72, 132; Samuel G. Freedman, "'From Swastika to Jim Crow': Finding Their Refuge in the Segregated South," *Refuge South,* January 28, 2001, www.racematters .org; and Christoph E. Schweitzer, "Ernst Moritz Manasse: A Black College Welcomes a Refugee," in Henry A. Landsberger and Christoph E. Schweitzer, *They Fled Hitler's Germany and Found Refuge in North Carolina,* Southern Research Report 8, Spring 1996, Center for the Study of the American South, University of North Carolina at Chapel Hill, 41–50. Another refugee scholar, Hilda Weiss, taught social studies at North Carolina College during the 1940–41 school year.

Even after Hitler took power, Manasse managed to have two works published in Germany: *Über Wahrheit in Platons "Sophistes"* (Berlin, 1936) and *Platons Sophistes und Politikos: Das Problem der Wahrheit* (Berlin-Schöneberg, 1937). His early professional publications at North Carolina College, which mirrored some of the very real issues in his own life, include "The Dance Motive and the Latin Dance of Death," *Medievalia et Humanistica* 4 (1943), 83–103; "Conversion and Liberation," *Review of Religion* 7, no. 4 (May 1943), 361–83; "Moral Principles and Alternatives in Max Weber and John Dewey," *Journal of Philosophy* 41, no. 2 (January 20, 1944), 29–48, and no. 3 (February 3, 1944), 57–58; and "Max Weber on Race," *Social Research* 14, no. 2 (June 1947), 191–221.

John Hope Franklin first told me about the secret gatherings of professors from Duke, North Carolina College, and the University of North Carolina. Mary Stewart Manasse and George Manasse later revealed Ernst and Marianne's central role in organizing the meetings, which were held in their apartment inside the large house at 1215 6th Street—now 1215 Clarendon Street—as well as of the threat by the KKK. The Durham Klan, however, may not have been the only group to have caught wind of these clandestine meetings. On August 6, 2013, I submitted a Freedom of Information Act request for any FBI materials on Ernst Manasse between 1938 and 1966. Two weeks later, I was informed that "records which may have been responsive to your request were destroyed March 15, 1971." The letter was from David M. Hardy, Section Chief, Record/Information Dissemination Section, Records Management Division, Federal Bureau of Investigation, and was dated August 20, 2013. We do not know, however, what the nature of these records were or why or when they were produced.

For John Hope Franklin's wartime experiences, see his *Mirror to America: The Autobiography of John Hope Franklin,* 103–30. Franklin, who blamed the US military for the premature death of his only brother, also had his own bus incident, in Richmond, Virginia, during the 1940s. See Raymond Arsenault, *Freedom Riders: 1961 and the Struggle for Racial Justice,* 34–35.

Nationally, the YMCA—as well as its even more liberal-minded counterpart, the Young Women's Christian Association—began grappling with segregation, both on its own turf as well as in the larger society, during the 1940s. See, for example, "Randolph Demands YMCA End Segregated Branches," *New York Amsterdam News,* April 24, 1943, and Doggett, *Man and a School,* 246–55.

A photograph of the thirty-six members of the 1943–44 North Carolina College chapter of the YMCA can be found in *The Maroon and Gray* commencement edition, May 1944, page 6. For the Duke YMCA chapter, see the 1943 *Chanticleer,* 155–59; the 1944 *Chanticleer,* 151–55; and "The Duke U. Y.M.C.A. Report of the President, 1943–44," "Religious Activities, the Woman's College Campus, Duke U., Durham, N.C., May 1944," and "Annual Report of the Y.M.C.A. of Duke University, 1943–1944" in the Young Men's Christian Association at Duke University Records, Duke University Archives, David M. Rubenstein Rare Book and Manuscript Library, Duke University. I also gleaned information from a telephone interview with John L. Powell conducted in Fremont, California, on November 30, 1995. On the Edgemont neighborhood and community center, see Anderson, *Durham County,* 206–7, 213, 276–77, 424–25; and the entries for "Durham Hosiery Mill No. 1" and "Edgemont Community Center" at www.opendurham.org.

The Young Women's Christian Association had two branches—one white, one African American—in Durham during the war. During the 1943–44 school year, the Social Science Club at North Carolina College "brought to the campus Mrs. Seabolt of the Race Relations Committee of the Y.W.C.A. of Duke University and Mrs. R. N. Harris, Chairman of the Durham Committee on Negro Affairs." See *The Maroon and Gray* commencement edition, May 1944, 12, and *Hill's Durham City Directory, 1944,* 340, 422.

Exactly *who* came up with the idea for the secret game remains cloaked in mystery to this day. While considerable evidence points to the joint YMCA meetings as the point of origin, and while the participants in the game agree on how it happened, we don't know for certain who actually proposed the idea or who carried the proposal to both teams. Dave Hubbell has long maintained that on the Duke side, a divinity student was the driving force. And while there are many likely candidates among students at the Duke Divinity School in 1943–44—including some who had played on the school's intramural basketball squad—efforts to identify who this person might have been have proved to be inconclusive.

Similarly, on the North Carolina College side, John McLendon always claimed that a male student named Vivian W. Henderson—who later became an economist, author, and the president of Clark College—had both cooked up the idea for the game and presented him with the invitation. According to the late Brooklyn T. McMillon, however, formerly the archivist at North Carolina College, Henderson was already in the Army at the time—an assertion that is partially borne out by both the "North Carolina College Service Honor Roll" that appeared in the May 1944 commencement edition of *The Maroon and Gray,* the North Carolina College yearbook, as well as in the entry for Henderson that appears in *Who Was Who in America* 6 (1974–76), 188. Nevertheless, I found McLendon's memory to be rarely faulty—"That man had the best memory," Pee Wee once stated, "of any man I have ever seen"—and given the fact that Henderson might have been in Durham on leave at some point in early 1944, he still remains the leading candidate for being the game's originator. See McLendon, *Tales of the Hardwood,* his unpublished memoir.

On Henderson, see "The New Black Presidents," *Time,* December 27, 1968; Vivian W. Henderson, "The Role of Predominantly Negro Institutions," *Journal of Negro Education* 36, no. 3 (Summer 1967), 266–73, and "The Economic Status of Negroes: In the Nation and in the South," Toward Regional Realism 3, Southern Regional Council; and James A. Hefner, "A Tribute to Dr. Vivian W. Henderson: Economist and Educator," *Review of Black Political Economy* 7, no. 2 (Winter 1977), 190–94.

Duke and North Carolina Central University share a long, complex, multilayered history together. McLendon recalled that at one time he received high-quality used basketball uniforms from Duke—which he welcomed. After the war he also took a group of female students on a field trip to Duke, an outing that resulted in the creation of a field hockey program at North Carolina College. On one prewar effort to create some contact between students at both schools, the Intercollegiate Fellowship of Cooperative Understanding, see the report of the director of religious activities of the Woman's College, 1938–39, Student Religious Activities, William Preston Few Papers, Duke University Archives, David M. Rubenstein Rare Book and Manuscript Library.

McLendon's experiences with travel and segregation in North Carolina during the 1940s were sometimes quite ugly. Once, in Raleigh, one of his Eagles teams was forced to move to an already cramped colored railroad car in order to make room for a handful of German POWs, who enjoyed the spectacle immensely. On another occasion, after the war, when he was driving—alone—through Alamance County after attending a coaches' conference, he was pulled over by a police officer who ordered him out of the car at gunpoint. The officer had McLendon lean up against the side of the car, spread-eagled, with both hands on the roof. But when the policeman asked for McLendon's driver's license, which was in his wallet in his back pants pocket, McLendon told the officer to get it himself. "I was worried that he was later going to claim that I had reached for a gun," McLendon recalled, "so he could shoot me."

The movie version of *Wuthering Heights,* starring Merle Oberon and Laurence Olivier, played in Durham in late May of 1939. See the *Durham Herald-Sun,* May 28, 1939, and the *Durham Morning Herald,* May 29 and 30, 1939.

On the dormitory incident, I relied for information on interviews with Edward "Pee Wee" Boyd.

CHAPTER 17: *"You Could See It in Their Eyes"*

Despite the fact that its coverage was often quite minimal, especially in comparison to the attention it gave Duke and other white colleges, the *Durham Morning Herald*—and its Sunday edition, the *Durham Herald-Sun*—is a vital source of information on the 1943–44 North Carolina College basketball season. See especially "NCCN Opens Season Friday," January 5; "17 Tilts Listed for Eagle Five," January 6; "Eagles Record 44–36 Victory," January 8; "Eagles Take Contest with Butner Quintet," January 16; "Eagles Preparing for 2 Court Scraps," January 19; "Eagles to Invade Raleigh for 2 Games," January 21; "Eagles Take Contest Easily from Bears," January 23; "Eagles' Star Cager Is Doubtful Starter," February 3; "N.C. College Tops A. and T., 62–43," February 6; "North Carolina Cage Club Faces Hampton Five Here Tonight," February 10; "Eagles Defeat Hampton Quint," February 11; "Eagles Defeat Bluefield Five," February 12; "North Carolina Eagles Unbeaten," February 13; "Leading Negro Quints to Play Here Tonight," February 14; "Eagles Defeat Charlotte in Cage Contest," February 15; "Eagles Facing Hard Schedule on the Court," February 17; "Eagle Quintet to Face Saints," February 18; "Negro College Eagles to End Home Season," February 28; and "Eagles Defeat Aggie Outfit to Win Title," February 29.

The *Norfolk Journal and Guide* also regularly covered the Eagles. See Lem Graves Jr., "Schedule Key to Basketball Hopes," January 1; "North Carolina Wins 5th Straight," February 5; "Thomas May Be Lost to Carolina for Entire Season" and "From the Press Box," February 12; "Thomas Back in Eagles Lineup" and "North Carolina to Honor Servicemen This Saturday," February 19; and "North Carolina, Lincoln Lead CIAA as Smith Beaten Twice" and "Eagles Homecoming Nets 200 Letters for Servicemen," February 26. Also see John T. Mitchell, "From the Press Box," February 26, 1944. Other sources include occasional stories—usually only a paragraph—in various African American newspapers, as well as the CIAA *Bulletin* for 1944.

The military draft, it should be added, also substantially reduced McLendon's talent pool. See Charles A. Ray, "Five Former All American Athletes of North Carolina College Now in Armed Service of United States," *Carolina Times,* December 18, 1943.

Equally important, however, in reconstructing the season were the personal memories shared with me—in recorded interviews, telephone conversations, and letters—by those who were there, including John McLendon, Aubrey Stanley, Edward "Pee Wee" Boyd, Ruth Boyd, and a number of former students at North Carolina College. This portrait also benefited greatly from the insights offered by Clarence "Big House" Gaines, Arthur Johnson, Alex Rivera, and other longtime associates of Coach McLendon.

On George Lindsey Samuel Jr.—a.k.a. Crazy Horse—see *The Campus Echo Review,* commencement edition, May 1945, and his World War II draft card. On Anthony Leroy "Smokey" Davis, see his family history profile, World War II draft card, and his entry in the 1940 US federal census, Smithville Township, Southport, North Carolina, all on Ancestry.com.

CHAPTER 18: *New York*

The classic work on basketball in New York City, and a marvelous book in its own right, is Pete Axthelm's *The City Game: Basketball from the Garden to the Playgrounds* (1970). By 1936, attendance at New York University basketball games was larger than that for the school's football team. Also see Cunningham, *American Hoops,* 9. For more information, I relied on interviews with Frank McGuire, in Myrtle Beach, South Carolina, on September 20, 1990, and with Bill Esposito, in Jamaica, New York, on February 9, 1988.

For an introduction to the life and times of Edward Simmons "Ned" Irish (1905–82), one of the architects of modern basketball, see Jerry Jaye Wright's entry in Porter, *Basketball: A Biographical Dictionary,* 225–26. On the doubleheaders at Madison Square Garden, see "College Quintets to Play in Garden," *New York Times,* December 5, 1934; Francis J. O'Riley, "Stanford Crushes L.I.U. Five by 45–31," *New York Times,* December 31, 1936; Zander Hollander, ed., *Madison Square Garden: A Century of Sport and Spectacle on the World's Most Versatile Stage,* 24, 45, 74–79; Hollander, *The Modern Encyclopedia of Basketball,* rev. ed., 13–31; and Sandy Padwe, *Basketball's Hall of Fame,* 43–49. Frank Keaney's use of smudge pots to re-create the atmosphere of Madison Square Garden in Rhode Island is from Woodward, *Runnin' Rams,* 25.

On the creation and early years of the National Invitation Tournament, see "Best U.S. College Quintets to be Matched in Writers' Garden Tournament in March," *New York Times,* February 1, 1938, and Brenner, *College Basketball's National Championships,* 604–6. For the beginnings and early years of the NCAA tournament, see Robert Stern, *They Were Number One: A History of the NCAA Basketball Tournament,* 7–25, and Joe Gergen, *The Final Four: An Illustrated History of College Basketball's Showcase Event,* 11–31.

In retracing the Eagles' March 1944 train trip to New York, my interviews with John McLendon, Edward "Pee Wee" Boyd, and Aubrey Stanley were key. Weather records from both the *Durham Morning Herald* and—for Washington, D.C., and New York City—at Tutiempo.net were also utilized, as were a number of period railroad maps and guidebooks, including *The Complete Guide to New York City,* World's Fair edition (1940); American Guide Series, *New York City Guide,* 164–67, 253–65; Hulbert Footner, *New York: City of Cities,* 282–94; Claude McKay, *Harlem: Negro Metropolis* (1940); Allon Schoener, *Harlem on My Mind: Cultural Capital of Black America, 1900–1978,* 123–202; Sharifa Rhodes-Pitts, *Harlem Is Nowhere: A Journey to the Mecca of Black America* (2011); and two superb love letters to the City of Dreams—Jan Morris's *Manhattan '45* (1987) and E. B. White's *Here Is New York* (1949).

Plans had been afoot for North Carolina College to play two additional games at the end of the regular season—against Virginia Union and Howard—but both were canceled. See "North Carolina College 'Eagles' vs. 1319th Engineers," a mimeographed schedule dated January 7, 1944, in the North Carolina Central University Archives, and "Negro College Eagles to End Home Season," *Durham Morning Herald,* February 28, 1944.

On the 1941 National Negro College Championship basketball tournament in Cincinnati, see Billy Packer and Roland Lazenby, *The Golden Game,* 237–38; Katz, *Breaking Through,* 33–34; and Arthur R. Ashe Jr., *A Hard Road to Glory: A History of the African-American Athlete, 1919–1945* 2, 55.

Overshadowed by the latter-day notoriety of the Apollo Theater and the Savoy Ballroom, the Renaissance Ballroom and Casino, which closed for business in the late 1970s, is today a largely forgotten player in the history of both the Harlem Renaissance and early African American basketball. While the building itself is still standing, a series of stunning 2012 photographs—see "The Harlem Renaissance Ballroom" at abandonednyc.com—reveals a ghostly moonscape of crumbling walls, dangling light fixtures, and button mushrooms sprouting on what remains of the ballroom floor. For an introduction to its larger story, see Christopher Gray, "A Harlem Landmark in All but Name," *New York Times,* February 18, 2007; Michael Henry Adams, "Renaissance Ballroom and Casino," www.harlemonestop.com; and "The Abandoned Harlem Renaissance Ballroom," August 3, 2012, desertedplaces .blogspot.com.

The Renaissance Big Five—more popularly, the Rens—were one of the wonders of early professional basketball. Arguably the best basketball team of their era, they also battled against the country's segregated ways during the prewar era. See Susan J. Rayl, "The New York Renaissance Professional Black Basketball Team, 1923–1950," PhD dissertation, Pennsylvania State University, 1996; Bob Kuska, *Hot Potato,* 120–85; Nelson George, *Elevating the Game,* 33–40; "Basketball in 1920s Harlem," digitalharlemblog.wordpress.com; and Gregory Lucas-Myers, "A Look Back at the Harlem Rens: 'They're Renaissance, Too,'" May 14, 2012, welcometoharlem .wordpress.com.

The Rens and their opponents, however, were not the only basketball teams to play in the Renaissance Ballroom. African American college teams occasionally played there, as did amateur teams playing in the various tournaments organized by the black Elks. Interestingly enough, the Twin City Elks team, from Farrell, Pennsylvania, was one of the best, and to this day there are aged locals in Farrell who believed that Big Dog himself not only once played on an Elks team but also that, in one game, he absolutely owned William "Dolly" King, the sensational Long Island University basketball superstar who later turned pro. See "Elks Play for Title on Renny Cage Court" and "Howard Takes Lincoln, 67–34," *New York Amsterdam Star-News,* March 21, 1942; and Barksdale-Hall, *Farrell,* 8.

On the 1944 Negro National College Championship basketball game and its buildup, see "North Carolina Scoring Ace," *Norfolk Journal and Guide,* March 4; "Lincoln U. Versus N. C. State College at Renny, March 10" and "College Basketball Star 'Coach's Dream,'" *New York Age,* March 4; "Sports Today," *New York Times,* March 10; "North Carolina College and Lincoln Lions Battle for National Honors in Harlem Contest, March 10" and "North Carolina College Eagles Claim CIAA Cage Title After Beating A. and T.," *New York Amsterdam News,* March 11; "Sensational Scoring Center of N.C. State" and "N.C. State College Cager to Invade

Renaissance Casino," *New York Age,* March 11; "Carolina, Lincoln in N.Y. Clash" and John T. Mitchell, "Press Box," *Norfolk Journal and Guide,* March 11; "Court Title to Lincoln U.," *Washington Star,* March 11; "Eagles Beaten," *Durham Morning Herald,* March 11; "Lincoln University Five Beats N.C. College Here," *New York Age,* March 18; "Lincoln Nips N.C. State Here, 57–52," March 18; "Lincoln Licks No. Carolina Eagles, 57–52," *Norfolk Journal and Guide,* March 18; and "Lincoln U. Issues Title Claim" and Don De Leighbur, "New Yorkers Don't Like Carolina Court Technique," *Norfolk Journal and Guide,* March 25, 1944.

My portrait of the game at the Renaissance Ballroom is also based upon my interviews with John McLendon, Aubrey Stanley, and Edward "Pee Wee" Boyd. And while McLendon firmly believed that the outcome of the game had been fixed, he did not feel that anyone from Lincoln had been involved. It bears noting, however, that in January of 1945 — less than one year after the Lincoln game — a college basketball betting scandal in New York hit the headlines when two Brooklyn College players were arrested for conspiring to throw a game. Indeed, enough money was being wagered on the doubleheaders at Madison Square Garden at the time that the NYPD had begun to arrest bookies. See "Effort to Quash Basketball Bribe Indictment Fails," *New York Amsterdam News,* February 17, 1945, and Aamidor, *Chuck Taylor, All Star,* 114.

Manuel Rivero, the legendary coach of the Lions, stayed at Lincoln University for decades. See "Manifest for Alien Passengers for the U.S. Immigration Officer for the Port of New York for the SS *Mexico,* Sailing from Havana, May 11, 1918," Ancestry.com; Larry Lewis, "M. Rivero, Pillar of Lincoln U. Sports," August 31, 2001, articles.philly.com; and Brett Hoover and Stephen Eschenback, "Ivy Blackball," www.ivyleaguesports.com.

McLendon's decision to play the game against the team from Duke may well have also been influenced by the fact that ten days later, on March 20, 1944, the basketball team from Morgan State College, another CIAA school, was scheduled to play a benefit game against Brooklyn College, a predominantly white school, at the Renaissance. See the *New York Age* and the *New York Amsterdam News,* March 18, 1944. McLendon's Eagles had, in fact, played Brooklyn two years earlier, in January of 1942, in what was later claimed to be the first integrated college basketball game in Washington, D.C. But despite its often Dixiesque ways, the nation's capital was *not* the South, and the Brooklyn ball club — which went 10–8 in 1942 and 6–14 in 1944 — wasn't a top-caliber team. As significant as both games were, neither would answer the basic question that haunted McLendon and other African American coaches during the Jim Crow era, namely, were their teams *good enough* to beat the best white teams? See McLendon résumés and interviews, in author's possession; North Carolina Central University Men's Basketball Media Guide, 2009–2010, 77; "1943–44 Independent Season Summary," www.sports-reference.com; "Post Season's Men's & Women's Basketball Records for Brooklyn College," www.luckyshow.org; and Patrick B. Miller and David K. Viggins, eds., *Sport and the Color Line: Black Athletes and Race Relations in the Twentieth Century,* 139.

On the game against the Orange Triangles, held at Lincoln Hall, see "Orange Triangles Bow to N. C. State" and "Tarheels Get Two," *New Jersey Afro American,* March 18, 1944. Lincoln Hall, where the game was played, is gone, but the immediate neighborhood is still noticeably Italian. See *Classified Directory of the Oranges, 1940,* 236, and Federal Writers' Project, *New Jersey: A Guide to Its Present and Past,* 339–42. In the *Durham Morning Herald,* March 9, 1944, the team was called the Triangle Riveters.

The depiction of the rail journey back to Durham is also based upon my interviews with McLendon, Stanley, and Boyd. In reconstructing the weather as well as the relative progress of spring for the journey, I utilized historic weather records for March 12, 1944, for New York City, Wilmington, Washington, and Richmond, available at www.tutiempo.net; *New York Times,* March 12, 1944; the Beaufort wind scale, which is posted online in Russ Rowlett's *Dictionary of Units of Measurement,* Center for Mathematics and Science Education, University of North Carolina, www.unc.edu; and extrapolated benchmarks—for 1944, using 1945 weather data—from Louis Halle's classic *Spring in Washington.* An absolutely first-class portrait of the seasons and natural life in central North Carolina is *The Piedmont Almanac: Central Region—A Guide to the Natural World,* written by naturalist Dave Cook, who once lived in a tent in the woods while studying at UNC. Also helpful is Stan Tekiela, *Birds of the Carolinas: Field Guide,* 2nd ed. (2004).

CHAPTER 19: *The Secret Game*

Intentionally clandestine events tend not to leave much of a paper trail.

Aside from Jack Burgess's letter home to his parents back in Missoula, there are no known period documents about the secret game. Thus while my reconstruction of the game makes use of numerous printed and written sources, it is primarily based upon my formal interviews, correspondence, and informal telephone conversations with some of the participants, namely, John McLendon, Aubrey Stanley, Edward "Pee Wee" Boyd, George Parks, David Hubbell, Jack Burgess, and Ed Johnson, as well as others who were aware of but did not actively take part in the game itself, including Lloyd Taylor, Barbara Taylor, and Herman Winberry. Not surprisingly, given how long ago the game occurred, some of the participants in the secret game occasionally had varying recollections of certain aspects of it. Dave Hubbell, for example, remembered the drive over to North Carolina College differently than the others. Another Duke medical student, Rufus Hambright, may have also played in the game.

Similarly, my reconstruction also benefited directly from the contributions of numerous individuals who lived in or near Durham in 1944 and provided key insights not only into the day-to-day nature of race relations at the time but also into small historical details—such as the fact that Dr. Shepard had the only automobile on campus at North Carolina College during the early months of 1944—which proved to be quite helpful. These individuals included Dr. Leroy T. Walker, Robert Seymour, John Hope Franklin, Alex Rivera, Brooklyn T. McMillon, Edith Stanford, Mabel B. Wright, Hubert L. Robinson, Bill Malone, Samuel Shepard, Roy D.

Moore, Rosemary Johnson, Ethel E. Lineburger, Carter Smith, John L. Powell, Mahlon Elliott, Roy Bell, James Allan Knight, and Art Jaffey.

Burgess's letters to his parents, however, have proven to be key in determining what was the likely date of the secret game, which I believe to have been Sunday, March 19, 1944. Even here, however, one must reach to make conclusions. For while Jack Burgess wrote to his folks regularly, he did not date his letters beyond writing such phrases as "Mon." or "Fri. Noon" at the top. Moreover, his mother did not save the envelopes for the letters, each of which would have included a dated postmark. But she did save the letters themselves. And, equally important, she placed them, in order, in a box once she had received them. Thus by going through the scores and scores of letters that Burgess wrote back home, one can, using clues here and there, determine the likely date of individual letters.

This was very much the case with the letter Jack sent to his parents in which he mentions the game. Simply dated "Sunday nite," it recounts a performance Burgess saw the night before by the Cleveland Orchestra, which played an evening concert in Page Auditorium at Duke on Saturday, March 18, 1944. "Sunday nite," then, must mean March 19. On the concert, which featured works by Beethoven, Brahms, and Wagner, see "Packed House Will Hear Symphony," *Duke Chronicle*, March 17, 1944; "Cleveland Symphony Will Play Tonight at Duke University," *Durham Morning Herald*, March 18, 1944; and the actual program for the concert, in the Dorothy Newsom Rankin Papers, Duke University Archives.

In this letter, Burgess writes that the game took place "a few nites ago." And while it is certainly possible that the secret game did, indeed, take place one night during the week of March 13–17, my guess is that it did not. The main problem is that practically every other participant in the game that I was able to speak with remembered the game as having been played on a Sunday morning. So why might Burgess have written this? Perhaps because he didn't want his folks to think that he wasn't going to church regularly. But the truth of the matter is that the exact date of the game has not been proved beyond the shadow of a doubt and perhaps never will be. That said, I remain confident that the game took place on Sunday morning, March 19, 1944.

On the cancellation of the 1944 basketball jamboree at Duke, see the *Duke Chronicle*, January 28, 1944.

Helpful sources on Camp Butner and its US Army General Hospital include Richard Stradling, "History Buffs, Soldiers Plan Museum for Camp Butner," November 30, 2013, www.newsobserver.com; "History of Camp Butner," www.butnernc.org; "Camp Butner History Tour," April 14, 2003, www.geocaching.com; "Camp Butner Summary," at the North Carolina National Guard website, www.nc.ngb.army.mil; the Camp Butner Society Facebook pages; and in the historic postcards held in the North Carolina Collection at the University of North Carolina at Chapel Hill, dc.lib.unc.edu. On POWs at Camp Butner, see Robert D. Billinger Jr.'s impressive study, *Nazi POWs in the Tar Heel State* (2008), as well as his article written with Jo Ann Williford, "Prisoners of War Held in North Carolina," on the NCPedia website, ncpedia.org.

The identity of the referee for the secret game remains in dispute. McLendon was confident that it was Frank Burnett, a CIAA-approved official who lived in Durham. When interviewed near the end of his life, however, Burnett told a reporter that he had no recollection of the game—something McLendon attributed to his age. Edward "Pee Wee" Boyd believed that it was either Burnett or Pete Williams, another CIAA-approved basketball referee, who lived in Raleigh. See the CIAA *Bulletin,* 1944, 25.

My key sources for the secret game itself were my in-person interviews, telephone interviews, and correspondence with its participants, including Edward "Pee Wee" Boyd, Jack Burgess, Dave Hubbell, Ed Johnson, John McLendon, George Parks, Aubrey Stanley, and Dick Symmonds. McLendon briefly mentions his strategy for pep talks in his *Fast Break Basketball,* 173.

Lillian M. Davis was the dietician at North Carolina College, while Annie P. Washington served as the "house directress" of the men's dormitory. See *North Carolina College for Negroes, Annual Catalogue, 1943–1944.*

CHAPTER 20: *"Did You Hear About..."*

For news of the war on the day after the game, see *Durham Morning Herald,* March 20, 1944.

On the Holocaust in Greece, see Errikos Sevillias, *Athens–Auschwitz,* 3–8; Steven Bowman and Isaac Benmayor, *The Holocaust in Salonika: Eyewitness Accounts* (2002); "Archbishop Damaskinos and the Jewish Holocaust," www.raoulwallenberg.net; Paul Isaac Hagouel, "The History of the Jews of Thessaloniki and the Holocaust: An Expose" (2006), www.academia.edu; and Martin Winstone, *The Holocaust Sites of Europe: An Historical Guide,* 409–20.

On the 1944 NIT and NCAA tournament, see *The Official National Basketball Committee Basketball Guide, 1944–45,* 30–47, and "National Basketball Tourneys Get into Full Swing," *Raleigh News & Observer,* March 20, 1944. As Robert Stern observed of the 1943–44 season in *They Were Number One,* his history of the NCAA tournament, "The best basketball teams in the country had 'fort,' 'camp,' 'base,' 'field' and 'station' appended to their names though none went to a postseason playoff" (page 33). John McLendon and a number of African American coaches, players, and sportswriters, however, would have made some further additions.

On Lin Holloway, see "Around the Town," *Carolina Times,* December 4, 1943; World War II draft registration for Burke Linwood Holloway; family member profile, Howard family tree, Ancestry.com; Durham city directory, 1943, 182; Durham city directory, 1944, 192–93; and North Carolina College for Negroes annual catalog, 1943–44.

The quotation from Jack Burgess's letter to his parents dates from March 1944.

In the long run, the game appears to have had a deeper impact on the Southerners who were members of the Duke medical school basketball team than it did upon their Northern and Western teammates. Indeed, by the time he left the South, Jack Burgess's anger toward Jim Crow had markedly dissipated, while Dave Hubbell's thinking about race clearly began to change. For this I drew on interviews and correspondence with Burgess and Hubbell.

Both McLendon and Edward "Pee Wee" Boyd believed that among the Cloudbusters and other white basketball players from Chapel Hill who came to North Carolina College during the summer looking for a game was Otto Graham, later a star quarterback for the Cleveland Browns.

For the Fort Bragg episode, I drew on interviews with John McLendon and Alex Rivera. Also see "Army Seeking Number of Civilian Teachers," *Durham Morning Herald*, March 20, 1944.

The murder of PFC Booker T. Spicely and the trial of Herman Lee Council were covered extensively in the *Durham Morning Herald, Durham Sun*, and *Durham Herald-Sun* from July 9 to September 17, 1944. For *State v. Council*, see Durham County Superior Court, Minute Docket, Criminal Term, v34, March 1943 through December 1944, and File Docket, v3, 1940 to 1956.

The legal affairs division of the National Association for the Advancement of Colored People also monitored the case. See especially the letter from C. J. Gates and M. Hugh Thompson to Thurgood Marshall, August 11, 1944, in NAACP Papers, Part II: Branch Files, Durham, North Carolina, 1940–45, Box 2-C135; Booker T. Spicely (1944) in Part II: Legal Files, 1940–1955, Box II-B152; and, Spicely, Booker T. (1944), in Part I: Board of Directors File, 1909–1959, Box 1-C410.

The US Army's Fourth Service Command, Security and Intelligence Division, also prepared a confidential report on the incident. It can be accessed online at the Northeastern University School of Law's Civil Rights and Restorative Justice Project website, at nuweb9.neu.edu/civilrights/north-carolina/booker-t-spicely/.

Other key sources include Timothy B. Tyson, "Wars for Democracy: African-American Militancy and Interracial Violence in North Carolina During World War Two," in David S. Cecelski and Timothy B. Tyson, eds., *Democracy Betrayed: The Wilmington Race Riot of 1898 and Its Legacy,* as well as an earlier, typescript version, courtesy of the author; *Hill's Durham City Directory, 1944;* and bus materials, photographs, and city maps in the Durham history room of the downtown branch of the Durham County Library as well as in the offerings found on the remarkable OpenDurham website, www.opendurham.org. During the war years, it appears that the number 5 Fayetteville Street route was combined with the number 1 Watts Hospital–East Durham route. See the Duke Power Company bus route map, 1948, in the Public Maps and Documents Division, Perkins Library, Duke University.

After his death, Spicely's body was taken by his family for burial in Nottoway County, Virginia. His name was later etched onto the Virginia War Memorial in Richmond, where he is noted as being one of forty-nine Nottoway County servicemen who died during World War II. At the memorial's website—www.vawarmemorial .org—visitors can make a virtual rubbing of his name. On Spicely, also see the 1910, 1920, and 1930 US federal censuses, Bellefonte Magisterial District, Nottoway County, Virginia, Spicely family entries; Philadelphia city directory, 1935; US World War II Army enlistment records for Booker Thomas Spicely; North Carolina

State Board of Health, Bureau of Vital Statistics, certificate of death for Booker T. Spicely, July 8, 1944; and US headstone applications for military veterans, for Booker T. Spicely, November 12, 1946.

CHAPTER 21: *Look Away*

On Big Dog's final weeks at North Carolina College, I relied on in-person interviews, telephone interviews, and correspondence with Edward "Pee Wee" Boyd and Ruth Boyd, Durham, North Carolina, as well as the recollections of teammates and classmates.

For the 1944–45 North Carolina College basketball season, see the CIAA *Bulletin*, 1945, 5, 20, 26, 34; *The Official National Basketball Committee Basketball Guide, 1945–46*, 110–12, 132; North Carolina College, *The Campus Echo Review*, commencement edition, May 1945; A. T. McDaniel Jr., "Morgan Breaks Eagles' Streak," *Pittsburgh Courier*, February 24, 1945; "Morgan Eliminates N.C. State from C.I.A.A. Cage Race, 50–44," *New York Amsterdam News*, March 17, 1945; and *A Decade of Greatness, 1937–1947.*

On Big Dog and the Orange Triangles, see "Triangles Oppose L.I. Pros," February 15, "Rens Get Revenge, Jar Triangles" and "Bronx Raiders to Battle Orange Triangles Sunday," March 29, and Dan Burley's "Confidentially Yours" column, April 12, 1947, all in the *New York Amsterdam News.*

For George Parks, I consulted the World War II draft registration card for George Brooks Parks as well as my correspondence and telephone interviews with George B. Parks, Los Angeles. On James Bugge Hardy, I relied on the 1940 US federal census, 5th Ward, Block 33, Gary, Indiana; and my interview with Edward "Pee Wee" and Ruth Boyd, Durham, June 13, 1997.

For information on Crazy Horse, I drew on interviews with John McLendon, Edward "Pee Wee" Boyd, and Ruth Boyd as well as Durham city directories, 1945–54.

For Aubrey Stanley in Watch Hill and leaving North Carolina College, I relied on interviews with Aubrey Stanley and undated correspondence from John McLendon.

On the Duke medical school basketball team after the secret game, see "Medical Students Play Benefit Game Tonight" and Jack Horner's Sports Corner, "Polio Twin Bill Offers Naturals," *Durham Morning Herald,* January 28, 1946.

Dick Symmonds: telephone interviews and correspondence.

Dick Thistlethwaite: correspondence and telephone interviews with Jeane Thistlethwaite; "James R. Thistlethwaite Dies at 78; Was White House Surgeon for Ford," *Washington Post,* July 14, 2000.

Ed Johnson: telephone interviews and correspondence.

Homer Sieber: correspondence with Charlotte Mock Sieber.

Harry Wechsler and the gold basketball: correspondence and telephone interviews with Helene Wechsler and Laura Broff; "Harry L. Wechsler, MD, 1923–1996," *Cutis* 58, no. 8 (December 1996).

Jack Burgess: interviews and correspondence with Jack Burgess, Donna Burgess, and family; "John R. 'Jack' Burgess," *Helena Independent Record,* July 22, 2003.

Dave Hubbell: interviews and correspondence with Dave and Barbara Hubbell.

Bus incident at Duke: Jack Burgess. On buses at Duke, interview with Lloyd and Barbara Taylor, Great Falls, Montana, July 2, 1997.

Harlem bar incident: interviews with Aubrey Stanley and his friends and relatives, Queens, New York.

On James "Boogie" Hardy, see 1940 US federal census, 5th Ward, Block 33, Gary, Indiana; *Polk's Gary (Lake County, Ind.) City Directories,* 1941, 1945, 1948; North Carolina College, *The Campus Echo Review,* commencement edition, May 1945; and interviews with John B. McLendon and Edward "Pee Wee" Boyd. The playground or schoolyard game could also be called the housing project game, as it first began to flourish among World War II–era housing projects built by government agencies for defense and war workers and their families, particularly in the North and West. Many were built by the federal government, while some, like the Delaney Community projects, were administered by local housing authorities. On the Delaney Community, see Raymond A. Mohl and Neil Betten, *Steel City: Urban and Ethnic Patterns in Gary, Indiana, 1906–1950,* 66–73.

The early history of the playground game in Indiana has not been written. Traces of it, however, as well as information about the milieu in which it was developed, can be found in Phillip M. Hoose, *Hoosiers: The Fabulous Basketball Life of Indiana,* 59–68, 143–93; Nelson George, *Elevating the Game: Black Men and Basketball,* 116–23; Aram Goudsouzian, " 'Ba-ad, Ba-ad Tigers': Crispus Attucks Basketball and Black Indianapolis in the 1950s," *Indiana Magazine of History* 96, no. 1 (March 2000), 4–43; and Ronald D. Cohen, "The Dilemma of School Integration in the North: Gary, Indiana, 1945–1960," *Indiana Magazine of History* 82, no. 2 (June 1986), 161–84. On Lockefield Gardens, see Robert G. Barrows, "The Local Origins of a New Deal Housing Project: The Case of Lockefield Gardens," *Indiana Magazine of History* 103, no. 2 (June 2007), 125–51; Lockefield Gardens apartments records, 1935–54, Collection Overview, Indiana Historical Society; the National Park Service, "Lockefield Gardens Apartments," www.nps.gov; and Leigh Darbee, "Lockefield Gardens," in David J. Bodenhamer and Robert G. Barrows, eds., *The Encyclopedia of Indianapolis,* 926–27.

The Shelbyville incident is from Tom Graham and Rachel Graham Cody's gem of a book, *Getting Open: The Unknown Story of Bill Garrett and the Integration of College Basketball,* 5–6.

On the growth of the playground game nationally, I drew on interviews with K. C. Jones, Boston, August 9, 1989; Willie Worsley, Spring Valley, New York, April 25, 1987; Hal Perry, Oakland, California, December 29, 1987; and Mike Farmer, San Francisco, August 27, 1987. Also see "List of Permanent Public Housing Projects Making Provisions for Negro Tenants, as of July 31, 1945," in Murray, *The Negro Handbook, 1946–1947,* 193–202. On this subject I also relied on in-person interviews, telephone interviews, and correspondence with John McLendon, Aubrey

Stanley, and Edward "Pee Wee" Boyd. See also Chet Walker, *Long Time Coming: A Black Athlete's Coming-of-Age in America,* 18–47.

On McLendon's post–secret game career at North Carolina College: interviews, telephone interviews, and correspondence with John McLendon, and Katz, *Breaking Through,* 46–57.

I observed the Springfield, Massachusetts, basketball clinic in person in May of 1996.

Clyde Hoey was the only North Carolina politician to have served as both a state congressman and state senator, as governor, as a US congressman, and as a US senator. On his life and career, see Susan Tucker Hatcher, "The Senatorial Career of Clyde R. Hoey," PhD dissertation, Duke University, 1983, especially 1–72, 106–26; T. Harry Gatton, "Clyde Roark Hoey," in Powell, *Dictionary of North Carolina Biography* 3, 158–59; and the North Carolina History Project's "Clyde R. Hoey (1877–1954)," at www.northcarolinahistory.org. On Hoey's dedication of the B. N. Duke Auditorium at North Carolina College, see David Leroy Corbitt, ed., *Addresses, Letters and Papers of Clyde Roark Hoey,* 160–61, and "Dr. Shepard Lauded in Dedicatory Program Here Sunday, *Carolina Times,* December 11, 1937.

"Clyde Hoey Discusses Peace in Talk at N.C. College Vespers," *Durham Morning Herald,* November 27, 1944. Mabel B. Wright, Ruth Boyd, and Edward "Pee Wee" Boyd were all present during the shoe-scraping incident. A brief audio recording of Senator Hoey was included on Edward R. Murrow's *This I Believe* radio broadcast and was later included on an eight-CD set. Two additional audio recordings of Hoey—including one from his 1944 senatorial campaign—were provided to me by the above-and-beyond efforts of the superb staff at the North Carolina Collection, Wilson Library, University of North Carolina at Chapel Hill.

EPILOGUE

For this incident I drew on interviews with Edward "Pee Wee" Boyd, Ruth Boyd, Alex Rivera, Aubrey Stanley, and John McLendon.

AFTERWORD: *The Ghosts of Jim Crow*

The Greenview Cemetery in Blackstone, Virginia, where Booker T. Spicely is buried, is located off Irvin Street, east of Main. On Blackstone, Virginia, and vicinity, see Federal Writers' Project, *Virginia: A Guide to the Old Dominion,* 594; US Department of Agriculture, *Soil Survey: Nottoway County, Virginia,* series 1954, no. 11 (July 1960), 78–82; John S. Salmon, *A Guidebook to Virginia's Historical Markers,* rev. ed., 79–80; and "Nottoway Training School," Virginia Department of Historic Resources, Historical Highway Markers, dhr.virginia.gov.

On the response to the Council trial verdict among the African American population in Durham, see Greene, *Our Separate Ways,* 18–21; and the US Army Fourth Service Command's confidential report on Private Booker T. Spicely, 1944, available online at Northeastern University School of Law's Civil Rights and Restorative Justice Project website, nuweb9.neu.edu/civilrights/north-carolina/booker-t-spicely/.

Martha's Chapel is located at the northwest corner of North Carolina Highway 751 and Martha's Chapel Road in northeast Chatham County, North Carolina. See also the Chatham County cemetery census for the church cemetery at www.ceme terycensus.com; Chatham County Historical Association, "Ceremony Celebrates Martha's Chapel," chathamhistory.org; and the official church website, www.Marthas Chapel.com. Jeffrey L. Thomas's "The Descendants of Robert 'Bobbie' Council (1768–1862) of Chatham County, North Carolina," thomasgenweb.com/council .html, is an impressive family history document.

On Herman Lee Council, see 1930 US federal census, New Hope Township, Chatham County, North Carolina; indexed register of marriages, Chatham County, Herman L. Council and Hazel Merritt, July 1, 1935, North Carolina Marriage Collection, 1741–2004; US Social Security Administration, application for account number filed by Herman Lee Council, December 3, 1936, obtained through a Freedom of Information Act (FOIA) request; Durham City Directories, 1936–1960; 1940 US federal census, Ward 1, Durham, North Carolina; World War II draft card for Herman Lee Council; North Carolina divorce index, May 6, 1971, for Herman and Inez Council; US Social Security death index; and North Carolina Department of Health, North Carolina deaths, January 24, 1982, for Herman Lee Council. When I was a graduate student in North Carolina during the late 1970s and early 1980s, I met, purely by chance, a member of Lee Council's family, who provided the quote.

Martin Luther King Jr., "Loving Your Enemies" in *Strength to Love*, 53–55. Also see Simon Wiesenthal, *The Sunflower: On the Possibilities and Limits of Forgiveness*, rev. ed. (1998).

Index

About the Author

Scott Ellsworth has written about American history for the *New York Times,* the *Washington Post,* and the *Los Angeles Times.* Formerly a historian at the Smithsonian Institution, he is the author of *Death in a Promised Land,* a groundbreaking account of the 1921 Tulsa race riot. He lives with his wife and twin sons in Ann Arbor, where he teaches at the University of Michigan.